ISLAM AND THE DEVOTIONAL OBJECT

In this book, Richard J. A. McGregor offers a history of Islamic practice through the aesthetic reception of medieval religious objects. Elaborate parades in Cairo and Damascus included decorated objects of great value, destined for Mecca and Medina. Among these were the precious dress sewn yearly for the Ka'ba and large colorful sedans mounted on camels, which mysteriously completed the Hajj without carrying a single passenger. Along with the brisk trade in Islamic relics, these objects – and the variety of contested meanings attached to them – constituted material practices of religion that persisted into the colonial era, but were suppressed in the twentieth century. McGregor here recovers the biographies of religious objects, including relics, banners, public texts, and coverings for the Ka'ba. Reconstructing the premodern visual culture of Islamic Egypt and Syria, he follows the shifting meanings attached to objects of devotion, as well as the contingent nature of religious practice and experience.

RICHARD J. A. McGREGOR is Associate Professor of Religion and Islam at Vanderbilt University. He is the author of *Sanctity and Mysticism in Medieval Egypt* (2004), coeditor of *The Development of Sufism in Mamluk Egypt* (2006) and *Sufism in the Ottoman Era (16th–18th C.)* (2010), and a translator of the Arabic edition of *The Epistle of the Brethren of Purity: The Case of the Animals versus Man before the King of the Jinn* (2012).

ISLAM AND THE DEVOTIONAL OBJECT

SEEING RELIGION IN EGYPT AND SYRIA

RICHARD J. A. McGREGOR

Vanderbilt University

CAMBRIDGE
UNIVERSITY PRESS

CAMBRIDGE
UNIVERSITY PRESS

University Printing House, Cambridge CB2 8BS, United Kingdom

One Liberty Plaza, 20th Floor, New York, NY 10006, USA

477 Williamstown Road, Port Melbourne, VIC 3207, Australia

314–321, 3rd Floor, Plot 3, Splendor Forum, Jasola District Centre,
New Delhi – 110025, India

79 Anson Road, #06–04/06, Singapore 079906

Cambridge University Press is part of the University of Cambridge.

It furthers the University's mission by disseminating knowledge in the pursuit of
education, learning, and research at the highest international levels of excellence.

www.cambridge.org
Information on this title: www.cambridge.org/9781108483841
DOI: 10.1017/9781108594233

First published 2020

Printed in the United Kingdom by TJ International Ltd, Padstow Cornwall

A catalogue record for this publication is available from the British Library.

Library of Congress Cataloging-in-Publication Data
NAMES: McGregor, Richard J. A., author.
TITLE: Islam and the devotional object : seeing religion in Egypt and Syria / Richard J. A.
   McGregor.
DESCRIPTION: I. | New York : Cambridge University Press, 2020. | Includes bibliographical
   references and index.
IDENTIFIERS: LCCN 2019051259 (print) | LCCN 2019051260 (ebook) | ISBN 9781108483841
   (hardback) | ISBN 9781108705219 (paperback) | ISBN 9781108594233 (epub)
SUBJECTS: LCSH: Islam–Liturgical objects. | Islam–Liturgical objects–Egypt. | Islam–Liturgical
   objects–Syria.
CLASSIFICATION: LCC BP184.95 .M33 2020 (print) | LCC BP184.95 (ebook) |
   DDC 297.3/9–dc23
LC record available at https://lccn.loc.gov/2019051259
LC ebook record available at https://lccn.loc.gov/2019051260

ISBN 978-1-108-48384-1 Hardback

CONTENTS

ILLUSTRATIONS

Figures

Maps

Table

PREFACE

I have had the pleasure of working on this book for more than a decade. My interest in writing about Islamic material culture and visual practice was stirred by two observations. The first was the presence of so many impressive objects in the living practice of Islam. Religion – at least modern voices tell us – is concerned with lofty and metaphysical things, and shuns the material world. We hear that Islam in particular is mistrustful and even hostile to images, representation, and sensory indulgences. Why then, I wondered, are the colors, forms, designs, images, along with the eyes, hands, and bodies, of adherents who respond to them, so prevalent? My experiences on the ground in one part of the Islamic world, and my explorations into Egyptian and Syrian history yielded one example after another.

The second observation was more abstract, coming out of my reflections on the modern study of religion. Despite the immense intellectual heritage available to us as scholars – inherited from the Middle East, Africa, and Europe – we still have only imperfect tools for making sense of what I came to call the objects of devotion. Arabic poetics, Kantian aesthetics, Islamic theology, and postmodern phenomenology, all have contributions to make, but they do so only in partial ways. It seems academics are only now beginning to find ways of accounting for the power and presence of religious objects.

Like much of the humanities, the study of religion has responded to the "material turn." Buoyed by what we now call the New Materialism, a recovery of the being, presence, and even agency of objects, religious studies is finding its voice in the field. Books have recently appeared, such as *Christian Materiality*, *The Embodied Eye*, *More than Belief*, and *Religion: Material Dynamics*, all of which chart different paths into the study of religion, with objects and their related human practices as their guides.[1]

The book before you follows in the wake of these and other studies. It opens with an introductory chapter, both a genealogy of my attempts to make sense of the observations outlined above, and a proposal for a way forward into the material study of this corner of the Islamic world. The chapter concludes with a proposal for a "machine" – that is to say, a dynamic object, operating within given and bounded environments, producing what the circumstances of history will allow.[2] The six chapters that follow, center on a series of Islamic objects as they engage with and occupy the complex religious landscapes they encounter. The objects of devotion, then, are the machines of religion.

ACKNOWLEDGMENTS

A large part of the research for this book was completed in 2012–2013 when I was a fellow at the Annemarie Schimmel Kolleg at Bonn University. I am grateful to Dr. Stephan Conermann and the many colleagues and friends I found that year in Bonn. Support for this project has also come from the Fulbright Scholar Program and the Department of Arab and Islamic Civilizations at the American University in Cairo. I have benefited from the helpful feedback and supportive gestures of many allies. I list them here, hoping they will forgive such a brief mention: Iman Abdulfattah, Ashkan Bahrani, Anna Bigelow, Daniel Demeter, Issam Eido, Yehoshua Frenkel, Kambiz Ghanea-Bassiri, Leor Halevi, Mimi Hanaoka, Ahmed Karamustafa, Aydogan Kars, Alexander Knysh, Matt Lynch, Mohammad Meerzaei, Birgit Meyer, Candace Mixon, David Morgan, and Anand Taneja, Nadirah Mansour, Abdulrhman Affaq, Nevine Abd El-Gawad, Avinoam Shalem, Alexandra Grieser, Irene Bierman-McKinney, Mustafa Bannister.

I could not have written this book without the support of my wife Katharine Loevy. I cherish deeply our adventures in affairs of both the head and the heart.

NOTE ON TRANSLITERATION AND DATES

For Arabic terms I have followed a simplified version of the transliteration system of the *International Journal of Middle East Studies*. The Arabic letter *'ayn* thus appears as ('), and the *hamza* appears as ('). I have not included macrons on long vowels, or subscript diacritics. My intention is to make the book more inviting to the nonspecialist reader. In the same spirit, I have provided only the most essential Hijri date equivalents to the Gregorian calendar years. Arabic terms appearing in common English dictionaries are not italicized. Unless otherwise noted, all translations are my own.

INTRODUCTION

One stubborn issue in the study of religion is that of location. The question is where do you locate the meaning of the phenomenon you have chosen to explore? Puzzled by this question, you quite reasonably might wonder what your options are. Let me propose that you have two. Indeed, the entire history of the study of religion seems to have divided itself into two camps on this issue: one side holds that meaning is found "elsewhere," removed from the context that produced the phenomena in the first place – while the other side insists that meaning remains anchored at the original site, and thus the place that holds a phenomenon up for us to consider is also its site of meaning. The first position I will simply call that of the *reductionist*, someone who deftly jumps the chasm separating the phenomena from the disciplined thinking that will supply distance, perspective, and ultimately meaning. The other, here perhaps awkwardly named the *non-reductionist* camp, insists on the uniqueness of each phenomenon, and distrusts relocation to an abstract, detached, and perhaps even obfuscating realm of meaning. So, reduction as I'm using it here isn't an interpretation that lessens the significance of phenomena. On the contrary, we might say that reduction actually seeks to expand or fully unfold the relevance of data, reaching wider understanding thanks to extensive conceptual structures that stand apart from those particulars. In contrast, the non-reductive forgoes such gestures, confident that either an internal logic or a self-sustaining structure simply awaits the eye of a careful observer. The seesaw between these two positions, like any good game, is never resolved fully in favor of one player over the other. In fact, this whole debate is significant not because one side will overcome the other, but rather together their conflict is the stage upon which a greater struggle is being waged. It is a struggle with an anxiety about the entire study of religion, with each side representing the unease of the other. I will return to this below, but first let us turn our attention to one camp, that of reduction, and its side of this seesaw.

In a recent book on material culture, Barry Flood defends his use of outsider or "etic" categories – most importantly his version of cultural *translation* – across the various religious and historical boundaries his research explores. His aim is to defend the reductionism inherent in making the history of religions speak to us today. For Flood, the specter of anachronism looms large, at least in the minds of his imagined critics, for whom he is writing. By accounting for iconoclasm and architecture as the material vehicles for ninth-century Muslim–Hindu encounter, through a narrative of translation, Flood worries he is open to charges of anachronism. He concedes that Muslims and Hindus of this period would not recognize themselves in his model; that is to say, these actors would never define themselves as "translators" of culture, as he is calling them. And yet Flood's approach is surely a sound one. His position is based on two claims, the second perhaps stronger than the first. Flood begins by pointing out that he is writing to his contemporaries, modern historians, and not to the participants in the original events. The implication is that the stories one community tells itself are not interchangeable with those of other communities. More precisely, for us as modern historians a description of the movement of objects and ideas across religious boundaries, usefully framed in terms of translation theory, makes perfect sense. A second observation Flood makes about his reductive gesture is one relating to the very nature of the study of history. He warns that his critics' accusation of anachronism and interventionism "obscures the historicity of history," deflecting attention from the formative prejudices and commitments that underlie any practice of history writing – his own included.[1] Flood's modeling might not be found in the self-conception of the Hindus and Muslims he is describing, but defending his approach to his fellow historians makes clear his own prejudices, and locates his work within the wider modern debates on what makes for good history writing. This reduction then is an opening beyond a simple account of events of the past: for Flood historiography is as much at stake as are the facts of the history of tenth-century Sind.

On the other side of the seesaw we find the complimentary position I've been calling the non-reductive. This is an approach that locates meaning in the immediate vicinity of, or even within, the object. From this perspective, the moment in history at which the object appears is singular, never to be repeated in quite the same way. A phenomenon is not – or at least very little emphasis is placed on it being — part of a wider pattern. No two dots on a graph are identical, even if line that purports to tell their story seems to connect them. This orientation to the local and the immediate, grounds the non-reductive in the logic of the object it addresses. Meaning inheres in the local and the particular, waiting to be unveiled by the neutral and receptive eye of the researcher. Description in its own right makes the significance of a phenomenon explicit, with no call for abstractions or comparisons. Descriptive histories, told ostensibly from the insider's perspective within the religious tradition, constitute such a form of reading. When abstractions are proposed, they are unique to the examples at hand, remaining untranslatable or incomparable to other phenomena. One critique of this approach challenges the assumptions made here about the self-apparent nature of the phenomena that come to be understood. In other words, the question is raised as to how these natural contours, these structures, themselves arise. The non-reductive technique must assume an entire array of concepts, usually theological, before it can allow its object to speak. If the concepts are not to be located elsewhere, as is the case with reductive readings, then they must emerge from this encounter with the phenomena.

These concepts then, if we are to share them with the objects before us, must be unchanging and fixed abstractions. If we are to explore the Middle East non-reductively we will need an unchanging concept of say, the Orient. Or if we are to let religious texts "speak for themselves," we will need to share with them, for example, a conception of subject voice. Since our relationship with the object is limited to this bare equation of viewer and the viewed, there is little place for contestation or relativizing the concepts that are to be put in play. Further in relation to the study of religion, the implications of non-reduction are significant. Russell McCutcheon makes the connection between what he calls the *sui generis* category and a fully non-reductive approach to religion. In other words, the perspective that assumes utterly unique attributes for a religious phenomenon implies that religion itself is unexplainable, irreducible, and untranslatable into any other register. The implications here are several, not the least of which is the foreclosing of the humanistic study of religion, whether it be of the reductive or the non-reductive variety.[2]

The non-reductive camp is a large one, but its exact boundaries are not well marked. Here meaning is inconceivable beyond the parameters associated with the object itself. This perspective is most commonly identified with the work of Mircea Eliade, and perennialists such as Henry Corbin. As historians of religion, these scholars were committed to better knowing religious phenomena by locating them within their chronologies and their social contexts, yet those contexts would never become the determining engines of meaning. In these scholars' analysis, religious phenomena require religiously coherent interpretations and explanations. Eliade reasoned that due to their essential uniqueness, religious phenomena belong to a category of their own. Attempting to explain them as if they were another sort of phenomenon – for example, a cultural product – would only disfigure them beyond recognition. Although he does not use theological terminology, Eliade often speaks of religious phenomena in ways that isolate them from other kinds of phenomena. For example, he tells us that objects are worshiped because they have "become *sacred*, the *ganz andere*."[3] He uses the latter phrase, meaning the *wholly other*, to underline their independent standing. Elsewhere, we are told explicitly that humanistic and social scientific accounts of religious phenomena are simply "false" because they miss "the one unique and irreducible element in it – the element of the sacred."[4] In the same spirit, Corbin would write in the introduction to his monumental *En Islam iranien* that he has sought in his encounter with any religious phenomenon to allow it to "show itself." Historical considerations are important for Corbin, but on condition they not impose an "alien category or consideration" upon the phenomena we are exploring.[5]

If the point of playing on a seesaw isn't to overpower one's opponent – after all, it's a game that takes two – then the goal is to find a balance. While there are many ways to conceive of such a balance, let me underline one proposal. The anthropologist and theorist of religion Talal Asad switches easily between reductive and non-reductive positions. In his now famous critique of Clifford Geertz's definition of religion, Asad points to the short comings of a universally valid descriptor for any cultural phenomenon. Asad at this point is defending the non-reductive. Geertz had claimed that religion was best seen as a system of symbols that convincingly advanced a cosmic order within a human perspective.[6] Asad's objection is that the crucial local histories behind these authoritative systems cannot be accounted for in such a definition. Surely the triumph of every symbolic system, or religion, is simply the last chapter in a long story of contention and conflict with rival systems. To say in essence as Geertz does that "religion is the system in place" is an erasure of the forces and struggles that made it what it is. Surely, Asad argues, knowing these local and historically anchored conditions, and how they contributed to the rise of the object under study, is essential to any profound grasp of religion. His corrective then, is to anchor the study of religion in the heterogeneous elements that have been uniquely put into play in each case. Following Michel Foucault's distrust of historical continuity and genealogy, Asad aims to recover the local interests and forces at play that have been hidden by narratives of the inevitable and the comprehensive. He distrusts the anthropological tendency to translate across cultural spheres.[7] And yet Asad will elsewhere tilt the other way. That is to say, at times this non-reductive posture will be the target of his criticism. On the question of the role of politics in religious formations, Asad is quick to object to those who would seek to insulate religion from secular power.[8] The story of religion then is to be told in terms that exceed its own accounting and its own language.

The need for such a balancing act should not surprise us. For Asad there is clearly a utility in shifting between perspectives and critiques. My point here is that although they are irreconcilable with one another, the reductive and the non-reductive may be usefully employed in succession or in parallel. Another insightful analysis – offered by McCutcheon – wonders if the reduction/non-reduction divide reflects a difference in content.[9] That is to say, these two perspectives address separate types of phenomena, with reduction speaking to complex social situations, and non-reduction focusing on disembodied experiences and states of being. This proposal awaits further exploration and indeed validation. Elsewhere McCutcheon nuances the category, distinguishing between two dimensions of reduction. One he calls *metaphysical reduction*, which is employed by Eliade, Marx, and Freud when they identify an essence behind their religious data.[10] McCutcheon's second dimension is the *methodological reduction*, which is the understanding produced through the interpretive lenses brought to bear by the researcher.

Wayne Proudfoot proposes another balancing model. His contribution redefines the reductive camp, splitting it into two independent procedures. Here reduction at the *descriptive* level – which would consist of a failure to contextualize a religious phenomenon in a way the subject would recognize it – is seen as problematic. A description should reflect the object in its context. To this, Proudfoot juxtaposes what he calls *explanatory reduction* (similar to the *methodological reduction* we just saw). In Proudfoot's eyes this kind of reduction is proper procedure. It offers explanations of a phenomenon that would not be shared by the subject, and might not be acceptable to her at all. In essence the proposal here is for non-reduction in description, and reduction in explanation.[11]

As I suggested earlier, the real significance of these debates is not one side prevailing, but rather it is a deeper anxiety that the objects of religion may be lost. As an academic discipline, the study of religion labors under a fear that its very object of study may elude it – or worse, may cease to exist the moment it is located under the scholarly gaze. As the brief survey above has made clear, there are clearly two sides to the seesaw, yet these poles are not mutually exclusive, and more than one model has been proposed in which both sides may be meaningfully embraced. Yet no matter how this tension is resolved, an anxiety persists for religionists, and it is as follows. The reductionist position can be seen as denaturing the religious object, and threatening to relocate it to an alien scholarly or disciplinary narrative. In this scenario, the study of religion then becomes a discourse on things like literature, social institutions, or politics. Thus, the object of study is lost, and the rationale for the entire discipline vanishes. Further, this anxiety is actually shared by the reductionist – but in a mirrored way – claiming that the non-reductive approach also loses the object of study, but does so by isolating it from wider regimes of meaning making. In other words, by preserving it, we are making it inaccessible.[12] Both positions are committed to the study of religion, yet both fear the other perspective threatens the very object of study.

As useful as my seesaw image might be as a descriptive device, its utility is clearly limited. Not only do reductionists and non-reductionists not line up cleanly on either side, but the analysis at play is also more complex. A simplistic model that contrasts description with interpretation – with the former supposedly self-apparent and mechanical, and the latter abstracting and purely conceptual – has largely been abandoned in our field. Theories of reading, for example, have overturned this account by pointing to the preconceived notions (from the text, or about the text) that are required to even begin the process of reading. In other words, the so-called abstracting that we think occurs after an encounter with a text, in reality must be in play before we start the very act of reading. And further, to complete the *hermeneutic circle*, the abstract meaning making that reading gives rise to is recalibrated and repeated in new instantiations at each reading of a text. In light of these insights, the argument goes, interpretation is not outside or after our contact with the object, and description is not mechanical, unchanging, or innocent. I rehearse this quick aside on hermeneutics not to suggest that religion can be accounted for as strategies of reading or language, but rather to claim that the reductionist and non-reductionist positions are mutually sustaining strategies for managing the anxiety of a threatened object of study. I say mutually sustaining since although they begin from different starting points, they can either be used in an alternating procedure, or as we have also seen, divided into further interrelated categories, as Asad, Proudfoot, Segal, and others have shown us.

BEAUTY AND ITS DISCONTENTS

In parallel to the anxiety that religion might disappear into unintelligibility or slip away into an alien discourse, another threat looms over the objects and images of religion. These objects have been obscured by two prominent mechanisms that we unthinkingly rely on every day. The first is the mechanism of signification, and the second that of representation. Both are familiar to us as techniques for getting at the meaning of the objects we encounter. In instances of signification, we interrogate the object for a "real"'meaning that we assume lies somewhere behind it. We are confident in this operation's efficacy, thanks to a necessary link that we can trace back to what is signified. We experience a remarkable leap from the sensorially tangible figure, image, or object, to a metaphysical realm of significance and meaning. The sign serves as the stepping-stone to where we really want to go; our aim is the signified, and the signifier is the path that gets us there. In the first half of the twentieth century this system was worked out in the context of language and culture theory. Building on the insights of Ferdinand de Saussure, Claude Lévi-Strauss developed theories around this structure, connecting the individual to the all-important signified meaning. For example, we might think of a hand gesture, which is meaningless until placed within its cultural context. Interpreting a gesture within its wider culture is hardly a technique we need to defend; we do this all the time. De Saussure's model of the mutually constituting relationship between overarching language and unique utterance is clearly behind much of the modeling here. The specific signifiers (the words, the gestures, the objects) are themselves the product of the wider meaning-making culture or system. However, priority is clearly given to the move from the signifier to the signified. Structuralism is, after all, about the *meaning* of signs, not the signifying objects. Post-structuralism is suspicious of this model, and has offered many criticisms, but for our purposes it will suffice to simply note one issue. Briefly, the concern is that the signifying dynamic of structuralism erases the object, relegating it to a vehicle for servicing the more valued goal, that of the signified. We rush past the signifier, intent on reaching the hidden meaning; a maneuver that not only blinds us to the object, but also denies those particular objects their significance, depth, and standing.

  Much in line with this process that at once enlightens and obscures – significance is attained while its indicator is pushed aside – stands another common mechanism, that of representation. While there are several ways to characterize the process of representation, they all suffer from the tendency to erase the object. Representations communicate by making the absent referent present to the viewer. For example, consider that a picture of a dog is not about paint or canvas, but is about a dog who sits elsewhere, if not in the next room then perhaps in history, or our imagination. If we talk about the content of such a picture, we address either the evoked dog herself or the rendering of her likeness, whether it's an accurate, or charming, or stylized rendering, for example. But whether we are concerned with the accuracy of the picture, or we want to discuss the interpretive gesture of the artist in the rendering, we continue to look past the object itself. We see through the representation, as if looking out a window, to something beyond. Our goal lies elsewhere. A common if naïve compliment for a representation is to declare that it's "just like the real thing." So just as the signifier effaced itself by deflecting our inquiry onward onto the signified, in the practice of representation, the image, as it stands before us in its uniqueness and material immediacy, quickly disappears as we look toward the distant subject being represented.

  These practices of representation and sign reading, however, are not exhaustive of the full communication that is at play. Despite their service as "stepping-stones" or "windows," these objects may be engaged more fully in their own right – in fact, some artworks began to force this reconsideration several decades ago. This turn to the object or image itself was given the dramatic name "The End of Art." In truth, it wasn't so much an end of art per se, but rather as Arthur Danto put it, the end of beauty as a defining element of an artwork.[13] With the appearance of non-representational art and abstraction, what most aesthetics had assumed was an essential marker of art, beautiful representation, suddenly fell away. Modern art was not beautiful, at least in the conventional sense, and yet it was clearly art. The ancient equation of beauty with the careful representation of well-proportioned, morally uplifting forms, had been overthrown by the history of artworks themselves. Now a Jackson Pollock drip painting could become a masterpiece, overturning the common, as well as the philosophical, assumptions about representation and beauty, and opening a framework in which to consider the immediacy of the art object itself.

Several new avenues for rethinking and redefining beauty, aesthetics, and art, have been opened up with the fall of the old paradigm. According to Susan Buck-Morss we may consider aesthetic experience simply the affecting of our senses. She wants to move past the focus on artworks, and widen out the field of encounter with objects. Picking up on Heidegger's claim that an object's "thingness" becomes clear to us only once its utility is negated – think of the new light in which we consider a tool once it is broken, or the artistic use of ready-mades – she proposes a redefinition of beauty that extends far beyond its old conception. For Buck-Morss any cultural object or aspect of nature, beyond objects traditionally defined as art, can be taken as beautiful in the sense that they are experienced as a materiality that resists instrumentalization.[14]

In an echo of the "End of Art" idea – but at a distance from aesthetics – Talal Asad has argued for a similar reconsideration and turn toward the object. In a discussion of cultural structures, the relationship between signifiers themselves can usefully be interrogated for interrelations, before the process of signification steers our consideration off to the realm of cultural systems. In other words, Asad wants to make room for the particular instantiations within a full vision of culture. Following in this direction, Webb Keane proposes that the particular and the historical be preserved along with the universalizing language of religion.[15] This is also an important re-anchoring of the objects, bodies, and signifiers within their cultural systems of meaning.

I will move to consider more fully the neglected object below, but before I do, allow me to caution against replacing one misconception with another. The danger in turning to the object is one of overcompensating and over-reaching. To turn to the object then should not entail isolating it from its cultural, historical, and ideological contexts. My complaint earlier was that the signifier deflects attention from itself; such deflections, however, are important functions that must be attended to in our full encounter with the object. In other words, while signification and representation do present a challenge to the consideration of the particular object, those particulars are never usefully considered in isolation from what they evoke, represent, or signify. The objects before us could never stand utterly on their own anyway. Adorno pushed back against such a narrow reduction of the experience of art when he placed aesthetic experience squarely within aesthetic language. An individual encounters the artwork not as a blank slate upon which she records her immediate experience, but rather via a developed language of art. It is thanks to this vast discourse around art that not only can artworks be located, but that they can be experienced at all. Adorno expands on this two-dimensional nature of experience, in which artworks require what they are not, their social other, in order to fully be themselves. He frames this it out saying, "...art on the one hand confronts society anonymously, and, on the other hand, is itself social, defin(ing) the law of its experience ... Its inner construction requires, in however mediated a fashion, what is itself not art."[16] Here he wants to recognize the importance of the individual's experience, while insisting that it is simultaneously anchored within, and limited by, the social understandings available at that moment of encounter.

Another proposal to avoid the dead end of isolated relativism was advanced much earlier by Kant. His strategy did not evoke the historically situated "language of art" that Adorno would point to, but rather Kant held that the individual encounter with an artwork was an experience that at heart was available to all of us. Yes, in each instance the aesthetic experience belongs to the individual, but that experience is the same one anyone else *would have* in that situation of encounter. When individuals push past their intervening desires, prejudices, and interests, they get to a subjective experience that is universally available to all. In pulling away from our interests and desires (Kant actually calls this a "disinterested" posture) we get to our truly subjective experience. Surprisingly, this subjectivity is not the product of an individual's whim or fancy, but instead anchors this experience in a shared human framework.[17] We shall see that later thinkers will return to Kant's disinterestedness claim, but for the moment I will simply note its function, in parallel to Adorno's position above, in rescuing our experience of objects and images from any individualistic relativism.

The point that emerges from these reflections runs counter to the way we usually think about images and objects. The typical account has us encountering an object, taking it in through our sense perception, which our reflective minds subsequently consider. In other words, we see the object, and then begin to think about it. Intuitively this feels right, but further critical reflection troubles this story. One strong objection, voiced best by Adorno, simply claims that objects would be imperceptible if approached before any mental reflection had taken place.[18] Thus, reflection can't be placed above or after the sensuous encounter. We must already possess a conceptual apparatus within which to locate the object. To begin to consider an object, we need sensory data, which itself can only begin to register with us once we can locate it in relation to ideas. Turning to religious objects then, we must bring an understanding of religion generally, including the specific tradition at hand, to identify the object, and begin to interpret the encounter. Reasoned reflection and concepts are not simply built over perception, coming after our innocent encounters as a tabula rasa, but somehow all of these components are in a reciprocal interplay. Scholars have taken various positions on this interplay between the immediate sensorium and reflective or conceptual procedures. We will explore some of these approaches shortly, but first we must turn to some of the key insights around "aesthetics," and their disputed utility in helping us think about objects, images, and religion.

In a basic accounting, we can identify two central concerns in this area. The first, actually known as *aisthesis* is a category defining itself against abstract ideas; it is simply a concern with the stimuli of the senses, individually or in concert. Aristotle took these procedures to be key generators of experience.[19] The word "aesthetics" appears in the mid eighteenth century, coined by A. G. Baumgarten, and is often taken to be a corrective to the harsh mind–body division that Descartes had formalized a century earlier. The rise of science, with its commitment to natural laws and the universal function of the "scientific method" made a receptive environment for the privileging of ideas and concepts. Baumgarten returned to a concern with the senses, in particular as they could serve as data for discerning the principles of beauty. He wanted to build on the senses rather than the intellect.[20] The second concern of aesthetics builds upon this project of recovery of the senses, but anchors itself more deeply in the relationship of the sensory to the conceptual. This formulation was articulated by Kant, and is key to modern thinking in aesthetics. Kant's central insight was not to recognize that ideas and sensory data were somehow connected; it was rather that sensory experience of particular objects is not fully reducible to the ideas that are at play with those experiences. Kant's aesthetics integrates the data of the senses, our impressions through them, the ideas behind them (and subsequently altered by them), while reserving space for the experience of the work that stands outside of these rational accountings. The aesthetic communication includes ideas and concepts, but crucially it also requires real and immediate objects for an encounter. Aesthetic experience is not "in the eye of the beholder," in the sense that it arises from whimsy or caprice. In your encounter with a particular artwork, the communication that is not reducible to ideas, is essentially the same as what I will discover in my encounter with that same object. For Kant, this untranslatable and irreducible experience, without goal or purpose, is available always to everyone.[21]

My characterization here of Kant's system sidesteps several important distinctions he makes – not to mention that Kant seems to have taken different positions on the topic in various places in his writing. Nevertheless, we can now consider some of the subsequent critiques and elaborations, particularly those that have been enlisted for theorizing about religion. We may start with three objections that seem to represent much of the current resistance among scholars to Kantian aesthetics. One concern is that Kant's system robs aesthetic experiences (or "judgments") of their visceral senses. Susan Buck-Morss worries that in this system we have no way to account for the procedures of our sensory intake, the mechanics and the experience, that connect us to the objects we are encountering.[22] While I agree that Kant's system does not cover the ground that later phenomenology would focus on, with its careful attention to the interaction of our senses and the world discovered around them, it seems only fair to note that in Kant's aesthetic theory the immediate sensory experience is foundational. He insists that concept formation is dependent upon the apprehension (via the body) of sensory particulars – that is to say, we can't think about art without engaging with real and specific artworks. While Buck-Morss's criticism is well taken, and we do need further thinking about how our senses do their work, it seems that Kant's system has the virtue of securing the place and function of the sensory encounter, even if it cannot account fully for them.

In the same direction as Buck-Morss's critique, Terry Eagleton sees Kant's treatment of bodily senses as insufficient. Eagleton's position is that Kant is only partially successful in accounting for our individual experiences of artworks. I mentioned earlier that for Kant it was important that part of our aesthetic experience (that part not reducible to concepts) can safely be assumed to hold for every other person, if they were to encounter the same object. That is to say, there is a certain universality at play in aesthetic experience. Eagleton seizes on this, and makes the point that while Kant may seem to be embracing the particular and the individual, the way he recovers this shared dimension of aesthetic experience actually erases our embodied presence in the system. I also mentioned above Kant's procedure for getting at the conceptually irreducible experience, which entailed pushing aside our personal prejudices and interests that we have generated around our aesthetic experience. This reduction, Eagleton claims, produces, "a 'subjective' but non-sensuous aesthetics."[23] While pleased that room has been made for the individual experience, Eagleton is nevertheless concerned that this has been done by proposing an abstracted subject, leaving us no way to account for the experiences of real bodies.

A third objection to Kant's aesthetics approaches the matter from the opposite direction, that is to say, it begins with the immediate apprehension of the object. While Eagleton's concern was that Kant didn't really get down to the embodied experiences, Birgit Meyer starts with the beholder of the aesthetic object. She claims that Kant's system only poorly accounts for this beholder's experience, and in the case of religious viewers, it misses the aesthetic phenomena completely. She contrasts the scenario of Kant's "disinterested" viewer engaging with an artwork, to the intense experiences religious practitioners typically have with devotional images and objects.[24] This objection is important in that it points to an important distinction in Kant's aesthetics. Meyer wants insight into the full experience of the aesthetic object, and sees the model of the "disinterested" viewer as missing the fullness of such an experience of religious aesthetics.[25]

While I agree with Meyer's focus on lived, embodied, and religiously informed experiences, I would argue that the Kantian model remains relevant. Meyer objects to a notion of disinterest that seems to exclude the intensity of feeling that is a play in typical religious aesthetic practices. And yet, for Kant it is disinterestedness, whether we are calmly viewing an artwork or gazing emotionally at an icon, that allows for aesthetic engagement at all. For him, disinterest brackets the surrounding conceptual world, making space for those experiences.[26] Let me recall the point I made earlier about Kant's aesthetics, which identifies the full experience as irreducible to concepts – and that this irreducible dimension can only be isolated through a procedure of disinterest. As Eagleton puts it, this points to experience that is both compelling and yet free from determining concepts. He describes it as a law that cannot be formulated: "The aesthetic in Kant short-circuits the conceptual to link concrete particulars in their very immediacy to a kind of universal law, but a law which can be in no sense formulated."[27] This unwritten and unspeakable law, giving aesthetic experience its force, is available through disinterestedness. The experience may be emotional or staid. The failure to distinguish between the two is exactly where Kant stops being useful to Meyer's inquiries. While Meyer has no further need of Kant on this point, and has moved on to successfully refine her own models and theories, I would claim that Kant's aesthetics nevertheless remains a useful reference for the field, since it helps us understand that the senses access objects and images in a way that exceeds our discursive registers. In this context, the disinterestedness that many have taken to indicate a cold impersonal disengagement (i.e. Meyer's concern) is actually the recognition of engagement with objects, which lies between sensory intake and conceptually informed experience.

With this stripped-down account of Kant's aesthetics, my intention has been to open a space between cultural determinism and a mechanistic sensory positivism. Any theory of religious aesthetic experience must account for both the irreducible power of the image or object as we encounter it, as well as the wider standing of such images and objects within the conceptual realms of theology, metaphysics, cosmology, etc. We noted earlier in our discussion the turn to object materiality and the rise of the "End of Art" thesis. There the development of art itself has shown that beauty and representation are not foundational to aesthetics. Kant had used beauty as his central illustration of aesthetic experience, but modern art has all but abandoned the identification with beauty. Likewise, the assumptions of Kant's age about the essential role of representation in an artwork no longer hold in our own. Yet duly noting the essential insights of his system – the non-conceptual and non-discursive communication at play in aesthetics – we can move forward. Leaving behind Kant's references to bourgeois art, Susan Buck-Morss proposes a reframing around the sensory, claiming provocatively, "My senses are affected. This is aesthetic experience." At this point we are far removed from the ancient definitions that located beauty in symmetry or identified it with the unity of the good. We have broadened out from a Kantian focus on high art as reference, to where Buck-Morss concludes of the "beautiful" that, "It doesn't matter whether that material reality calls itself art or not. It could be the experience of any cultural object – or a person, or an aspect of nature."[28]

With this liberating of aesthetics from a narrow focus on high art, reflections on the nature and function of the aesthetic object can proliferate. This post-Kantian discourse has turned much of its attention to the social life of artworks and objects. A central insight in discussions of objects in relation to the world around them is the inescapable tension that lies within these objects, one that both constitutes them as aesthetic objects, and destabilizes them in relation to the wider world. They are connected to, but not fully determined by, the world around them. And it is this indeterminacy that becomes the opening for change and for ethics.

Adorno starts to get at this indeterminacy of artworks when his aesthetic theory turns to a foundational paradox. On the one hand, every culturally charged object is autonomous in the sense that it stands as a unique individual. Cultural theorists now talk about the biography of an object, an idea that is predicated on the historical particularity of objects.[29] Each articulates its own aesthetic communication with the viewer who encounters it. And yet, any such communication is also predicated on the object being recognizable, so that it can get a foothold in our visual field. This traction is supplied by a negotiation with the wider cultural system, allowing for the object to be considered as an artwork, as well as permitting reflection on it. We noted this earlier, in relation to Adorno's claim of the artwork inhering in the language of art. Thus, art is at once autonomous and social, with its own construction requiring its other. This "other" constantly stands within the experience of the work, even ensuring the work's coherence. In a rough parallel to Kant's model, which links sensory apprehensions to reflective thinking, Adorno ties together the autonomy and the dependence of a work, grounding the aesthetic experience upon a dual consciousness of how an object is unique and new, and yet resonant and recognizable. For Adorno, artworks are neither reducible to their cultural contexts, nor are they utterly self-making; their autonomy is real, but like all freedom in the end a negotiated one. "Only when art's other is sensed as a primary layer in the experience of art does it become possible to sublimate this (outside) layer ... Art is autonomous and it is not; without what is heterogeneous to it, its autonomy eludes it."[30]

This internal and essential plurality of artworks not only speaks to their indeterminacy, but it also sheds light on their role as gestures of destabilization. This plurality means these objects have leverage against the existing order; in their autonomy they can challenge, while in their familiarity they can facilitate real change. One version of this insight hinges on the interplay between individual and society. Eagleton describes the dual function of aesthetics, which at once embeds us within a continuity and yet also serves as the voice for our individual expression and by implication the voice for historical change.[31] In its autonomy, the artwork can challenge, while in its social anchoring it speaks the language of the world around it. However, this leverage is not ideologically pre-determined. The point is that an artwork, by its very nature, constitutes a site for possible change. Adorno talks of art as turning against what "merely exists," while it may simultaneously replicate the status quo. Its "form" is its disruptive capacity, while its "elements" are its continuity with the social. Adorno's form is the novel and autonomous standing of the artwork, and its elements are the components that are familiar to the world around it.[32]

While Adorno typically underlines the essential neutrality of this capacity, Susan Buck-Morss sees a clearer trajectory for the unruly force of aesthetics. She emphasizes aesthetic communication's disruptive abilities, calling it a "knowing" that resists culture. As any historian of art would tell us, successful artworks after all are often revolutionary. But this capacity, Buck-Morss reminds us, is deeply seated within the constitution of the artwork. Culture is always part of the equation, but the autonomy of the artwork gives it a foothold outside its social configuration, allowing it a critical stance. The aesthetic experience then, "... is the body's form of critical cognition."[33] These perspectives point then to an important capacity for change inherent in the aesthetic experience. An opening is thus made for disruption, distance, and critique.

A POETICS OF THE MUNDANE

Historians of Islamic art have long labored under their own version of many of these challenges. One problem is that when trying to move beyond a descriptive approach to Islamic art, questions quickly arise around the production and reception of artworks. On the one hand, we can try to reconstruct the social worlds in which these objects were crafted and viewed, with the goal of decoding the references within the artwork, or determining the wider conditions to which a piece is responding. On the other hand, we also begin to ask questions about the universally applicable dynamics of this art. Islamic art is after all a human civilizational achievement, and something of that operation must be universally available, and thus recoverable to historians. The two sides of this equation seem irreducible, with historical reductionism standing against an ahistorical psychological reconstruction. In a book on medieval geometric designs, Gülru Necipoglu has wrestled with these issues, reflecting on the non-representational designs that many scholars have dismissed as simply decorative, operating independently of cultural codes. Her great insight is to avoid the juxtaposition of iconology and non-figural decoration – that is, images that can be decoded, and designs that cannot – in its place proposing that the communication at play with abstract designs is culturally grounded.[34] The debates in Islamic art history around iconology and ornamentation will continue, but for our purposes Necipoglu's move to anchor non-figural art in the specifics of the Islamic culture that produced them, is an important opening. The implication is that not only images, but also design and ornamentation, are sites of enculturation; both images and objects then are bridges between individuals and the order of the world around them.

Following Necipoglu, we can now move past the unhelpful binary that opposed psychological explanation to historical semiotics, and toward a model that embraces these dimensions, but does so by focusing on the object itself. That is to say, the dynamics of perception and its historical contexts can be refocused through objects because they tie the individual to the world around them. As Eagleton points out, social order connects to the body directly. It does this through the habits, sentiments, and pieties of the body, becoming its impulses and sensibilities "lived in everyday unreflective custom."[35] Power and order thus inhere in the aesthetics of the individual subjective life. This subjective experience, formed through contact with objects and images, is the site of order, law, and religion. Objects, and the aesthetic communication that informs them, are essential to our knowing the worlds that created them.

While the struggle between idea and object generates religious phenomena, the outcomes are not predetermined. Beyond the discursive claims with which an object is associated, it also employs its non-discursive aesthetic communication. This communication is only possible in the confrontation with real and individual objects, and thus the outcome is historically and culturally grounded, never determined in the abstract. Each event of religious practice entails a unique encounter with an object within a discursive world. These events normally are continuous in their character, facilitating a cultural continuity, and yet, as Adorno pointed out to us earlier, an opening for change is always there. When we observe individual objects operating in the world, indeterminacy is part of the equation.

The object might not speak in the way that a concept does, but that doesn't mean it's empty and meaningless, or that its communication operates beyond our range of understanding. This is the crucial insight of aesthetics. *I would like to propose we think of such communication as emerging out of resistance.* That is to say, rather than assuming that religious objects are passive vessels driven solely by theological agendas, we should envisage objects negotiating with those ideas. Objects resist the concepts they are intimately connected with. Such a model of negotiation allows both ideas and objects their standing, and yet points to the central constitutive dynamic of an undetermined outcome. Objects thus rely on concepts, and yet resist any complete appropriation. The object of religion is constituted through this resistance and negotiation.

This relationship between the object and the concept – or the sensory and the semiotic – will remain the central concern of this book. Through the course of our study it will be seen that religion is founded upon, and produced out of that relationship. And yet, this approach seems to run counter to religious discourse itself. After all, religion speaks with a voice that is above the mundane; its celestial source is by definition beyond the historical and the material. Clifford Geertz long ago pointed out the irony that the transcendent position of the religious voice is always grounded in historical particulars.[36] This book then, with its focus on objects, swims against the self-descriptive current of religious traditions. Islamic religious language does not speak in terms of contingency, history, or materiality; these variables are of course relevant to it, but they are subordinate to the ultimate truths that religion is speaking for. Thus, my task in the chapters that follow is not to expose these discursive limitations, the blind spots that hide the contingent and the material of Islamic practice. Instead, by recovering the relationships forged between objects and ideas, a blurry dimension of Islamic religion will be brought into focus.

With my focus on the interrelatedness of object and idea, and the recovery of the activity of the former, we can move away from analyses of religion that overstate the determining role of ideas and conceptual models in the history of Islamic practice. Legal reflections, theological discourses, and other normative Islamic formulations will instead be put into dialectical relationship with materiality, rather than being deferred to as final determinations of historical practice, belief, or experience. The remainder of this book then will consist of studies in this vein, bringing out the creative tension that is generated when an object resists such reduction. Earlier, I described this as the labor of the machines of religion. The chapters investigate historical scenarios through which objects and ideas intertwine to negotiate themselves and their futures.

In this light, I will tell the stories of pilgrimage and parading objects, of relics and banners, idols and iconoclasts – all of them enlisted in the religious lives of Muslims. Our starting point will be pre-modern Egypt and Syria, but in order to tell these stories, we will have to follow these objects across various geographies and time periods. These resisting objects generate complex equations of visual practice, object and bodily display, theological disputes, religious revivalism, political authority, and public controversies over religious ritual. No single story will emerge from these case studies – beyond that of images and objects negotiating their immediate and evolving circumstances – but each scenario will produce a unique episode in the materiality of Islamic life.

ONE

OBJECTS OVER DISTANCE

Felicitous Egypt has no rival for her three sources of delight: the sultan's processions, the flooding of the Nile, and the rightly guided *mahmal* moving by day.

Al-Jabarti, 1814

It is significant that in his description of the most captivating moments of Egyptian life the historian 'Abd al-Rahman al-Jabarti pointed to parades. In the pre-modern period sultans and their deputies used large public processions to display their wealth and power, both on their way out on military campaign and hopefully even more conspicuously upon a victorious return. These gatherings displayed military might, but were also claims to legitimacy. Investiture ceremonies sent important messages to the population that continuity at the top of the social hierarchy was being assured. But order is not only political; it is cosmological and religious too. Al-Jabarti thus lists the Nile flood as the second source of national delight. This yearly spectacle, which around Cairo included lavish parading, was far more than just an occasion for communal celebration; it guaranteed the agricultural cycle, and thus the survival of Egypt for another year. All along the Nile, farmlands would be fertilized by the silt arriving when the river burst its banks each year in the fall. The official rituals around measuring the rising waters – prognosticating a sufficient or an inadequate flooding, and even petitioning the Nile itself – were ubiquitous from ancient times up until the modern era. This ritual negotiation with the natural order was typically successful, and famine though not unknown, was rare in Egypt. In Cairo the flood cycle was most evident in relation to the cutting of the dam of the city's canals. The sovereign's symbolic actions around the opening of these waterways were numerous, and parading figured prominently. The cosmic order was also preserved through religion, the third of Jabarti's delights of Egypt, and was embodied in the processing *mahmal* or holy palanquin. These elaborate and striking litters circulated widely in Cairo, Damascus, and other cities, performing rituals associated with the Hajj. Provocative in their size and expense, *mahmal*s from every region and era played key roles in the organization and experience of the pilgrimage to Mecca. We will return to parading practices in Chapter 3, and attend to some of the ritual objects associated with the Nile in Chapter 4, but first let us turn to the *mahmal* (also pronounced *mahmil*) and the dramatic career it enjoyed on the public stage of Islamic practice.

The Hajj is one of the five pillars of the faith. Along with salat, fasting during the month of Ramadan, paying yearly alms, and openly declaring one's belief in God and His prophet, the Hajj is incumbent upon every Muslim who has the means to make the journey safely. While many have made the great pilgrimage – earning the honorific Hajji or Hajja – the numbers have always constituted only a small proportion of the global Muslim population. In the past the vast distances, expense of travel, and dangers along the pilgrimage routes, made the trip a daunting one. Even in the twentieth century, with its long-distance communications and travel by air, the numbers remain a small proportion. The dangers of disease and mass stampede – remember that the Hajj in 2016 was estimated at just over two million – along with the logistics of managing so many bodies within a fixed ritual space, mean that quotas on admission to the modern Hajj will continue to significantly restrict numbers. This situation means that although a central ritual, relatively few Muslims can actually leave on the Hajj. A Muslim will know the obligation, may have celebrated another Muslim's successful completion of the Hajj, but likely never have herself gone to Mecca. And yet as we shall see below, the situation is not one of utter frustration; on the contrary, the Hajj has been woven into shared religious life in several ways, rendering it immediately available to all. For centuries the Hajj, particularly for Egyptians, was literally within arm's reach; the body and its senses, particularly those of vision and touch, ensured the Hajj as a religious practice was always a local practice. We shall explore some of these practices in this chapter.

To say that the Hajj is local is not to deny its global and even cosmological significance. It played an important role in the foundational narratives of the Islamic community. In the arc of Muhammad's prophetic mission, it served as both a past to be recovered and a future to be redeemed. Muhammad overcame resistance from the Meccan elites, and secured access to the great shrine. He purged it of its many pagan idols, and a few years later redirected Muslim salat away from Jerusalem and toward Mecca. As we shall see below, the Hajj space and the objects and bodies that inhabit it, are the essential raw material for the construction of Muslim practice.

While the Hajj processions traveled the major arteries of a particular city, they were part of the immense wider web of bodies, objects, and terrain that stretched across the Muslim world. Yet despite its universality as a religious obligation upon all Muslims, in important ways the Hajj remained deeply grounded in the visual and material life of all Cairenes. The pilgrimage procession, along with its attendant escorts, texts, fabrics, images, palanquin, mounts, itineraries, and audiences, embodied this central duty and belief. The Hajj then was not simply something done out in the desert wastes of Egypt and the Hijaz; it did not begin with the departure from Cairo, nor did it end in Mecca by simply reaching the Ka'ba. The Hajj occurred as much within the cities of Cairo or Damascus as it did in Mecca or Medina.

My focusing on these local practices of the Hajj should not be seen as a turn away from formal religious practice, in favor of 'popular' religion. I resist this popular vs. elite model because such a position would reduce the Egyptian and Syrian pilgrimage practices to cultural accretions sitting uneasily upon a "properly" religious concept. It would also be saying that viewing a mural celebrating a retuning Hajji, or joining a queue to venerate an object that has been to the Prophet's tomb in Medina, are isolated and idiosyncratic religious gestures that are not fully Islamic. In the study of religion, such normative claims very problematically locate the essence of religion in an abstract, disembodied, and ahistorical realm. I reject such a proposition, as I hold that religion essentially inheres in culture. Even at its most abstract, religious conceptions are cultural, embodied, and historically positioned. While voices within a religious community may debate the boundaries between proper and improper beliefs and actions, for the scholar such categories are of little use. As I suggested earlier, a wider perspective on the interplay between religious objects and ideas is called for. The story of the *mahmal* and related objects of the Hajj shows how Islamic law, theology, and the politics of the Hajj evolved in relationship with material practices. The objects in ritual use were more than the symbolic sensory expression of doctrine; they shifted in form and presence, and resonated in tension with the abstractions to which they were intimately connected. Uncovering the transfiguring of objects and ideas within this wider history ultimately shows the *mahmal* to be a dynamic object that destabilizes several important boundaries. Debated among jurists, appropriated by sultans, cherished and venerated as a devotional object, the *mahmal* served to undo distinctions between distance and presence, the profane and the religious, as well as those between objects and persons.

The two central objects of the Hajj parades were the *kiswa*, a large elaborately inscribed covering destined to hang over the Ka'ba, and the *mahmal*, a large decorated empty palanquin or litter, which would accompany the *kiswa* on its journey to Mecca. Figure 1 shows a *mahmal* from the end of the nineteenth century, sent from Egypt by the Khedive Muhammad Tawfiq. We shall turn in more detail to *mahmals* shortly, but for the moment note the elaborate decorations and calligraphy displayed on the litter. The *kiswa* – literally the "dress" of the Ka'ba – was also decorated, particularly its *hizam* or belt which bore both religious text and profane identifiers. Figure 2 shows a section of the belt displaying a passage from the end of the third chapter of the Qur'an, on the right on a black background, promising success to those with patience and constancy. A lower band in black bears text of the last chapter of the Qur'an, warning of Satan's temptations. Both panels are visually contrasted with the name Selim II to the left on a red backing. The Ottoman sultan would have commissioned this piece around 1570. A new *kiswa* dress was sewn and dispatched each year on the Hajj, while the *mahmal* made the return journey, with its decoration changing only when its royal patron was replaced by his successor.

The origins of the practice of covering the Ka'ba predate the Islamic period, and the practice continues today, but the career of its accompanying *mahmal* has a clearly marked start and end point within Islamic history. As we shall see below, although *mahmals* could originate from just about any capital within the Islamic world, in practice the vast majority came from Cairo. From its first appearance around 1270, to its official demise in 1953, the *mahmal* was associated with Egypt. These objects were the focal point of the Cairo processions, with the *mahmal* making a striking impression on the vast crowds who would turn out to see, and if possible touch it. A visitor to the city in the mid-nineteenth century described the intensity of this interaction. At one procession he reports, "Many of the people in the streets pressed violently towards it (the *mahmal*), to touch it with their hands, which, having done so, they kissed; and many of the women who witnessed the spectacle from the latticed windows of the houses let down their shawls or head-veils, in order to touch with them the sacred object."[1]

As these preliminary images demonstrate, an important component of this drama is the identifying features of the *kiswa* and *mahmal*. I shall return to these in detail below, but for the moment it will suffice to note that these objects do not easily align according to the traditional distinction we make between profane authority and religion. Islamic political theory has often set this binary in the terms *din* (religion) and *dawla* (dynasty/empire). Interestingly, both are represented in the features of the *mahmal* and *kiswa*. The *mahmal* always displayed prominently the emblem of its patron – as we saw in Figure 1,

1 Le *mahmal*, after 1886, Cairo. Credit: ARC, p. 163; Hajj and the Arts of Pilgrimage. Khalili
Collections. © Nour Foundation. Courtesy the Khalili Family Trust

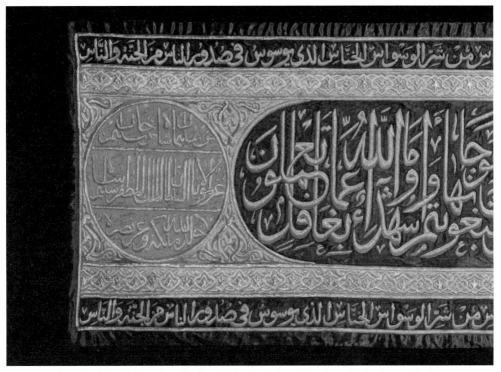

2 Section from the belt of the Ka'ba. Credit: TXT 280; Hajj and the Arts of Pilgrimage. Khalili Collections. © Nour Foundation. Courtesy the Khalili Family Trust

Tawfiq placed the sultan's monogram, clearly visible, in the middle of the upper triangular panel. At the same time the *mahmal* made explicit reference to its religious function by displaying Qur'anic passages and pious phrases. Likewise, the *kiswa* dress, as we noted in the example above, bore the name of its patron – normally the sovereign – alongside its prominent scriptural components. Here the connection I noted earlier between concepts and objects is clearly at play. Below we shall see that sending a *mahmal* was not only an expensive proposition but it was often a contested one, jealously guarded. But here the important point is the claim to authority that the *mahmal* itself makes possible, which is the display of the sultan's name, materializing his authority explicitly on nothing less than one of the central rites of Islamic tradition. In exploring the history of the *mahmal* we shall see that it presented a new vehicle for mobilizing concepts of political authority. At the same time, as I argued above, our objects often resist or reframe concepts. The material and aesthetic capacities of the *mahmal* offer clear if narrow parameters for the claims of authority. *Mahmal*s were conspicuous for their elaborate decoration; their beauty was expected to be striking, making an unrivalled impression. Although

3 Modern Kaʻba with *kiswa* dress. Credit: S. M. Amin/Saudi Aramco/SAWDIA

each *mahmal* was unique in its embellishments, and no formal rules ever developed around their design, they clearly needed to be extravagant if they were to be successful. Egyptian rulers projected power in many ways, and the *mahmal* was prominent among them.

Although essentially an empty structure – and entering it does not constitute part of the Hajj rite – the Kaʻba makes a dramatic impression on pilgrims as they enter the *Haram* complex in Mecca. In its current form, it rises almost 13 m from the ground, with a length at about 12 m and a width about 10 m. The overall form is roughly that of a cube (Arabic: *kaʻba*). Three of the four corners are named according to their geographic orientation – the northern corner is the Iraqi, the eastern the Syrian, and the southern the Yemeni. The eastern corner holds the Black Stone, embedded about 1.5 m off of the ground, in a silver frame. The eastern wall of the structure holds the single access point, a door raised 2 m from the floor. In its immediate context within the Great Mosque, the Kaʻba dwarfs the series of lesser objects that occupy the sanctuary courtyard with it. Of these the most important are the well of Zamzam, the Station of Abraham (*maqam Ibrahim*), and the Enclosure (*hijr*) of Ismaʻil, marked by a low wall (*hatim*) forming a semicircle across the northwestern face of the Kaʻba.[2] In Figure 3, showing the Kaʻba with a modern *kiswa* covering, the *hijr* is partially visible on the left side of the image. The dimensions of the Kaʻba have seen some change, most significantly in the first century of the Islamic era it was rebuilt to temporarily include a second door, and lengthened to include the *hijr* enclosure.[3] The early historian of Mecca, al-Azraqi tells us that it was ʻAbd Allah ibn al-Zubayr who opened a second door, and expanded the building's foot print when he rebuilt it after it suffered significant damage in the course of his rebellion against central Umayyad rule. This 'D' shape floor plan seems to have been the original pre-Islamic form. The present dimensions – the square shape, with the semi circled *hijr* enclosure outside – were determined by the Umayyad general al-Hajjaj, after he defeated Ibn al-Zubayr in 692.[4]

As the daily salat prayers are oriented toward Mecca, so too the trek of each pilgrim leads to the Sacred Mosque (*al-masjid al-haram*) and the Kaʻba. The pilgrimage consists of a series of rituals: the circumambulation of the Kaʻba, kissing or pointing to the Black Stone embedded in the southeast corner of the Ka'ba, drinking from the nearby Zamzam well, running back and forth between the hillocks of Safa and Marwa, traveling out to Mount Arafat, and the symbolic stoning of Satan on the return road to Mecca.

The Black Stone's origins are unclear. There are various mythological explanations for its presence – we shall see some below – but all agree that it has been part of the shrine from well back in the pre-Islamic period. As a ritual object, the Stone seems to sit uneasily within the Islamic devotional rationale. On the one hand, it is treated aniconically, as an object without inherent significance. Al-Azraqi recalls a set of hadith reports that understood the Black Stone to be God's right (*haqq*) on earth, and that whoever was unable to pay allegiance in person to the Prophet could rub the Stone to make clear their obeisance.[5] The second caliph, 'Umar ibn al-Khattab, apparently shared this perspective on the Stone, seeing it essentially as a site at which Muslims may demonstrate their fealty. Quoting from the hadith, Al-Azraqi tells us that while circumambulating the Ka'ba 'Umar stopped before the Black Stone and said, "By God, I know you are a stone and can do neither good nor evil, and if I had not seen the Prophet do it, I would refuse to kiss you."[6] In the caliph's view, venerating the Stone was simply a way to emulate the Prophet, and recognize his example. In contrast, however, the Black Stone could also be thought of quite differently. The same hadith report that Al-Azraqi was quoting goes on to present 'Ali ibn Abi Talib's view of the Stone, which attributes to it agency and even an intercessory role to be played in the hereafter. 'Ali responded to 'Umar, saying that the Black Stone "can indeed do good and evil!" and cited the Qur'anic passage 7:171, in which God drew out of Abraham all of his posterity and recorded their covenant with Him. The hadith continues, "The Stone had two eyes and a tongue; and God said to it, 'Open your mouth and swallow this document.' Then God placed it there, saying, 'You will serve as witness on the Day of Judgement for all who fulfilled their commitment.'"[7] In as much as it celebrates the superiority of 'Ali's grasp of scripture, the passage seems to be pro-Shia, but the two attitudes toward the Black Stone coexist within the hadith tradition across sectarian lines.

While the Stone's origins and significance may be disputed, its history has at times been traumatic. During the Carmathian revolt of the early ninth century not only was the Stone broken into several pieces, but was torn out of is frame in the Ka'ba wall, and taken to al-Ahsa, and eventually to the Iraqi city of Kufa. The great mosque of Kufa was the seat of the Carmathian state, and it was from that mosque's seventh pillar that the Stone was hung, apparently in an effort to divert pilgrims from Mecca. Twenty-one years later, in 959 it was returned to Mecca and restored to its position in the Ka'ba wall.[8]

The Ka'ba and the Hajj in the pre-Islamic period are well attested to in the Islamic sources, having been key to a series of different pilgrimages, and hosting a variety of deities and idols.[9] A highpoint of Muhammad's prophetic career was his cleansing of the idols from the sacred precinct of Mecca. According to some Islamic sources there were hundreds of sacrificial alter stones around the Ka'ba and in Mecca.[10] This foundational act of iconoclasm marked the reconfiguration of the shrine, aligning it with the new Islamic expression of worship. The Islamic tradition linked the restoration of this central sacred space to the triumph of monotheism among over its many rivals in the Near East. Such a triumph was understood – starting with the Qur'an – as also a recovery of an obscured Jewish and Christian revelation of monotheism. Several Islamic narratives of the Ka'ba connect the control and definition of its space with the foundational monotheistic mission of Islam. One account of the prophet Solomon has him passing by a saddened Ka'ba, which bemoaned its condition as a site for polytheistic devotions. When traveling through Mecca Solomon,

> saw idols around the House (i.e. Ka'ba) which were worshipped instead of God. So he went by the House, and when he had passed on, the House wept. And God, revealing Himself to the House, said: "What makes you weep?" It said: "Lord, this is one of your prophets and party of Your saints, and they have passed me by, and did not alight by me, and did not pray in me, and did not mention You in my presence, while these idols are worshipped around me instead of You." The story continues that God revealed to it: "Do not weep, for verily I will fill you with faces worshipping Me. . . I will impose upon My worshippers a religious duty which shall hasten their walk to you with a gait as hurried as the swift flight of eagles to their nests, and they shall yearn for you with the yearning of the female camel for her young, and the pigeon for her eggs. And I will purify you from idols and from devil-worship."[11]

This agent of purification would of course be Muhammad, who would cleanse the site, reconnect with the ancient line of prophets, and restore the Ka'ba to its original function. In the *sira* biography of Muhammad the "breaking of the idols" is commemorated by a poet thus: "Had you seen Muhammad and this troops / The day the idols were smashed when he entered / You would have seen God's light become manifest / And darkness covering the face of idolatry."[12] In an interesting twist on the iconoclastic gesture so central to Muhammad's mission, another connection is offered, this time to the Christian tradition, and apparently the eastern Christian devotional sensibilities around icons. The story is told that at the time Mecca was conquered, the interior of the Ka'ba was decorated with a variety of images of prophets, angels and trees, in addition to portraits of Jesus and Mary. The Prophet's purging of the shrine did away with all of these images, except those of Jesus and Mary. More than a century later, Al-Azraqi tells us, these images (*suwar*) were still in existence.[13]

The details around these images are scant, and it seems unlikely they were preserved within the Ka'ba structure itself. Nevertheless, the important point here is the negotiation of the sacred space of the Ka'ba as a proxy for the wider Prophetic mission that was underway.[14]

The Ka'ba is also woven into the earliest narrative of human history through its association with Adam and Eve. By the third century of the Islamic era the Ka'ba had been clearly identified as the earthly parallel to God's throne, the center of the Earth, and the point in creation nearest to heaven. Upon their fall from the Garden, Adam and Eve are informed that their exile is not absolute, and that the Ka'ba will stand in for the lord's throne. "God sent down one of the sapphires of the Garden, and set it down at the place of the House in the size of the Ka'ba... Then God inspired Adam: 'I have a Sanctuary located directly under My Throne; so go to it and circumambulate it, as (the angels) circumambulate My Throne, and pray there, as they pray at My Throne, for there I shall answer your prayer.'"[15] This Ka'ba of heavenly origin would remain in place until the Flood, at which time it was raised up to Mount Abu Qubays, saving it from destruction.[16] It's foundation was never completely lost, since during its travels across the vast expanses of the watery globe, Noah's ark stopped for a week to piously circle the site from far above.[17] The history of the Ka'ba is restarted with new narratives identifying it with the prophet Abraham. Here the site is restored, and the origin of some of the related Hajj rituals is established through the figure of Hagar. To guide Abraham as he worked to build a "House on Earth" for God, one account describes a gale (sakina) with two heads, another relates a cloud "in the form of the Ka'ba," being sent down to indicate the required location and dimensions of the structure.[18] In the same story, Hagar is sorely tested in the desert, running between the hills of Safa and Marwa in search of water – an act recreated in the Hajj ritual of sa'y. Likewise she is at the origin of the well of Zamzam, with Gabriel revealing it to save her and Ishmael from thirst.[19] Another important component of the Ka'ba complex is the Station of Abraham, a stone bearing his footprints marking the moment at which he positioned the final stone into the structure.[20]

Few descriptions of the interior of the Ka'ba have come down to us, but the traveler Nasir-i Khusraw provides some precious details from the mid-tenth century. He describes a red slab of marble on the northern edge of the Ka'ba floor marking the spot where the Prophet had prayed, from which those in the know would take their cue and pray in emulation of him. A similar site was marked outside the Ka'ba within the semicircular hijr, by a slab of green stone in the shape of a mihrab, which could accommodate one person performing prayer. Unfortunately, Nasir-i Khusraw provides no explanation for the six silver mihrabs, the height of a person, set up on the western side of the room, however these were almost certainly precious gifts sent by Muslim rulers. The interior walls were made of marble of various colors, and at this point in history were adorned with small silver plaques bearing the names of the caliphs of the Fatimid empire – the Shia rulers of Egypt and Mecca at the time.[21]

The Ka'ba and the sanctuary around it, the *haram sharif*, have seen a seen a series of renovations and rebuilding. Today almost none of these earlier materials have survived. After Nasir-i Khusraw's time several floods seriously damaged the site, and in the twentieth century the Saudi regime rebuilt both the *haram* and the Ka'ba completely, preserving only the Ka'ba's stones in its rebuilt walls. The evolution of this site has been dramatic, but the local historians of Mecca do not provide enough information for anything approximating a full reconstruction of those stages. We are left with snapshots, some of which are indeed telling, of a devotional and politically charged space that contrary to its fixed position at the heart of Islamic ritual, has been constantly in flux. The early sources speak of the pre-Islamic Ka'ba as an open-air enclosure, with the roofed structure having been built only in the seventh century, in the generation before Muhammad. Despite this and other changes, one constant has been the fabric coverings. The tradition of covering extends back beyond the historical record. The earliest record of Ka'ba dressing is likely the report found in the *sira* literature, in which an invading Yemeni king is convinced by two of his Jewish captives to spare Mecca. The king decides to make the pilgrimage, and receives a divine vision commanding him to embellish the Ka'ba with fine striped fabrics.[22]

Indeed throughout its life as both a building and a ritual object, the Ka'ba has been embellished with *kiswa* coverings. Beyond the hadith reports cited above, at least one account of the Ka'ba's mythical foundations identifies it as a tent. We are told that after the Fall, Adam was consoled by a gift from the angels, one of the tents (*khiyam*) of Paradise, which covered the site of the future Ka'ba.[23] Another reading of Ka'ba dressing has been to liken it to a woman dressed in her finery. Each year on the 27th of Dhu al-Qa'da, the Ka'ba, like the pilgrims as they approach the sanctuary, goes into a state of ritual purity by donning the simple white seamless *izar* garment. One account, from about 929, describes the Ka'ba in its white silk cloth during the Hajj, like a pilgrim, however at the completion of the pilgrimage it donned a red *kiswa* of silk brocade, with circles in which devotional phrases were inscribed.[24] The famed medieval Tunisian traveler Ibn Battuta witnessed the hanging of the Ka'ba's undergarment in the fifteenth century, and describes the "tucking up" (*tushammar*) of the dress. See Figure 3 for a modern example of this tucking. He adds that upon completion, this is understood to put the Ka'ba into its state of ritual purity. An Egyptian official in the early twentieth century likewise describes the under dressing of the month of Dhu al-Qa'da, calling it a pilgrim's garment (*izar*) of white cloth.[25] The earliest leaders of the Muslim community are recorded as adorning the Ka'ba with brocade and white cotton coverings.[26] A variety of styles and material are mentioned in the sources: a white veil in the summer, a "shirt" (*qamis*) in the winter, red brocade, green or black silk. In the early twentieth century one pilgrim notes that just before the start of the Hajj, the Ka'ba is stripped and dressed in its seamless white under-cloth, in imitation of its visitors' dressing in ritually pure *ihram*.[27] In the nineteenth century a traveler reports that when the Ka'ba is between cover-ings, it is referred to as "naked."[28]

From pre-Islamic times violence in the vicinity of the Ka'ba was prohibited, and in accord with the sanctuary status of the site, the kiswa is understood to offer safety to all afflicted pilgrims. This asylum, however, did not protect the many who died in the Carmathian rebel attack of 930, and whose bodies were unceremoniously dumped into the Zamzam well. These victims are recorded as having sought shelter by grasping onto the *kiswa*.[29] The section of the Ka'ba between the Black Stone and the door – the *multazam* – is identified as the most efficacious point to seek asylum. This protective function of the Ka'ba and its *kiswa* is even extended to the drama of spiritual salvation. In one medieval account of the virtues of the Dome of the Rock in Jerusalem, we are told that at the end of time the Ka'ba will be presented to the Rock as a bride. With every person who ever came to her on Hajj clinging to her garment, she will then ascend with her consort to heaven.[30] The analogy here is not to a tent or to a simple dress, but rather to the cloak of a chieftain or sovereign. As we turn to explore another Hajj related object, the *mahmal,* we shall notice similar anthropomorphic framings.

Although the term *mahmal* can refer to a variety of litters and palanquins, the shape of the Hajj *mahmal* over the centuries has been quite consistent. As we saw in Figure 1, the object consists of two components, a cubic lower section, and an upper section in a tent or pyramid shape. One modern Egyptian writer makes the formal association of the lower half with the Ka'ba, and the upper with the pyramids.[31] This is a rather fanciful explanation, which ignores the fact that *mahmal*s were sent from various countries in the Islamic world. *Mahmal*s were mostly from Egypt, but there is nothing to connect them to the pyramids. For a more substantial theory on the origins of the *mahmal* we may turn to the Arabian tradition of covering and transporting betyls or sacrificial stones. Lammens, and later in more detail Ettinghausen, have pro-posed that the *mahmal*'s sanctity was a vestige of the nomadic portable gods of pre-Islamic Arabia. Betyls were set up near a chieftain's tents for rituals and to offer asylum to anyone who could reach them. Representations from as far back as the eight-century BCE have come down to us of a betyl being carried in a litter. Literary sources on the subject later called such a litter a *qubba*, which usually means "dome" but here refers to covered litters. In Bedouin society, an open litter (*hawdaj, markab, 'ammariyya*) could be used in battle as a site for asylum, or carry noble women of a tribe to encourage their fighters.[32]

Ettinghausen argues that the tradition of circulating a sacred object like a betyl in a covered litter was adopted by Muhammad and others in the prophet's lifetime. The sacrificial stone or deity was removed, but the vehicle was preserved as a symbol of power, with early historians describing red leather *qubbas* in circulation.[33] The connection between these early Arabian domed or tented litters and the advent of the Egyptian *mahmal* some six centuries later is unclear, as Ettinghausen admits.[34] We may at least note that there were several precursors to the *mahmal* that like it, evoked political power and social standing along with a distant – at least from the medieval Islamic perspective – association with venerated religious objects.[35]

The *mahmal* sent by sultan Qansuh al-Ghawri (d. 1516) is preserved in the Topkapi museum in Istanbul, likely seized as a trophy marking the last gasp of Mamluk resistance to the expanding Ottoman empire. In Figure 4 we see that the lower section (1.5 m high, 1.6 m long, 1.1 m wide) and upper (1.75 m high) are adorned with calligraphic text.[36] The lower and upper panels repeat the sultan's name along with various honorifics: "Abu al-Nasr Qansuh / All power to our regal lord the most noble / al-Ghawri, may his victory be confirmed!" The upper panel repeats the ruler's name, but on two of the four sides the middle line is shortened to "the regal most noble," the honorific by which he was most commonly known. The frames for these texts recall Mamluk blazons or coats of arms, which were also typically round and divided into three horizontal sections. A horizontal band joins the two sections on all four sides, and displays devotional text expressing the pilgrim's desire to see the Ka'ba (*nanzur al-ka'ba*), and to be rewarded in this world and the afterlife for fulfilling the duty of pilgrimage, all thanks to the intercession of the Prophet.

Later *mahmal*s similarly displayed a combination of texts identifying the royal patron, along with pious and devotional messages. The *mahmal* of King Fu'ad I – preserved in the National Geographic Society's Ethnology Museum – is similar to that of al-Ghawri in proportions and ornamentation. We see from a sketch, Figure 5, that the lower section measures 1.55 m high, 1.35 m long, 1.75 m wide, with an upper section extending 1.67 m, topped with an onion shaped ball with a finial, adding another 30 cm. Its total height is 4.10 m – making for an impressive object, especially once mounted on a camel. The fabric is red, and the embroidery silver. One observer calls it, *un petit monument*.[37] The cipher of King Fu'ad on the upper panel identifies him as the patron, while the remaining inscriptions are taken from the Qur'an. Text is displayed on the band of the lower section. On the front is the *basmala* followed by "Allah! There is no god but He," followed on a second panel with the Qur'anic verse (2:255), "The Living and Eternal! Neither sleep nor slumber may seize Him," which continues on the right side, "To Him are all things in heaven and earth. Who can intercede with Him without His permission?" and the verse continues around the back and sides of the *mahmal*,

4 Sultan Ghawri's *mahmal*. Credit: TSM 31/263 Topkapi Palace Museum, Istanbul

"He knows what is at hand (for His creation), and what is behind them. They may only grasp," continuing on the next panel, "of His knowledge what He wills. His throne encompasses," continued with, "heavens and the earth, feeling no burden in preserving them, for He is exalted and great." On the

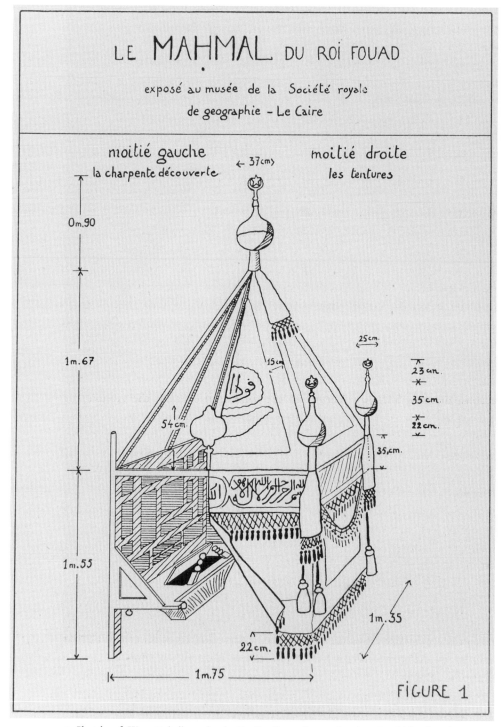

LE **MAḤMAL** DU ROI FOUAD

exposé au musée de la Société royale
de geographie - Le Caire

moitié gauche
la charpente découverte

← 37cm)

moitié droite
les tentures

0m.90

1m.67

15cm

25cm.

23 cm.

35 cm.

22cm.

35.cm.

54cm

1m.55

1m.35

22cm.

|← — — — 1m.75 — — — →|

FIGURE 1

5 Sketch of King Fu'ad's *mahmal*. Credit: From JacquesJomier, *Le Mahmal et la caravane Égyptienne des pèlerins de la Mecque (XIII-XX siècles)*. Cairo: Presses de Institut Français d'Achéologie Orientale, 1953. © Institut français d'archéologie orientale

top of the upper section small round panels read, "This noble *mahmal* covering was made by our master Sultan Fu'ad the First, in the year 1336 [i.e. 1918 CE]."[38]

In addition to the crowning finial, there are the four silver balls, set at the four corners. These are attested to in photographs of various modern *mahmal*s, but their use in earlier periods can only be surmised. The background fabric could be a variety of colors. Al-Ghawri's *mahmal* at the turn of the sixteenth century was yellow. In accounts from the end of the seventeenth century, travelers describe a black background,[39] which seems to have been common, although we have reports from the middle of the eighteenth and nineteenth centuries of red and green *mahmal*s.[40] Istanbul has preserved Syrian *mahmal*s from the twentieth century in both gold and black.

*Mahmal*s were dispatched from several capitals other than Cairo, including Baghdad, Damascus, and in the Ottoman period Istanbul. Lesser known centers sending *mahmal*s were Yemen, and in Syria Aleppo.[41] Regardless of the wider diplomatic and political realities, in which Egypt's status variously rose and fell over the centuries, the Egyptian *mahmal* aggressively asserted its pride of place over all competitors, regardless of origin. Between the thirteenth and fifteenth centuries, on the occasions the Syrian *mahmal* was sent to Mecca, it seems to have been humiliated each time by its Egyptian counterpart.[42] The first *mahmal* was sent on the Hajj by the sultan Baybars in 1277. It seems to have always been accompanied by a *kiswa* covering. In the thirteenth century, the Rasulids of Yemen tried on several occasions to send their own *kiswa* to Mecca, which at least once included both the interior and exterior dresses. As Baybars' position grew stronger, he was able to rebuff subsequent gestures from Yemen through diplomacy and threat. The Rasulids however continued to challenge the Mamluk ritual monopoly over the *kiswa*, trying on several occasions up to the year 1430 to hang their own dress.[43] In the first half of the fifteenth century the Timurid ruler Shah Rukh tried on several occasions, all of them unsuccessful, to send the interior *kiswa*. The judges of Egypt denied Shah Rukh's request to Barsbay in 1435. However, under Barsbay's successor Jaqmaq, Shah Rukh successfully sent an interior *kiswa,* which arrived in Cairo in 1444, and despite popular Egyptian disapproval, managed to complete the Hajj, to be hung until 1452.[44] In 1473 the amir of the Aq-Qoyunlu federation, Hasan al-Ta'wil, sent two *kiswa*s, which were never hung.[45] The first record of an inner *kiswa* being sent by the Mamluks comes from 1359. It was from Sultan Muhammad ibn Qalawun, and it was in black silk, with a golden embroidery with an upper section in red silk.[46] Barsbay sent a new inner covering in 1423. Both Barsbay's and Shah Rukh's, apparently hung together, were replaced by Jaqmaq's covering in 1452, and that in turn by Sultan Qaytbay in 1478.[47]

As the history of rival *kiswa*s is complicated, the sending of *mahmal*s is similarly difficult to account for in full detail. Several anecdotes of conflict between *mahmal*s have come down to us. A report from 1320 describes the Egyptian *mahmal* leading the Iraqi and the Yemeni *mahmal*s without incident,[48] yet in Mecca in 1472 the Iraqis threatened to put their *mahmal* before that of the Mamluks. The following year the amir al-Hajj of Egypt forbade the Iraqi *mahmal* from entering the city at all. The heads of the Iraqi caravan – who had the sermon in Mecca said in the name of their ruler Uzun Hasan, thus claiming authority over the holy places of Islam – were then taken prisoner, and sent to Cairo in chains, along with their offending *mahmal*.[49] Under Ottoman rule – that is from the turn of the sixteenth century – Egypt was reduced to the status of a province within a vast empire ruled from Istanbul. While the occasional *kiswa* and even *mahmal* would be sent from Istanbul, Egypt continued to supply the Ka'ba hangings, and to send a *mahmal* each Hajj season, all carried out by the Porte's representatives in Cairo. In the sixteenth century, there were occasionally three *mahmal*s sent: one from Istanbul, one from Cairo, and one from the Ottoman-controlled areas of Yemen.[50]

The cities of Syria were also important players in this game. Under Mamluk rule, up to five *mahmal*s set out from various points in Syria in 1311, and in the next century Karak and Aleppo on at least one occasion added their own.[51] The earliest descriptions we have of these palanquins are from Pierre Belon in 1552.[52] In the nineteenth and early twentieth centuries Damascus produced red, light green, and dark green *mahmal*s. Their formal dresses were made in Istanbul, and they bore the names of the ruling sultan of the day. Under the Mamluks we know that there were serious altercations in Mecca between the *mahmal*s from Damascus and Cairo in the years 1293, 1312, 1407, and 1408.[53] Figure 6 shows the Egyptian and Syrian *mahmal*s meeting on the Hajj in the early twentieth century. They awkwardly and aggressively bump up against one another at an important stage of the pilgrimage, the standing at Mt. 'Arafat.[54]

Like the Ka'ba adopting a white pilgrim's dress, the Syrian *mahmal*, at least in the modern period, wore white when in the holy precincts of Mecca, and likely at the Prophet's tomb in Medina.[55] The last Syrian *mahmal* was retired to the National Museum in Damascus sometime after 1924, and it has appeared recently in a British Museum exhibition on the Hajj. This *mahmal* was green, and completed the Hajj five times. Its measurements are: lower box, 135 cm

6 The Egyptian and Syrian *mahmal*s meet at Mt. 'Arafat. Credit: Ibrahim Rif'at, I *Mir'at al-Haramayn*. 2 vols. Cairo: Dar al-Kutub al-Misriyya, 1925. Image in public domain.

high, by 200 cm, by 115 cm; the pyramid is 230 cm high, the copper ornaments on four corners and on top are 80 cm. Its inscription mentions the date 1911. The silk covering was made in Istanbul. Under Abd al-Majid it had been red, under Abd al-Aziz it was light green, and for Abd al-Hamid it was dark green.[56] It wore its formal dress when parading in cities, and a white dress when on display in the sacred precincts of Mecca and the Hajj.

In the 1807 Hajj season, with the Wahhabis in control of Mecca, the Egyptian *mahmal* itself was attacked and burned.[57] The religious reform movment of Wahhabism would have a great impact on the Hajj and the wider religious landscape of Arabia.[58] Along with a heavier guard the following year, another *mahmal* was sent, and its right of way was reopened. The Wahhabis would later retake Mecca, and redouble their opposition. In the nineteenth century, shipping and rail travel became the more reliable means of travel in the region, and from this period onward the *mahmal* was only borne by its camel when parading within urban centers, or as it made its way from the port of Jeddah to Mecca and then Medina (see map 2). In the early twentieth century, the Khedive of Egypt, Muhammad ʿAli, waged largely successful campaigns against the Saʿudis, yet the Wahhabi-Saʿudi alliance would slowly extend its influence, consolidating its hold on the on much of the peninsula by 1926. In this year, an attack – supposedly by Bedouins on their own initiative – upon the Egyptian *mahmal* caravan near the valley of Mina was thwarted, but opposition from the Saʿudi regime would only intensify. We shall see in the next chapter how these conflicts would sweep the *mahmal* and *kiswa* up in a tide of politics and religious reform that engulfed mid-twentieth-century Egypt.

A *mahmal* parading through Arabia and the sacred sites of the Hajj, bearing the name of the sultan who had sent it, clearly served a political purpose. The Mamluk sultans, the Ottoman governors, and later the Khedives, had all projected their authority over the central Islamic landscape by asserting and jealously guarding their *mahmals'* right of way. As the Saʿudi regime found its footing, however, it openly resisted such encroachments on its sovereignty. Resistance, significantly, would be determined by the parameters of the object itself. That is to say, the discourse of Wahhabi religious reform came to cluster around the *mahmal*, its parading and its display within the Hajj. The disputes over religion in the public sphere, the role of sharia law, and the legacy of traditional theological interpretation, would all be arranged around the *mahmal* by both its defenders and its detractors. Of course, the religious objects of the Hajj were not the only site for modern debates about religious reform, but by virtue of their prominence and function, they remained at center stage. We shall investigate these debates further in the next chapter, but for now let us simply note that beyond their roles in symbolically asserting power, the *mahmals* also served to frame the very ideas that competed to define them.

The fabric for the *kiswa* background typically consisted of eight vertical bands, two for each face of the Kaʿba, with a band (*hizam*) running around the entire

7 Black satin dress of the Ka'ba. Credit: T.387-1960; Victoria and Albert Museum. Given by Mr. W. Hastings

structure near the top. As we saw earlier in Figure 2, this band (93 cm high) displays several verses and even entire chapters of Qur'anic text. *Kiswa*s were produced in several different colors, which will be described below. This fabric however, was more than a simple background for the inscriptions it bore. In Figure 7 we see a sample in black satin (69.5 cm by 82.5 cm) from the early twentieth century, into which is woven the shahada in a zigzag pattern, with "Allah" repeated below, and the pious phrase "May His majesty be increased" in mirrored text above. Travelers have provided some details on the fabric of other modern *kiswa*s, and further examples can be seen in Cairo's Textile Museum (e.g. TM427).[59]

The pre-Islamic practices of hanging at the Ka'ba apparently involved the use of either woolen material (*burud*) that was commonly used in Yemen as a garment, pieces of leather, material woven of hair (*musuh*), and sack cloth. These were piled one on top of the other, and remained on the Ka'ba. This practice persisted through the Prophet's lifetime, and that of his immediate successors including 'Umar,[60] up to the caliphate of Mu'awiyya (d. 680). The governor of Mecca petitioned the caliph to remove the old accumulated hangings, the earliest of which he claimed from an Islamic perspective were ritually unclean. Mu'awiyya sent a new *kiswa* make of silk, Egyptian white linen known as *qubati*, and striped wool. The caliph then made it his practice to send two *kiswa*s to Mecca from Damascus each year, one *qubati* and the other silk (*habara*). Al-Hajjaj, who we saw earlier had been involved in one of the rebuildings of the Ka'ba, is known to have secured annual *kiswa*s each year from his brother who was serving in Iraq as an administrator. Another source for Ka'ba coverings, but only the simpler undergarment, apparently was the Christian community of Najran. They supplied hundreds of garments (*hulal*) to the Umayyads as part of their annual tax tribute (*jizya*).[61]

From early on, the *kiswa* was more than simply a decorative object. It's status as a devotional object was established not only by its relationship to the Ka'ba, but also with the tomb of the Prophet in Medina. Around the year 692 the caliph 'Abd al-Malik sent his *kiswa* but insisted that on its way it be hung for a time between pillars in the Prophet's mosque. And as early as the ninth century the discarded coverings began to be distributed to the people of Mecca, or even stolen by marauding Bedouin.[62] Of course, displaying one's *kiswa* in the Prophet's mosque, or conversely managing to steal one from under the authorities' noses, had clear political implications; and distributing valuable silk and cotton textiles demonstrated a capacity for charity. Yet as we shall see with more detail from later periods, these practices clearly also had a devotional rationale.

Apparently, the earliest details on Egyptian production are recorded by the ninth century chronicler al-Fakihi. He describes a number of *kiswa*s made for the Abbasid caliphs in the towns of Shata and Tinnis in the Egyptian delta near Dimyat. The names of the reigning caliph are inscribed, as is that of his representative in Egypt. In one account al-Fakihi recalls a visit to Shata:

> There I saw one of the *kiswa*s made of fine Egyptian cloth for (the caliph) Harun al-Rashid, Commander of the Faithful. It was inscribed with the following text: 'In the name of God. Blessings upon Harun, Commander of the Faithful, servant of God. May God preserve him. This (*kiswa*) was commissioned by Al-Fadl ibn al-Rabi', the client of the Commander of the Faithful, made from Shata tiraz; a *kiswa* for the Ka'ba in the year 191 (805 CE)'.[63]

The conflation of political claims with religious invocations becomes the rule for future *kiswa*s, as they advertise the piety and authority of the rulers that send them. Not surprisingly then, strife arising from religious and political disputes have also been recorded on these objects. In the beginning of the ninth century a Shia revolt under Abu al-Saraya al-Shaybani deposed the Abbasid governor of Mecca. He then tore down the Abbasid *kiswa*, and replaced it with a new one that read: "By order of al-Asfar ibn al-Asfar Abu Saraya, protector of the family of the Prophet, (this is) a covering for the Holy House of God, which has been cleansed of the coverings of the usurpers, the sons of Abbas. Written in 199 (815 CE)."[64] Here too the patron is mentioned by name, and immediately connected to his religious interventions – cleansing the Ka'ba of the presence of the usurping Sunni Abbasids – which in this location, through Shia eyes would recall Muhammad's purging of the idols some two centuries earlier.

There was no color scheme mandated for the *kiswa*, or for its decorative components, beyond the expectation that there be an under garment and belt. As with the *mahmal,* as we shall see shortly, no two were identical, and significant departures in design and color were common. The rebel we just met, Abu al-Saraya, had torn down the caliph's *kiswa* in a gesture of revolt. Fortunately, some of the physical details of this doomed *kiswa* have been preserved. The caliph al-Ma'mun (d. 833) had decided that the Ka'ba should wear a white Khurasanian fabric for its ritual *ihram*, a Qubati undercoat of Egyptian cotton, and a red exterior covering adorned with brocade.[65]

In the mid-tenth century one report describes the hangings sent from Baghdad by the Abbasids: a white linen *kiswa* while the pilgrims were performing the Hajj rituals, over which a red silk *kiswa*, embellished with medallions (*darat*) was later hung. The medallions were inscribed with devotional petitions and praise.[66] Another historian records the Fatimid caliph's elaborate offering for the year 973, which displayed twelve outward spans (*shamsa*) from a center of circular Arabic text containing Surat al-Hajj.[67] The first *shamsa* however to appear on a *kiswa* had been sent by the Abbasid caliph al-Mutawakkil sometime before 861. Al-Mu'izz's 973 commissioning was recognized by contemporaries as a conscious imitation of the Abbasid practice. "When it was displayed in al-Mu'izz's palace, the Egyptians, Syrians, Iraqis and Khurasanians who had been on the pilgrimage said that there was none equal to it: although the 'Abbasid *shamsa* was more finely worked, it was only one-quarter the size."[68]

In the mid-eleventh century the Persian traveler Nasir-i Khusraw took note of the *kiswa* that hung on the Ka'ba when he arrived in Mecca. He describes it as being white, with two bands of tiraz calligraphy about 50 cm wide. There were three mihrab niches embroidered into each side, a larger one in the middle flanked by two smaller mihrabs. They were woven in colored silk, with geometric designs provided in gold thread. The two bands of tiraz were placed at equal points up the *kiswa* symmetrically dividing it into three even horizontal layers.[69] This use of the niche motif on the *kiswa* was apparently not repeated, although it did appear elsewhere, for example on the façade of the Aqmar mosque built in 1125. Another mosque object that became a design motif is the lamp, which embellishes some of the earliest copies of the Qur'an and appears widely as a carved form in religious architecture.[70]

While few material details have come down to us, the Abbasid caliphs engaged in a centuries long rivalry with the Fatimid's to supply the *kiswa*.[71] The Abbasids were of course the champions of majority Sunni Islam, while the Fatimids were the most successful Shia power in the Islamic world at the time.

Controlling the central site of Islamic ritual, the Ka'ba, and the unparalleled visibility it afforded, was clearly advantageous. Ibn Jubayr reports on the hanging of a *kiswa* by the Abbasid caliph al-Nasir (r. 1180–1225). He recounts the procedure used to install the *kiswa*, much as it is done today, along with the impact this *kiswa* had on those there to see it. He describes caliph al-Nasir's *kiswa* thus:

> The covering was placed on the noble roof above the Ka'ba. On Tuesday the 13th of this blessed month, the Banu Shayba began to unfold it, a rich green cloth, with a beauty enchanting all who looked upon it. Above there was a large strip of red embroidery with inscriptions; on the side that faced the venerated Station of Abraham and where the holy door opened, that is, on its blessed face, one read, after the *basmala*: "The first house that was founded for humanity (was that at Mecca – blessed and a guidance for the worlds.)" (Q. 3:96) and on the other sides the name of the caliph, and invocations on his behalf. The encircling inscription was on two red bands, and small white medallions were adorned with Qur'anic verses and the caliph's name, all in a fine script.[72]

Ibn Jubayr goes on the mention the need for pulling up the lower fringes of the *kiswa* to keep it beyond the reach of overzealous worshippers. He concludes that this *kiswa* was ". . . the most beautiful sight, a salvation to those who gazed upon it. Like a bride lifting her veil of green brocade, God gives pleasure to whoever looks at her, wishing to approach her, desirous of an audience with her."

A detailed record of the inscription on another *kiswa* is preserved for us by Taqi al-Din al-Fasi (d. 1429). He records the name of the Mamluk sultan who supplied the *kiswa*, with the remaining three sides displaying lengthy Qur'anic passages recalling the divine command to perform the Hajj, the patriarchs Abraham and Isaac who set up the Ka'ba, the sanctity of the *haram* and the holy months.[73] Figures 8 and 9 are of *kiswa* belts from the mid-twentieth century, but their complexity and proportions of scale in relation to the human bystanders were likely just as striking in al-Fasi's time. Perhaps a decade earlier the Egyptian chronicler al-Qalqashandi (d. 1418) made his own record of the *kiswa* design.[74] He describes it as being of black striped silk, with an inscription at its top in white thread of Qur'an text: "The first house that was founded for humanity was that at Mecca (blessed and a guidance for the worlds)" (Q. 3:96). By the end of the reign of sultan Zahir Barquq (d. 1398) it was woven in yellow with gold thread.[75] In the reign of Barquq's son al-Nasir, the tiraz was changed from white to yellow, with the yellow writing in silk and gold on the black background. The former however was more impressive for the contrast between the white and the black. Al-Nasir had the phrase, "There is no got but God, and Muhammad is His messenger" woven in white onto the black sides of the Ka'ba.[76] Surveys of the *kiswa*s of the medieval Mamluk period do

8 *Kiswa* on its way to Mecca. Credit: Newsreel, British Pathé

9 Hizam parade in Midan Farouq. Credit: Jacques Jomier, *Le Mahmal et la caravane Égyptienne des pèlerins de la Mecque (XIII-XX siècles)*. Cairo: Presses de Institut Français d'Achéologie Orientale, 1953. © Institut français d'archéologie orientale

not reveal any clear line of stylistic or decorative evolution. Between 1408 and 1463 for example, yellow, white, but predominantly black were the colors of the *kiswa*; there could be two bands of calligraphy but usually there was only one. The medallions were variously placed, they could be few or many, and appeared in white, black, or gold.[77]

The production of the *kiswa* in the fourteenth century seems to have taken place in the state-run *dar al-tiraz* in Alexandria, but later in the same century a second report has it being made in the *mashhad* of Husayn.[78] In the eighteenth century, the *kiswa* was made at the Citadel, in Qasr al-Ablaq.[79] Despite the

Ottoman victory over the Mamluks in 1517, the *kiswa* continued to be made in Egypt. Competition would come first from the Hereke factory in Turkey, founded in 1844, which began to produce textiles for the structures associated with the Ka'ba.[80] In Egypt, Muhammad 'Ali Pasha established the Khurunfush workshop in 1817, which produced a variety of fine coverings for various state purposes, until the 1960s.[81] We shall revisit this complex history in Chapter 2, in relation to the production of the *mahmal* and tomb coverings.

Within the Egyptian capital, the *mahmal* and the *kiswa* were usually paraded three times a year. The fist occasion was mid Rajab, the seventh month of the Islamic calendar. The second was just before the departure of the Hajj caravan, and the third as part of the return parade of the pilgrims. The *kiswa* was paraded in Cairo least from the year 1263, which saw the covering processed on mules, accompanied by judges, jurists, Qur'an reciters, Sufis, and preachers.[82] This preceded the advent of the *mahmal*, which joined the parading in 1266.[83] In 1282, another notice mentions the *mahmal* and the *kiswa* leaving Cairo in the month of Shawwal, under the Amir Nasr al-Din.[84]

In the mid-fourteenth century one visitor reports a Rajab procession of judges, jurists, heads of guilds, and officers of the state, forming up at the citadel, where they are greeted by the amir of the Hajj, designated for that year, and the *mahmal*. Joined by detachments of soldiers and water-carriers on camels, the entire group processed around the city. These displays must have been impressive since we are told that, "resolves (for the Hajj) are inflamed, desires are excited, and impulses are stirred up."[85] This procession became a major event in the city's life. In the fifteenth century, we are told of the great crowds that gathered at the foot of the citadel to celebrate and take in the martial games of Mamluk soldiers, the fireworks, the bonfires, and the music. These festivities kept up all night.[86] Soldiers' displays included mock battles, tossing and catching lances, and riding tricks. They also dressed in frightening costumes, and were known as the "demons ('*afarit*) of the *mahmal*." They colored their faces, and some wore false beards and teeth.[87] By 1467, after several instances of excess – including the abduction of women and boys, and the looting of local shops – the "demons" were apparently suppressed by royal decree.

At some point in the sixteenth century the Rajab procession was delayed, taking place only two or three weeks before the Hajj departure. The carnival-esque atmosphere however, continued to be part of the procession. One account from an eighteenth century European notes a dizzying array of banners, symbols, and sounds:

> I afterwards saw nothing, but an amazing number of Scheks (rulers of the church) divided into troops, and Dervices (who are the same amongst the Turks as Monks among the Papists) all on foot. There were ensigns of different colours to each troop, some green, others yellow, others red,

and others white and red, &c... All repeated in high tone of voice, but without the least harmony, the Mahometan confession of faith. They all continually cast their heads backwards and forwards... With each troop were some that had disguised themselves in different manners.[88]

Here the European Christian tourist is doing his best to describe the paraders in terms that will make sense to his readers. The "Dervices" are the Sufis, who processed with banners identifying their allegiances to particular mystical orders, all the while reciting the *shahada*. The passage ends by noting a contingent in costume – a practice recalling the supposedly outlawed "demons."

And a century later, another Western visitor, Sophia Lane Poole, recounted the *mahmal* procession in some detail, noting a figure who appears to be either mocking the entire ceremony or poking fun at the religious authorities. She begins her account saying,

The first person who passed, belonging to the procession, were two men with drawn swords, who engaged occasionally in mock combat. Next came a grotesque person, well mounted, and wearing a high pointed cap, and an immense beard of twisted hemp, and clothed in sheep-skins. He held a slender stick in his right hand, and in his left a bundle of papers, on which he pretended, with a tragicomical expression of countenance, to write judicial opinions. Next followed the gun of the caravan, a small brass field-piece...[89]

As with the "demons," this satirical judge panders to the audience's appetite for theatrics and entertainment. The connection to the *mahmal* and the Hajj are tenuous. One scholar has proposed that this dimension of the parade constituted a playful transgression of social order.[90] Sophia Lane-Poole continues her description of the ranks of Sufi processors and their instruments:

The soldiers were followed by a long procession of Darweeshes. First came the Saadeeyeh, with numerous flags, bearing, in many cases, the names of God, Muhammad, and the founder of their order, on a ground of green silk. Most of these Darweeshes were beating a small kettle-drum called báz, which is held in the left hand, and beaten with a short thick strap. Some beating cymbals, and all repeating religious ejaculations, chiefly names and epithets of God. They were perpetually bowing their heads to the right and to the left during the whole repetition, and this motion was rendered the more apparent by many of them wearing very high felt caps; then, the variety in their costume, and, more than all, the gravity of their deportment, combined to rivet our attention. These Darweeshes were followed by a body of their parent order (the Refá-eeyeh), bearing black flags, and also beating bázes and cymbals, and repeating the like ejaculations. Their sheykh, a venerable looking person, wearing a very large black turban, rode behind them, on horseback.

Then passed the Kádireeyeh Darweeshes: their principal insignia were borne by members of their order; viz. palm-sticks, for fishing-rods; and fishing-nets strained on hoops, and raised on long poles, with many small fish suspended round them. They carried white flags. Next followed the Ahmedeeyeh, and Baráhimeh Darweeshes, bearing red and green flags; and immediately after these came "the *Mahmal*." The *Mahmal* is a mere emblem of royalty, and contains nothing; but two copies of the Kurán, in cases of gilt silver, are fastened to the exterior. It is an imitation of a covered liter, borne on the back of a camel; and it accompanies the caravan yearly, forming, if I may use the expression, the banner of the pilgrims. Many persons have understood that it contains the Kisweh, or new covering for the temple of Mekkah; but they are mistaken...The half-naked sheykh who has for so many years followed the *Mahmal*, incessantly rolling his head, for which feat he receives a gratuity from the government, rode on a horse immediately after it.[91]

Mrs. Poole notes the various Sufi (or Darweesh) orders by name. We shall return to consider their "flags" and "insignia" in greater detail in Chapter 3, but for the moment let us examine her presentation of the *mahmal*. Here she correctly notes that it does not carry the *kiswa*. More contestable though, is her off-hand remark that it is "a mere emblem of royalty." As the inscriptions we noted earlier make clear, the *mahmal* was not limited to that function.

In the pre-Hajj procession of 1874 the ranks of soldiers were followed by various Sufi groups, including,

howling dervishes – a ragged, wild-looking, ruffianly set... The sheikhs of the principal orders of dervishes came next in order, superbly dressed in robes of brilliant colours embroidered with gold, and mounted on magnificent Arabs. Finest of all, in a green turban and scarlet mantle, rode the Sheykh of the Hasaneyn, who is a descendant of the Prophet; but most important, the Sheykh el Bekree, who is a sort of Egyptian Archbishop of Canterbury and head of all the dervishes, came last, riding a white Arab with gold-embroidered housings. He was a placid-looking old man, and wore a violet robe and an enormous red and green turban... Then came the Sheykh el Gemel. Rolling his head for the entire Hajj.[92]

This was clearly a significant parade, with the full hierarchy of Sufis represented. The leading shaykhs are here identified as "Sheykh of the Hasaneyn," that is, the leader of the Sadat al-Wafa'iyya, and the "Sheykh el Bekree" (presumably these were Ahmad 'Abd al-Khaliq and 'Ali ibn Muhammad al-Bakri). The narrator Amelia Edwards makes the awkward comparison of the latter to the "Egyptian Archbishop of Canterbury" in an attempt to convey the preeminent position the Bakris had held from the early part of that century. This was official state recognition of the privilege of the Bakris to represent all the Sufi orders in state matters and at public functions.[93] We will revisit this modern effort at centralizing and controlling Sufism in Chapter 4, when we consider further the dynamics of public processions. The description of the *Sheykh el Gemel* (Shaykh of the Camel) notes a curious figure – unlikely to be a Sufi – whose function is unclear. He is known by various names, and we shall meet him again below.

At roughly the same time as Amelia Edwards was taking notes in Cairo, Isabel Burton was observing similar parades in Damascus. The scale of those processions was smaller than those mounted in Cairo, but many of the components were similar: the banners, soldiers and Sufi troops, jurists and judges, and a *mahmal*. One significant ritual object used in Ottoman-era Damascus was the processional flag known as the *Sanjak Sherif*. This object, which appeared in public only once a year, was identified as the flag of the caliph 'Umar.[94]

For the year 1799, the historian al-Jabarti provides the following colorful details describing the various high level functionaries in parade:

> The procession of the *kiswa* dress of the noble Ka'ba from Black Square (Qaramaydan) was announced... The procession passed along: in front the Leader of the pilgrims and the Market Inspector, and all the banner bearers with their drums, pipes, and cymbals; then Bartholomew, Vizier of the Guardians, wearing a huge fur, and before him 200 or more Muslim Janissaries and a great number of Greek Christians in arms, officers in capes; after that, marching groups of police guards; then the superintendent of the *kiswa*, who was a retainer of Mustafa, Vizier of the pasha; behind him a band of Turkish musicians. This procession was one of the most extraordinary and wondrous pageants including as it did, a diversity of figures, a variety of images, an assemblage of different people, and elevation of the lowliest, a multitude of crowds, of wondrous creatures, a union of contrasting things and a change from the ordinary.[95]

Al-Jabarti does not identify the "wondrous creatures," but it is not inconceivable that these were exotic animals such as monkeys, hunting birds, or tigers.

In the twentieth century, the *mahmal* procession proceeds on a well-organized and official itinerary. As during the time of the fifteenth century "demons," the central stage is the large square, Qaramaydan, at the foot of the Cairo citadel. Details, including photographs, of the various military units, groups of scholars, government officials, and of course Sufis, abound. The enigmatic Shaykh al-Gamal, also known in the modern period as Abu al-Qitat (Father/Master of the Cats), continues to participate. After various rites are performed in the square, the *mahmal* sets out northward, about six kilometers, through the densely populated Darb al-Ahmar neighborhood, to reach an open ground in the Abbasiyya quarter. After a week or two, the *mahmal* would usually set out from the Abbasiyya train station for Suez, where it would travel

CAIRO · LE CAIRE

PROCESSION OF THE HOLY CARPET · PROCESSION DU TAPIS SACRÉ

10 The *mahmal* and *kiswa* processing below citadel. Credit: Travelers in the Middle East Archive (TIMEA) 7 × 4.5 in. "Procession of the Holy Carpet" from the collection of Paula Sanders, Rice University

by boat to the port of Jidda.[96] Upon its return from the Hajj, the route would be followed in reverse, all the way back to an official ceremony at the citadel square.

The ceremony in 1908 at the foot of the citadel saw the *kiswa* and *mahmal* circle three times around the square. Figure 10 records the event, with the *mahmal* being visible in the lower left of the photograph. After soldiers and musicians on camels, beating drums, have passed, the Sultan's Egyptian representative, the Khedive, is then presented with a decorated bag containing the key to the Ka'ba. The *kiswa*, along with a decorated covering for the stone of the Station of Abraham, are further displayed by foot soldiers carrying them before the crowds.[97] Another report of this ceremony seven years earlier, describes seven rather than three circles – evoking the number of circumambulations the pilgrims will make of the Ka'ba – and of the amir of the Hajj kissing the reigns of the *mahmal* camel after having received them from the Khedive. The procession then moved off across the city: the *mahmal* to Abbasiyya, and the *kiswa* to the shrine-mosque of al-Husayn. The latter was displayed for two weeks, hung upon the mosque walls, where people would come to visit, and if possible, touch the *kiswa*, even cutting small pieces from it for the *baraka*. The crowds that gathered were often over-enthusiastic, and required the intervention of shrine attendants to restrain them.[98] Temporarily hanging the *kiswa* in a devotional space had been a longstanding practice.[99] Al-Waqidi claims that in the early eighth century, the caliph 'Abd al-Malik sent a *kiswa* made of silk to

Mecca once each year – and that before being delivered to Mecca, it was displayed in the Prophet's mosque at Medina, where sections were hung between the pillars.[100]

The devotional responses to both the *kiswa* and the *mahmal*, were spontaneous – no formal rituals were developed around these devotional practices. The reactions, however, were remarkably consistent across the centuries. The accounts of such responses from the earliest period of *kiswa* and *mahmal* parading are rather scant, but details from later periods are abundant. Perhaps the earliest such report is from 1679, where a Maghrebi traveler describes the *kiswa*, circulating in pieces, mounted on wooden frames and being touched by crowds seeking blessing (*baraka*).[101] European visitors were also impressed by the significance of these behaviors, and seem invariably to have noted them in their accounts of Egyptian religious life. From the mid-eighteenth century, we read the following:

> It was pleasant enough to see how the mob crowded towards the camel as he passed, in order to touch the pavilion, which they esteemed holy. Those that could not come so near as to touch it with their hands, threw their handkerchiefs or sashes on it, that they might at least possess something which had touched so holy a thing.[102]

The sympathetic tone of this and other foreigner accounts is notable. A century later, Amelia Edwards described the parade, capturing some of the intensity of the reception of the *mahmal*. In her account of the pre-Hajj procession of the 21st of Shawwal, she describes the climax of the display and the responses to it:

> But the crowning excitement was yet to come, and the rapture with which the crowd had greeted the Sheykh el-Gemel was nothing compared with their ecstasy when the *Mahmal*... was seen coming through the gateway. The women held up their children; the men swarmed up the scaffoldings of the swings and behind the carriages. They screamed; they shouted; they waved handkerchiefs and turbans; they were beside themselves with excitement.[103]

The enthusiasm of the crowds and the intensity of the community's experience of the *mahmal* on such occasions is clear. Figure 11 reflects the liveliness of the event, including its appeal to curious outsiders such as the British officers, shown at the bottom viewing the procession from the edge of the crowd.

The *kiswa* did not have to be made in Cairo for it to elicit devotional responses from Egyptians. For the year 1802, the chronicler al-Jabarti notes the joyous, if unusual, event of the arrival of a *kiswa* from Istanbul. People were told in Cairo that the Sultan ordered it made when he heard his forces had defeated the French in Egypt. The *kiswa* was met at the Bulaq port of Cairo by shaykhs, banner carriers, a detachment of sergeants, soldiers, judges, jurists, and

11 *Mahmal* procession. Credit: Travelers in the Middle East Archive (TIMEA) "Fête du tapis sacré" from the collection of Paula Sanders, Rice University

the representative of the descendants of the Prophet, as well as the leading candidate for the position of Amir of the Hajj for that year.

> The *kiswa* was brought; they passed in front of it. Pieces of the bands made of canvas were removed: three such pieces and five woven, as well as a veil (*burqa'*) of the Maqam Ibrahim. All this was made of fine cloth and bold lettering, hollow and carefully executed. The rest of the (*kiswa*) carpet was in crates carried by camels. Over the crates were covers of green broadcloth. The people rejoiced; it was a memorable day.

An additional passage in the original manuscripts adds the following:

> They all walked in procession until they reached the Husayn Shrine with it (the *kiswa*). Along with it was the veil of the Maqam Ibrahim. All this was made of superior cloth and arranged most carefully. The trimmings and bands of canvas were spread on an elongated wooden structure. The rest of the cover was in crates carried by camels.[104]

Although the origin of this *kiswa* was unusual, the rituals required for its proper reception and display were quite clear. The wider political context is relevant here, as the French occupiers had recently been expelled, and the renewed heavy British and Turkish military presence in Egypt made public life uneasy. Under the French, the production of the *kiswa* had been disrupted, and the Egyptian pilgrims at Mecca are reported to have stripped the Ka'ba of her dressing when they first heard the Europeans had invaded their homeland. The link between ritual and public order was clear to Napoleon and the French governors – and Jabarti tells us of the significant, yet ultimately failed, efforts made by the French to repair and send an Egyptian *kiswa* in 1799 and 1801, in the name of the French Republic.[105] In this context, it seems the arrival of the 1802 *kiswa* from Istanbul would have provided some reassurance, and the sense of a restoration of order through a shared devotional ritual.

Although not a formal rite, devotional impulses toward the *mahmal* were promoted and facilitated by various actors in the public sphere. In his stipulations for the renovations of the Aqsunqur mosque, the sixteenth-century amir Ibrahim Agha Mustahfizan provided money for Sufis to recite the *fatiha* and other prayers for the *mahmal* as it passed each year in front of the mosque.[106] The *mahmal* was also installed at various sites for public veneration. From the year 1700, the Qaramaydan had a *mastaba* or platform specifically for displaying the *mahmal*. Records only mention rituals of Qur'an recitation associated with this display for the year 1901, but this was very likely a long-held practice.[107] Likewise, the site for viewing the *mahmal* in Abbasiyya, before it was loaded onto a specially made railway car, was carefully organized. Soldiers stood guard, and fabric screens were erected to set the object off from the surrounding space. Although temporary, these boundaries provided individuals a clear sense of sacred space. Figure 12 shows such a *mahmal* set up in 1911 as a temporary shrine,

12 The *mahmal* in camp at Abbasieh. Credit: Simon H. Leeder, *Veiled Mysteries of Egypt.* New York: C. Scribner's Sons, 1913. Image in public domain

and Figure 13 records some of its visitors. The rationale is described in terms typical for visitation of shrines, i.e.: "that those seeking blessing may visit."[108]

The *kiswa* would end its Hajj being placed over the Ka'ba, while the *mahmal* continued the pilgrim's circuit. Figure 14 records the *mahmal* on the plane of Arafat, an important stage of the Hajj. One report from 1901 describes the *mahmal*s of Egypt and Syria, in parade dress, making five circles outside of the *Haram*.[109] An account from the early twentieth century, by an official of the Egyptian delegation, draws a vivid picture. Ibrahim Rif'at describes the placement and dressing of the *mahmal*, noting that, "While in Mecca, and resting between the Gate of the Prophet and the Gate of Peace (i.e. at the eastern edge of the *Haram*), it wears its common covering. There it is visited by all kinds of people. When it moves from this spot, setting out for Medina, it is escorted in an official procession." The *mahmal* typically traveled on to the Prophet's tomb in Medina, and at certain places sat in display for visitors. As at the Qaramaydan and the Abbasiyya site in Cairo, the *mahmal* here played a central role in the rite of the Hajj. Figure 15 records individuals from Medina coming out to visit the *mahmal* before it reaches the city. Rif'at continues his description with an account of the pilgrimage to the Prophet's tomb:

> It arrives at Medina, entering the city by the 'Anbariyya Gate, to a great reception including a twenty-one-gun salute. It continues to the

13 Egyptian women visiting the *mahmal* at Abbasieh. Credit: Simon H. Leeder, *Veiled Mysteries of Egypt*. New York: C. Scribner's Sons, 1913. Image in public domain

Egyptian Gate, with its entire escort on foot out of respect for this the Station of the Prophet. When they reach the Gate of Peace, the Shaykh al-Haram takes the camel's bridle, and leads it up the steps of the Gate, and has it kneel there. The *mahmal* is unloaded, and brought inside to its place, on the west side of the (Prophet's) minbar. Its formal covering is then replaced by its green cover.

14 The Egyptian *mahmal* at Mt. 'Arafat. Credit: Ibrahim Rif'at, *Mir'at al-Haramayn*. 2 vols. Cairo: Dar al-Kutub al-Misriyya, 1925. Image in public domain

15 The *mahmal* met by women from Medina. Credit: Ibrahim Rif'at, *Mir'at al-Haramayn*. 2 vols. Cairo: Dar al-Kutub al-Misriyya, 1925. Image in public domain

The shaykh of the shrine-mosque of the Prophet's house ritually receives the *mahmal*, bringing it into the enclosure of the open-air prayer space. At this point the dress covering – literally the '*kiswa* of the *mahmal*' – is taken off its frame in order to continue its pilgrimage.

On entering the holy site, the Amir al-Hajj and his entourage wear the garments of servants, loose white coverings fastened with a belt. In a solemn ritual, they then transport the *kiswa* of the *mahmal* into the Noble Sanctuary by way of the Syrian door, placing it near the Station (or grave) of Fatima (next to Muhammad's grave). The formal covering remains here until the *mahmal* is ready to leave Medina. The ritual processions upon departure from the city are similar to those of arrival.[110]

The *mahmal*'s ritual approach to the Prophet's grave illustrates a progressive crossing of the physical boundaries that encircle the shrine. The *mahmal*, on its frame, upon its camel, enters Medina; the camel is stopped outside the shrine-mosque; the frame and the green travel covering stay in the open-air mosque; and the formal covering enters the immediate vicinity of the tomb. This accession is apparently not an occasion at which the formal covering is displayed – in other words, it is not the object being visited, rather it is making its own devotional visit.

In the sacred topography of Islamic pilgrimage, the house-mosque of Muhammad is a high-point second only to the Noble Precincts of the Ka'ba. While the complete history of *mahmal* parading in the Hijaz has yet to be written, for our purposes, the descriptions above are enough to indicate the important interaction the *mahmal* had with the Prophet's tomb. This association constitutes a significant dimension of the *mahmal*'s life as a religious object. We shall see later this association reappears in some unexpected places.

The *mahmal* returned to Egypt loaded with *baraka*, that currency of blessing associated with sanctity and pious deeds. As a commodity *baraka* is normally understood to be transferable; it may be accrued through personal devotion, or acquired from an object that has collected it in surplus. *Baraka* abounds at the shrines of the saintly dead, and is easily conveyed by the simple objects, or human bodies, that come into contact with it. It is an intangible force resting upon the very material objects of religious culture.

Interpretations of the official ceremony at the foot of the Citadel, signaling the departure of the Hajj, hint at this identification of the *mahmal* with the Prophet's tomb. In 1672, the Turkish traveler Evliya Celebi attended the event and noted that the Pasha led the camel around the square. Other accounts make it clear that this was common practice, but Evliya's explanation of the ritual is telling. He claims that by this self-abasing gesture the Pasha was proclaiming himself the Prophet's camel driver and humble servant. This emotive ritual, evoking the Prophet, was repeated upon the pilgrim's return, when the Pasha rode out to meet the *mahmal*, and dismounted in order to lead the camel back by his own hand. Evliya notes both the Pasha and the religious elites in attendance recited prayers in honor of the Prophet, but even more interesting is Evliya's assertion that the *mahmal* received such reverence because it constituted a tangible link to Muhammad. Although it appears

nowhere else in the written records that have come down to us, Evilya claims
the *mahmal* originally carried the Prophet's personal belongings, in particular
his gown, shoes, a twig for cleaning teeth (*miswak*), and an ablutions bowl.[111]
These objects are well known relics of the Prophet, and were also preserved
from other leading figures in Islamic history. We shall return to the practice of
relic veneration in Chapter 3, but for the moment I will simply underline
their function as evidence of the association of the *mahmal* with the Prophet's
grave.

This identification of the *mahmal* with the Prophet is made in similar terms
at the turn of the twentieth century by the Egyptian functionary Ibrahim
Rif'at. In his account of Hajj parades, both in Cairo and other cities, he notes
how children were brought out by their parents in order to touch the passing
mahmal, as well as the practice of placing onlookers' handkerchiefs briefly
inside the litter, all in order to capture its *baraka*. Rif'at is not a superstitious
man, but he explains the efficacy of these practices, saying that people want the
blessing that has accrued to an object that has visited the holy sites. Rubbing
oneself against the Prophet's tomb enclosure (*maqsura*) may have been impossible in 1901 – due to the distance of travel to Medina, and the recent
obstructions by the Wahhabis – but these practices of *mahmal* veneration, he
tells us, are seen as the next best thing.[112] It is notable that he is not attributing
the curative power of the *mahmal* to its having visited the Ka'ba, instead it
functions here as an extension of the sanctity of Muhammad's tomb.

Thanks to the *mahmal*, the ideas and objects of the Hajj were realigned, and
new possibilities for both emerged. With the appearance of the *mahmal* and the
associated practices it generated, a successful pilgrimage evolved new criteria.
The visual displays, the parading, the public celebrations, and the *mahmal*'s
own program of pilgrimage – along the stations of the Hajj and to the
Prophet's tomb – were all occasions to be newly negotiated within the
constellation of ideas that structure Islamic ritual and religious duty. The Hajj
as both religious practice and concept, became an intimately shared and local
event. No longer was pilgrimage simply the lonely experience of the Hajji
wandering through silent desert tacks. The *mahmal* served to collapse that
distance, as it played with the distinction between subjects and objects; it
crossed complex boundaries within the sacred spaces of Mecca and Medina,
while becoming itself a mobile devotional site. The *mahmal* as we saw, also
engaged with political concepts. Legitimacy, authority, and force – whether
monetary or military – were all asserted and resisted in new ways. The *mahmal*
was thus a new opportunity to practice the Hajj, and perform statecraft, but it
also brought a unique of challenges. The sultan, amir, or Pasha had to manage
a successful *mahmal*, and like the women photographed making their pilgrimage to Abbasiyya (Figure 12), had to engage with objects that actively negotiated the world around them.

TWO

AN EXUBERANT AND ELUSIVE PALANQUIN

The hero of this trek was surely the camel. He shared with the pilgrims their thirst, their fear of robbers, and the threat of pillaging.[1]

By any measure the *mahmal* had a long and dramatic career on the public stage of Egyptian religious life. We have seen that for seven centuries it was venerated and celebrated in its many exuberant instantiations. The following pages will explore this career further because, as will become clear, mahmals and kiswas in effect scattered themselves. They did so as forms, as objects, and as disarticulated material remains, dispersed throughout the country. I consider this scattering a material exuberance, the seemingly irrepressible reappearance of these objects and practices throughout the landscape often in unexpected ways. Such exuberance extends the story of *mahmal*s and *kiswa*s in ways that uniquely illuminate how the graves of prophets and saints were conceived, envisaged, and revered. In a related sense, *mahmal*s and *kiswa*s were also elusive because their theological and doctrinal standing, along with the reformist politics that would later swirl around them, continued to be contested. We shall see that proponents and detractors alike spun a complex and at times confused discourse around *mahmal*s and *kiswa*s. Particularly illuminating in this context was the role of that formidable colonial institution, the museum. Conservative religious reformers mobilized the Egyptian museum in their campaign for a postcolonial reshaping of public Islamic religious life.

16 Procession of cover for Station of Abraham. Credit: British Pathé

Let me begin this story by noting that dressing religious objects other than the Ka'ba with elaborate coverings became a rather common practice.[2] Venerated stones, walls, and even pulpits were candidates for such honors. Perhaps it is not surprising to find that the Station of Abraham, the stone bearing his footprints as he put the final stones in place on the Ka'ba, has received such attention. The stone's proximity to the Ka'ba kept it a prominent feature in the Hajj landscape. We read of the Ottoman sultan sending such a dress in 1802, which is described as made of "superior cloth" and displaying "bold lettering, hollow and carefully executed."[3] The hollow lettering refers to the more elaborate technique of raised stitching. Another covering for the Station of Abraham, parading some 137 years later, is presented in Figure 16.[4] This *kiswa* seems to be less elaborate than the earlier one described by al-Jabarti but is nevertheless impressive. There are upper and lower calligraphic panels on each side in addition to arabesque infills and what appear to be column and arch style bordering along the bottom. Another object located near the Ka'ba, the enclosure (*hijr*) of Isma'il, also received a covering. The Mamluks had sent it in 1448, but it was hung only two years later. Whatever the misgivings were that delayed its display, likely also discouraged further dressings from being sent – this being the only recorded instance of a *kiswa* being made for the enclosure wall.[5] The Black Stone of the Ka'ba had been reverentially veiled while the Ka'ba was being rebuilt in the time of Ibn al-Zubayr, although no descriptive details have come down to us.[6] Another revered stone, that of the

Sakhra in Jerusalem, was for a time regularly dressed. More than one source from the mid fifteenth century describes a rich brocade *kiswa* covering the rock.[7] At one point, even the Prophet's minbar, preserved in in the courtyard of his home in Medina, was covered with a veil of white Egyptian *qabati* cotton.[8] As we noted in the previous chapter this fine material had often been used to make the inner dress of the Ka'ba itself. Though none of these dressing practices can be considered central to the pilgrimage, and some were rather short-lived, together they mirror an active and even experimental religious culture of veiling.

The most intensive site for dressing beyond the Ka'ba however was the Prophet's tomb in Medina. This practice goes back to the first century and a half after Muhammad's death. We shall explore this history in detail below, but some of the wider debates and conceptions at play around the relationship of Mecca to Medina are important here. The sanctity of Mecca was never in dispute, with the Qur'an and the Prophet having explicitly recognized its status as a sacred precinct or *haram*. However, the status of Medina, the Prophet's adopted home, including his grave and that of his family members and immediate followers, along with many important nearby sites in early Islamic history, was never a settled question among jurists. Generally, the Hanafi school of law denied the sacred status of Medina, while other schools recognized it.[9] A related debate revolved around pilgrimage to the Prophet's grave. While the Hajj always enjoyed canonical status as an obligation upon all able Muslims, extending one's visit to Medina was until the rise of Wahhabism in Arabia, widely practiced, and even encouraged. Some hadith reports disapprove of visiting graves, while others recommend the added trip, promising rewards for the devotee upon judgment in the afterlife.[10] Textual evidence for the explicit linking of the Hajj to pilgrimage to Medina seems to only be available in sources after the mid ninth century, but historically we know that several early caliphs included the *ziyara* to Medina as part of their Hajj itinerary.[11] The complex debates around the status of the Prophet's grave, along with the pilgrimage to other commemorative sites in Medina – which I shall explore further in Chapter 4 – constitute the conceptual matrix within which *kiswa* veiling practices evolved. Let us turn now to consider some of the long and colorful history of dressing Muhammad's grave.

According to one early historian of Medina the first to hang a full *kiswa* over the tomb of the Prophet was the Hamdanid ruler Sayf al-Dawla (d. 967). This would have only been possible with the permission of the reigning Abbasid caliph, perhaps as compensation for not being allowed to send a *kiswa* for the Ka'ba. The early Abbasid caliph, Harun al-Rashid (d. 809) had perfumed the grave and covered it in silk, which in the opinion of the historian al-Samhudi did not count as a *kiswa*.[12] Al-Samhudi also describes a *kiswa* sent by the Fatimids in the late twelfth century. This white covering (*sitara*) displayed text, and was adorned with striped medallions (*jamat marquma*).[13] Additionally, a red silk sash bearing the text of sura YaSin, the thirty-sixth chapter of the Qur'an, was hung around the grave. The Shia identity of the Fatimids clearly came into play, not least because they were the great rivals of the Abbasids for leadership of the Muslim world and control of the central sites of Mecca and Medina. We are told that the governor of Medina blocked its installation while he sought permission from the Abbasid caliph Al-Mustadi bi-Amr Allah (d. 1180). Surprisingly, the request seems to have been granted, since the covering hung for two years. Abbasid authority was not to be ignored for long however, and a replacement was sent, which clearly displayed the caliphal title of Al-Mustadi bi-Amr Allah. The covering was a violet silk, with inscriptions and striped medallions. The earlier Fatimid covering was removed and sent to the *mashhad* shrine of 'Ali in Kufa. Al-Samhudi continues the story, describing how the Abbasid caliph Al-Nasir li-Din Allah (d. 1225) commissioned a covering of black silk, which was hung over that of his predecessor. Al-Nasir's mother had a third covering hung on the grave after her return from the Hajj.[14]

Over the course of the following century and a half the *kiswa* of the Prophet's grave would make several appearances in the historical record. Coverings for the inside of the chamber typically consisted of a patterned fabric and a *hizam* belt.[15] In 1256 a fire destroyed the roof of the Prophet's house, several valuable Qur'ans, the Prophet's minbar, and the tomb covering of the noble precinct (*kiswa al-hujra al-sharifa*).[16] A few decades later we hear of a *mahmal* parade in Cairo, which included a new covering for the Prophet's shrine (*al-hujra al-nabawiyya*).[17] In 1353 sultan Salah al-Din ibn Muhammad established a permanent endowment (*waqf*), the revenues of which would cover the cost of producing new *kiswa*s for the Prophet's tomb and his pulpit every five years.[18] Records from the late fourteenth century note further endowments established for the Prophet's tomb.[19] In the late sixteenth century, a covering for the Prophet's tomb was ritually bestowed upon the Amir al-Hajj, along with the *kiswa* of the Ka'ba, with both being processed within the city. The covering was triangular, with gold lettering on a green velvet background, at a height of approximately 65 cm.[20] A modern survey of *kiswa*s dating from the sixteenth to the twentieth centuries identifies the coverings of the Prophet's grave as a stylistically distinct group of hangings. Typically, a black background was used for Ka'ba coverings, a red one for the *kiswa*s that hung inside the Ka'ba, and green fabrics used for the Prophet's tomb. As we noted in our earlier discussions of Ka'ba *kiswa* colors, these typologies are far from airtight. At best, we can speak of tendencies toward certain colors rather than hard and fast rules.[21] These categories are also apparently based upon the textual content displayed: Coverings of Muhammad's grave include verses and prayers related to him and the listing of his successors, the four Rightly Guided caliphs.[22] Another covering (Figure 17), from the sixteenth century, displays

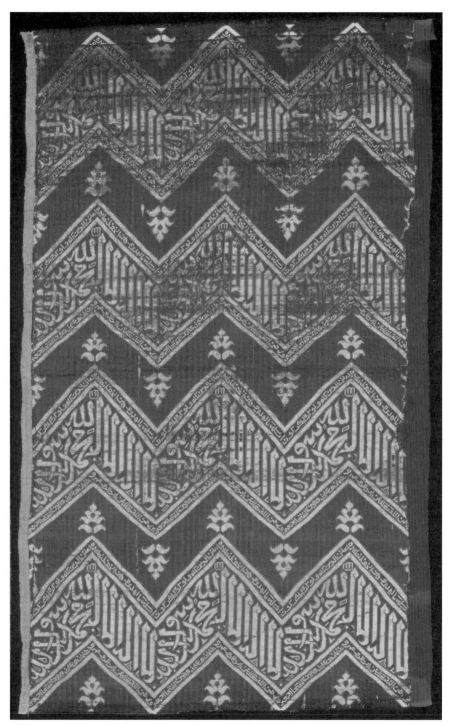

17 Green silk dress for the Prophet's tomb. Credit: 779–1892; Victoria and Albert Museum. Larger parts of this hanging are preserved in Cairo's Textile Museum (TM430)

the confession of faith "There is no god but God, and Muhammad is the messenger of God" in its main zigzag panel. The smaller inscription in the upper panel recalls the divine nature of Muhammad's mission and his status as prophet: "It is He Who has sent His messenger with guidance and the religion of truth, to proclaim it over all religion, however much the idolaters dislike it." (Q. 9:33) The text in the lower panel calls for divine blessings upon Muhammad's successors, "Abu Bakr, 'Umar, 'Uthman, 'Ali, and all of the early companions."

The impact of the *mahmal* on Egyptian religious culture was of course not limited to Cairo. In Chapter 1 we saw that as an object of veneration, a signifier of the Hajj, and a link to Muhammad's grave, the *mahmal* came to be identified as an expression of belief and religious practice in its own right. The history of the diffusion of the *mahmal* beyond its primary association with the Hajj caravans is not linear, but rather a story of unexpected boundary crossing. The exuberance I've been claiming for the *mahmal*s and *kiswa*s is thus also manifested in their mobility. We noted earlier in some detail the processions of the *mahmal* around Cairo, Mecca, and Medina. These cities however were not the only urban centers to see the parading of the *mahmal* and the *kiswa*. In the age of rail and steamer travel the Egyptian port of Suez saw such processions every year. In 1902 this first leg of the Hajj was completed directly from Cairo, a distance of about 130 km. The previous year however, the *mahmal* and *kiswa* made a detour of at least 175 km, detouring from the normal Hajj route and traveling through several cities in the Delta before arriving at Suez. From Cairo this route led north to Tukh, and Banha, then east to Zagazig and Abu Hammad, continuing eastward to Nifisha and Isma'iliyya, then turning south to Fayid and finally Suez (Map 1). At each stop the *mahmal* processed and was greeted by adoring crowds.[23] In 1910 an even more significant detour was made. Al-Batanuni tells us that the *mahmal* traveled by train to Alexandria, where "it was received with great celebration," and then by boat to the port of Jaffa in Palestine, travelling by train to Medina and Mecca (Map 2). Its return route took it by boat to the small town of al-Tur in the Sinai, then on to Suez, and finally back to Cairo by train from there.[24] These detours covered significant ground, but seem to be mentioned in our sources in a matter-of-fact way, leading us to wonder how much more traveling the *mahmal* and *kiswa* did throughout Egypt and the region that was not recorded in the sources. These journeys outside of the direct Hajj routes may have also taken place further up the Nile, since in the pre-modern era the Hajj route of choice ran south, crossing the Red Sea to Arabia from ports such as Qusayr (Map 2). Figure 18 shows a *mahmal* in its traveling dress. It is at sea, likely heading out from the post of Suez. The upper panel to right, although obscured appears be a Qur'anic passage calling believers to the Hajj: "(and purify My House for those who circle around it) and for those who

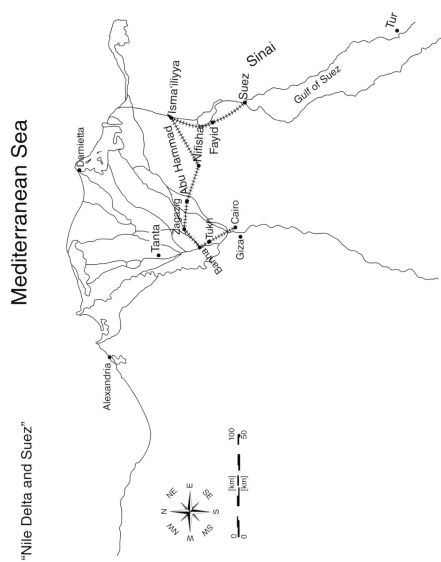

Mediterranean Sea

"Nile Delta and Suez"

Alexandria

Damietta

Tanta

Zagazig

Abu Hammad

Nifisha

Isma'iliyya

Fayid

Suez

Sinai

Gulf of Suez

Tur

Bilbais

Tukh

Cairo

Giza

N
NE
E
SE
S
SW
W
NW

[km] 100
      50
[km]

0
0

MAP 1 Nile Delta and Suez

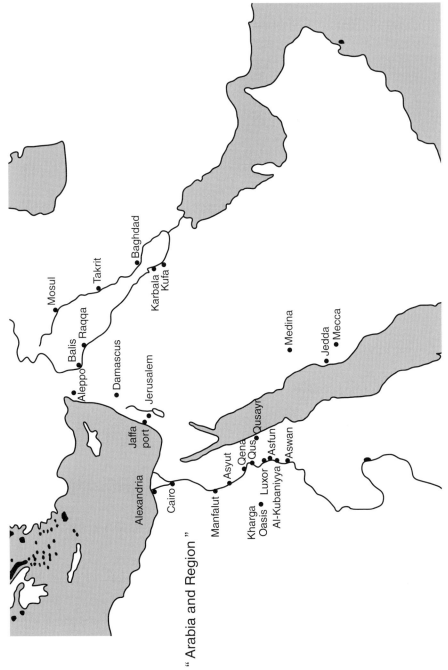

" Arabia and Region "

Mosul

Takrit

Baghdad

Raqqa

Balis

Karbala

Kufa

Aleppo

Damascus

Jerusalem

Jaffa port

Alexandria

Cairo

Manfalut

Asyut

Qena

Qus

Luxor

Asfun

Qusayr

Aswan

Kharga Oasis

Al-Kubaniyya

Medina

Jedda

Mecca

MAP 2   Arabia and region

18 *Mahmal* crossing Red Sea in travel dress. Credit: AGE Photostock America Inc. 11″ × 16″

stand, and who bow down in prayer" followed on the panel to the left: "(Proclaim to the people the Hajj, and they will come to you on foot) and on every kind of camel; they will come from every distant ravine." (Q. 22:26–27)

Transportation of the *kiswa* was always a primary concern of these tours, and after leaving Cairo it appears not to have been taken out of its traveling crates until it reached Mecca. The *mahmal* clearly became the primary if not exclusive object for public display on these long excursions. Not surprisingly then, the *mahmal* loomed large within the visual culture of Egyptian religious life. Iconic examples of the camel with its palanquin abound on jewelry and talismans.[25] In an account of festivities in 1814 Cairo, one chronicler describes floating images formed of lights in the Azbakiyya lake. The renderings must have been rough, but nevertheless were easily identified as representing lions, boats, and a *mahmal*.[26]

The *mahmal* processions were also the occasion for the decoration of private shops and homes. Descriptions of colorful silk streamers and thematic pictorial representations seem to have been common as far back as the fourteenth century.[27] Beyond this, and much more common, is the adornment of the homes of returning pilgrims with *mahmal* images. Exposed to the elements, these paintings typically last for only a few years, but in the modern period as well as the medieval they are well attested to, and likely go back much further.[28] These decorations are not limited to Egypt, being common in Syria and Palestine. Figure 19 is a modern Egyptian painting showing the entrance of the *mahmal*, followed by a camel train of pilgrims, into Mecca. The *mahmal*

19 *Mahmal* caravan in Hajj mural. Credit: Ann Parker and Neal Avon Neal, *Hajj Paintings: Folk Art of the Great Pilgrimage* (Cairo: American University in Cairo Press, 2009). © American University in Cairo Press

camel is led by a forceful Amir al-Hajj waving a sword as if to deter any rival *mahmal*s or Wahhabi objections. The train is typical in such compositions, as is the airplane. This painting conflates train travel with the traditional march by camel. Another house painting, this one from Upper Egypt likewise depicts the *mahmal* along with more modern modes of travel. Figure 20 depicts the front of a returning pilgrim's home in the year 1988. At the bottom right are two women carrying water, perhaps an identification with the local village identity. To the left is an iconic rendering of the Ka'ba and its *kiswa*, with the dome of the Prophet's mosque in Medina awkwardly positioned behind. To the left of the house's front door is a horseman in traditional dress with the long stick that is often used in equestrian games at popular festivities. Running above is the notice: "(This is the home of) the Hajji and pilgrim to the tomb of the Prophet, Muhammad Hasan al-'Ummi in the year 1988." Text from Qur'an 3:97 runs, "Pilgrimage to the House (of God) is a duty the people owe to God, those among them who are able." At the top right, a pilgrim dressed in *ihram* is reciting the Hajji's *labayka* prayer. To the left is a lion, a common symbol of power and courage; a modern airliner is also depicted. A camel and a simplified rendering of a *mahmal* on the far left complete the facade. This rendering of the *mahmal* is rather simple, and displays no details that would link it to an existing exemplar. As we shall see below, the royal *mahmal* stopped circulating in public in the early 1950s, and thus the artist who produced this rendering would likely never have seen a *mahmal* in person. The

20 *Mahmal* in house mural. Credit: Ann Parker and Neal Avon Neal, *Hajj Paintings: Folk Art of the Great Pilgrimage* (Cairo: American University in Cairo Press, 2009). © American University in Cairo Press

form and afterlife of the *mahmal* thus clearly persists, even if this representation only refers to its original as a type, rather than a specific religious object. Another example, from roughly a century earlier, shows the persistence of some of the same elements of Hajj compositions. Figure 21 records a late nineteenth-century *mahmal* image, along with a pennant, positioned above a stylized palm tree, the latter typically referencing an oasis. The tree is flanked by birds above two beasts of prey. The birds appear to be parrots, and the predators are likely a lion and a leopard. The artist would almost certainly have seen "real" *mahmals,* but the significance of this rendering is not that it preserves a likeness of the original, but rather it demonstrates the iconic status that the *mahmal* had in this devotional visual culture.

Although the historical record provides uneven accounts of the matter, the identification of the *mahmal* with the Prophet's tomb was well established in public religious practice. A contemporary image (Figure 22) shows the armed Amir al-Hajj leading the camel, with the title provided above, "*Mahmal* of the Prophet." This popularly conceived connection with the Prophet is further illustrated by a shift in the visual identification of the *mahmal*. In a study of Egyptian Hajj paintings, Juan Campo noted that when asked, typical viewers of these compositions called the *mahmal* the "*tabut al-rasul*" or "coffin of the Prophet."[29] Campo conducted his fieldwork some thirty years after the *mahmal* had disappeared from the national Hajj rites. This suggests that as the popular memory of the *mahmal* in official ritual faded, the image and form continued to

21 Arabic decorative painting. Credit: Georg Ebers, *Egypt: Descriptive, Historical, and Picturesque*, 2 volumes. Translated by C. Bell (London: Cassell and Co. 1898). Image in public domain

circulate, gradually losing any direct connection to its original reference, and coming to be associated with Muhammad's grave. While this appears to be the case, I would suggest that the wider picture is even more complex and interesting. It seems that this identification of the *mahmal* with tombs goes back much further, and was not simply the result of it losing its position in the Hajj caravans.

Examples from at least the early eighteenth century attest to local shrine practices imitating – or perhaps better "scattering" – the materials and rituals

22 *Mahmal* of the Prophet. Credit: Ann Parker and Neal Avon Neal, *Hajj Paintings: Folk Art of the Great Pilgrimage* (Cairo: American University in Cairo Press, 2009). © American University in Cairo Press

associated with the *kiswa* and the *mahmal*. Perhaps the most prominent monument in Cairo to the family of the Prophet is the shrine of his martyred grandson Husayn. We shall consider this mosque-shrine and its founding relics in Chapter 4, but for the moment only its role as the site of *kiswa* displays will concern us.

Under the Shia Fatimids various shrines were established over the bones of the *ahl al-bayt* or descendants of the house of the Prophet. The intrepid twelfth-century traveler Ibn Jubayr left us an account of some of the devotional activities at the shrine. He comments on devotees crowding around the grave, throwing themselves upon it, kissing it, and tenderly running their hands over its *kiswa* covering.[30] However, it is not until the mid-nineteenth century that we read of any details on this tomb covering. Stanley Lane-Pool describes a green silk covering, with a white band, bearing Qur'anic inscriptions.[31] This grave covering is likely similar to the one donated 50 years earlier by Husayn Pasha al-Qubtan, who made a pilgrimage from Gaza to the shrine, distributing meat to the servants of the shrine and the local poor, in addition to presenting a new *kiswa* to the shrine.[32]

As we noted earlier, the Husayn shrine-mosque also displayed sections of the Ka'ba *kiswa*. Sources from the end of the nineteenth and early twentieth century tell of the *kiswa* hanging for public viewing for anywhere between three days and two weeks.[33] The formal and ritual parallels with tomb covers are intriguing. The historian al-Jabarti notes that in 1712, Amir Azaban al-Jalfi undertook improvements to the shrine of Husayn in Cairo. He enlarged the building, and commissioned a new ebony inlaid casket. "He also provided a cloth of embroidered and brocaded silk. When the work was finished, he had the cloth placed on a frame made of palm branches, carried by four men. Fixed on its sides were four knobs of silver overlaid with gold. Before it walked the Rifa'iyya Sufis with their drums and banners, carrying silver censers burning aloes-wood and amber, and flasks of rose water with which they sprinkled the people. They marched this way until they reached the shrine and placed the cloth cover over the tomb."[34] In light of the accounts of the *mahmal* and *kiswa* parades we saw earlier, and the fact that the Husayn shrine was the display space for the *kiswa* indoors, and the *mahmal* outside – another source describes women seeking blessings by scurrying under the *mahmal* camel in front of the shrine[35] – al-Jabarti's account is very evocative. Amir Azaban had apparently made his *kiswa* and organized its procession along the lines of the *mahmal* and *kiswa* parades. As was the case for the Hajj rites in the Citadel Square, this embroidered covering was placed on a wooden frame, and carried before crowds by footmen. Much as the *mahmal* appeared with five silver balls adorning it, Azaban's tomb covering sported four silver and gold knobs. Likewise, ranks of marching Sufis were mustered, their task being to excite the human senses – the ear with music, the nose with incense and rose water, and the eyes with their banners – all mobilizing a solemnity and sanctity recalling that of the *mahmal* departure rituals.

Another bridging between the *mahmal*/Hajj and funerary practices is recorded in Syria in the 1730s but is very likely much older. Around Damascus the shrines of descendants of the Prophet, Zaynab bint 'Ali, and Ruqayya bint Husayn, would receive remnants of the *kiswa* that had been brought back on the Hajj. Likewise, the tomb of John the Baptist and the shrine of Shaykh Arslan, the Sufi and patron saint of the city, were bestowed *kiswa* fragments.[36] Many of these sites also received tomb coverings. The Mamluk sultan Baybars (d. 1277) embarked on a campaign to renovate the great shrines in his domain, including the tomb of the Patriarchs in Hebron, the grave of Joseph at Nablus, the tomb of Moses at Jericho, and that of the companion of the Prophet, Abu Hurayra, located at Yanbeh. This revival included the regular supply of new tomb *kiswas*.[37] Details have not come down to us, but sultan al-Ghawri had seven black curtains of silk made, each designed and decorated for the specific prophetic tomb it was intended for. These small *kiswas* were paraded around Cairo, led by the custodian of the shrine of Abraham, accompanied by musicians and troops of Sufis.[38] Near the end of the fifteenth century, Sultan Qaytbay sent an elaborate covering with a floral motif, for the tomb of Abraham.[39] One later example has survived. Dating from 1789–1807 this piece has been preserved in the Islamic Museum, al-Aqsa Mosque, in Jerusalem. It measures 180 cm by 210 cm, and consists of light green silk with silver silk thread used for the inscriptions. This covering was made for the tomb of

Abraham, with texts reading across two panels: "This is a noble cavern" – a reference to the shrine complex itself. The *kiswa* also bears the *tughra* of the Ottoman sultan Selim III (r. 1789–1807). There are several large stylized mosque lamps represented on the lower portion.[40]

The connection between shrines and *kiswa*s is multifaceted and shifting. We saw that the Prophet's grave, along with those of his descendants, and other prophets, shared in the veiling practices associated with the Ka'ba. This shift goes further however, with *kiswa*s becoming more than the object of pilgrimage, in effect actively taking up their own pious visits. And we shall see that not only *kiswa*s but also *mahmal*s perform in this way. The ritualized feeding of the *mahmal* camel was one way to associate a tomb site with the Hajj and the *mahmal*. As part of the departure ceremony in Damascus, the *mahmal* would leave the city, accompanied by pilgrims and various local elites, stopping at the mosque-shrine of Sa'd al-Din al-Jibawi al-Shaybani (d. 1335) of the Sa'diyya Sufi order. We noted earlier the mid-nineteenth-century description by Isabel Burton. How the Sa'diyya became associated with the *mahmal* and Hajj is not clear, but the fact that one of its leaders, Sa'd al-Din, died on the Hajj in 1626, may be part of the explanation.[41] This mystical order was founded in the thirteenth cent by Sa'd al-Din al-Shaybani al-Jibawi, whose father, Yunus, was from the Banu Shayba, the tribe with the right to drape the Ka'ba. Sa'd celebrated this association, calling himself one of "the protectors of the Ka'ba," and a direct spiritual acolyte (*murid*) of the Prophet. The Sufi order has a presence in Cairo, through the shrine of Yunus al-Sa'di, located near Bab al-Nasr. For a time, the Egyptian Hajj rites also associated the Sa'diyya with the *mahmal*; and in the mid nineteenth century, the Sa'di family ran the workshop in Khurunfush were the *kiswa* was produced.[42] Upon its return to Cairo, the *mahmal's* dress covering was preserved for use the following year, while its green traveling dress was regularly replaced, with the old one donated as a covering for the grave of Yunus al-Sa'di.[43] The history of this shrine is confusing, and the identity of Yunus al-Sa'di – beyond being popularly called the *renewer of the Sa'diyya in Egypt* – awaits further research. In his comments on the shrine, the nineteenth century historian 'Ali Basha Mubarak notes that according to al-Maqrizi this was originally the late-fourteenth-century tomb of Amir Yunus al-Nawruzi al-Dawadar.[44] Mubarak doubts this is actually the resting place of Yunus al-Sa'di, but notes that common belief, and the subsequent interment of Sa'diyya shaykhs in the immediate vicinity, have redefined the location as a Sa'diyya site.[45] Not only was the green *mahmal* covering used to honor the reputed founder of the Sa'diyya in Egypt, but its members were accorded pride of place in the official processions. Reports from the mid-nineteenth century describe the ranks of Sa'di dervishes leading the *mahmal* parades, bearing green flags and banners – the same color as the traveling *mahmal*.[46] As the origins of this Sufi order are obscure, so too is the end of its ritual association with the *mahmal*. By 1953, Jacques Jomier reports he could find no one at the *kiswa* workshop in Cairo (*Dar al-Kiswa*) or anywhere else who knew of the practice of retiring the green covering to the tomb of Shaykh Yunus.[47] There is likely more to this Sa'diyya story, but for the moment we may simply note that in this practice of adorning a tomb with pieces of returning *mahmal* fabric, we see a relocation of the *mahmal*'s active role as pilgrim. The fabric has accrued baraka through its association with the Ka'ba and contact with the tomb of the Prophet, and as a tomb covering becomes itself an object of veneration.

The Hajj *mahmals* of sixteenth-century Damascus, accompanied by flutes, drums, and singers, and the political and religious elite of the day, would visit the most prominent mosques and shrines of the city.[48] As we noted in the previous chapter, there was no set itinerary for the Egyptian *mahmal*, however beyond the Qaramaydan, the shrine-mosque of Husayn is the most frequently mentioned location. Further research into the itineraries of such parading would likely produce interesting maps of the urban networks religious and political significance.

We noted earlier the association of tomb coverings with Ka'ba veiling. The processing *mahmals* and *kiswas* of the Hajj also had their local counterparts in the parading of coverings for the tombs of great saints. The yearly festival or *mawlid* of Abu al-Hajjaj (d. 1244) in Luxor is a most prominent example.[49] The festivities are highlighted by an elaborate parade, which incorporates processing tomb coverings. Commemorations of Abu al-Hajjaj have included prominent boat imagery, with various explanations being proffered – none of them very convincing. Some point to the importance of Nile boating, and presumably the symbolic importance of ferries transporting people from one side of the river to the other. Another perspective stresses the prominent boat imagery still visible in the many Pharaonic inscriptions around Luxor, and particularly in the great temple in the middle of which the saint's shrine is located.[50] Entering into what seems a more fruitful line of enquiry, we may instead explore the boat theme as it is used to mobilize the objects of parading at the festival. On the evening before the parade, a boat is prepared, painted with bands of blue, white, and red, and mounted upon a four-wheeled flat cart. An image from the turn of the twentieth century shows the painted boat adorned with flags bearing the confession of faith. The tomb covering of Abu al-Hajjaj is placed on this float, which leads the parade, and is followed by several other boats, most of which are occupied by members of a particular trades and guilds.[51] A group of *mahmals* also circulates, the dressings of which include the coverings from the graves of Abu al-Hajjaj's five sons. The *mahmals* are preceded by a group of eight to ten standard bearers. Vast crowds attend this event, crowding the *mahmals* for a chance to touch them and receive baraka.[52] Figure 23 shows the *mahmals*, also known as the "coffins" (*tabut*) in

23 Procession of Abu al-Haggag in Luxor. Credit: Sharif Sonbol and Tarek Atia. *Mulid! Carnivals of Faith* (Cairo: American University in Cairo Press, 1999). © American University in Cairo Press

procession.[53] They display the names of the tombs' occupants, along with the
names of God, invocations for the saintly departed, and Qur'anic passages, such
as those on Abu al-Hajjaj's covering – the fourth one in the procession line –
which runs, "We have granted you a clear victory." (Q. 48:1) By processing
together, there is a clear intention to reinforce the connections between shrine
sites. A century ago Legrain recorded some of the songs sung in the parade,
one of which makes the bond with the Prophet's grave explicit: "His (Abu
al-Hajjaj) tomb is here with us, but the other is in Mecca, near the grave of
Abraham. . ."[54] Legrain has misheard as "grave" of Abraham, what could only
be the Station (*maqam*) of Abraham next to the Ka'ba. Consensus has it that
Abraham is buried in Hebron. Nevertheless, it is significant that the crowds of
the devotees in Luxor are explicitly identifying Abu al-Hajjaj's tomb *kiswa*
with that of the Ka'ba. This tomb *kiswa* also visits prominent religious sites
around Luxor, a practice we saw elsewhere associated with the Hajj *kiswa*.
Along its parade route the colorful processing "coffins" stop at several local saint
shrines – Legrain mentions the tombs of Saboun and Megachgiche – where the
fatiha prayer is recited to mark the visit.[55] The path taken through the city has
been changed at least once in the modern era due to new roadworks, the
building of parking lots, and an urban renewal project in the area.

At another *mawlid* of Upper Egypt, in the city of al-Qina, many of the same
practices and objects are put into circulation. The tomb of 'Abd al-Rahim
al-Qinawi (d. 1196) provides its *kiswa*, which becomes the *mahmal* for the main
saint-day parade, when it is hung upon a quadrangular frame with a pyramidal
top. A late nineteenth century anthropologist observed that this *kiswa-mahmal*
was embroidered with gold and silver thread.[56] He also noted the presence of
several other saints represented in the parade by their grave coverings. Some
forty years later another report describes a great number of saintly *mahmals*
(locally called *tabuts*, as in Luxor) joining al-Qinawi in his ghostly procession.
At least in this period, the parade traveled out of the city, through the
graveyard, and out into the desert, upon its return stopping at the tomb of
the prophet Lot.[57] This ritual visiting of the prophet Lot's tomb has apparently
been discontinued for some time, but its significance remains as a parallel to
earlier examples we have seen of *kiswa*s making local pilgrimages.[58]

Other *mahmals* have continued to appear in a number of public religious
processions. In some cases, these have been simply recreations of the departure
parades for the Hajj, as had been practiced in Cairo, while in other instances –
we have seen two from Luxor and al-Qina – the *mahmal* has been refocused on
local saintly tombs. One example of the former type comes from the oasis of
Kharga, a remote settlement in the southern desert some 300 km west of
al-Qina (Map 2). A report from 1923 describes a *mahmal* being taken from the
mosque of 'Ain al-Dar each year at mid-Sha'ban, and loaded upon a camel.
This *mahmal* is clearly a model of those that would have circulated in Cairo,

with the words *Allah* and the profession of faith sewn in appliqué upon a crimson background. The anthropologist recording the event correctly identified the parts of the *mahmal*, but was confused by what he called, "representations of an object rather resembling a badly drawn cup and saucer."[59] This was very likely either an imitation of a Sultan's cipher (*tughra*), barely recognizable as such since it would likely refer to no ruler in particular, or a rendering of a Mamluk era blazon.[60] Accompanied by musicians, the camel would carry its sacred load around the outskirts of the town, ending up in the public square. Veneration for this *mahmal* is evident, and the anthropologist records instances in which sick children are held under the *mahmal* covering, in the hope of a miraculous cure. In keeping with the practices in the capital, but of course on a much-reduced scale, the community gathered to celebrate the occasion with a common meal. Later that evening, the *mahmal* was loaded back on its camel and returned to the mosque where it remained until the following year's festivities.

In 1990, an Egyptian journalist filed a story with the headline "The *Mahmal* of Manfalut – Superstition!"[61] He related that this city's *mahmal* procession had been discontinued in 1890, but revived a few decades ago. At the end of Ramadan each year, those intent on the Hajj would gather in the city of Manfalut at Mahmal Road, and together with a *mahmal* would parade down the town's streets before well-wishers. The reporter notes that people would compete for the chance to lead the camel on such an auspicious occasion. He also claims that in recent years the event attracted up to twenty thousand people for the procession lasting up to seven hours. However, authorities vowed to discontinue the procession due to public disturbances. It seems the size of the crowds, along with the tradition of bearing arms on the occasion, led to violent incidents, including the deaths of six people. Although the Coptic community had participated safely in the celebrations in previous years, they had by the mid-1980s often become targets for abuse.[62] The same reporter however presents a confusing account of the history of this procession, thanks to his conflating of the *kiswa* of the Hajj – which before the opening of the Suez Canal would have passed through Manfalut on its way to the port city of al-Qusayr, to cross into the Hijaz – and the *kiswa* of a local saintly tomb. Another account, dating from the 1870s of the *kiswa* of Manfalut, describes in some detail a shrine and the wooden frame which carries the "saintly patron" (presumably his grave covering) as a *mahmal* in his annual festival.[63] We shall return to the story of the Manfalut *mahmal* below, and in particular within the context of debates over the licitness of its public circulation and veneration.

On a smaller scale, just north of Esna, similar processions take place in the town of Asfun. Here as part of another saint day *mawlid* a camel, bearing a *mahmal*, circles several times the tomb of Shaykh al-Amir Ghanim. It also carries the new dressing, called a *kiswa*, for his tomb. Figure 24 gives a sense of how simple the *mahmal* procession can be. Further south, at al-Kubaniyya, the

24 Procession of a *mahmal* in Asfun, Egypt. Credit: Nicolaas H. Biegman, *Egypt: Moulids, Saints and Sufis* (New York: Kegan Paul, 1990). © Taylor & Francis (UK)

festivities in memory of Sidi Abu Zayd al-Bistami culminate in a series of circumambulations of his grave. Evoking the *mahmal* rites at the Citadel in Cairo – and the pilgrims circling around the Ka'ba itself – groups of adults, then camels, then boys with donkeys, walk around the saint's grave seven times. They are preceded in this by a *mahmal* and a drummer riding a camel, who first process through the town, before beginning their circumambulations at the shrine.[64]

Of note regarding these provincial *mahmal* parading rituals is the presence of riders. Famously, the official *mahmals* of the Hajj were empty, the covering itself being the object of veneration. In the instances just noted from Asfun, al-Kubaniyya, and Luxor, we find that riders are included. In some cases, these are shaykhs, religious leaders associated with the shrines, children of prominent families, or the descendants of the venerated saints themselves. Not surprisingly, Egypt shares this innovation with Syria. Isabel Burton recounted the *mahmal* parade in Damascus when, "Out of the Mahmal gazed a man of the people; he looked like a Majnun, or madman, and probably was one. They are much respected, as their souls are supposed to be already with God."[65] It is not clear from the evidence available, when or how riders became a part of these local *mahmal* processions.

As mentioned in the last chapter, the 1920s and 1930s saw conflicts with the Wahhabi rulers of Arabia, which led to first the Egyptian *mahmal* and then the *kiswa* being discontinued.[66] In 1926, the Egyptian caravan had stopped to allow stragglers to catch up, and was blowing horns to attract their attention. Some Wahhabi-inspired pilgrims on the same route took offense and began to throw stones at the *mahmal*. The Egyptians ordered them to withdraw, but when the attack persisted the military escort opened fire, killing 25 and wounding many others. Ibn Sa'ud himself came to intervene and restore order. For the next ten years Egypt did not send its *mahmal*, and stopped sending a *kiswa* for the Ka'ba. Over the following decade tensions subsided, and in 1937 the Egyptian *mahmal* sought to resume its pilgrimage. It was transported to Suez by truck, but once it had arrived at the port of Jidda, the Sa'udi authorities denied it further access on the Hajj route, and it was obliged to stay in the port city, to await the return trip to Cairo.[67] The *mahmal* continued in subsequent years only to send off pilgrims, and welcome them back home. The two parades of the *mahmal* and *kiswa* were consolidated into one. The rituals remained much as before, but now took place in Abbasiyya, from 1937 to 1940, and in a field just north of the Sultan Inal funerary complex in the Northern Qarafa from 1940 to 1952. At the last ceremonies, there were only seven camels; the first carried the *mahmal*, the second a flag, the third carried a shaykh, and the rest carried musicians with their instruments of tambourines and flutes. They processed to the Husayn mosque where the *mahmal* and the *kiswa* were put into crates, with only the latter being sent to the Hijaz. In the return ceremony for 1937, the *mahmal* was carried out to the Al-Ghafir square for assembly. The Amir al-Hajj returned the camel's reigns to a government official. At the 1945 return ceremony, there were British officers in attendance, along with a military band. The mounted lancers were there, but did not perform. The Sufi orders were not included on the field, but waited down the street, and led the lancers and the *mahmal* in procession to al-Husayn. The military on the parade square did not process.[68] The police held the crowds back from touching the *mahmal*, which apparently had not lost its ability to dispense baraka.

The *kiswa* continued to be sewn in Egypt and sent to Mecca until the 1960s, when production was taken over by the Sa'udi state.[69] Members of the Nada family, with a long history of service in the Dar al-Kiswa workshop in Cairo, travelled to Saudi Arabia in the 1970s to assist in the production. When the processions were halted altogether, the *mahmal* was relegated to Cairo's Museum of Islamic Art, effectively neutralizing it as a devotional object. The celebrations of the *mahmal* and the *kiswa* thus came to a halt amid a variety of factors, some political, others religious. The end of these rites – practiced variously for seven centuries – marked a dramatic turn in the practice of Islam in the public sphere. In the remainder of this chapter we shall explore the constellation of events, discourses, objects, and institutions that came together to make this change possible.

Over their long history, *mahmal*-related practices had both their critics and defenders. Jurists, academics, government officials, and even popular opinion, all contributed to an ongoing debate on the licitness of such practices. On one side, proponents defended the devotional practices associated with it as harmless enthusiasm, inspired by a noble impulse to promote the Hajj. They claimed that the practice is essentially a calling of fellow Muslims to good behavior (*al-amr bi al-ma'ruf* or "enjoining the good"). On the other side, critics objected to the wastefulness of such displays, and some ultimately claimed the rituals constituted an objectionable sacralizing of parts of the caravan and parading traditions. Here we shall see that Wahhabi resistance in Arabia to the objects as projections of Egyptian political power, along with the availability in Cairo of a national museum to redefine and reconceive of the *mahmal*, played contested but key roles. More generally, *kiswa*s and *mahmal*s would emerge as sites for the modern reform of Islamic thought and practice.

In the previous chapter, we saw some of the accusations of excess that were leveled against the medieval *mahmal* processions in the Qaramaydan square below the citadel. Such festivities were typically criticized as opportunities for the public to indulge in immoral behavior. Similar large celebrations, including the yearly cutting of the Nile dam, and the great saint days of Egypt, were attacked as occasions for alcohol consumption, gambling, and prostitution.[70] Of course, the details of daily life in medieval Cairo are largely irretrievable to us, and a certain rhetorical license taken by the moralizing chroniclers and jurists of the day can be taken for granted. Nevertheless, we may assume that objections to certain practices, when made in some detail and repeatedly, do reflect activity happening on the ground. The conservative critic Ibn al-Hajj describes fourteenth-century practices generally in line with those we have noted. He argued not against the *mahmal* per se, nor even against the celebrations associated with it, he simply seeks to limit the excesses. He makes the typical call for greater supervision of the lower classes, objecting to the uncontrolled mixing of sexes so common at *mahmal* parades. But his objections went further, to deal with the circulation of images. Citing the authority of the Maliki school of law – in particular a passage condemning the production of images on cloth and clothing – Ibn al-Hajj attacks the shopkeepers' habit of displaying pictures in their establishments related to the festivities.[71] We are not told exactly what was represented, but in light of our survey earlier of formal themes relating to the Hajj and *mahmal*, we can imagine that these were images of the *mahmal* on its camel, pilgrims in procession, and various animal figures such as the lion and the hoopoe. Images of the Ka'ba itself or the Prophet's mosque in Medina would also seem likely, but we are not provided with sufficient detail to know Ibn al-Hajj's limit of acceptable images.

In a review of earlier fatwa opinions on the nature of the *mahmal* and its celebrations, the modern Muslim reformer Rashid Rida (d. 1935) cites a variety of positions for and against. He himself clearly opposes the rite, and most of the medieval predecessors he cites, al-Shatibi (d. 1388) being the most prominent, confirm his position. In line with the established prohibition on wearing silver – and the identification of the Ka'ba covering as a "dress" – some rejected the use of silver thread in decorating the *kiswa*, extending their objection to the covering for the Prophet's grave, claiming the veneration that these coverings attract constitutes a major sin. Rashid Rida concluded that the proper legal position is one that discourages, if not prohibits, the public display and celebration of these objects.[72]

In addition to the consensus of negative legal positions Rida has collected, he follows his mentor Muhammad 'Abduh (d. 1905) in adding politics to his critique.[73] A wider historical survey of opinions and practices shows an equivocal standing for the *mahmal* and its associated rites. For centuries, it had been enthusiastically supported by sultans, pashas, emirs, and officials at every level of the bureaucracy. Their presence at the Qaramaydan and other key sites is well established. Likewise, the religious scholars were well represented, parading alongside the Sufis every year. The popular reception of the *mahmal* was, as we have seen above, positive and widespread. Rida's critique did not challenge these facts, but rather took a different tack, one that addresses the object in its historical specificity. He begins by recasting his critique within the wider context of religious reform. Here the problem is not limited to debates in legal practice, but rather concerns the condition of the religious class itself, its independence from government interference, and in Rida's opinion, its duty to lead society.

Rida begins his account of the *mahmal* by identifying its origin with the long-established practice of sending stipends to the inhabitants of Mecca, via the Hajj caravans. The sending of money to Mecca is unobjectionable, dating back to the earliest period of Islamic history, but Rida argues this honorable gesture has been progressively distorted and debased. He claims the *mahmal* should have remained simply a symbol of this philanthropic gesture, but once it sat for display in the Haram sanctuary at Mecca and in the Prophet's mosque, toured the sacred stations of the Hajj, it itself became a source of blessing in the popular mind. Rida supplies no evidence to support his narrow view of the *mahmal*, nor does he account for the continued sending of financial stipends from Cairo long after the *mahmal* became an object of devotion. Nevertheless, Rida claims that the ruling authorities intervened to redefine it as a proper Islamic rite (*min sha'a'ir al-Islam*), and supported it with official religious celebrations (*ihtifalan diniyyan*). In this degenerate situation, he reasons, the religious class of the ulama have shirked their duty as guardians of proper religion, and have been co-opted by a meddling and morally suspect government. Rida sees this crisis literally embodied by the participants at the official ceremonies below the citadel. He declares scornfully, "Kings, princes, and scholars have taken turns holding the reins of the (*mahmal's*) camel." For Rida the real culprits are the religious scholars, whose failure to resist the political authorities has opened the door to "polytheism and depravity" throughout the Islamic lands.[74] While he admits that many leading shaykhs at al-Azhar have indeed condemned *mahmal* practices as a blameworthy innovation (*bid'a*), just as many have supported it, most importantly by their participation in the rites and rituals.[75] Yet the crucial point for Rida is his claim that in essence the rite is a misunderstanding of the original practice of the stipend donations, a development that saw a licit non-religious practice transformed into a deeply flawed religious rite. From a wider perspective, we can see in Rashid Rida's intervention precisely the insight behind our paradigm of the interaction of objects and concepts – what I have been calling the object that resists determination. In this case, albeit from a hostile perspective, Rida puts the object's identity into play, shrewdly relocating it, and thereby asserting for it a new significance.

As Egypt approached independence some 35 years later, the dispute over the *mahmal* erupted once again. Positions were not substantially different from what they had been on both sides of the divide back in Rida's day, but new circumstances would bring the debate to a head. This time the government would not position itself as the defender of the *mahmal*, but instead would ultimately side with jurists like Rida to abolish it. We shall return to consider these new conditions below, but let us turn first to the public dispute over the licit nature of the *mahmal* and its related festivities. In the newspaper *al-Ahram*, between 1950 and 1953, a number of legal opinions on the matter were reported from Egypt's leading jurist Hasanain Muhammad Makhluf. This shaykh served as the grand Mufti of Egypt, the highest legal authority in the country, from 1946 to 1950, and 1952 to 1954. Over this three-year period, the pages of *al-Ahram* document an intense exchange between the Prime Minister 'Ali Mahir and Muhammad Makhluf – a negotiation that saw the Mufti's position progressively harden, and the Prime Minister's give way, resulting in the official abolition of the *mahmal* rites.

We shall explore these developments, but first let us note the modern Muslim anxiety that arose around the propriety of public religious practices. To his fellow Egyptians Makhluf pleads: "Do you not see that this theatre evokes mockery among the foreigners when shown in their cinemas, daily newspapers, or broadcast news?"[76] Despite his anxiety around the broadcasting of such images, it seems that Makhluf himself was recorded in at least one such newsreel. A British Pathé reel from 1946 shows him attending the Qaramaydan ceremonies. Perhaps more interesting than the Shaykh's apprehension under the colonial gaze, is another kind of anxiety around modernization and Western viewers. In 1946, the journalist Husayn Mazlum Riad criticized the *mahmal* procession not as a cultural accretion masquerading as "proper" religion, but rather for the outdated way this important Islamic rite was carried out. In the weekly *al-Thaqafa* (December 24th) Riad worried that Europeans would mock such a display. He argued the ceremony should be modernized; for example, the *mahmal* could be mounted on an automobile rather than a camel.[77] Perceptions, real or imagined, around the *mahmal* in the context of the colonial mid-twentieth century were important. Not only the Hajj rites, but national Egyptian identity, as well as discourses around what it meant to be Muslim and "modern," were being worked out. We shall return to these themes below in our discussion of the Museum of Islamic Art.

In August of 1950 a story was run describing a gathering between 'Ali Mahir, Shaykh Makhluf, and other jurists, to discuss the licitness of the practices associated with the yearly departure of the *mahmal*. The upshot was a declaration condemning four specific parts of the rite as blameworthy innovations. These were

1. the circling of the *mahmal* around the Qaramaydan,
2. the procession of camels in the square,
3. the Amir al-Hajj kissing the rein of the *mahmal* camel, and
4. the accompanying processions of the representatives of the Sufi orders. Two years later however, 'Ali Mahir requests another fatwa from Shaykh Makhluf, who responds with essentially the same criticism. In a story dated August 19, 1952, he
1. dismisses the circling of the *mahmal*,
2. condemns the procession of musicians,
3. rejects the kissing of the rein,
4. rejects the prayerful supplications of the Sufis, and
5. spurns the claim that these practices are acceptable innovations in religious practice.

The last point is in line with a position taken two years earlier, in November 1950, in which he attacked the most prominent defender of the *mahmal*, 'Abd al-'Aziz Fahmi (d. 1951), leader of the Dustur party. In Makhluf's account, during a speech made to political supporters, Fahmi had defended the *mahmal* rites as resonant with the Islamic religious culture – the *sunna* – established by the Prophet. In Makhluf's opinion this position was an affront to proper practice on three accounts: first, the *mahmal* was only paraded from the medieval period of Shajar al-Durr, and not among the earliest Muslims; second, such considerations and appeals to the *sunna* should be left to those who are expert in religious affairs; and third, that these rites constitute an imitation of the rites that should only take place in Mecca – circumambulation is only proper around the Ka'ba, and the only proper object worthy of being kissed is the Black Stone.

A newspaper article appeared two days later under the headline, *Celebrations of the Departure of the Mahmal to Be Free of Innovations and Accompanied by a Reduced Military Display*. Clearly Makhluf's fatwas were having an impact. The story reported that the Prime Minister had dropped some of the offending rituals, in particular the kissing of the rein and the seven circles of the *mahmal* camel. The charge of *bid'a*, or blameworthy religious innovation around rites and practices not practiced by the Prophet and the earliest Muslims, had apparently hit its mark. However, this accommodation was only partial, since these debates did not touch on the *kiswa*, which was paraded as usual. Further, the *mahmal* continued its procession from the Qaramaydan, along with its Sufi escorts, throughout the city to be displayed finally in the Abbasiyya district.[78]

Nine months later however, the Ministry of Interior – basing its decision on a fatwa from the Grand Mufti – announced it was doing away with the *mahmal* celebrations completely. The display of the *kiswa* would continue, for the purposes of marking the start of Hajj season, but the *mahmal* would no longer appear in public rituals. Three days later, on May 13, 1953, the fate of the *mahmal* was sealed when the Ministry of Interior ordered its removal to the Museum of Islamic Art (then known as Dar al-Athar al-'Arabiyya), and the disbanding of its small stable of camels. The *mahmal* would henceforth be displayed in the museum as simply one among many artifacts (*mukhallafat*) preserved from the various bygone eras of Islamic history.

For many, however, the status of the *mahmal* under religious law remained an open question. In the decades that followed, voices both for and against were raised. One Egyptian historian, Ibrahim Hilmi, defends the *mahmal* observances, reasoning that they constituted a popular (*sha'bi*) journey to God's holy house. He echoes the widely held opinion that the *mahmal* rites should not be rejected as blameworthy innovations, because they were a long-established practice among Muslims.[79] Although Hilmi is not making a formal legal argument here, he is alluding to the wider juridical concepts of "public good" (*maslaha*), and "licit innovation" (*bid'a husna*). The debates among jurists, administrators, and religious scholars have however faded from the headlines. After 1953, there was never any serious effort made to revive *mahmal* and *kiswa* parading rites. However, the question about what exactly to do with a decommissioned *mahmal* will be explored below since it represents a new stage for the object's resistance and negotiation of meaning. Let us note first, however, the parallels in the story of the parading and veneration of local *kiswa*s and *mahmal*s. For example, opinions on the *mahmal* of Manfalut mirror the variety of positions that circled around the rites in Cairo. As mentioned above, the practice of *mahmal* parading and public display continued into the 1990s in Upper Egypt. In the city of Manfalut the occasion of these rites had been lately marred by violence. In a striking parallel to 'Ali Mahir's decision in Cairo to consign the *mahmal* to the Museum of Islamic Art, the patrons in Manfalut also relegated their *mahmal* to a museum. When confronted by local authorities objecting to the *mahmal* celebrations, the representative of the Ayyub Jamal al-Din family responded that although he saw no harm in such a custom – we are reminded of Hilmi's defense above – he would acquiesce and end the parading. His solution for dealing with the local *mahmal* was to confine it to the large family home, "behind glass, in a special room, as in a historical museum."[80] We shall return to the effectiveness of such a strategy detail below, with special attention as to how displaying a *mahmal* in such circumstances works to redefine it.

The opinions in Manfalut on the status of the *mahmal* rites varied across much the same spectrum they did 40 years earlier in the capital relating to the official Hajj *mahmal*. In an informal street survey, a newspaper reporter asked if people considered the *mahmal* a properly religious occasion (*min al-din*). One person responded that in his opinion this celebration was a long-established practice, an uplifting event that people have always enjoyed. Average folk dress up for it, and enthusiastically revel in the occasion. As this informant notes, unfortunately, in recent years, various disturbances and even fighting have broken out, threatening public security to the extent that the event should be discontinued. Another individual, a schoolteacher, concurs. He says that the *mahmal* parade was an occasion for fun, like any other saint day *mawlid* celebration, but that now it has become unmanageable and dangerous. A third voice from the street, this time a university student, is more categorical and dismissive. Also identifying the *mahmal* with *mawlid*s, he rejects both, declaring that, "No thinking person could celebrate such superstitions, which have no connection to religion... [True] Muslim youth distance themselves from such things, and call for their reproof, as well as the protection of the people's religion from such evil things. How nice it would be if *mawlid*s were abolished, so that people would no longer waste their time at them, instead concentrating on their trades and their productivity."[81] We noted above that many of these criticisms were given voice in the 1920s and 1950s – much in line with the medieval objections we heard from Ibn al-Hajj to the squandering of resources, both material and moral, at such celebrations.

The religious authorities of the area also opposed the Manfalut *mahmal* generally, although some recognition of its status as a harmless tradition persisted. Shaykh Ramadan Haykal of Asyut represents the more permissive approach. In his opinion, such well-established and well-loved observances, "similar to *maw-lids*," should be preserved, but controlled much more carefully for the violence and crime associated with them. Dr. 'Abd al-Sabur is of the opinion that the bad behavior of the revelers and the armed riffraff disqualify the entire event as a licit practice. The Imam of the Sayyida Zarifa mosque in Manfalut is of the same mind. He calls it a blameworthy innovation in Islamic practice, one that is a categorical affront to Islamic values. It is remarkable how constant the positions have remained for over sixty years on both sides of the debate.

Not insignificant here is the gesture toward the museum as a solution to controlling the object, and managing the conflict. It is obvious to note that the strategy of retiring *mahmals* to museums was possible only in the colonial era. The European presence in Egypt was in some ways epitomized by the museum. Orientalist notions of progress, science, and even Egyptian history itself were given tangible expression in the design and organization of these institutions. In the nineteenth and early twentieth centuries, several European powers, most prominently among them France, contributed personnel and expertise to the training of Egyptian specialists whose task it was to bring their country into the "modern era" through urban planning, architectural restoration, and various institutional reforms. Inspired by the *Encyclopédistes*, the French had begun the nineteenth century with their vast scientific survey, the *Déscription de l'Egypte*, which sought to record every aspect of the country. Beyond the explorers and archeologists who were attempting to recover a lost Pharaonic civilization, various colonial administrations were setting the stage for a modern Egypt, and museums were to play their part.[82]

Initially, a museum of Egyptian antiquities was established in 1835, under the direction of Rifa'a al-Tahtawi (d. 1873). Although its creation was part of the rising sensibility around protecting Egypt's national patrimony, Pasha Muhammad 'Ali failed to fully support the *Antiqakhana* as it was known, and it quickly fell into obscurity.[83] In 1858, a second museum was established under the direction of the French Egyptologist Auguste Mariette (d. 1881), which eventually became the Museum of Egyptian Antiquities, located in Tahrir Square. This institution was contested among European powers vying for influence and control. The United States also had its strategy to appropriate the narrative of Egyptian nationalism through the control of antiquities.[84] Another institution, the *Madrasat al-funun al-jamila* (l'École des beaux-arts), was established in Cairo in 1908, with the express intention of replicating European sensibilities around art.[85] The material culture and history of Islamic Egypt was less of a concern for most Europeans, and thus the Museum of Arab Art (Dar al-Athar al-'Arabiyya) emerged somewhat late in the game and with less support than other museums. It was established by Max Herz in 1884, spending its first twenty years in the courtyard of the crumbling al-Hakim mosque.[86] The present site of the museum is a neo-Mamluk style building on

Port Sa'id street, designed by Alfonso Manescalo, a member of the *Comité de conservation des monuments de l'art Arab*.[87] The top floor of the building originally housed the Khedival Library, which later became part of the Egyptian National Library, and moved much of its growing collection to new facilities in Bulaq. Although the Museum of Arab Art was funded by the Khedive Abbas, and its opening in 1903 was attended by the Grand Mufti of Egypt, Muhammad 'Abduh, and Sufi elite in the persons of the Shaykhs of the Bakri and Sadat orders, its direction remained largely in the hands of Europeans for the next 50 years.[88] Criticism of this control of cultural institutions, and resistance to the colonial influence on Egyptian art and architecture, were deeply held among many, but voiced most famously by leading figures such as Ahmad Zaki and 'Ali Basha Mubarak.[89] Their cultural resistance would be overtaken by overt political resistance and the nationalization of the Suez Canal in 1951, the Free Officers coup in 1952, and the founding of an independent Egyptian state the following year. The Museum of Arab Art was also essentially nationalized, in that its direction in 1952 was assumed by Zaki Muhammad Hasan, who was replaced shortly thereafter by Muhammad Mustafa.[90] Now known as the Museum of Islamic Art, this institution acquired at least one *mahmal*, that of king Faruq (r. 1936–1952).

A second museum representing Islamic culture was founded at roughly the same time as the Museum of Arab Art. This was the ethnography museum of the Egyptian Geographical Society.[91] Its collection is peculiar in that it is closely identified with the research agenda of the Geographical Society, and fits awkwardly into the common nationalist narrative public museums typically tell. The Society was established in 1875 primarily to facilitate the exploration of lesser-known (to Europeans, at least) regions of Africa. Initial support was enthusiastic, but in the twentieth century, and more so after Egyptian independence, the institution lost momentum. Few resources have been devoted to its museum, and visitors are rare.[92] In December 2011, the building was damaged when the library adjacent to it, belonging to the Institut d'Égypte, was burned in the course of rioting. The ethnography museum had become the unlikely home of the *mahmal* of Fu'ad I, who ruled from 1922 to 1936. Significant for our discussion is the context of that *mahmal*'s display. In the museum it is located in the Cairo Hall, grouped together with nineteenth century artifacts of daily life such as cooking utensils, musical instruments, jewelry, writing tools, and amulets. The context for the *mahmal*'s display is revealing. The object sits uncomfortably in these surroundings. It represents a ritual tradition dating back to the thirteenth century, but here is surrounded by nineteenth-century artifacts. In its original performative context it was revered for the baraka it had accumulated from many trips to the Ka'ba and the grave of the Prophet, but here it is surrounded by objects chosen specifically because they represented common and everyday life. The *mahmal* was designed to make an extraordinary visual impact, to be a resplendent beacon at the head of the Hajj caravan, not an object seen casually in the typical Cairene home. Like every other *mahmal*, this object was designed and fabricated to be unique. It's presence among objects chosen because they are typical representatives of Egyptian material culture is discordant.

Established in 2010, the Egyptian Textile Museum in Cairo houses three bands of twentieth century Ka'ba *kiswa*. The circumstances of their acquisition illustrate some of the issues we identified around the relegating of *mahmal*s to museums. The week of June 21 issue of the 2012 *Al-Ahram Online* reported that in March two of the five *kiswa* panels displayed in the royal mausoleum of Khedive Tawfiq, located in Qubbat Afandina (1894) Qaytbay, had been stolen. Their custom display cases had been broken into by thieves overnight. The story points out that up to that point there had been no official control of these *kiswa*s beyond their legal status as endowed goods (*waqf*), which technically put them under the protection of the Ministry of Endowments. The robbery precipitated a crisis by illuminating the ambiguous status of these objects. In response to the theft, the Ministry of Antiquities took charge of the three remaining *kiswa*s and placed them in the Textile Museum. This latest chapter in the story of Egyptian museums encapsulates the drama and tensions that swirled around the *mahmal*. More precisely, it is the process of denaturing a religious object that is at stake. The *kiswa* panels had sat for decades, displayed reverentially at the tomb of the Khedive, with an unambiguous status as a devotional baraka-ladened object. As the *kiswa*s are moved from one site to another (from a mausoleum to a museum), their status is changed from active religious objects in a pious endowment, to passive "antiquities," and their location within the Egyptian bureaucracy shifts from one ministry to another.

We noted above the shift in religious and political culture after Egyptian independence, which tipped the balance against *mahmal* practices. Not only did the colonial origins of the museum manifest themselves in this process, but the very procedure for abolishing the *mahmal* was predicated on a postcolonial Egyptian appropriation of the museum. This institution, orphaned from its original purposes of serving the European imperial project, was redirected for this task specifically because it was a contested and conflicted space. The museum as a home for a *mahmal* or the *kiswa* belts, then is well suited as a site for denaturing, for depriving the object of its original active capacity in religious life. The museum is then a space that is foreign, static, and isolated. As a contested space, it served the conservative reformers well. In their view, it constituted a non-Islamic space easily controlled and available as a safe holding pen for problematic objects like the *mahmal*. Islamic reformers like Rashid Rida, and movements that developed in his wake, such as the Muslim Brotherhood, and Salafism more widely, sought to Islamicize society, and public space in particular.[93] The museum thus served as a convenient island of secularism to which those projects could banish inconvenient objects such as the *mahmal*.

In Ottoman Turkey, scholars have argued that the museum was embraced, modified, and ultimately enlisted in the effort to resist European imperialism.[94] The circumstances for our religious objects in Cairo are rather different. Here religious reformers reimagined the museum as a place to resist parts of Islamic tradition they opposed. A quick example from the career of Rashid Rida shows this logic at play. In 1916, British and French military missions into the Hijaz were at a high point. A British warship had even transported the *kiswa* and *mahmal* for a time. Rida was unnerved by the retreat of the Muslim Ottomans from Arabia. A manifesto he had penned before the war had become timely and was reprinted, to be distributed among the Hajj pilgrims of that year. In it Rida raised the specter of European presence in Arabia, and declared that France's intention was to destroy the sacred sites of Islam, and to abscond with the Black Stone and the relics of the Prophet, in order to display them at the Louvre.[95] The theft of these precious objects would be bad enough, but displaying them in a museum would also negate their sanctity and redefine them as simple ethnographic items.

This sense of not only violation by stealing them, but also by re-signifying them, is at play in Rida's warning of the French conspiracy toward the Black Stone and Muhammad's bones. Carol Duncan has described the museum as a secular temple, which transmutes cult objects into artifacts.[96] For example, once removed from circulation as political and religious objects, Aztec artifacts are open to reclassification as artworks when installed in a Spanish museum. In a similar process, Greek sculpture that originally stood in a temple, embodying the divine presence, is transformed into a symbol of conquest when it reached Imperial Rome. But Duncan reminds us that the Western museum does not simply display safe, secularized, nationalistic objects; rather these objects maintain much of their character, becoming the focus of serious rituals and intense devotional gaze. The museum, not the church, she says, has become the site for iconoclasm – a sure sign that these objects have not lost their powers.[97] But this is certainly not the case in Cairo, where the "resacralizing" of objects via museum display has not happened. The nightmare Rida envisaged at the Louvre assumes the objects to be utterly defeated, being held as victory trophies, and displays of their own helplessness, in the hands of Egypt's colonial oppressors. Surely some of this was envisaged as the fate of the *mahmal* relegated to the Museum of Islamic Art – but in this case, the museum stood isolated within a wider re-Islamicized Egypt, as a vanquished memorial to those Islamic practices that had been exposed as illicit, and made obsolete by the ascendant Islamic revival.

Viewers of such museum artifacts are expected to have lost their connection to them, and to be distanced from them both physically and conceptually. Of Christian artifacts put on museum display, Philip Fisher has claimed that, "To abolish (the original) context means more than taking the cathedral out of the crucifix. Context includes the signals that permit or deny access. The museum signs that warn us not to touch the sculpture are one example of a denial of access."[98] Access is now controlled according to a logic and regime utterly foreign to those in effect around the Khedive's tomb for example. In the case of the *mahmal*, its new regime of access is a dramatic reversal. Instead of appearing in the streets of Cairo at the start of the pilgrimage season, and triumphantly parading upon its return, the *mahmal* in museum display is both overexposed and inaccessible. When any curious member of the public can at will view the *mahmal*, this condition robs the object of its performative impact, and the charged experience that represented its baraka. Simultaneously, the viewer is distanced from the artifact by the culture of the museum, which historicizes its artworks. The museum-going Cairene is thus presented with an object that the museum is proposing as a highlight in the (future) historical record. In other words, as Fisher puts it, "To see the present as history is to estrange our relation to it in the act of imagining it as the future's past."[99] The original devotional and performative relation between the viewer and the parading *mahmal* has been replaced by one in which the viewer is pushed to imagine its relationship to a distant future. Within the parameters laid out by the museum, the *mahmal* will not only become an obsolete relic of the twentieth century, but just as importantly it must be considered as such by its viewers today.

The *mahmal* sits awkwardly in the museum, historicized to be today the past of tomorrow. Yet in its immediate context it fails as a cultural display; and this failure is surely intentional in the minds of the *mahmal*'s detractors. On the experience of museum collections, one scholar has pointed out that an object does not communicate if it is not understood to be part of a collection. The "collection" rescues all the individual examples within it from the danger that they might be arbitrary or unrelated.[100] A successful museum object is also one that is taken as representative of a style, a stage in the history of the production of such objects, or a mirror to a moment of cultural expression.[101] In the museum, the *mahmal* fails on all of these counts. It stands disconnected and isolated from any others of its kind – trapped in the museum, it is neither fine art nor good ethnography.

THREE

PROCESSIONS, BANNERS, AND THE RELIGIOUS SPECTACLE

The Caliph al-Ma'mun looked upon a document written in a beautiful hand, and declared, "How wonderful is the pen! It weaves the fine cloth of royal power, embroiders the hem of dynasty, and raises aloft the banners of the caliphate."[1]

Long before the rise of modern advertising billboards proclaiming the virtues of dish detergent, Coca-Cola, or the titles of the latest blockbuster movies, texts were presented to the public in many less flamboyant ways. Though less eye-catching, medieval public inscriptions were ubiquitous and fairly prominent across the cityscape, addressing myriad topics and serving many different purposes. For example, the mosque of al-Juyushi, built in 1085 on Muqattam mountain, overlooking Cairo, bears long inscriptions of Qur'an text. While the precise function of this isolated building remains a mystery to us, the Qur'anic passages were clearly chosen to underline the divine right to rule of Juyushi's employers, the Fatimid dynasty, and to vilify the recently defeated local rebels who had resisted their Isma'ili Shia overlords. Inscriptions lauding the Fatimids include: "Truly, We have granted you a clear victory" (Q. 48:1) and "It is He who has made you regents upon the earth; and whoever disbelieves, it will be upon his own head" (Q. 35:39). The rebels are disparaged with passages such as, "Those who spread slander are only a small group among you..." (Q. 24:11) and "O men, your rebellion will only turn against you..." (Q. 10:23). A quick survey of the cityscape shows that the most significant public writings were the foundation texts adorning many of the monumental structures of premodern and medieval Islam.

Beyond scriptural passages evoking a blessed future for the builders and the users of such edifices, these texts typically record in stone the date and the purpose of the construction. From the eleventh century, public baths, drinking fountains, mosques, shrines, schools, and even hospitals typically bore stylized inscribed panels. These textual markers were part of the vast system of patronage and public works that functioned thanks to the juridical institution of the *waqf* or pious endowment, which sheltered private assets invested in property made available for public welfare. The legal structures behind this Islamic institution were significant, extending beyond law into economics, politics and statecraft. While interrogating the *waqf* endowments for the light they can shed on the history of building practices, scholars of Islamic art and architecture have also debated the significance of the inscriptions as compositions in their own right.

Political and social history can thus be illuminated through texts that stand as little monuments, strategically placed within the built urban environment. One issue that arises – and is particularly relevant to our focus on objects – is the relationship between the connotative and the denotive dimensions of these publicly displayed documents. In other words, how is their literal reading connected, if at all, to what they communicate visually? And by visual communication I mean the expressive force or the "tending toward the visual" that is at play in stylized writing.[2] Scholars have taken a variety of positions around the connotative force, of public texts. Following Irene Bierman's earlier speculations on the symbolism at play in Fatimid public uses of Arabic script, Yasser Tabbaa has tried to link the changes in calligraphic style to shifts in imperial policy and gestures toward religious legitimation.[3] However, Sheila Blair has pushed back against this type of analysis, emphasizing instead aesthetic considerations internal to the inscription styles, which she argues evolved to better balance the angularity of the carved letters and to fill the empty spaces that Arabic script opens up.[4]

This exploration of the visuality of public texts is a promising exercise that awaits more careful consideration of historical processes,[5] as well as some account of the mechanics at work in the interplay of connotative and denotive dimensions of public texts.[6] Oleg Grabar began the interrogation of this interrelation by proposing a threefold typology of reception. At the first level, a viewer may be impressed by the skill on display in the production. Here Grabar was thinking of the fine and steady hand on display in official writing, along with the carefully planned forms by which some inscriptions seem to be pointing to an opening, or hanging as if on a background made of fabric. Secondly, in some cases the writing essentially becomes subordinate to the ornamental forms within or among which it sits; typically, short texts such as the profession of faith or the names of God are almost an afterthought in relation to the visual impact the media around them are making. And finally,

Grabar noted the effective illegibility of an inscription, which the viewer responds to either by reflecting on the visual impact that such writing makes, or else returns to in order to reread it in an attempt to get at the denotive meaning. The inscription – here Grabar is thinking of complex calligraphy – is encountered at a first glance, making its visual impact and then requiring a long and enquiring interrogation from the viewer before it starts to give up its literal meaning.[7] In this chapter I will expand on Grabar's insight on the near illegibility of inscriptions. Moving beyond the connotative and denotive binary, and following the dynamics of aesthetic negotiation described earlier in this book, I will turn to religious banners and argue that their resistance to reading is key to their full meaning and significance.

Beyond epigraphic foundation documents, the decorative use of Qur'anic text is a predominant feature in the visual landscape, commonly found in mosques, shrines, madrasa colleges, and Sufi convents. However, Robert Hillenbrand has noted that the choice of Qur'anic citations in mosques, typically do not follow any pattern, and are often "surprisingly undirected."[8]

The texts of interest in this chapter, however, are ambulatory: banners traveling across the cityscape as mobile objects on display. In our survey of parading practices, we shall see that banners become more than texts, and as Grabar, Tabbaa, and others have noted earlier regarding inscriptions, they are both word and artwork. We might say they are simultaneously "read" as texts by onlookers and "viewed" as processing artifacts of a parade. Beyond this, and here perhaps is a paradox, these mobile text objects also stop functioning fully as either texts or artworks. In a real sense, they become artworks representing nothing, and texts that are not to be read. In order to make sense of this peculiar form of religious textuality, I propose we turn first to the notion of performativity that lies behind parading, and from there consider the aesthetic function of banners as they negotiate the formation of themselves and their processions.

Before encountering the banners, we must first understand what the public dramas of parading are doing, and more precisely what is at stake and what they are putting into play. The list of occasions that could be marked by parading was indeed long. Not surprisingly, they marked official events such as the annual cutting of the Nile dam, royal accessions and investitures, the arrival of important foreign dignitaries, departures on military campaigns which would hopefully be followed before too long with a victory march upon return. For families that could afford them, marriages, deaths, and circumcisions, were also marked by parades. Religious and civic associations also paraded; important holidays of the Islamic calendar often supplied the occasion, as did the *mawlid* saint day celebrations.

At first consideration, we might take a procession to be the assertion of power, a public advertisement of a ruler's authority, or a claim to fame by a public figure. In this uncomplicated reading, processions are simply authority inscribed onto the cityscape. This perspective will call for some reconsideration when we move to consider the function of banners, but first an overview of the history of parading practices is in order.

I begin by echoing earlier scholarly observations that these official ceremonials were surprisingly inconsistent.[9] That is to say, the contents of a parade, its itinerary within the city, and the occasions it was marking, varied greatly. Under the Fatimid regime, public displays were focused on the Caliph himself, with an emphasis on the thoroughfare of Bayn al-Qasrayn.[10] The early part of Mamluk rule saw a concerted focus on the annual Eids of al-Adha and al-Fitr. During the later years, the Burji Mamluks revised some of the Eid processing, and moved it from the hippodrome near Qaramaydan up to the Citadel.[11] Doctrinal assumptions can be seen at play behind the Fatimids' ritual; as Shia, the Imam-Caliph figure wielded not only temporal but also cosmological import. We would be remiss, however, in thinking that easy explanations are discernable behind all public ceremonials. Some interpretations seem to suggest themselves, but the specific content of a parade along with its route, seem to have been newly negotiated in each instance.[12] Although there was no set itinerary, processions in both Cairo and Damascus typically took place in the most densely populated parts of the city. Not surprisingly, the Citadel was the usual starting point. In Cairo, parades then headed north into the desert cemetery with its many monumental religious sites, turning west to pass through the Gate of Victory (Bab al-Nasr) or the Gate of Conquests (Bab al-Futuh), and onto the main artery of Bayn al-Qasrayn (Map 3). Processions continued out through the Zuwayla Gate, and either stayed left to follow Darb al-Ahmar, or continued onward to the Qaramaydan and up to the Citadel.[13] The chronicler al-Maqrizi describes several versions of this parade route over the thirteenth century.[14]

Through their itineraries and the makeup of parades, patrons of course aimed at elevating their profiles and their reputations. Identifying themselves with certain locations of public space was an important strategy. The landscapes crossed were filled with sites of symbolic religious, cultural, and social significance, which could all be incorporated into a parade's itinerary. City squares, shrines, mosques, tombs, etc. each offered their own reasons why one might process through them, or stop in front of them, or avoid them completely. Nasser Rabbat has recently shown how monumental buildings of the Mamluk period were often designed with parading and viewing practices in mind.[15] Politics is clearly at play here: through parade decisions one made symbolic claims to allies and ancestors – newly elevated princes might stop at tombs of sultans, or a madrasa associated with their patron. Such self-identification was particularly important in the Mamluk polity, which drew so heavily for its personnel on slaves, who had to work their way up

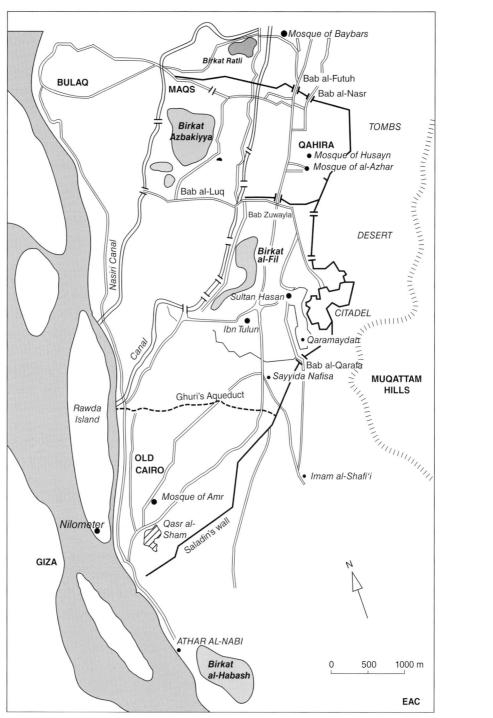

MAP 3 Cairo

the military and political hierarchies. A pious image could also be important, and might be fostered by processing in the funeral of a deceased religious leader, or paying homage to a Sufi shrine by halting at its door. In addition to choices about landscape, a parade also elevated its patron by publicly, framing him or her with symbolically charged adornments; objects and ornaments carefully chosen to enrich and empower the image of the patron.[16]

In 1257, nothing less than an "awe-inspiring procession" was organized to mark the accession of al-Mansur ʿAli ibn Aybak to the sultanate. He descended from the Citadel in full regalia and made his way to Qubbat al-Nasr, a Fatimid hospice established to house Persian Sufis, at the far northeastern edge of the city. His route apparently took him through the northern Qarafa cemetery, returning through Bab al-Nasr, to finally reach the Citadel where he took his royal seat. He was accompanied by his amirs, who had dismounted during his return, and marched before him on foot in a show of loyalty and deference. Surrounded by his amirs, and passing along a well-chosen route, Aybak was also framed by objects that signaled his status: collectively these were the markers or insignia of the sultanate (*sha'a'ir al-sultana*).[17] Ibn Taghribirdi doesn't tell us precisely which objects accompanied the sultan, but other chroniclers of the Mamluk period have identified a large stock of items the patron could have chosen from: a decorated saddle, a yellow silk parasol, an inscribed mantle for the horse, drums, flags, and banners bearing inscriptions of the sultan's name and titles, etc.[18]

Many such processions were made by subsequent rulers. When Al-Malik al-Ashraf Inal ascended to the sultanate in 1453 he rode down from the Citadel into the heart of the city, wearing the black robe the caliph had bestowed upon him, carrying the emblems and insignia of royalty (*shi'ar al-mulk*).[19] Although the Abbasid caliphs had long ago lost any real power – as evidenced by their virtual imprisonment by the Mamluk regime – they continued to play a symbolic role in legitimating the authority of each new Mamluk sultan.[20] The person of the caliph himself could also be put on processional display; on at least four occasions in the fifteenth century a caliph is recorded riding alongside the sultan.[21] In military parades also, the sultan surrounded himself with key individuals. Setting out for Syria, in 1516, on an ill-fated campaign against the armies of the Ottoman Sultan Selim, Qansuh al-Ghawri led a spectacular procession out of Cairo. The chronicler Ibn ʿIyas noted that al-Ghawri made the unusual choice of parading through the city in a reverse itinerary, taking him from Bab Zuwayla northward to Bab al-Nasr. The precedent for military campaigning had been to leave the city via the northern cemetery and only as a victory parade to pass through the heart of the city. Presumably his choice can be explained by the great investment this campaign represented. No expense was spared and every asset, material or symbolic, was mobilized. For dramatic effect three elephants carrying banners led the way, followed by 50 camels carrying the entire Mamluk treasury.[22] Al-Ghawri, wearing a black and white tunic embroidered with gold, was preceded by the caliph, officers on caparisoned horses, and lower officers on foot. The sultan's horse had a golden saddle and saddle cloth, with a headdress to match. The heads of the most prominent Sufi orders of the day, the Rifa'iyya, the Qadiriyya, and the Ahmadiyya, were also in the procession, as was the son of the shaykh of the Sayyida Nafisa shrine. Judges, administrators, Qur'an reciters, doctors, masons, carpenters, blacksmiths, musicians, and singers were also part of the parade. Not be left out, the head of the beggars' union, the Harafish, participated; as a "sultan" in his own right he brought his own drums and a banner.[23] Al-Ghawri ultimately took to the battle field near Aleppo, accompanied by the caliph, the shaykhs of the Sufi orders – all with their banners of various colors – and a contingent of civilian nobles. The latter carried with them copies of the Qur'an wrapped in yellow silk, the official color of the Mamluk regime. These displays of military and religious assets may have raised morale, but by the end of the day the Egyptians were defeated and their sultan killed.[24]

We noted earlier that in the mid-thirteenth century, Aybak had processed out of the city to the Sufi hospice of Qubbat al-Nasr, yet many other high-points on the religious landscape were available to a regal parader. Like many other rulers, Barquq fostered a personal relationship with prominent Sufi figures. Early in his reign, in 1383 the sultan visited the ailing shaykh Akmal al-Din, and later walked in his funerary cortege. The Sufi master had been appointed the first director of the Shaykhu Sufi Hospice, and it was to this complex not far from the Citadel that the sultan accompanied his body for burial.[25] It is no surprise that a sultan's parading network could also include sacred spaces that evoked communal and even cosmological concerns. In one parading foray, Khushqadam made his way from the Citadel to the Nilometer, perhaps simply for inspections but more likely to participate in the devotional rituals that were maintained there. Along the way, however, he also stopped to visit the relics of the Prophet housed in the Ribat al-Athar mosque (Map 3). On the return leg of trip, Khushqadam paid a pious visit to a *zawiya* overlooking the Nile established by his secretary Janibak.[26]

The visual impact of these large parades was significant, and the messages they sent were various, and at times mixed. A triumphal return to the city could also include a display of despair and defeat. On several occasions prisoners of war were marched in large numbers, with their humiliation carefully choreographed. The first Mamluk parade in 1250, included the inverted flags and broken war drums of the recently deposed Ayyubid ruler. After a victorious campaign against the Mongols, Ibn Qalawun paraded 1,600 prisoners in chains, each with the severed head of one of their companions tied around his neck, with another thousand heads displayed on pikes. From 1472 to 1498, with their flags turned downward, Ottoman prisoners were on several occasions paraded in shackles, to their execution outside the gates of the city. On one occasion an enemy was skinned, stuffed with straw, and paraded – although this was apparently too much for the sultan's sensibilities, and did not become common practice.[27] Ashraf Khalil captured Acre, and making his triumphal entry into Damascus, paraded Frankish prisoners, carrying a reversed Crusader banner, and a spear to which were tied the scalps of slain soldiers.[28]

The brutality on display was a visceral assertion of the sultan's power, yet rather different communications were possible. In 1419 the population of Cairo was summoned to collective supererogatory prayer in the northern cemetery. The crisis at hand was yet another devastating wave of the plague.[29] The sultan arrived in procession with the leading religious officials, yet the presentation was intentionally subdued and even contrite. By dressing in a simple Sufi cloak, Sultan al-Mu'ayyad was playing on the image of a penitent ascetic focused on his devotions to God. The reversal is clear, the sultan's wealth and worldly power are set aside by his spiritual poverty and piety. He bore no insignia of royalty, and his horse was unadorned. He was met by crowds carrying banners and copies of the Qur'an, petitioning the divine for mercy. Prayers for intercession were made, and al-Mu'ayyad left in procession to the Sufi hospice of al-Faraj, to pray there at the tomb of Sultan Barquq.[30] A similarly doleful spectacle played itself out the following year at another gathering, but this time for the collective petitioning prayer for rain.[31] Processions were complex phenomena that relied on both their content, human and inanimate, as well as their context, to have the desired effect. The aesthetic dimension was at times commented upon explicitly. One of the Hajj parades of 1799 we noted earlier in our discussion of the *mahmal* was touted as utterly extraordinary by the chronicler al-Jabarti. The procession of the *kiswa* around the Qaramaydan is described in detail, starting with the governor and the inspector of markets, accompanied by banners, drums, pipes, and cymbals. Bartholomew, lieutenant of the Janissaries, passed by wearing a huge fur, preceded by 200 Muslim soldiers supported by a great number of Greek Christians in arms, with their officers all wearing capes. A detachment of police was followed by the guard of the *kiswa* and a Turkish music band. Al-Jabarti applauds the pageant, remarking on the variety of forms used, the diverse assemblage of people, and multitude of onlookers and wondrous creatures; he concludes that it was a "union of contrasting things, and a diversion from the ordinary."[32]

While the components of a procession could be organized in various ways, and the Hajj parade just mentioned was a successful tableau in motion, the examples above of the sultan as Sufi show that dramatic re-workings of those components were possible. But beyond this, the landscape itself could be put into play, intentionally transformed for semiotic purposes. A series of victory parades, beginning in the late thirteenth century, illustrates this. As part of their reception in Cairo, the processions of Qalawun, and later each of his two sons who succeeded him, passed by decorated wooden castles that lined the most densely urbanized stretch of the route, running between the northern gate of Bab al-Nasr and Bab Zuwayla to the south. These parades were indeed lavish affairs, with silk fabrics hung on the walls and rugs lining the streets.[33] This landscape of decorated castles seems to evoke the various forts and castles that the sultans would have encountered on their campaigns in Syria and elsewhere. Along with the humiliated prisoners who made up part of these victory parades, the fortified landscape in miniature would function as a trophy, symbolizing the success of the sultan's campaigns and the extension of Mamluk rule in the face of its enemies. These castles, however, could also be reversed in their connotations. Some 80 years later, they would reappear, ostensibly to celebrate Sultan Barquq's restoration to the throne. They were decorated, and each even had a commander in charge along with a communication system linking the castles. But in one popular district of the city, al-Husayniyya just outside the northern gates, the castle became a focal point from which to assert the local rule of the quarter. The neighborhood disturbances that followed led to the Sultan's order for the "castles" to be removed. This transformation of the landscape, symbolically and in miniature, seems to have earned the mistrust of the authorities, disappearing from the historical record after 1388.[34]

Although sultans certainly produced the largest and most lavish parades, such displays could be mounted by a bewildering variety of actors. Established Sufi leaders in particular, were regular paraders. One such actor was Shaykh al-Hanafi (d. 1443) whose processions to his home on Ruda island included such large retinues of soldiers, merchants, and nobles that they elicited criticism that such displays were more appropriate to a sultan than a saint. Al-Hanafi's processions included disciples chanting *dhikr* invocations, and merchants responding with prayers and blessings.[35] Parades could be *ad hoc*, serving to mark fortuitous events, such as the departure of the occupying French forces.[36] In 1690, Sufi orders and religious dignitaries in Jerusalem organized a parade, with banners and chanting, to celebrate the arrival of the scholar and mystic al-Nabulusi, who had traveled on pilgrimage from Damascus.[37] Parades could also be cyclical, as in the yearly processions to mark the beginning of the month of Ramadan, which in Cairo included the chief judge, the inspector of markets, and representatives of various guilds.[38] Small-scale parades persisted into the modern era. In the year 1807, we find that a saintly pretender from the Delta arrived in Cairo and managed to enlist a number of locals in a victorious entrance ritual. We do not know if this upstart ascetic managed to find a permanent following in the capital.[39]

Another occasion for such ritual parading was the appointment of judges. Usually each of the four schools of Islamic law had a state-appointed head, but the most prestigious legal rank was that of the chief judge or *qadi al-qudat,* literally "judge of judges." The jurist Abu Zakariyya al-Ansari (d. 1520) was appointed to this position. Chroniclers tell us that a large procession was organized to celebrate the occasion. Mamluk notables, judges, scholars, and students gathered at the Citadel and marched to the Salihiyya madrasa – the first and largest college to train students in all four legal rites – and from there to al-Ansari's home.[40] The celebration of such appointments continued to be marked publicly with processions. The traveler Evlia Celebi recounts the typical seventeenth-century celebrations of the appointment of the new chief judge. Typically, he enters Cairo and joins a welcoming procession that includes government officials, military officers, religious leaders, a contingent of the *ashraf* descendants of Muhammad's family, and the imams and preachers of the most prominent mosques. A banquet is held for the new judge, and then the participants reassemble for a mounted parade, which "made for an impressive scene," as Celebi puts it. These included judges, hadith scholars, teachers, the professors of al-Azhar university, and the representative of the descendants of the Prophet (*naqib al-ashraf*). Celebi wryly comments that many in the procession demonstrated less than perfect horsemanship, and that their real talents lay in scholarship, rather than parading.[41]

Beyond his skills as a judge, Abu Zakariyya al-Ansari was also a Sufi shaykh. One of the ways he demonstrated his piety and mystical affiliation was by only eating bread that had come from the famous Sufi hospice of Sa'id al-Su'ada.[42] Founded by Saladin in 1173, this was the first *khanqah* hospice established in Egypt, which for more than three centuries housed a community of Sufis, some three hundred strong in the fifteenth century, supporting them with clothing and food. The Sufis, however, did not remain secluded in their cloister, inaccessible to the wider population; in fact, they paraded regularly. We are told that each Friday people would gather at the *khanqah* from throughout the city to witness the Sufis' procession to the mosque of al-Hakim for prayers. This viewing practice was understood to generate baraka and blessings for all who participated (*yushahidu sufiyyat khanqah sa'id al-su'ada... kai tahsul la-hum al-baraka wa'l-khayr bi-mushahadatihim*). The procession was led by the shaykh of the *khanqah* followed by his attendants, the tallest of whom carried decorated boxes containing booklets of the Qur'an divided into sections for recitation. In a dignified silence the Sufis made their way to al-Hakim, entering the door nearest the minbar. The shaykh began the session with greetings to those in attendance. They sat, the Qur'an booklets were distributed, and together they recited until the adhan called them to prayer. The Friday sermon follows the salat prayers, and is in turn followed by supererogatory devotional prayers (*du'a*). One of the Sufis then stands to recite a few passages from the Qur'an, and the group invokes blessings upon both the Sultan Saladin and the Muslim community as a whole. The shaykh then leads his Sufi followers out of the mosque, and back to their *khanqah*. This was considered "one of the most beautiful customs" in all of Cairo. The historian al-Maqrizi reports that in his own day the common folk used to do a bit of their own parading, walking through the hall of the *khanqah* with their shoes on in order to collect baraka through direct contact with the site of the Sufi processions.[43]

Sufi parading could take many forms. Since investitures of judges and sultans received so much attention, it should be no surprise that the appointment of a new shaykh to the head of a Sufi order could occasion regal processing. In contrast to the practices that developed in the large state-run Sa'id al-Su'ada, autonomous Sufi groups could develop their own rituals. One prominent Sufi order of the Mamluk period developed an elaborate series of rituals around the person of the shaykh and a set of key locations in the cityscape. The order of the Wafa'iyya was established at the turn of the fourteenth century by Muhammad Wafa'. His family had come to Egypt from the Maghreb as scholars, establishing themselves in Alexandria, but Muhammad would establish himself in Cairo as a prominent poet and mystic. His family-based Sufi order would be active for more than 500, cultivating an elitist aura for itself, attracting high-profile adherents from the religious and military classes. The family owned several properties in Cairo, but the most important were their lodge in the Khurunfush quarter, and the large family funerary complex in the southern Qarafa cemetery, which included a mosque, living quarters, and later a minaret and courtyard. Muhammad's sons 'Ali (d. 1405) and Shihab al-Din (d. 1412) would in turn succeed their father as head of the order. Their appearances were carefully choreographed, apparently keeping themselves out of the public eye, only to appear in full display on special occasions. These events included parading from the Khurunfush quarter along Darb al-Ahmar street, through Zuwayla Gate, past the Citadel, and on to the funerary complex in the southern Qarafa cemetery. Their "lavish parades" (*mawkab hafil*) became a "well-established tradition" ('*ada qadima*).[44] They gave the public a glimpse of the otherwise inaccessible holy man, while assertively occupying the main thoroughfare of the city, and processing past the center of worldly political power, the Citadel.

This tradition continued for at least three hundred years. In the late seventeenth-century the accession rite of Abu al-Takhsis is described. Accompanied by princes and religious scholars, the new shaykh of the Wafa'iyya recited prayers at the Khurunfush lodge, in accordance with the devotional rites of the order. He then departed in procession to pay homage to his ancestors in the Qarafa cemetery. The parade was led by a group of scholars and jurists on foot, followed by the shaykh on horseback, accompanied by princes and a second group of religious men. Further details are not provided, but the pageant is described as outdoing its predecessors in pomp and solemnity.[45]

Once the Sufi orders began to proliferate in the Mamluk period, their impact on the official Hajj parades was significant. While the early thirteenth-century descriptions included the famous, if troublesome, "devils," they did not include formal Sufi groups. However, later accounts of *mahmal* parades invariably mention the participation of Sufi orders. The rivalries among such groups, each seeking to distinguish itself on such a grand public stage, was surely in part behind the evolution of these parades. Banners became ubiquitous, and color schemes developed to distinguish one order from the next. The historical record does not allow a full accounting of this evolution, yet a broad picture does emerge. The travelogue of one European visitor in 1657 describes many Sufi figures in the Hajj procession, with a multitude of banners distinguishing their various groups.[46] Some 16 years later, another traveler confirms the abundance of Sufi flags and banners, adding that many dervishes carried wooden "sabers." By sabers he was likely referring to the traditional long Egyptian staffs that are still used in martial games at festive gatherings.[47] A century later, another visitor describes the many troops of Sufis and their shaykhs, each with its ensign in green, yellow, red, or white with red stripes.[48] The Egyptian historian al-Jabarti reports on the *mahmal* parade of 1788, noting the great number of shaykhs of the Sufi orders processing with their banners alongside the *kiswa* as it crossed the city to the mosque of Husayn.[49]

Sufi parading in relation to the *mahmal* ceremonies was increasingly formalized from the middle of the nineteenth century onward. Egypt itself was being transformed into a modern state, and the spirit of a centralizing bureaucracy extended into the organization of key public rituals. The Bakri shaykh of the day, 'Ali ibn Muhammad, had been appointed to the newly created position of *shaykh al-sajada al-sufiyya* – an office intended to centralize and control all the Egyptian orders. In 1872 we have a report of al-Bakri playing his role as overseer of the orders, as he fixes the sequence of the *mahmal* procession. The Marzuqiyya branch of the Ahmadiyya order were to guide the *mahmal* camel to the Qaramaydan. After the rituals in the square, the Qadiriyya lead the way, followed by a contingent from the Burhamiyya and then the Hamidiyya-Shadhiliyya.[50] In the last years of *mahmal* parading, participation by the Sufi orders continued, but as with the event generally, this was increasingly subdued. A photograph from 1938 shows a procession of the orders in Cairo, who have come out to one of the *mahmal* parades (Figure 25). In 1945, the return ceremony was attended by mounted lancers, who did not perform. The Sufi orders were not included in the initial ceremony at al-Ghafir Square, but waited down the street to lead the lancers and the *mahmal* in procession

25 Sacred carpet starts on its way to Mecca. Credit: Newsreel, British Pathé

back into the city. In a gesture reflecting the changing policy toward public acts of veneration, the police held the crowds back, preventing them from the touching the *mahmal*.[51] Sufi banners, however, continued to be a common and impressive site at important religious observances. We shall return to inspect some of these flags and banners in more detail below.

So far in this chapter we have seen that parading was a vast enterprise, spanning historical periods and locations. Royal parades were common, as were Sufi processions, and the two often overlapped: Sufis appeared in state processions, and sultans, amirs, and other functionaries participated in Sufi processions, in addition to incorporating religious sites into their itineraries. Yet this sketch does not fully capture the complexity and variation of the phenomenon. On many occasions, Egyptian and Syrian processions crossed the confessional boundaries that usually separated Muslim from Christian, and Sunni from Shia. A variety of processions represented such boundary crossing. One was the shared religious culture that developed around the display of sacred books. We shall revisit the use of scriptures as relic objects in the next chapter, but for now let us note one account from 1261, in which the new caliph al-Mustansir was welcomed by a contingent consisting of the sultan, his vizier, judges, religious figures, and a group of Christian Copts bearing a copy of the Gospels. Such official ceremonies could also include the Jewish community. In the late fourteenth century, Sultan Barquq's reinstatement to the sultanate was marked by a large parade of Sharifs, Sufi orders, "Jews with their Torah, and the Christians with their New Testament."[52] The Jews and Christians also processed with candles, which would seem to be a further appropriation of liturgical objects mobilized in these shared displays.

Parading opened a window for cooperation among religious communities. Their coordinated displays could be uniquely effective in matters of this world and the next. In 1348, with the city of Damascus suffering a return of the plague, Jews and Christians joined with Muslim processors to petition for divine relief, each community displaying copies of its scripture as part of the procession.[53] In Cairo, the ceremonies around the Nile, and the importance of water generally, are of course hard to overstate, and so it is no surprise that Muslims should process yearly with the Melkite Christians to the Nile to mark the Day of Epiphany.[54] Saintly *mawlids* had long been sites for multi-religious participation. Examples of Muslim saints being celebrated by Christians are numerous, and the gesture was regularly reciprocated. In Upper Egypt, perhaps the most significant example is that of Muslims taking part in the Coptic processions marking the saint day of the Virgin Mary.[55]

Interreligious parading certainly points to a shared religious culture, yet differences remained, and were sometimes quite disruptive. Tension around the 'Ashrua mourning parades of the Shia could provoke violence. Fourteenth-century accounts of the processions around al-Azhar and the nearby shrine of al-Husayn describe the antagonism stirred by the ritual Shia cursing of the early Islamic figures seen to have frustrated the claims to leadership made by 'Ali and his descendants. On the tenth of Muharram, Shia mourners would parade from the shrines of Umm Kathum and Sayyida Nafisa, presumably passing in front of the Citadel and through the Bayn al-Qasrayn, ending up at the shrine of al-Husayn. Their cursing of those responsible for the hero Imam's death at Karbala would have been a provocative gesture as they passed through the heart of the majority Sunni city.[56] The history of this minority Shia parading, and even that of Shi'ism in Egypt more generally, remains to be written.[57] Although Shia populations dwindled after the fall of the Fatimid regime, the Sufi hospices continued to house Shia, and thus some form of these Muharram observances persisted into the early twentieth century. Up to World War I, on the tenth of Muharram, Shia Sufis gathered in procession behind a young boy on a white pony – apparently stand-ins for the martyred al-Husayn and his beloved horse Dhu al-Janah – and processed to the "Persian Takia, slashing themselves with swords and crying, Ya Hasan! Ya Husein!"[58] Calling out to the imams al-Hasan and al-Husayn, along with practices of self-flagellation, is common in Shia Muharram processions across the Islamic world. These displays of charged religious devotion and ritualized mourning, when practiced to their extremes, have often stirred antipathy between Shia and Sunnis.

As we saw above, parading could be used to lay claim to royal authority, and often symbolically subordinated the ulama, the caliph, or the Sufis to the power of a sultan, yet we would be remiss in conflating that subordination, that specific display of agency, with any essential account of the nature of parading. We have seen that high-ranking jurists, Sufi shaykhs, and others, appropriated such performances, and turning them to their own purposes, made their own bids for recognition. These appropriations were forays into the complex web of politics and religion of the day. Donald Preziosi's observations on the nature of visual fields illuminates the indeterminate character of our parading. As he puts it, any intervention into a visual environment disrupts the existing elements, causing them to be re-sorted and re-narrativized.[59] Thus, the components of a procession are themselves not determinative of meaning before they are mobilized and negotiated within historical practice. While in their familiarity they are recognizable, ultimately they are performative elements with which actors interact and reckon with their environment; through these "reckonings" they push toward reorderings that will better suit their interests. In putting aside any fixed or predetermined readings – in other words, simply decoding the symbols of a procession – we make openings for the historicity, contingency, and the uniqueness of each parade. Following Preziosi's insight, our parades become the stage upon which agency and accident are worked out. The objects of devotion then are players amongst others, all sharing the same stage.

The debates that raged around the denunciations of Sufism, stirred by the theologian and jurist Ibn Taymiyya in the early fourteenth century, set the stage for one intervention. The most prominent Sufi of the day, Ibn 'Ata Allah al-Iskandari, joined by the shaykh of the Sa'id al-Su'ada hospice, followed by some five-hundred Cairenes, marched to the Citadel in angry protest.[60] Ibn Taymiyya, along with most critics of Sufism, would fail to gain the sultan's ear.[61] In this historical moment, the great figures of Sufism were not just appropriating the practices of power, they were reconfiguring the landscape, "reckoning" as Preziosi would say, a new environment for all.

Many examples of protest could be cited. The events of 1713 illustrate nicely the indeterminacy of such performances. When one of their number is killed by a Turkish soldier – Egypt having been integrated into the Ottoman Empire two centuries earlier – the native Sharifs of Cairo rose up in protest. They closed the local markets, and under a banner, marched to the residence of the head treasurer of the administration to express their rage. The *Daftardar* took the situation seriously, and called the army to protect him and to disperse the marchers. The Sharifan leaders of the event were arrested, but thanks to the intercession of certain Sufi shaykhs and jurists, were soon released.[62] The context of this skirmish, the simmering tensions between a long-occupying Turkish force and its subject Arab-Egyptian population, served as backdrop for the protest procession, a performance the outcome of which not even its organizers could have known.

These quick examples should suffice to illuminate the indeterminacy of parading. The objects that were mobilized for a protest parade were some of the very same ones that appeared in the processions asserting, celebrating, and enacting the authority of the Sultan. The procession itself could do such double duty, being reappropriated, and turned into a tool for civilians to wield against the authorities. In one episode of popular dissatisfaction at the levying of new taxes, a diverse group of Damascenes, including "commoners,"preachers, and judges, came together to protest. But this was not simply an angry mob; they carried with them the ancient Qur'an copied some seven centuries earlier by the hand of none other than the Caliph 'Uthman. The parade wielded further clout by including a sandal of the prophet Muhammad, along with various caliphal standards.[63] The central monument of the city, the Umayyad mosque, was itself at times appropriated for such protests. In 1485 another protest march was mounted with banners and participants chanting the *takbir* or 'Allahu akbar!" Their ire had been stirred by the injustice of fines levied against a Sufi shaykh, who was being punished for attacking the local hashish sellers and damaging their stock. Five years earlier, a similar protest march was mounted after a popular shaykh was arrested for having incited the population to resist the levying of new taxes.[64] There was a long tradition of Sufis channeling community frustrations and anxieties. At times demonstrations were directed against the political powers of the day, but more frequently a rabble-rousing shaykh driven by moral outrage, exercised what one scholar has called "unauthorized moral regulation."[65]

In 1494 one episode in Damascus turned particularly violent. Two incendiary Sufi shaykhs who had forbidden the sale of alcohol in the city were imprisoned, but crowds broke into the jail to free them. Resistance to the authorities escalated to a violent pitch, and in the ensuing clashes some one-hundred and fifty people were killed.[66] In Cairo, the sacred scriptures were also enlisted in protests. In the year 1341 alone, two demonstrations were held. The first march protested the judiciary's turning a blind eye to the local trade in hashish. The ringleaders are not identified, but the participants marched behind one of them, carrying a copy of the Qur'an. The second march is described as a protest against the moral laxity of the judiciary, where the banners of the caliphs were held up as symbols of religious rectitude. It is not clear from the sources what these banners were exactly; the caliphs themselves, reduced to figure-heads under the Mamluks, would not have been directly involved. More likely these banners simply bore the names or titles of the caliph, who at that point would have been either al-Wathiq Bi'llah or al-Hakim al-Thani.[67]

These examples of the reversal of agency, with the commoners or the local religious leaders forming their own processions behind various sacred objects,

help underline the essential indeterminacy of performance. In fact, this indeterminacy, contemporary theory tells us, is essential to performativity itself.
Austin's now famous speech-act theory eloquently brought the precariousness
of any act into full view. The act is thus redefined to include its inherent
capacity for misfire. As Stanley Cavell puts it, every instance risks missing its
goal. The meaning of any gesture then is never assured, and always carries
within it a dimension of failure, real or unconsummated.[68] Judith Butler speaks
of this sense of indeterminacy, the wager that every staging makes, and extends
it into bodily performance. For Butler – as for our "commoners" and Sufi
rabble-rousers – the indeterminacy of performance is not a failure, rather it is
an opening, an opportunity to reorient and redefine a practice.[69] A subversive
potential lurks behind every supposedly normative performance, representing
the possibility of failure or reversal. Thus, the Qur'ans, the banners, the relics,
carried aloft by paraders in their noisy marches, could be transformed from
symbols of regal authority into markers of local empowerment, resistance, or
moral critique.

   For the ruling elite, each instance in which they displayed their power put it
at risk. Things would likely turn out as expected, but by the nature of such
performances, there were no guarantees. For Sultan Muhammad ibn Qalawun
this was made only too clear when on one occasion he and his royal retinue
approached Qaramaydan square, only to find that it was empty, devoid of
spectators. Crisis was averted, however, once criers were sent out into the city
"calling people to the spectacle in the square," and finally crowds gathered to
"attend the event in their usual way."[70] In another instance, in Damascus a
century later, the governor was not so lucky, and could not salvage his parade.
The event was interrupted by a popular (*'amma*) protest at the high price of
meat in the city, which quickly transformed the occasion into a demonstration,
and a platform for criticizing the governor and his administration.[71] Another
hundred years later, we see a similar transformation of an official procession.
A local official in the town of al-Mahalla al-Kubra was attacked; his house was
looted, and he met his end in the public square at the hands of an angry mob.
Cairo moved to restore order. The unfortunate Shihab al-Din Ahmad, simply
the acting governor at the time, had stoked the ire of the inhabitants of the city
with his manipulation of food prices. After his death, his brother, a well-placed
official in Cairo, a royal steward, dispatched a troupe of soldiers to the
provincial city. The ring leaders were identified, arrested, and taken to the
capital for exemplary punishment. In addition to flogging them outside the
city, the bereaved steward intended to humiliate the rebels by parading them
down the main avenues of the capital. However, the tables were turned when
spectators not only failed to jeer or mock, but instead began to sympathize
with the prisoners. Making the event a complete fiasco, the crowds began to
hurl insults and curses at the steward himself. Disapproval turned to anger,

which so frightened the official that he abandoned the parade, and went into hiding.[72]

If indeterminacy lurks behind every performance, then the objects in play at each event are also in flux. As we saw earlier, the parading of humiliated prisoners might not yield the anticipated results, or the holding aloft of a Qur'an in procession can mean rather different things, depending on the situation. This is the framework then within which we can turn to consider the spectacle of banners. Recalling the discussion of what I've been calling the aesthetic negotiation between an object and its referent, this indeterminacy and its resolution come into sharper focus. More specifically, although indeterminacy is ubiquitous, it can be resolved, at least temporarily, through the playing out of such aesthetic negotiations. Parading, banners, and their special form of textuality, come together within religious, political, and cultural contexts to determine each performative occasion. The calligraphic writing on banners plays a key role, and reflection on those dynamics illuminates the mediation between objects, their viewers, and the negotiated meaning of such events.

We shall see that textual presentations on banners are complex phenomena, which challenge any easy explanation of our common reading practices. Banners are not read in the same way that everyday ink and paper writing is. In fact, these ambulatory calligraphic banner texts hinder such easy reading. More specifically, in order to assert themselves as aesthetic objects, they resist any simple reading that would make them transparent – any quick reading that pushes past the material instantiation of the writing to get to the "meaning" that it signals. I discussed this effacing gesture above in relation to artworks resisting their erasure in the face of reductive readings. The implication here is that our parading banner texts assert what we noted earlier as a tending "towards the visual."[73] The immediacy of the performance is also an important element at play, one that is absent from our typical pen-and-paper reading practices. The Egyptian spectator engaged these processing text objects with an immediacy that required different reading strategies. The gazing spectator must take everything in at once. In a parade, nothing repeats itself, and objects are constantly moving, shifting, and changing their aspect. The great theoretician of optics, Ibn Haytham (d. 1040), pointed to this sort of dynamic viewing in his reflections on reading. His idea was that readers do not need to decode words one letter at a time; familiar words are recognized ". . .at the moment of their being perceived before every one of their letters has been inspected."[74] Ibn Haytham was not talking about the materiality of the text *per se*, instead his observation related to the fact that textual communication can take place in various ways, in this case reading by an instantaneous grasping of entire words rather than letter-by-letter.

This glancing operation is at play in the peculiar legibility of our banners. It makes possible the kind of material force Benjamin was describing, and what

I've been calling the aesthetic resistance of the writing. More specifically, we shall see below that banner texts foil the kind of reading that would erase them by seeing past them, in two important ways. First, they resist simply by being located on unsettled and moving surfaces. Banners of course are normally fluttering in procession, bouncing along with the bodies that transport them, all with the expectation that audiences will view them in such fitful perform-ances; the moving surface is only intermittently legible. The transportability of banners also brings to the texts a kind of ephemerality, limiting its presence and obstructing visual access. By virtue of its design and function, every banner carries with it the sense that it could be elsewhere, that it might not be where the viewer sees it for long. The second way banner texts resist transparent reading is through their complex calligraphic style. While the ostensible reason for writing in an intricate style is simply beautification, the effect in this case is to unsettle and resist any quick and simple reading.

Bearing in mind these two ways that banner text resists reading – its mobile display and its unusual letter composition – we can begin to account for its place within processions. We saw earlier the contested and undetermined nature of parading. In that context banner texts constitute material, visual, and aesthetic gestures against such indeterminacy. Rather than simply labeling a parade, and then passing into insignificance, banner texts insist on their continuing presence. They move along with the paraders, claiming a continu-ity and immediacy that persists for the duration of the event. Against the uncertainty inherent in every performance, the banner text stops the reading eye that would otherwise pass through it.

Not every dimension of banner textuality outlined here will be fully at play in the cases we explore below, but various instantiations of these two forms of resistance to reading are clearly at play. We now turn to consider the military and religious banners. As was the case for the *mahmal*s we encountered in Chapter 1, banner colors varied widely. This variation did not preclude certain tendencies, however. In the days of the Prophet, a limited set of colors were displayed. In conflicts with his Meccan adversaries, Muhammad carried black banners, which the Abbasid revolution some one-hundred and twenty years later would also adopt, explicitly evoking their genealogical connection to the family of the Prophet.[75] The early *liwa'* banner typically identified a military formation, and the term in later generations even came to apply to a military command. The *ra'ya* standard, by contrast, usually indicated membership in a kinship group. The hadith sources distinguish between the Prophet's banner (*liwa'*), an elongated piece of white fabric, and his black standard (*ra'ya*), square in shape. Accounts of such colorings, however, vary, and we also have reports of Muhammad bearing a white and a yellow *ra'ya*, in addition to a black *liwa'*.[76] While the Qur'an says that on judgment day the chosen will wear green (Q.18:31), this does not seem to have dictated color choices for public displays. At the battle of Siffin (657), according to some sources the rebel forces under Mu'awiyya carried red banners, but some report black.[77] The Abbasid empire was invariably associated with the color black, as was the office of the caliph which survived its fall in the thirteenth century. Reduced to a figurehead, the caliphate was moved to Cairo for the duration of the Mamluk era. Here the caliphs' ceremonial functions rarely exceeded the ritual bestowing of their black robes and turbans upon each successive sultan.[78]

The Mamluks had adopted yellow as their own dynastic color, in clear contrast to the black of the Abbasids – the Ottoman successors to the Mamluks would use red. Color, however, could also be used to distinguish one religious community from another. In medieval Syria, non-Muslim men at one point were required to use specific colors for their turbans: Christians were to wear blue, Jews yellow, and Samaritans red.[79] Far more enduring than these temporary dictates aimed at minority communities, however, was the development of color branding to distinguish between the major Sufi orders. The Rifa'iyya typically used black for its banners and turbans, the Ahmadiyya red, the Qadiriyya white, and the Shadhiliyya and Burhamiyya green.[80] These associations have largely persisted up into the contemporary period. Theories around color developed in speculative Sufism to some degree – and philosophers had recognized the aesthetics of color – but they do not seem to have been behind their associations with the various orders.[81]

Color was also a component of the blazons that Mamluk princes and sultans adopted. These consisted of stylized representations that either symbolized the heroic character of the individual, or indicated his area of expertise within the bureaucracy or the military. Sultan Baybars famously represented himself as a panther in his blazons, while Muhammad ibn Qalawun adopted the eagle, single or double-headed. A sword, cup, or pen-box, could also be represented, indicating both rank and responsibility of a highly placed amir.[82] Black, red, and blue were commonly used for blazons, but there seems to have been no significance behind these color choices.

Returning to our wider concern with banners and textuality, we note early and famous examples deploying Qur'anic text in claims for political and religious legitimacy. Among the black banners that the Abbasid rebels hoisted on the battlefield, was one that bore one of the longest words found in the Qur'an. The text (Q. 2:137) runs *fasayakfikahum,* which translates as, "Surely (Allah) shall sustain you against them."[83] A sense of how unusual this is can be gleaned from the fact that Arabic words often appear as three, sometimes four consonants, with vowels being left unindicated – here there are eight consonants. Moving across a battlefield, fluttering in the wind, even hung around a tent, this text, likely set against a black background, would have made a striking impression. Such a display was clearly laying claim to religious authority and legitimate revolution. Quoting this Qur'an passage evoked divine

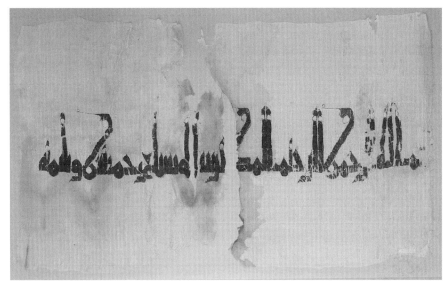

26 Tenth-century *tiraz*: Egypt. Credit: T.24-1942; Victoria and Albert Museum. Presented by Art Fund

providence and favor for the Abbasid cause against Umayyad central authority. The scriptural reference is to the earliest Muslim community as it struggled against its Christian and Jewish foes to find footing. The banner itself pushed this reading to the fore. Through resisting easy reading, the banner wrests *fasayakfikahum* out of its original scriptural context, isolating it, and setting the stage for discursive reworking and rereading. Thus, our banner text – both despite and thanks to its Qur'anic roots – became a claim to legitimacy and favored divine providence, all within the revolutionary politics of the Abbasid claim to the caliphate.

Displays of moving text were also found on clothing. Largely from Egypt, fabrics known as *tiraz* were often woven with colored threads forming words. Precious robes of honor could be decorated with *tiraz* texts.[84] One surviving example from Fatimid Cairo (Figure 26) dates to 968. The middle section of the red inscription is missing, but the beginning *basmala*, and the year can be made out. Robes were so valuable, they were the main currency for the tribute exacted from the Christians of Najran after they were expelled from Arabia. In Iraq, the governor al-Hajjaj required them to furnish 1,800 robes per year, "of the kind adorned with images."[85] With the new Abbasid regime established, in the year 770 the second caliph, al-Mansur, insisted that all of his courtiers wear black clothing with Qur'an verses inscribed on the back. Bestowing robes of honor had long been an established tradition, but this was something quite different. Black had been adopted by earlier generations of the Abbasid cause, and was reinforced in its association with their rule by al-Mansur himself through a dream in which both he and his brother – whom he has succeeded as caliph – were invested with black banners by the Prophet himself at the Ka'ba.[86] By dressing in dynastic black, al-Mansur's entourage served as visual extensions of his presence and thus authority. This control was extended to the population at large, with black becoming a sign of one's loyalty to the caliphate.[87] The visual dynamics at play were carefully framed. In displaying Qur'anic text on their clothing, the caliph's entourage were acting much like banner displays, reframing and reworking scripture through complex calligraphic displays on their persons. Thanks to its ambulatory and calligraphic contexts, this writing resists easy reduction to its Qur'anic origin, insisting on its own immediate presence in the visual field, and opening up a play of indeterminacy of meaning. This presence becomes the site for a new association, one that is intended to serve al-Mansur's political interests. Specifically, the caliph's authority is thereby visually anchored within revelation and scripture, and presumably divine providence itself.

Banners were to play an important role in the subsequent investiture ceremonies of the Abbasid empire. In Egypt, the waning Fatimid dynasty of the Isma'ilis gave way to the upstart vizier Saladin who would establish the Ayyubid dynasty, returning the rule of Egypt and Syria to the Sunni creed, and to the nominal authority of the caliphate. Saladin's 1174 investiture was ceremonially endorsed by the caliph with the arrival of a black banner that bore in white lettering the latter's official title "al-Mustadi bi-Amr Allah." Saladin would go on to heroic campaigns against the Crusaders and rival Muslim powers in the Levant. While we might read the banners at the coronation ceremony as a metonymic presence of the caliph in Baghdad[88] – in other words, the banners acting as stand-ins for the person named – the stage that is set puts much more into play. The inscribed banners "hoisted above (Saladin's) head" (*yanshuru 'ala ra'sihi*)[89] did more than simply represent the authority of the caliphal office, symbolically approving the coronation. Paradoxically, they also communicate the caliph's absence. Rather than being conflated with al-Mustadi, the elaborate calligraphy hanging above Saladin points to the weakness and ephemeral position of the caliph. Having set his empire on a strong foundation, Saladin's need for the caliph was only ceremonial. Essentially, the real power of the caliphs was ebbing, and they were fast on their way to becoming subjects of the military and political powers around them.[90] In their distant connections to the caliph in Baghdad, and the precarious authority they represented before the rising status of Saladin, the banner texts of al-Mustadi bi-Amr Allah communicated the fragile standing of the caliph as much as it authorized the accession of one of his loyal subjects.

For 500 years the caliphs ruled a vast empire from their capital at Baghdad. While the Mongol invasions of the thirteenth century put an end to their rule – the execution of al-Musta'sim by the Mongols being only a small example of their ruthlessness – the caliphate, however, was revived in

1261 from Cairo, where Sultan Baybars reestablished the office, but reduced it to a ceremonial position.[91] A set of relations was thus established, which continued the power reversal that Saladin had begun. In one investiture ceremony accompanied by the captive caliph, Sultan Baybars wore a golden collar and shackles, capturing perfectly the nature of his 'slavery' as a Mamluk, and his 'submission' to the caliph.[92] In this new context, the rituals of investiture were key to maintaining the newly defined power structure. Standard practice saw the caliph send robes of honor (*tashrif*) to the newly invested sultan, and in keeping its Abbasid association, the robes were invariably black in color. Additionally, the Mamluk sultan would typically receive a scepter, a turban, and a royal seal. Other indispensable objects were banners or standards (variously called *sanjaq, rayyat, a'lam*),[93] two of which would be black, bearing the caliph's name and titles embroidered in white, along with two yellow silk banners bearing the new sultan's name.[94] In parading with these banners, the new sultan set the stage upon which this collection of names, titles, and coloring are all put into play. The relationship between the individuals named, and the calligraphic banners themselves, is thus more complex than a simple process of naming and labeling. We noted Saladin earlier sitting below the Baghdad banners, thereby upholding the authority of the caliphs as much as himself benefitting from their patronage. The investiture banners of the Mamluks brought the caliph and the sultan into the latest configuration of an intertwined and multivalent relationship. The processing banners, in both yellow and black, more accurately negotiated an equipoise between two parties that needed the other, along with the political reality that the caliph was more indebted to the sultan upon whom he was ostensibly ordaining the right to rule.[95]

Not only might the calligraphic banner serve as the site for renegotiating power relations, it could also put the categories of religious and military charisma themselves into play. As we saw earlier, the *mahmal* serving at once political and religious functions, a royal banner could negotiate similar boundary crossings. One illustrative example comes from North Africa. In 1281 supporters of the deposed Hafsid ruler al-Wathiq arrived in Cairo with a plea for help. At the sultan's court, they petitioned Qalawun for assistance in regaining control of the Maghreb. Although the Mamluks had recently been victorious on the battlefield, Egypt and Syria remained under threat from the Mongol invaders. Unable to divert forces to intervene in the Maghreb, sultan Qalawun only agreed to send his royal banner. This gesture, however, was far from hollow, as the banner figured prominently in the accounts of the retaking of Tunis. As the historian Ibn 'Abd al-Zahir recounts, the taking of Tunis, "was accomplished by the *baraka* of Qalawun's name and by the good fortune of his noble banner."[96] The ambulating, and rampart-storming, banner was thus more than just a signal of the Mamluk sultan's support for the cause. This inscription of name and titles was not simply a label recording the sanction of a distant political authority; instead it evoked the charisma of a heroic and successful ruler, making his banner a tangible force joining in the assault on the city.

Banners designed for a purely martial context also played with the lines dividing religious and worldly authority. The Mamluk empire would fall to the Ottomans after the disastrous battle of Marj Dabiq at which Sultan al-Ghawri himself met his end before the forces of Sultan Selim "The Grim." Not only was the empire lost, but even the seat of the caliphate would be taken, removed to Istanbul. A surviving banner attributed to Selim displays an inscribed double-sword, the *dhu al-fiqar* associated with the early Islamic hero 'Ali ibn Abi Talib, who reportedly received if from his uncle the Prophet during the battle of Uhud. Inscriptions include the Qur'anic text from sura 48 beginning, "We have granted you manifest victory..." running along the sword blades and again across the top horizontal band. Four crescent moons are represented, cradling the vocative devotional phrase "Ya Muhammad" and filled with the text of the Islamic profession of faith: "There is no god but God; and Muhammad is his messenger."[97] Religious authority and spiritual evocations were to remain standard elements in the visual vocabulary of imperial and military banners.

Flags and banners were also common sights on the Hajj, heading up the pilgrims' caravans and serving as signals and rallying points for various ritual stations. While the historical documentation for Hajj standards is less than we have for its more prominent partner, the *mahmal*, it is clear that the display of standards was a long-established practice. The use of military standards was ubiquitous, for the obvious utility they provided as visual reference points for soldiers in the confusing fog of battle. The various groups of pilgrims at every Hajj relied on similar signals. Perhaps the earliest account comes from the year 686, when four standards were raised on mount Arafat in the course of that year's Hajj. The first was that of Ibn al-Zubayr (d. 692) the grandson of the caliph Abu Bakr. Ibn al-Zubaryr had established a short-lived counter caliphate in Mecca and Medina, with the aim of overthrowing the Umayyads, who were also represented on Arafat by their standard. Additionally, the Kharijites and the Shia were gathered under their respective standards. No detailed descriptions of these or other Hajj standards seem to have come down to us, but for the modern period the record is more substantial.

As I claimed above, in playing across the boundary lines that divide the religious and the martial, these standards make their own complex statements within their time and place. Hajj standards, which in the Ottoman period often became known as *sanjaqs*, relied little on the legibility of their calligraphic inscriptions. Their formal visual communication, either of a sunburst pattern, or sword and crescent shapes, was their primary reference. The *sanjaqs* thus became far more than decorative objects. The calligraphic forms they displayed facilitated their wider role as beacons leading and rallying the pilgrims. This intimate relationship with the Hajj pilgrims, and more importantly the *sanjaq*'s repeated presence at the most holy sites of Islam, and its association with the pilgrimage, elicited intense veneration at both the official and the popular levels.

In the modern era, the Hajj flag displayed alongside the Egyptian *mahmal* was an impressive site in its own right. What was likely the last *sanjaq* in circulation appears in photos from the turn of the twentieth century: see above Chapter 1, Figures 1 and 11. One late nineteenth-century report describes the flag (*bayraq*) being taken into the Prophet's grave, in Medina.[98] In one photo the flag is carefully rolled up, but in the second we can clearly see a sunburst calligraphic pattern, framed by a rectangular border. Jomier was very likely describing this flag in the 1940s, which he describes as being 150 cm by 130 cm. The background color is red with the embroidery in silver. The central oval or medallion contains the *tahlil* "There is no god, but God" with lines radiating outward.[99] Unfortunately the photograph is not of sufficient detail to allow a confirmation of Jomier's reading of the calligraphy, but the flag preserved in the Khalili collection (Figure 27) is similar to the one he was describing. The inner text displays the *tahlil* formula, with the outer band running, "In the Name of God the Merciful the Compassionate; There is no God but He, the Living and Eternal! Neither sleep nor slumber may seize Him. To Him are all

27 *Mahmal* banner with inscriptions. Credit: TXT 290; Hajj and the Arts of Pilgrimage. Khalili Collections. © Nour Foundation. Courtesy the Khalili Family Trust

things in heaven and earth. Who can intercede with Him without his permission?" (Q. 2:255) It is clear that the size, the bold color contrast, and the calligraphic design, worked together to make an effective flag.

In Damascus, records of a *sanjaq* accompanying the *mahmal* go back to 1672, although it was almost certainly an essential part of the Hajj rituals long before.[100] While accounts of precise inscriptions are lacking, there is plenty of evidence for the veneration of the standard. Damascus celebrated not only the Day of the *Mahmal* (*yawm al-mahmal*) but this was followed immediately by the Day of the *Sanjaq*, which in the mid-nineteenth century included the Amir of the Hajj ceremoniously receiving the flag, rubbing his hands upon it and then passing them over his face in a ritual partaking of blessing through the flag's *baraka*. The popular understanding is that the *sanjak* has been handed down from the time of the Prophet or the caliph 'Umar. Perhaps not surprisingly, as the case has been for the *mahmal*s, the Syrian flag – which like the late Egyptian *sanjaq* had a red field – was relegated to the National Museum after the demise of the *mahmal* rituals.[101]

The Ottoman sultans preserved and deployed a *sanjaq*, variously known as the "Noble banner" (*liwa-i sherif*) or the "Prophet's flag" (*'alem-i nebewi*). This *sanjaq*, or more precisely a series of *sanjaqs*, served functions well beyond those associated with the Hajj – starting in the late fifteenth century and extending up into the twentieth century. Official chronicles give various accounts of the flag's origins, but they all associate the *sanjaq* with the Prophet or members of his family. Following Sultan Selim's conquest of Egypt, and the taking of the Hijaz, the flag came into Ottoman possession. It was kept in the provincial capital Damascus and associated with the Hajj rituals we noted above, but at the same time the *sanjaq* appeared on several occasions at the head of Ottoman armies leaving the capital or on the battlefield itself.[102] By the late seventeenth century, the flag in Damascus was worn beyond repair. Pieces from it were woven into three new green silk flags, thus preserving the *baraka*. One flag went to the military, one was kept with the sultan's person, and the third was stored in the Topkapi Palace along with other relics. Until 1908 soldiers guarded the spot – essentially a small impression in the courtyard of the palace – where the *sanjaq* had been ritually presented. As of 2015, this space has remained roped off and identified with a small plaque.

The Hajj banners are striking because of the complex interplay between text, form, and the ritual performances of which they were an essential part. It should not surprise us then, that much of the same interplay is found in the banners of the Sufis. Whether on pilgrimage to a saintly shrine, or as part of the annual celebration of holy days, or even as part of parades marking regal accessions or victory marches, Sufi groups displayed their banners. While almost no Sufi banners have survived from more than a century ago, one valuable example nicely illustrates the complexity we have been exploring.

A red banner (Figure 28) preserved at Harvard, dates to the late seventeenth century. With its shape and the central display of the two-headed *dhu al-fiqar* sword, it clearly resembles a *sanjaq*. It would not have looked out of place on a battlefield, but its true use was quite different. The upper panel contains Qur'anic inscriptions, and the text on the sword likewise is from Qur'an 48:1–2, "Truly, We have granted you a clear victory; That God may forgive your sins of the past, and those to come, perfecting His grace upon you, and guiding you upon a straight path." Reference to being put on a "straight path" seems quite appropriate for a pilgrim's banner. More significant, however, is the text in the rectangular panel above the sword, (Figure 29) which praises Muhammad, and calls for blessings upon the Sufi saint 'Abd al-Qadir al-Jilani (d. 1166). There are 18 lines in each of two columns – in small text, difficult to read. The first column praises Muhammad: "(His) mother and father (being) from the highest of the nobility. From his light comes the light of law. Were it not for him, the pilgrims would not get to Mina. Were it not for him, there would be no circumambulating of the Ka'ba. Were it not for him, there would be no running to al-Safa. (He is) most noble of creation. . ." Of the Sufi saint, the inscription reads, "Jilani 'Abd al-Qadir. . . God's blessings upon him, and may they increase. . . If one visits his grave, one's desires will be granted. (He is) sultan to the people of the east and the west." The banner is from the Maghreb, and seems to have been used by adherents of the Qadiriyya Sufi order on their Hajj.[103] Details of the ritual context are lost to us, but internal evidence suffices to show us a Sufi banner playing out its polyvalent meanings, appropriating the form of a military banner for the purposes of a Sufi community and its pilgrimages to Mecca, but also likely to other holy sites and shrines. As part of this indeterminate identity, the banner's resistance to easy reading – particularly the lines in the central panel – is also at play.

Not surprisingly, as with the variety of processions we explored earlier in this chapter, the Sufi parades have carefully chosen itineraries. Yet unlike the typical sultan's procession, Sufi banners from different shrines or Sufi orders often cluster together in temporary displays. Sufi processions and their banner texts can operate in an imbricated or layered fashion, with several separate groups and banners incorporated into one event. Through this visual multi-layering – one Sufi group after another presenting their banners – issues of legibility and ornamentation are still at play, but an additional dimension of interpretive framing is supplied. Here a Sufi banner text incorporates the denotive power of the banners that have processed before it as well as those that follow, while itself contributing to the impact of those banners.

The imbrication of text can take many forms, with inscriptions integrated into wider visual compositions. In our discussions above of the *mahmal* parade in Luxor, we noted that not only the great saint's *tabut* processed, but it is

28 Pilgrim's banner. Credit: 1958.20; Harvard Art Museums/Arthur M. Sackler Museum. 369.6 × 211.8 cm. Gift of John Goelet. Photo: Imaging Department © President and Fellows of Harvard College

29 Pilgrim's banner (detail). Credit: 1958.20; Harvard Art Museums/Arthur M. Sackler Museum. 369.6 × 211.8 cm. Gift of John Goelet. Photo: Imaging Department © President and Fellows of Harvard College. Detail

accompanied by the *tabuts* of local affiliated shrines. The collocation of these devotional inscriptions and saintly titles in a sequence within the parades generates a web of association between the objects, the saintly figures they are associated with, and the various shrines that house them. The practice of

30 Cairo: feast of the Prophet. Credit: Travelers in the Middle East Archive (TIMEA). From the collection of Paula Sanders, Rice University

displaying banners at the front of the tents of Sufi pilgrims, attending the many saint day celebrations though out the year, generates similar textual webs.

One account from 1842 describes Sufis parading as part of the *mahmal* celebrations, noting the prominent orders of the day such as the Saʻdiyya, the Rifaʻiyya, the Qadiriyya, and the Burhamiyya. Each group displayed it flags, typically bearing the shahada, short passages from the Qurʾan, and the names of the shaykhs and founders of that order.[104] Although dating from the twentieth century, the Figure 30 "Feast of the Prophet" captures some of the visual multi-layering Sophia Lane-Poole was describing in the mid 1800s. Here more than a dozen red flags of an Ahmadiyya group are aligned in a procession to mark the birthday of the Prophet (*mawlid al-nabi*), with the shahada visible in the oval panels of the first banner. Another image, from about the same time, gives a wider view of Sufi banners. In Figure 31 we can see at least two Sufi groups, with their clusters of banners, processing uphill toward a reviewing stand, itself marked by smaller and more regular flags than those of the orders. The caption describes them coming from "saluting the Sheikh-el-Bekri" the government appointed head of the orders. This photo may actually be show-ing them on their way to the Sheikh. State officials would typically be seated together with head of the Sufi orders, and in this case probably all sitting in the elevated reviewing stand.

This practice of grouping banners together in Sufi processions was not limited to the capital. Local celebrations in the countryside took up the practice also. One anthropologist describes in her field work from the 1920s

THE BIRTHDAY OF THE PROPHET.
A deputation of one of the Mohammedan Orders on its way from saluting the Sheikh-el-Bekri.

31 The birthday of the Prophet. Credit: Travelers in the Middle East Archive (TIMEA). Sladen, Douglas. *Oriental Cairo: the City of the "Arabian Nights"*. J. B. Lippincott Company: Philadelphia and Hurst & Blackett, Ltd: London, 1911

a small *mawlid* celebration in Upper Egypt. She details a humble parade in honor of shaykh Umbarak, which included a banner from the saint's shrine, accompanied by the banners from the tombs of shaykhs of the neighboring villages.[105]

The *mawlid* celebrations for the prophet Moses, outside of Jerusalem, were also an occasion for banners to process together. Accounts from the early twentieth century describe a procession through the city, led by Moses' green banner with gold embroidering and black silk panels bearing inscriptions. As the parade moved along, it was joined by flags from neighboring local shrines.[106] At the end of the twentieth-century, the parading and banners are restricted to the shrine property.[107]

The Rifaʻiyya in Cairo were avid paraders, and often contributed to the complex and imbricated displays of banner text. A 1965 photograph of the Rifaʻiyya shows them participating in New Year's celebrations – parading in a succession of Sufi orders. Their black banners display the word Allah against a white panel, and the names of the Prophet, the first four caliphs, and the profession of faith. Some appear on rounded rectangle panels, recalling hieroglyphic cartouches, with others on crescent or diamond shaped panels. One banner carries the image of a sword, recalling the practices of self-mortification the Rifa'is were famous for. The preponderance of texts, however, serves to identify the sub-branches of the order, and their leaders. One banner reads, "Abu Bakr (in diamond shaped panel) The order of the Rifa'iyya, 'Umar (in diamond shaped panel); Shaykh Muhammad Ibrahim... head of the noble Rifa'iyya; 'Uthman (in diamond shaped panel) From Giza, Muhammad, 'Ali (in diamond shaped panel)." A light-colored banner behind it, also displays the names of the first four caliphs in each corner, and identifies one shaykh Mustafa. Two of the banners are topped with rows of stylized fleur-de-lis, recalling the middle Mamluk architectural feature of cresting found on the top of many monumental walls.[108]

An account of the saint day *mawlid* for the twelfth-century poet and saint 'Umar ibn al-Farid describes a procession in the 1980s from the saint's shrine at the foot of the Muqattam hills, through the City of the Dead, to the shrine of Sayyida Aisha. While attendance for the spectacle was rather limited, the Sufi orders marched onward, with the black Rifa'i banners taking the lead, followed by the red flags of the Ahmadiyya and the green flags of the Burhamiyya.[109] A set of photographs from 40 years earlier, with banners being paraded by a succession of Sufi groups, nicely capture the flow and complexity of these displays of religious text (Figures 32 and 33).

At first glance, one might be struck by visual messiness of these parades. But upon closer inspection, a wider organization comes into focus. The bodies and objects are not moving about randomly; the various Sufi orders, the military

32 Sufi parade in Cairo with flags. Credit: Jacques Jomier, *Le Mahmal et la caravane Égyptienne des pèlerins de la Mecque (XIII–XX siècles)* (Cairo: Presses de Institut Français d'Achéologie Orientale, 1953). © Institut français d'archéologie orientale

33 Sufi parade with *tariqa* banners. Credit: JacquesJomier, *Le Mahmal et la caravane Égyptienne des pèlerins de la Mecque (XIII-XX siècles)* (Cairo: Presses de Institut Français d'Achéologie Orientale, 1953). © Institut français d'archéologie orientale

units, and the religious and political elites, are certainly not interchangeable. Likewise, the story I've been telling in this chapter of parading and banners, might seem disorderly, but I hope that the object itself has remained our focus. Like any good pilgrim or parader, we would be wise to keep the banners within view at all times. Throughout this chapter, the performative context of parading was key to setting the stage – and here the negotiated, indeterminacy, and even reversibility of parades, was explored. While scriptures made various appearances in these parades, the role of banners was most in question. The examples we saw made it clear that inscribed banners are texts that play in strange ways with their audience. Banners are announcements and declarations, and yet they resist reading. Though their ornamentation and their dynamic display, banners resist easy reading – thus preserving for themselves ongoing occasions for meaning making. In the next chapter, we shall continue to explore this resistance to reduction. Our focus will be on relics, how their viewers related to them, and the complex polyvalency that they maintained as object of devotion.

FOUR

THE RELIC AND ITS WITNESS

No perfume is as beautiful as the dust that embraces his bones. Blessed are those who kiss them, or catch their scent.

Al-Busiri, Qasidat al-burda, lines 61, 62

At the southern end of Cairo, near the Nile, stands an unassuming mid-sized mosque and shrine, known as the Convent of the Relics of the Prophet (*Ribat Athar al-Nabi*). While this is not the only place in the city visited for its relics – we shall explore this rich landscape in the following pages – it has long been an important site for such encounters. Contact with relics was an intense experience. People found a variety ways to make sense of these encounters, and to share those interactions. In the early fifteenth century Sibt ibn al-'Ajami visited the Cairo relics. He recounts how he and his friends later that day came across a scholar and friend, Jalal al-Din ibn Khatib Darya al-Dimashqi, at one of the Cairo book markets. Al-'Ajami continues,

> He asked where we were coming from. I told him that along with a number of friends and scholars, we had visited the relics and were now just returning. He asked if any of us had composed poetry while we were there, and I had to admit that we had not. Jalal al-Din then revealed that a few days earlier he too had visited the relics, and had versified the following lines, which he then recited for us: *O my eyes! Return to the beloved and his precious abode. You have longed for the spring rains and the welcoming shores of his shrine. Though you have not seen him directly, bliss and utter triumph are yours, for these are his remains.*[1]

While al-'Ajami and his literary companions might have felt chastened by Jalal al-Din, the episode was not too embarrassing to be recorded for posterity. We get the sense that al-'Ajami knew he had missed an opportunity to reflect upon the inspiration that viewing relics can offer, and that his learned friend had made much more of the experience.

The word Jalal al-Din used for shrine was *mazar*, literally a place of visitation. The cognate *ziyara* denotes a visit, and is often best translated as pilgrimage. Islamic shrines have taken a great variety of forms, with such diversity that it is difficult to identify any essential architectural feature shared by all.[2] A pious visit to the dead could be to a tomb structure, a graveyard, a mosque, or even a library. In contrast, a more formalized pilgrimage was the Hajj, which of course was always undertaken with great attention to proper practice and a well-established itinerary. Lesser pilgrimages, to tombs of the prophets, saintly graves, and other sacred sites, have long been practiced. While not a religious obligation, and at times criticized for frivolity and excess, regional pilgrimages were widespread and loosely formalized through the conventions of established practice. But more germane to our discussion in this chapter is the Arabic term for relic: *athar*. In the vignette above, Jalal al-Din had been to see the relics of the Prophet (*athar al-nabi*). While the ritual context leaves no doubt as to where he was, the semantic range of the term *athar* itself is rather broader. The basic sense is that of a trace, sign, or vestige – operating at either a conceptual or a material level. Thus, *athar* can refer to the reports of the Prophet and his companions, passed down through the ages as part of the teachings of Islam; as well as a physical sense of an impression, for example of a footprint in sand, or an ancient monument, the vestige or trace of a bygone era.[3] A recent comparative study highlights the "handed down" sense of relics at play across religious traditions.[4] The semantic range of *athar*, extending to both the immaterial and material, is mirrored in devotional conceptions of the prophet Muhammad, through the memory of his deeds and sayings, in addition to his physical remains. Key related terms, often used as synonyms to *athar* are *amanat* (objects in trust), and *mukhallafat* (heritage).

Jalal al-Din's poem elegantly navigates this boundary between the immaterial and the material. The object of his devotion, the figure of the Prophet, both is and is not immediately available to the senses. That is to say, the gaze of the pilgrim reaches beyond the physical confines of simple visual observation. The "utter triumph" that Jalal al-Din's poem celebrates is precisely this availability of the Prophet, beyond the simple presence of his bodily vestiges. At the same time – and essentially so – it is these relic objects that the pilgrim encounters, views, and interprets. We saw another version of this insight at the beginning of this book, where we noted aesthetics' insistence upon access to real and individual objects. Sufi masters recognized this boundary crossing in the encounters with relics and saintly tombs, enlisting those experiences for the spiritual training of their adepts. Pilgrimage to the grave of a revered teacher was edifying because the departed spirit would continue a watchful presence over its body; a presence that the devout could approach through visual engagement with the tomb. Another explanation of this "crossing" held that vestiges or traces left behind by the long departed continue imprinted upon the sites in which those individuals once stood. We are told that in these spaces, thanks to those lingering presences, the pilgrim's heart is profoundly affected and advances in spiritual progress.[5] Identified by poets and mystics – and as we shall see below by jurists and theologians too – this is the dynamic site at which the object of devotion may resist a static or marginalizing determination, and as I have argued earlier, engage anew in negotiation of its meaning. The indeterminacy of the relic, or in less elegant but more accurate terms, the multideterminacy of the relic, will be the subject of this chapter. To tell this story, I will explore the diversity of relic practice along with the religious discourses and bodily engagements that were essential parts of it.

As a category of object, the relic is surprisingly difficult to define. In the explorations below it will become evident that there is no natural typology. I will turn more fully to the formal characteristics of these objects, but first let us consider the question of medium. What the objects are made of, and to what extent our viewing or touching the object engages with that materiality, provides a benchmark against which we can situate these objects. As we shall see, this benchmark covers a wide span of experience, ranging from witnessing absence, to encountering an impervious and immediate presence. Hans Belting gets at part of this question of the medium by pointing out its inverse relationship to form, or what he calls the image. It is in the nature of each medium to either draw our attention to itself, or to conceal itself in the image. That is to say, the more we are concerned with the image, the more its medium disappears. We saw a version of this back in the introduction where I made the point that symbolic reading displaces or erases the object status of the symbol. But Belting's contribution here is to recognize this shifting relationship between the medium and the image as undetermined and yet essential to engagement with objects. "The more attention we pay to the medium and its navigating force, the less we concentrate on the image it carries. Conversely, the less we take notice of a medium's presence, the more we are captured by the image, until it seems to us that the latter exists by itself."[6] In the context of Buddhist relics, Robert Sharf focuses on one side of this equation, one type of medium, that of human flesh and bone, and underlines the force of its presence. We are not struck by the bearing of these relics, he says, nor by what they might symbolize, rather "It is their unabashed yet impenetrable corporeality that evokes such a powerful response."[7] By corporeality Sharf is not referring primarily to the bodily origin of a relic, but rather to the immediate physical presence of the relic's medium, that is to say the body of the object, not the body of the "saint." Sharf is drawing attention to one end of the spectrum, where the relic medium arrests our attention by its brazen and startling corporeality.

However, the other kind of presence identified by Belting is also available, one that relies on us taking less notice of the medium. This sort of presence is the "visible absence" that images generate in pointing to their referent. In evoking a person or a body that is no longer there, the relic stages, or perhaps better put, witnesses that distance and absence. What I will be calling contact and imprint relics below, quickly come to mind. Here the media almost disappear as the image comes the fore to "perform" the absence that it is making visible.[8] My position, however, is not that contact relics are simply evocations of an absent original, while by contrast relics of bone and flesh are reducible to their medium. The insight is rather that between these two positions on the medium, neither of the two is more central than the other, and both are always at play in every type of relic. Every object is after all both medium and image, and at each viewing a position is taken somewhere between the two. A relic of bone can be viewed with its medium as either prominent or receding. Likewise, a contact relic can be considered primarily for its medium or the "present absent" it is indicating. And yet in their aggregate, a typology has emerged among relics, which can be made sense of in reference to their medium. Bodily relics are clearly distinguished by virtue of their corporeal medium, whether we are focused on that medium or on the person being evoked. And likewise contact relics share a type of medium, one that is marginal, circumstantial, and contingent. The leather of a sacred sandal, or the specific cloth used for a saint's preserved turban, constitute the medium, but it is a medium that is incidental, and quickly gives way to the presence of the absent.

While the medium continues as a variable within every instance of viewing, it is to its tendency in the formation of relic category that we next turn. We shall explore them more fully in the pages below, but a quick list seems in order at the outset. The first group of relics consists of body parts, in particular hair, fingernails, blood, and severed heads. I will use the term **corporeal relics** to denote this category. The second group, much less bounded than the first, is that of **contact relics**. A wide variety of objects have been preserved for the virtue and baraka they have accumulated thanks to their contact with holy persons. These may be clothing, such as a shirt, cloak, or sandal; they may be tools such as a cup, awl, or stylet; or weapons such as a sword, lance, or shield. A third category is that of **imprint relics**, bodily impressions typically left in stone – the most common examples being those of feet and hands. While these three categories account for the vast majority of relic objects, two additional categories suggest themselves. One group I am calling **animated relics**, objects that speak or move of their own volition; and the last are **stage relics**.

Often incorporated into shrines or mosques, stage relics are the locations preserved and marked off as sites of events in the lives of revered individuals.[9]

We shall return to these categories to explore their material history along with some of the religious and political contexts in which they operated. But first I would like to thematize some of the interaction or intersubjectivity that seems to be at play between the relic and its witness. By virtue of the embodied framework in which these interactions take place, it should be no surprise that multisensory registers are employed. Turning to these sensory regimes will avoid the reductive explanations that can be generated when we forget that we are dealing with experiences of real and unique objects. One such analysis sees the relics of Muhammad in just such a light. In his reading of the collection and dispersal of the Prophet's corporeal relics, Brannon Wheeler argues for a "sociogonic" or society-founding explanation. In a conventional if outdated style of mythological analysis, Wheeler equates the dismembered body of Muhammad with the foundations of Islamic civilization, and the dispersal of his body parts with the extension of the boundaries of Islamic land.[10] This approach makes little room for the individual object and its reception, locating its significance within the abstract mapping of the center of civilization against its peripheries.

For our purposes, however, insights like those of the tenth-century litterateur al-Jahiz on eloquence and meaning, are more immediately useful. As part of his theory of *bayan* (meaning) he points to the *hal* (state) of supposedly mute objects, which he claims can speak volumes to the attentive ear. A line of poetry recited before the corpse of Alexander the Great, "He could speak before, but he is more telling today," captures for al-Jahiz the many possible evocations that an object may carry. In an echo of the Qur'anic vision of creation as imbued with signs of the creator's wisdom and providence, al-Jahiz connects the "state" of a complex spider web to the perfection of the creator of all nature Allah.[11] An even more direct positioning of meaning upon the body-object is, however, possible. In an argument on embodiment as the fundamental way that individual subjects relate to each other, Terry Eagleton points out that embodiment is simultaneously the condition of our individuation and our connection to one another. He claims that, "To encounter another human body is thus to encounter indissociably, both sameness and difference. The body of the other is at once strange and familiar. It is exactly the fact that we can relate to it which highlights its otherness. Other things in the world are not strange to us in the same sense at all."[12] It is this insight into sameness as inextricable from difference that I would like to underline. While al-Jahiz's "state" of an object gestured to its unspeakable cache of evoked meanings – i.e. Alexander's corpse becomes a cipher for his conquests – Eagleton's model goes further, to close the gap between bodies through a widening of the self in the intimate experience of otherness. If this gap between viewers and relics can indeed be closed, then certain embodied and sensory impressions come to the fore. As the examples below will show, these are most characteristically experiences of pleasure (love) and fear (death).[13] My proposal is that at each viewing devotees relate to relics in ways that stimulate devotional love, while recalling the experience of death.

In this framework love is understood as the encounter with another body that reflects powerfully on one's sense of self and the universal. Expanding on Plato's *Symposium* where love is an absence seeking fulfillment in beauty and the infinite, and resonating with Eagleton's claim that nothing is so familiar and yet strange to us as the other's body, is the characterization offered by Jean-Luc Nancy of love as the intertwining of self and other. Here the presence of the other has the power to open new dimensions of the self; through the encounter of the body, the self is opened in an unbounded and uncontrolled way.[14] This experience of the beloved – at once outside and within – is visceral and sensible, yet an opening out of the self infinitely. The Sufi poet 'Umar ibn al-Farid (d. 1235) points to this consuming and liberating transformation in the context of mystical love when he writes: "By her, I departed to her / from me, never to return / one like me never speaks / of coming back... And I was made to witness / my absence when she appeared / so I found me, her there / in the bridal chamber of my seclusion."[15] From a similar perspective, a century later in Cairo Muhammad Wafa' would describe the apotheosis of love more concisely: "Serene love is the obliteration of the lover in the essence of the Beloved."[16]

Love and desire as embodied practices, however, show up at the boundary between seeing and touching, often playing back and forth across that sensory distinction. Descriptions of love between devotees and their objects of desire also flitter across the categories of sensory experience. As Margaret Miles has put it in relation to the Orthodox Christian experience, "The ultimate goal of religious desire is not vision but touch, the metaphoric touch of the visual ray or the literal touch of the kiss."[17] Here Miles is proposing a concept of "touch" wide enough to include these otherwise distinct bodily gestures. For Merleau-Ponty also, our experience of vision resists any easy division of the visual and the tactile. For him, the viewer and the object are in such an embrace that in important ways they are inseparable – the look is best described as a reaching out to gently touch, or palpate the object, rather than passively recording its form.[18] In an echo of the lover internally transformed by the encounter with the beloved, Merleau-Ponty's vision assumes both an experience in which there is no barrier between the self and the visible/touchable, and yet of course the two cannot be collapsed into one.

If love is experienced as an unlimited expansion of the self, then approaching death is a turn to the finitude and vulnerability of the body. This vulnerability is uniquely generated by relics in a way that resists the typical functioning of an image. In other words, the present absent model of an image is transformed into a "present present" model. Having lost the capacity to symbolize or to stand in for something absent, the relic denies the opening facilitated by the absent, insisting instead on its own presence. This presence at once precludes the perfection and vitality of a body that is absent, replacing it with its own brokenness and incompleteness. Thus, my claim that a relic recalls and revisits death. Rather than being a symbol for a lost person, playing a metonymic role, it is the making present of death. In the examples below, we shall see that the disjointed "not-belonging," the disaggregated and broken nature of relics, and the fear that attends them, are key to their presence.

Before we turn to particular relics and their associated viewing practices, note should be taken of the devotional discourses at play around images of the Prophet and the saints. These constitute significant resources in the conception of holy bodies and saintly appearances. Descriptions of the prophet Muhammad were collected among the hadith reports of his life and sayings, and within a little over two centuries constituted their own subcategory of religious literature known as the Virtues (*shama'il*) and Proofs (*dala'il*) of Muhammad and his prophecy. The tenth-century editor Muhammad ibn 'Isa al-Tirmidhi composed what is likely the first Virtues work.[19] There is little narrative structure across the book as a whole, and instead it presents hundreds of reports on the Prophet, thematically collected under headings such as how he kept his hair, what kinds of shoes he wore, how he walked, and how he spoke. Several personal objects, such as his weapons and his clothing, are inventoried and described. Al-Tirmidhi opens with a quote from Malik ibn Anas, "The Prophet was neither exceedingly tall nor was he short. He was neither very light nor very dark. His hair was neither curly nor completely straight and flowing."[20] Balanced and moderate personal features are enumerated, alongside humble comportment and healthy habits, all evidence of the Prophet's beauty of character and appearance. It was out of this descriptive material that textual images, known as the Ornaments of the Prophet (*hilya*, Tr. *hilye*) evolved. Beginning in the late seventeenth century, Ottoman calligraphers composed portraits of Muhammad, and occasionally of other prophets, consisting of descriptive and devotional phrases drawn from the early Virtues collections. A variety of forms were explored, but horizontal bands of text above and below a circle or crescent panel containing physical descriptions of the Prophet, were most typical. Representations of various relic objects were at times incorporated into the compositions.[21]

While the Ornament compositions never took hold in Egypt and Syria, the devotional imagining of Muhammad and other saintly figures continued in other ways – all inspired by the early Virtues and Proofs literature. The envisioning of holy figures was encouraged by the often asserted claim in the hadith literature that a dream in which the Prophet appears should be given full credence, since the devil cannot assume Muhammad's appearance.[22] Divinely inspired visions, both in a sleeping or a waking state, were also recognized as a channel for minor prophetic revelations – more specifically, containing one fortieth, fiftieth, or one seventieth of revelation.[23] Focus on the person of Muhammad though mental portraits in the course of Sufi spiritual exercises became a widespread practice. 'Abd al-Karim al-Jili (d. 1424) provided physical descriptions of Muhammad so that his students might internalize the image, and focus all the more intensely on the Prophet.[24] Beyond the didactic use of these images in devotional meditation, episodes of visionary encounters with holy figures were also common.

The saintly family of the Sadat al-Wafa'iyya, prominent in the religious life of Cairo throughout the Mamluk and Ottoman eras, were a typical source of such miraculous envisioning. One of the venerated descendants of this family of Sufi masters was shaykh Abu al-Fadl (d. 1483). An admirer, Abd al-Wahhab al-Sha'rani, recounts his dreaming encounter with the recently departed saint. It was the occasion of the celebration of the saint's day, when al-Sha'rani was visited by none other than Abu al-Fadl himself. The shaykh led him to a picnic laid out at the family shrine in the Qarafa cemetery. Sometime later, Abu al-Fadl appeared again, but now at al-Sha'rani's house, announcing: "I have come to take you and your family to live with me." To which al-Sha'rani tactfully deflected: "Tomorrow. God willing!" But the saint insisted. "He carried my daughter Ruqayya on his shoulder, and took her sister Nafisa by the hand, and together with their mother we all reached the shrine, to sit between the saint's grave and the tomb of Umm al-Sultan Kamil who is buried behind him." Al-Sha'rani recounts that the funerary dome above them opened, swinging up like a trap door, with something like cotton or white plaster continuing to fall from it, piling around them up to the saint's head. Abu al-Fadl explained that this material was the *sakinat al-haya min Allah* that is, the divinely sent tranquility of modesty, which "God would provide to whomever gazed upon it." Al-Sha'rani told his family to gaze upon it immediately.[25]

Al-Sha'rani also recounts a vision of the prophet Muhammad and his grandson Husayn. Having visited the shrine that houses the martyr Husayn's head in Cairo, al-Sha'rani's companion, shaykh Shihab al-Din, had a dreaming vision in which he saw the occupant of the shrine rise up from his grave. Shihab al-Din followed the apparition all the way to the tomb of the Prophet in Medina, where Muhammad gave the martyr instructions to embrace Shihab al-Din, and to forgive him for the doubts he once had as to whether the tomb actually contained Husayn's head.[26] The saintly founding figure of the Wafa' Sufi order related several waking visions of the Prophet, each confirming the saint as an inspired spiritual master: once as a child he was tutored in Qur'an recitation by the Prophet, and later at the age of 21 he was bestowed a white cotton shirt off the Prophet's back.[27] Manuals for dream interpretation had been written from at least the seventh century, and many dream journals from Egypt have survived.[28]

The best-known dream of the prophet Muhammad, however, is surely that of the Sufi poet al-Busiri (d. 1295). His encounter with the Prophet, and more precisely the healing relic of his mantle, evoked key concepts at play around the devotional gaze. Suffering from a condition that paralyzed one side of his body, al-Busiri petitioned Muhammad, who appeared to the poet and wrapped him in his mantle. The result was immediate, and al-Busiri awoke the next morning cured.[29] This dream evokes an episode from the early career of the Prophet in which he wrapped himself and his immediate family under his cloak. Chapters 73 and 74 of the Qur'an describe Muhammad as the "enwrapped one" – identified in the commentary literature as the shaken Muhammad sheltering under his cloak upon hearing the first revelations. Al-Busiri's dream encounter inspired the *Mantle Ode* (*Qasidat al-burda*), which would become one of the most widely recited devotional poems.

AN ATTEMPT AT CLASSIFICATION

As al-Jahiz implied earlier, for living human beings perhaps nothing is as compelling as dead bodies. That we are attached to the dead of our communities almost goes without saying. Bodily relics play on this connection, through both medium and image; that is, they are both the immediate presence of (part of) the body, and an intentional form put on display for consideration. We shall see that the responses to these objects reflect both of these dimensions.

The preservation of martyrs' blood has produced a number of corporeal relics. The blood of al-Husayn, killed at Karbala in 680 has been venerated by Sunnis, but in the Shia tradition it became a central theme in the mourning rituals that were to structure communal religious practice. We will return to the blood of al-Husayn below in relation to the relic of his severed head. Blood of other martyrs, however, was also revered. The third caliph, 'Uthman – no friend of the Shia who would see his leadership as a usurping of Ali's rightful place at the head of the community – is one case. In 656, internal strife within the Muslim community precipitated 'Uthman's assassination in Medina. Tradition has it the pious caliph was cut down while reading the Qur'an in his home, blood from his wounds marking the precious book. Ritual use of this relic is recorded from the twelfth century at the western edge of the Islamic world. The great Mosque of Cordoba would begin prayer services by removing the Qur'an, written in the 'Uthman's hand and bearing traces of his blood, from a chamber along the qibla wall, bearing it in a candlelight procession to the mosque's mihrab. Here it was placed on an ornate stand and read aloud. Under the Almohads, this Qur'an was transferred across the Mediterranean to their capital at Marrakesh, where it continued to be the focus of veneration.[30] The vehicle for the blood relic, 'Uthman's Qur'an, is doubly significant. Not only is it a record of the revelation, but according to tradition, 'Uthman established the single authoritative recension of the text, famously sending his "official" copies out to the regional capitals of the empire, with the command that all other versions be destroyed. More 'Uthmanic Qur'ans will appear in our relic inventory below.

Devotional use of relics was known from the earliest period of Islamic history – the companion Khalid ibn al-Walid had conquered Damascus with a hair of the Prophet concealed in his hat.[31] The first Islamic ruling dynasty, that of the Umayyads, seized power from the Rightly Guided caliphs, Muhammad's four immediate successors, the last of whom was 'Ali, the son-in-law and nephew of the Prophet. Ali's defeat came at the hands of Mu'a-wiyya, who perhaps because of the unfortunate association he had with the death of the Prophet's son-in-law, made a point to be known as a great lover of Muhammad's relics. Mu'awiyya was buried in a shirt that he had received from the Prophet, along with clippings of Muhammad's fingernails, and strands of hair placed in his nose and mouth as well as over his eyes.[32] The practice of collecting Muhammad's nail and hair clippings, and even his saliva, for curative purposes is attested to in the hadith literature.[33] In having relic hairs placed over his eyes, the caliph was continuing a devotional tradition that persists up into the modern period.

This ritual of the relic hairs is not so much a viewing practice as it is an engagement with the faculty of vision, with the eyes themselves. One report from the nineteenth century describes the rituals one Sufi lodge in Cairo practiced with its relic hairs. On two occasions of the year – the celebration of the Prophet's birthday, and the night of Muhammad's ascension (mi'raj) – religious and state notables gathered at the Naqshbandi lodge to witness the Sufi shaykh ceremoniously bring out a hair of the Prophet, which was kept in three ornate boxes, set one within the other, and rub it against his eyes.[34] The city of Bursa paraded its hair during the month of Ramadan, Cairo's mosque and shrine of Husayn has several housed in its relics room, open to the public on religious holidays. Examples abound across the Islamic world, from Morocco to India.[35] A hair is preserved next to the Dome of the Rock in Jerusalem.[36] Medina not only held hairs, but its Shubayka cemetery was also the resting place of a tooth of the Prophet; the Topkapi palace in Istanbul likewise contained hairs and a tooth.[37] Hairs were also venerated by incorporating them into religious architecture. We will see more examples of relics and the construction of such sacred spaces later in this chapter. For the hairs of the Prophet, the most prominent Egyptian example was that of the mosque of Siryaqus. Upon his return from a successful campaign, Sultan Barsbay fulfilled a vow made upon his departure by constructing an impressive mosque, building nine hairs of the Prophet into its mihrab.[38] Madrasas in

Damascus also had these tiny relics incorporated into their structures.[39] While the hairs are not visible, their relationship in this ritual space to worshipers seems to be twofold. The permanent presence of the relics avails the worshipers of their baraka; in fact every person to use the mosque would accrue such a benefit, even if they were not aware of what lay ensconced within the mihrab. At the same time, the position of the relic hairs within ritual architecture was clearly intended to guarantee their veneration. Although actually praying to a relic was not a ritual option, and is unknown to me in the historical record, organizing prayer space in order to channel the merit of salat was a well-established practice.[40]

Despite their great variety, bodily relics constitute a category based on their medium, which of course is the body. A second category of relics, which I am calling contact relics, is also predicated upon the body, but in a rather different way. Instead of acting as the medium, the body here is evoked and made present by the objects with which it has been in contact. The medium of these relics, again in contrast to our first category, is coincidental or inadvertent – almost any material can serve as the medium for a contact relic. While bodily relics evoke the broken and even violent ends of a person, contact relics are everyday objects pulled out of their usual environment, and repurposed as bridges to distant holy bodies. What moves across those bridges is of course baraka, the invisible but transferable currency of blessing. The contact relic serves as an inexhaustible source of contagious baraka. One example is the practice of touching the decorative grill housing the tomb of a saint or prophet, which is ubiquitous across the Islamic world. It is an engagement in the economy of baraka. This can be simply by the touch of a hand, or an object can be used as a repository. In Chapter 1, we saw examples of handkerchiefs, scarves, and even babies, being rubbed against the *mahmal* as it passed, all in order to collect baraka.

As the sense of touch is central here, so too is that of sight. Greek and Islamic theories of vision as developed among philosophers and theologians, addressed the mechanics of seeing; opposing positions usually argued for either a model intromission or extramission. Plato held an extramission theory – the eye emitting some kind of ray to its object – although Aristotle rejected this. In the second-century CE Galen proposed that the eye excites the air around it, which when reaching its object, and illuminated by the sun, constitute visual contact. Ibn Sina (d. 1037) rejected extramission, while al-Kindi (d. 873) defended a theory of extramission, with rays emanating from the eye in a cone shape.[41] In the thirteenth century, Ibn 'Arabi echoed Plato's extramission, when he described the collapsing of distance between the viewer and the object, by sight's extending outward to make contact.[42] In the following generation, Sitt 'Ajam took this further, with a complex theory of witnessing culminating in an outflowing (*jari*) from the spiritualized self onto the object of devotion.[43] Other mystics and philosophers would speak of the "eye of the heart" and the "vision of the heart."[44] Much in line with Betancourt's recent nuancing of the sight/touch divide in Byzantium, we shall see that this overlapping of what might otherwise be held as two utterly independent senses, are instead intertwined around contact relics.[45]

A survey of this type of relic reveals a wide variety of media, ranging from personal items, such as clothing, to weapons, and domestic objects. Weapons, the tools of war and symbols of authority, have a long history as relics. The Ziyada gate of the Great Mosque in Damascus once bore a piece of Khalid ibn al-Walid's lance. A companion of the Prophet, and the most prominent Muslim general of his day, he is revered by posterity for extending the boundaries of the early empire. The lance relic commemorates his providential conquering of the city of Damascus in 634.[46] Swords were, however, a more common relic from the earliest period. Muhammad's swords have been preserved, some inherited, others captured in raids and battles. They each bears a name, such as *al-Rasub* (the penetrating) or *al-'Adb* (the cutting), and often come with origin stories. Early tradition records a raid in which 'Ali was dispatched to plunder and destroy the rival shrine center of Manah. 'Ali carried away two swords, which had been donated to the shrine by the king of the Ghassanids. As a reward for his service, Muhammad gave *al-Rasub* and *al-Mikhdam* to 'Ali.[47] Another sword, *Dhu al-Faqar* (the notched), given to 'Ali by the Prophet at the battle of Uhud, would play an important role in later Islamic iconography, with its split end constituting a double-headed sword. The *Sira* records Muhammad as saying: "There is no sword but Dhu al-Faqar, and no hero but 'Ali!"[48] Holding the swords of the Prophet and his companions became a part of any claim to leadership of the Muslim umma. In the eleventh century, to assert his independence from his Fatimid overlords, the amir of Mecca not only appropriated the caliph's title of Commander of the Faithful, but he also claimed to possess among other relics, the famous *Dhu al-Faqar*.[49] The Fatimids themselves claimed to have the swords of the Prophet and several of his companions, stowed away in their Cairo armory. With the overthrow of the Fatimids and the plundering of their treasuries, the swords were expropriated by the Abbasid rulers.[50] The history and the provenance of the surviving swords are unclear – one is preserved in the Husayn shrine in Cairo – but their association with imperium continued well into the modern period. In the Topkapi palace, the heart of the Ottoman empire, no fewer than 30 have been collected, joined at some point by lances, bows, and shields, all displayed as relics.[51]

Another set of contact relics, more evenly distributed across the religious landscape, was that of clothing. These objects were more ritually accessible, and thus more engaged with gazing and touching practices. The veneration of prophetic sandals in Damascus is particularly striking in this regard. The

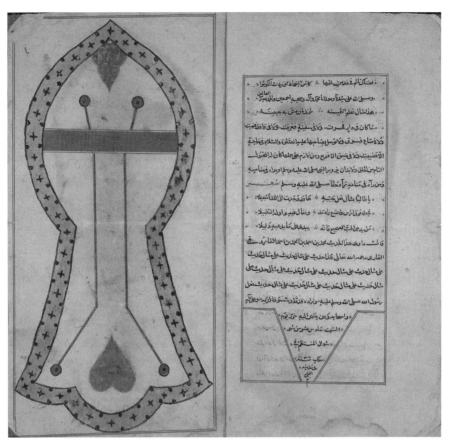

34 The Prophet's sandal. Credit: From MS *These Are the Virtues of the Tracing of the Prophet's Sandal* (*Hadhihi siffa timthal na'l al-Nabi*) by Ahmad ibn Muhammad Abi Bakr al-Fariqi al-Qadiri. The National Library of Israel Ms. Yah. Ar. 353

Ayyubid ruler al-Malik Ashraf was very fond of this relic. In 1228 he had one installed in his newly completed madrasa college, named Dar al-Hadith al-Ashrafiyya. This was not the only sandal in town, however, and 12 years later the Madrasa Dammaghiyya would be founded, displaying another sacred sandal. Although Ashraf's relic would eventually be looted by the invading Mongol Tamerlane in 1401, it enjoyed a great deal of attention in the interim. Ashraf touted its virtues, and encouraged others to visit it and gaze upon it. It could also go on the road; Ashraf had it sent to Ba'albekk so that an elderly admirer could venerate it. This was the grandmother of the historian al-Yunini, who records the episode in his *Dhayl mir'at al-zaman*.[52] As a devotional object, the sandal – often reduced to an iconic minimum, as pictured in Figure 34 – would give rise to a significant literature.[53] Ashraf's devotion to the relic endured to the end of his life. A report has come down from 1237, the year of his death, which describes him in the madrasa, taking the sandal in his

35 Al-Badawi's relic case: Tanta. Credit: Photo courtesy of Iman Abdulfattah

hands, kissing it, placing it upon his eyes, and weeping.[54] As with the devotional encounters with the hairs of the Prophet we noted above, al-Malik al-
Ashraf engages the relic with a combination of seeing and touching, two
versions of contact with the eyes.

In the mid thirteenth century, we have notice of the iron stirrups of the
Prophet, one of which was sent from Damascus to Baghdad. The historian Ibn
Hajar al-Asqalani tells us that the Caliph received it and placed it in the
Abbasid treasury along with the Prophet's cloak (*burda*) and staff.[55] In
sixteenth-century Istanbul, a royal ritual was developed for mid-Ramadan,
in which the Sultan washed the *burda* mantle preserved in the Topkapi palace.
The soiled water was preserved, bottled, and handed out as gifts to the Sultan's
favorites.[56] In the mid-nineteenth century, the mosque of the Noble Cloak
(*Hirka Sherif*) was purpose-built to store and display the Prophet's *burda* during
Ramadan. Part of the cloak is preserved in the Husayn collection in Cairo.[57]
The great shrine of Ahmad al-Badawi (d. 1276) in the Egyptian Delta houses
some of the saint's relics. His turban, cloak, and large prayer beads can be seen
in Figure 35. Not all relic practices, however, have stood the test of time.
Under the funerary dome of Qalawun's Mansuriyya complex, built in 1285,
some of the clothing of the Sultan and his successors was preserved in a
wardrobe locker at his graveside. The function and display of these articles of
clothing is not clear, although the space was used for religious ceremonials,

including day and night Qur'an recital, Sufi gatherings, and prayer.[58] It is not clear how long this wardrobe was preserved.

The Topkapi relics collection holds several items of clothing, including Muhammad's sandals, a shawl that belonged to his wife Aisha, robes belonging to al-Husayn and Abu Hanifa, a bowl that belonged to the Sufi poet Rumi, and the caps and turbans of 'Abd al-Qadir al-Jilani, al-Sha'rani, and Uways al-Qarani, three important figures in the history of Sufism.[59] The trade in caps of important Muslim figures seems to have been strong; we are told that upon his death, Ibn Taymiyya's personal items, like the water used to wash his corpse and a cord he used to wear around his neck, were all sold. His cap apparently brought 500 dirhams.[60] Once in contact with the body of a venerated person, even waste water was recognized for its powers to bless and consecrate. Tradition has it that when the prophet Muhammad had suggested the Arab Christians of the region of Yamama tear down their church and put up a mosque in its place, he provided them with his ablution water to help purify the ground.[61]

Personal domestic items could also be taken as relics. In addition to the various examples of clothing just noted, jewelry is also notable. The signet ring of Muhammad is mentioned several times in the hadith literature, and the tradition recalls the powers of Solomon's magical ring. A square stone sat above the mihrab of the mosque al-Walid built in Medina; highly polished, it was said to have been the mirror of Muhammad's wife Aisha.[62] While not a prophet in the fullest sense, Mary holds a prominent place in the Qur'an. A pair of her earrings was stored in the Ka'ba until 930, when the Carmathians overran Mecca and made away with the Black Stone, the horn of Abraham's ram, and Mary's jewelry.[63] Some 40 years later, the Fatimid Caliph al-Hakim sent an envoy to collect relics from the house of Ja'far al-Sadiq in Medina. They returned with several objects, including the Prophet's cup.[64] The *Ribat al-Athar* on the banks of Nile, and eventually the Husayn mosque, held several personal objects as relics. The Prophet's kohl jar and applicator are preserved there, along with tweezers, an awl for piercing leather, and a piece from a broken bowl.[65]

Written documents may also serve as contact relics. We saw earlier the bloodied Qur'an of 'Uthman ritually circulated in the Great Mosque of Cordoba. Qur'ans written in his hand were also preserved in Damascus, where they were powerful relics. In 1148, with the Crusaders besieging the city, the precious codex was brought out of the Umayyad mosque to join in communal prayers for divine aid. Beyond these rites in times of crisis – recall in Chapter 2 above, scriptures parading outside of Cairo during times of drought – this Qur'an copied in the Caliph's own hand regularly received pilgrims, who through their pious gaze sought the blessings of the Codex (*al-tabarruk bi-nazar al-mushaf*).[66] An incomplete copy of the Qur'an made in 650 in the hand of

Zayd ibn Thabit was preserved in the haram enclosure of the Ka'ba, and used in ritual supplication for relief in times of famine.[67] Muhammad himself had also left written documents. The biography of the Prophet notes his sending letters to the "kings of the Arabs and the non-Arabs," inviting them to join the new religion of Islam. These included the rulers of Oman, Bahrain, Egypt (i.e. Muqauqis of Alexandria), the Caesar of Rome (i.e. the Byzantine emperor Heraclius), the Negus of Abyssinia, the governor of Syria, and Khusraw II the Persian king of kings.[68] Some of these letters are preserved in the Topkapi relics collection, with the letter to Muqauqis having only been discovered in the mid-nineteenth century in an Egyptian monastery.[69]

Another contact relic associated with the Prophet was a piece of wood preserved in a pillar standing in the *rawda*, or courtyard, of Muhammad's house in Medina. In his twelfth-century travelogue, Ibn Jubayr describes pilgrims kissing it and rubbing their cheeks against it. This wood was from the palm tree that had miraculously moaned and cried when Muhammad left it, once a minbar had been built for him to preach from. To quiet the tree's anxiety, the Prophet came down from his minbar, placing his hands on it, at which point its crying ceased.[70]

The minbar in this story itself also became a revered object. It consisted originally of a seat upon two steps, which the caliph Mu'awiyya had raised upon a platform, adding six additional steps. Ibn Jubayr reports on crowds of people gathering around the minbar to rub their hands on the seat, and then upon themselves to gather the baraka. In the thirteenth century this minbar was lost in a fire.[71] Additional accounts of now lost prophetic relics have come down to us. While on the Hajj in 1050, Nasir Khusraw gained entrance to the Ka'ba, where he found planks from Noah's ark. In pairs, these were fastened to the wall at three of the corners of the shrine by silver nails.[72] These relics did not become a permanent feature of the Ka'ba. In fact, Nasir Khusraw's seems to have been the only report of their presence there. Although their career in the Ka'ba may have been short-lived, they reappear briefly three centuries later in Cairo. Al-Sha'rani relates a Sufi claim that Noah preserved a plank from the Ark with the name of 'Ali ibn Abi Talib inscribed on it. Thanks to its miraculous powers, 'Ali ascended to heaven riding on the plank.[73]

Seeing and touching are further intertwined in our next category, that of imprint relics, also known as petrosomatoglyphs. The impressions made by holy feet, hands, elbows, and heads, cross the boundaries that normally separate the body, in its fleshy malleable presence, from the hard and inert presence of stone. The imprint signals an absence, but just as importantly, it is a record of presence. The force of imprint relics lies not in their ability to capture and preserve the appearance of an original body, but rather in their recording with precision a one-time contact, allowing the pilgrim to share that space and place. While the imprint miraculously violates the natural physical properties of both stone and flesh, it also connects the pilgrim and the object of devotion by capturing and making available the location of that holy body. Pilgrims can thus share the space, collapsing the distances of space and time that lie between them and the saintly body. In a poem about the imprints at the Ribat al-Athar, al-Nabulusi wove together these elements of seeing, touching, and location:

> Ta Ha (Q. 20:1), the Messenger's passionate heart,
>> Most noble, he trod upon this rock.
> Although my eye has missed him,
>> It contents itself to see his relic (athar).

And in the following verses:

> We gather 'round the Prophet's foot in Egypt,
>> Blessed by its radiant light.
> Upraised under a mighty dome,
>> Its light as bright as lightning flashes.
> Upon him lie the exalted adornments and secrets,
>> Guiding hearts to recall their original covenant (with God).
> The fate of the pilgrim's felicity and aspiration,
>> Shall be determined by him.
> A noble relic has shown itself in stone,
>> And those who lay hands on it will be cured of their ills.[74]

Here al-Nabulusi speaks of his visionary engagement with the trace of the Prophet. Further, contact through the pilgrims' hands – seeking Muhammad's intercession and relief from affliction – intensifies the interaction.

Imprints of hands and fingers were readily available to facilitate contact with the Prophet and other important figures. In the pre-Wahhabi period, the landscape of Mecca was dotted with sacred sites that were identified by their imprint relics. We read of pilgrims visiting a variety of sites associated with the Prophet and the earliest Muslim community. In 1184, Ibn Jubayr visited the house of the Prophet's birth. The precise spot was indicated by an impression in the floor of the house, accompanied by a green marble plaque, framed in silver. The pilgrim rubbed his cheeks upon the impression.[75] An early sixteenth-century painting by Muhy al-Din Lari shows a small building at the bottom of the composition, marked as "location of the birth" (Figure 36). The early historian of Mecca, al-Azraqi, tells us that upon the Hijra migration to Medina, the house was sold to 'Ali's older brother, 'Aqil ibn Abi Talib, who had not yet embraced Islam. It was by the patronage of the most formidable woman of her age, Khayzuran, the wife of one caliph and the mother or two more, that the site was transformed. While on the Hajj in 788, she bought the house, expanded it, and turned it into a place of prayer.[76] In the mid sixteenth century the building was renovated, or perhaps rebuilt, by order of the Ottoman Sulayman the Magnificent.[77] At some point, however, pilgrimage was suppressed, and the building was turned into a library. In 1951, the

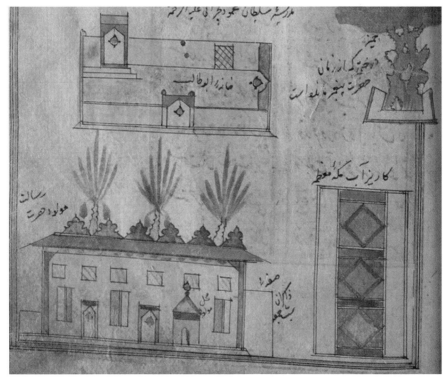

36 Location of the Prophet's birth. Credit: From the MS *The Book of Longing* (*Kitab shawq-nama*) by Ali Husayni. 49 fols, 24 color drawings. 23.3 × 15 cm. National Maritime Museum, Haifa, Inv. No. 4576. Given by Mr. Joseph Soustiel

building was replaced by a modern construction, which was given over to the Sa'udi Ministry of Information, and then the Ministry of Pious Endowments, continuing to serve as a library.[78]

Pilgrims also visited the house of al-Arqam, the building in which Muhammad and his earliest followers secretly met to practice the new faith.[79] In Ibn Jubayr's day, an attached building housed pilgrims in rented rooms. In the main room, which lay under an exquisite dome, one found the Prophet's seat, a simple stone upon which he sat. To the right, one found the places of Abu Bakr and 'Ali ibn Abi Talib. This stone was anchored in the wall, like a mihrab. We are reminded that it was in this house that 'Umar converted to Islam. Ibn Jubayr proclaims that, "God has graced us with the blessings of these noble sites and venerated relics, so that we may end our days in loving devotion to those who have honored these places and given their names to them – May God's praises be upon them all."[80] The queen-mother, Khayzuran, also acquired this site, and developed it for religious pilgrimage.[81] In the modern period, under the Wahhabi regime, the building was closed to visitors, and given over to a family as a private residence. While on Hajj at the turn of the twentieth century, the Egyptian novelist Muhammad Husayn Haykal recalls the importance of this occluded site, and laments such a loss "to the spiritual heritage of the world."[82]

Another important stop on the pilgrim's route was the house of the Prophet's first wife, Khadija. She spent her adult life in this home, where she gave birth to their children, four girls, and two boys who died in their youth. When the Hijra took place, the house was sold to 'Aqil ibn Abi Talib, who eventually sold the property to the caliph Mu'awiyya. The site was transformed into a square-roomed building, replacing its older round style, typical of Meccan houses in the pre-Islamic era. The original home included two covered rooms, and an uncovered courtyard in two sections, all of which Mu'awiyya preserved, and to which he attached a mosque. One of the original rooms was called the Dome of Revelation, where Muhammad would sit when he received the revelation of the Qur'an. Mu'awiyya's new rectangular prayer space, half of which was covered, had its own entrance, a mihrab, and was divided lengthwise by pillars supporting seven arches. Fatima was born in this house, with the exact spot being marked by an impression in a round stone, in which sat a black stone.[83] In the same room, Fatima gave birth to her two sons, al-Hasan and al-Husayn. The spot, against a wall, was indicated by two dark stones. Ibn Jubayr also mentions an impression in one of the walls of Khadija's house, marking the spot where Muhammad used to sit, sheltered by a stone ledge extending out from the wall. As part of his pilgrimage, Ibn Jubayr rubbed his cheeks on these sacred places, each of which was covered by a small cupola in wood, which the pilgrim lifted, in order to touch the site.[84]

At some point before the mid-seventeenth century, the shrine hosted regular devotionals, which included weekly prayers of remembrance (*dhikr*) and a yearly celebration of Fatima's birth – something that had become a widespread observance throughout the Islamic world commemorating saints, prophets, and various descendants of Muhammad.[85] The site was kept in this form, receiving upkeep and renovations over the centuries thanks to various 'Abbasid, Mamluk, and Ottoman rulers. This changed in the early twentieth century, when the site was repurposed as a Qur'an school, thanks to the efforts of the mayor of Mecca, Shaykh 'Abbas Qattan, who had also been behind the redevelopment of the house of Muhammad's birth.[86] The three-story Qur'an school itself was demolished in 1989, to make way for expansion of the Sacred Mosque. A brief archeological survey was allowed, before the site was covered over.[87]

In an account of his late nineteenth-century Hajj, the Azhari scholar Isma'il al-Hamidi describes stones in and around Mecca bearing imprints of the Prophet's elbow, hand, and his back as he leaned on a large stone. Al-Suyuti (d. 1505) mentions the imprints of the Prophet's elbow and shoulder upon the wall of Abu Bakr's house in Mecca, which then became known as the Alley of the Elbow. Commenting on these accounts, Ahmad Taymur suspects that the relics were destroyed by 'Abd al-'Aziz ibn Sa'ud when he seized the Najd region in 1925.[88]

Despite the Saudi regime's hostility toward relics, the history of these objects shows clearly that they figured prominently in the religious landscape of the region. In al-Harawi's twelfth-century pilgrimage guide, relics of all sorts are identified and mapped out as stages in the regional itineraries of pious travelers. In the city of Hims, 'Ali appeared in dreams to local inhabitants telling them that imprints of his fingers were to be found upon a stone column in his *mashhad,* the shrine of the Prince of Believers.[89] The Mosque of Abraham, in the citadel complex of Aleppo, incudes a stone venerated from at least the eleventh century – which the prophet is believed to have rested upon.[90] In the southern Qarafa cemetery of Cairo, above the tomb of Ibn al-Farid, lies another shrine, that of the Stone of Moses, which bears the imprint of his fingers left when he was hiding from Pharaoh.[91] With a few days travel up the Nile, the pilgrim is encouraged to visit an imprint of the hand of Jesus, preserved in the Coptic Church of the Hand.[92] The city of Nisibin in northern Syria boasted an imprint of 'Ali's hand in the oratory of the Roman Gate, and the Iraqi city of Mada'in, the ancient Ctesiphon, preserved another of 'Ali's handprints. A Baghdad cemetery was the site of a lodge (*zawiya*) in which was found a stone bearing the imprints of 'Ali's fingers.[93] Baghdad also had the Shrine of the Palm. In the early eleventh century, the Prophet appeared to a woman in a dream telling her of his handprint on the qibla wall. Restoration after the flooding of 1010 was an occasion to further highlight the relic, with the addition of a sandal wood plaque, clamped in silver, identifying the imprint, which sat behind a protective railing.[94]

Other well-known imprints are those associated with the Sakhra Rock in Jerusalem. Famously, it bears the impressions of the fingers of the angel Gabriel, who had placed his hand upon it in order to prevent it from floating upward, to follow Muhammad as he made his heavenly ascension (*mi'raj*). During his 1047 visit to Jerusalem, Nasir Khusraw described seven footprints attributed to Isaac sunken into the large unfinished stone.[95] A century and a half later, with the city under Crusader rule, 'Ali of Herat claims that the footprints on the Rock are actually those of Muhammad.[96] The late fifteenth-century writer Shams al-Din Suyuti, also attributes the footprints to the Prophet, but reduces their number to one, and locates it on a separate smaller stone next to the Rock.[97] In the modern period, some have attributed the footprints on the nearby stone to the Qur'anic prophet Idris, who also ascended to the heavens.[98] Below the Rock, is the Cave of the Souls, with its stone ceiling that apparently made way for the Prophet so he would not strike his head while praying, leaving a permanent indentation.[99]

Footprint relics constitute the largest category of imprints, and a typical set of visual and tactile practices has developed around them. Since an empty space might seem hard to use as a relic, two prominent strategies were developed. The first was framing, and the second was the use of water as an intermediary between the negative space located in hard stone and the human body. The writer and pilgrim al-Nabulusi describes some of this in his account of a visit to the Sakhra. He describes a small silver dome being set up on the Rock over the Prophet's footprints. Out of concern for theft, he notes that a grille of yellow copper with two doors in it was placed over the silver dome. In addition to the double framing of the grille surrounding the dome, al-Nabulusi also provides us an account of the pilgrims' interactions with the imprints. He tells us that the space was opened to the devout upon their arrival, allowing them to stroke the blessed relic while reciting blessings and prayers. The shrine attendants sprinkled the imprints with rose water, which the pilgrims then took up with their hands and wiped across their faces. The visit ended with attendants reciting verses celebrating the wonders of this "sign of flesh and blood appearing within hard stone."[100] Al-Nabulusi is describing the impressions upon the Rock, confirming accounts going back to the early twelfth century. Ibn Kathir (d. 1373) described these prints as resting on columns next to the Rock, as they had from as far back as the early 1190s.[101] On the Mount of Olives, not far from the Dome of Rock, the graves of several early Muslim figures were visited, along with the imprints of Jesus, venerated by both Muslims and Christians.[102]

Near Mecca, another site associated water with prophetic imprints. At the caravan halting spot known as Majid Pond, a shelter was constructed over the nearby spot where Muhammad stood on one foot, his right foot, to pray for rain. Muhy al-Din Lari's Persian pilgrimage manual renders both the shrine immediately above the pond and the rock (on the far left) bearing the footprint in Figure 37. The site regularly received visitors, who brought votives to the shrine, and rubbed their faces against the imprint.[103] Ibn Jubayr tells us that water drawn from the well of Zamzam is drunk out of the stone at the Ka'ba bearing the footprints of Abraham (maqam Ibrahim). Describing his visit, he praises his Lord, "who has softened this stone under the passing foot, leaving its trace; a foot that left no imprint on the softest sand." The relic made a strong impression on pilgrims, and one feels a "pious fear that shakes the soul, and rattles the heart and the mind." These pilgrims, with lowered gaze, eyes swollen with tears, humble themselves and praise their Lord.[104] Less central was the Prophet's footprint that once sat in the south wall of the Haram mosque, at the Gate of Felicity. According to the eleventh-century traveler Nasir Khusraw, the impression was made in black stone, which had been cut out and set into a white stone, presumably already within the wall, and oriented so that the toes faced inward toward the Ka'ba. For blessings, some pilgrims placed their foreheads upon the impression, while others slid their feet into the impressions.[105]

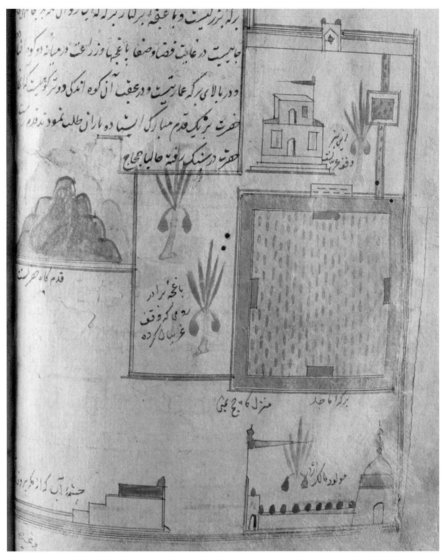

37   Muhammad's footprint near Mecca. Credit: From the MS *The Book of Longing* (*Kitab shawq-nama*) by Ali Husayni. 49 fols, 24 color drawings. 23.3 × 15 cm. National Maritime Museum, Haifa, Inv. No. 4576. Given by Mr. Joseph Soustiel

In Cairo, a popular imprint relic could be found in the tomb of Sultan Qaytbay (d. 1496). Located in the northern Qarafa cemetery, the complex includes a mosque and lodgings, along with a mausoleum. Lying near the sultan are the graves of his son and sister. The mausoleum houses two imprints in black stone, one near the head of Qaytbay, which bears the faint imprint of Muhammad's two feet, and a second near his sister's grave, which is the more sharply defined single footprint of Abraham (Figure 38). The late seventeenth-century traveler al-Nabulusi visited the site twice, and describes inscribed domes of silver and copper installed over the relics. He recites from the

Qur'an, adds supplicatory *du'a* prayers, and kisses the imprints.[106] Another traveler from the same period also visited the relics, and describes rose water being sprinkled on the imprints, which pilgrims would rub on their hands, faces, and heads in hopes of acquiring baraka.[107] These relics were clearly accorded great value. Various accounts have circulated, and one story has the Sultan buying the imprints for his mausoleum at a price of twenty thousand dirhams; another suggests he appropriated them from a madrasa in the Bulaq neighborhood, after the death of its founder Shams al-Din ibn al-Zaman.[108] The relics were so prized that even from the afterlife, Sultan Qaytbay would jealously guard them. After a visit to the relics, the Ottoman Sultan Ahmad I reportedly had them transferred to Istanbul. Later in a dream, in which

38 Footprint in Mausoleum of Qaytbay. Credit: Photo courtesy of Iman Abdulfattah

Qaytbay pleaded his case to the Prophet, it was made clear to the Ottoman Sultan that the relics must be returned to their rightful place in Cairo.[109]

Footprint relics were also found at the Convent of the Relics of the Prophet (Ribat Athar al-Nabi). We shall return to the evolution of this site below, but for the moment let us consider the imprints and the practices associated with them. The site was a popular destination for visitors, and because of its proximity to Ruda Island, seems to have often been part of the pilgrimage itinerary that included the Nilometer.[110] The mediating role of water is again apparent. The Nilometer, which measured the level of the rising river waters, in many ways served as a shrine; the Qur'anic inscriptions and its function as a place for supplicatory rituals clearly suggest this – as we noted in Chapter 3. In 1373, fearing an impending drought, the caliph joined other religious leaders at the site to pray for rain. Some from among the religious class brought relics associated with the Prophet and ritually washed them in the well of the Nilometer.[111] Specifics have not come down to us, but these may have been relics taken from the Ribat Athar al-Nabi. In 1504, Sultan al-Ghawri brought relics to the Nilometer, as part of the public invocations petitioning the Nile waters to rise.[112]

The Ribat Athar al-Nabi housed the footprint of the Prophet, which one pilgrim writing around 1680 describes as resting in a niche, submerged in rose water, and covered with a silver lid. Enthralled visitors would throw themselves on the ground before the relic.[113] A report from a decade later describes the sprinkling of rose water upon the footprint, in a vault on the qibla wall, and concealed behind a curtain. Crowds prayed beside the relic, and some recited laudatory verses.[114] The precise positioning and display of the imprint is unclear; the immersion in water in the earlier account would require a horizontal positioning, while the later account of a curtain hanging before it suggests a vertical display. We shall see later in this chapter that the current relic does not appear in the shrine until much later.

Footprint relics play a prominent role in other Egyptian shrines, with the most notable being that next to the grave of Sayyid Badawi in the Delta city of Tanta. The yearly celebration of the saint's day in early October attracts vast numbers of pilgrims. A footprint of the Prophet is on display near the saint's grave, in a cabinet built behind a gilded frame, across a corner wall. Descriptions from the fifteenth century confirm the presence of such imprints at the shrine in apparently the same location.[115] The modern inscriptions inside the cabinet are of the Islamic profession of faith, and the text running horizontally above the frame reads, "Truly God and His angels confer blessings upon the Prophet," which is from Qur'an 33:65 – with the unwritten remainder of the verse running, "O ye who believe, call for blessings and peace upon him" (Figure 39). Footprints of the Prophet were also reported to be preserved upon green stone, in the shrine-mosque of one of Sayyid Badawi's disciples, Marzuq al-Yamani. South of Cairo along the Nile, nearing the Fayyoum oasis, an open-air imprint of the Prophet's foot could be found east of the station (*maqam*) of the enigmatic saint Uways al-Qarani.[116]

In Chapter 2, in relation to the Hajj parades leaving southward out of Damascus, we noted the Sa'diyya shrine, which marked one of the ritual stopping points. Nearby is found the town of Qadam, which from at least the turn of the thirteenth century, boasted a shrine in whose mihrab sat a stone bearing footprints; sources differ on the identity of these imprints, some said they were those of Moses, others claimed they were Muhammad's.[117] In the nineteenth century, Isabel Burton reported on this mosque, but located the imprint of the foot upon a windowsill. She was told that a second imprint, that of the angel Gabriel, had sat on an adjoining sill, but that it had been removed to Istanbul.[118] While these two accounts sound irreconcilable, it would be reasonable to propose that at some point the moveable relic in the mihrab went missing – perhaps stolen, sold, or appropriated by an Ottoman Sultan. As a pious fiction, this event may have been re-narrativized as the loss of an imprint of Gabriel, leaving open the possibility that the Prophet's imprint had remained. The latter could rather easily have been "discovered" on the windowsill, preserving the shrine's status and its future as a pilgrimage site. The early thirteenth-century pilgrimage guide of al-Harawi also describes the

39 Footprints in Al-Badawi's shrine. Credit: Photo courtesy of Iman Abdulfattah

relic of the foot of 'Ali, impressed upon a large rock, housed in the Bitter
Orange Mosque (*masjid al-naranj*) on the banks of the Qalit river. This relic,
however, survived only a century longer. In the year 1305, the jurist and
moralist Ibn Taymiyya rallied a mob, among them some local stone-cutters,
and attacked the mosque and stone. The jurist's student, Ibn Kathir, celebrated
the destruction of the relic as a blow against superstitious practices.[119]

Imprint relics have also been left by notable animals. The mythical al-Buraq,
a winged white steed, smaller than a mule yet bigger than a donkey, famously

carried the Prophet on his night journey from Mecca to Jerusalem, and upwards on his heavenly ascension. The story appears in the hadith literature, where various descriptions of the steed are offered. Several sources note the hole at the side of the Sakhra Rock, where Buraq was tied, while the Prophet made his ascension.[120] The hoofprints of al-Buraq are preserved upon a small separate section of the Rock, which in the modern period is found under its own small dome.[121] Although no longer extant, Ibn Jubayr described a mosque on the Nile, dedicated to Abraham and preserving the hoofprints of his mount.[122]

The traveler Isabel Burton mentions a footprint of the Prophet's camel, preserved at al-Qadam outside of Damascus. I have not found supporting claims in the written sources for such an identification, but the site's close association with the *mahmal* camel makes such a relic almost foreseeable.[123] This camel also apparently left imprints in the Syrian city of Bursa. The shrine of the kneeling she-camel (*mabrak al-naqa*), built in the early twelfth century, housed a stone bearing her knee prints.[124] The historian of Arabia, al-Hamdani, reports that two mosques in Sana'a were built over the kneeling-place of the Prophet's she-camel.[125] It was not only Muhammad's mounts who were responsible for such imprints. In al-Harawi's pilgrimage guide, mention is made of a relic associated with the camel of the prophet Salih. This warner had been sent to the people of Thamud in northern Arabia. They were tested with a command to allow Salih's she-camel to forage and roam freely in their territory, but their impudence led them to ham-string her, prompting divine chastisement (Q. 7:75–79, 11:65–68). Although the site was apparently lost by the time al-Harawi was writing, he claims there once was a *mashhad* shrine of Salih in the Syrian town of Qinnasrin, which preserved the she-camel's hoofprint in stone.[126] Ibn Battuta, however, claims the spot is south of Tabuk, where a mosque used to mark the spot of the camel's kneeling, and where pilgrims still gather to pray.[127]

Within this typological sketch, note must also be made of animated objects. In both their speech and movement, these otherwise inanimate objects miraculously display obeisance and homage. One example we met earlier as a contact relic is that of the weeping palm, which needed to be consoled by Muhammad after he abandoned it in favor of the newly installed minbar. A portion of the tree's wood was preserved, displayed in a pillar standing in the courtyard of the Prophet's house. While this example constitutes a contact relic by virtue of the Prophet's touch, it is also a relic thanks to its miraculous animation. A further example of animated relics is that of the stones that spoke to the Prophet, who had come to pay a visit to his companion 'Umar, telling him that the latter was away. Pilgrimage guides of the early sixteenth century encouraged visitors to stop and pay their respects at the enclosure built over these stones.[128] Richard Burton describes the site of the stone that blessed

Muhammad and informed him that Abu Bakr, for whom Muhammad had been knocking at the door, was away. We are told the miraculous stone, reddish-black in color, about a foot wide, was fixed within a wall, and attended by servants.[129]

A much larger oratory was built over another stone, the famous Sakhra in Jerusalem, which also performed miraculous deeds. On the night of his ascension, when Muhammad approached it, in response to the Prophet's greeting, the Stone said, "I am here at your service! Peace be upon you, prophet of God." After Muhammad had prayed near the Rock, in a gesture of respect, it stood up straight. The Prophet placed his hand upon it to set it back into place, although it remains partially raised, presumably to make space for the cave beneath it.[130] Animated relics may also be found among the legacies of Muslim saintly figures. The patron saint of Damascus, Shaykh Arslan (d. cir. 1145–1146), worked for 20 years as a carpenter. His prized tool was a saw, which on occasion miraculously spoke to him. Arslan knew he was destined for greater things than carpentry when one day the saw broke itself into pieces, and told him to take up the life of religious devotion. One of the shaykh's students was buried with a piece of the saw, wrapped in his funeral shroud.[131]

Devotional obedience was also displayed by the tree that upon hearing Muhammad's call that it come to him, pulled up its roots and shuffled across the ground, to present itself before the Prophet. Having displayed the appropriate reverence, the tree was then ordered to return to its original place. This site, just outside Mecca, was preserved, and in commemoration the *Mosque of the Tree* was built over it.[132] This memorial practice – one that marks off and preserves a location – constitutes our final category, that of the stage relic. In a recent survey of the Alid shrines of Syria, Stephennie Mulder nicely captures the sense of many such sacred sites. To her eyes, these places together constitute a "landscape of deeds," a map that marks the actions of holy figures.[133] The twelfth-century writer al-Muqaddasi would have approved of Mulder's term, as his impressions are similar. He opens his description of greater Syria, with a dizzying list of sites, many of which commemorate holy deeds. Bilad al-Sham he tells us is the refuge and tomb of Abraham, the habitation and the wells of Job, the oratory and gate of David, the wonders of Solomon (Q. 27:18–19), the tomb of Isaac and his mother, the birth place of the Messiah and his cradle, the village and river of Saul, the place where Goliath fell, the prison of Jeremiah, the dome and gate of Muhammad, the Rock of Moses, the oratory of John, the villages of Job, and the habitations of Jacob, the Mount of Olives and the grave of Moses, the meeting place of the two seas (Q. 18:60), the dividing place of the two worlds (Q. 57:13), and the station of the Ka'ba.[134] Building upon Mulder's term "landscape of deeds," my category of stage relics emphasizes the status of each site in its peculiarity and uniqueness, requiring preservation, framing, and marking. As a site, a stage, and an object, such relics function as the legacy and inheritance from holy actors, but also importantly, these sites must be preserved, and not repurposed to serve other functions. In other words, if a stage relic has been put to alternative uses subsequently, it loses its status as a relic; framing makes room for the relics to negotiate their meaning, and to make their claims.

A fine example of such stage relics is found in the village of Quba, on the southern edge of Medina. Ibn Jubayr describes a section of the mosque that has been cordoned off, preserved as the place where the Prophet's camel lay down. He notes that this stage relic drew pilgrims to it, seeking its baraka, and considering prayers performed near it to be particularly effective.[135] In his description of the Umayyad mosque in Damascus, Ibn Jubayr mentions another stage relic. Across the courtyard from the shrine-mosque to 'Ali, a section of the colonnaded wall is draped with a curtain, marking the spot that Muhammad's daughter A'isha used to sit and collect hadith reports.[136] Examples of stage relics abound. Earlier, we noted another preserved site, a shrine outside of the city of Kufa, built over the spot where the camel carrying 'Ali's corpse knelt to rest. At Mount Abu Qubays near Mecca, a site associated with the Prophet and his family is preserved. In a cave lies a black stone marking the place where Muhammad once sat. Further up in the cave is the trough of his daughter Fatima, where she kneaded dough for bread to feed her family.[137] Several locations were marked in the architecture of the Temple Mount, including the mihrab of Mary, the spot where an angel brought her food during her seclusion, and the Cradle of Jesus, the place from which he miraculously spoke in defense of his mother's virtue.[138]

Pilgrims were also encouraged to visit the site of Muhammad's birth in Mecca. Al-Azraqi describes the location of Muhammad's birth briefly, noting it had been turned into a mosque.[139] In 1184, Ibn Jubayr visited this building, and the impression, three hand spans wide, indicating the spot where Muhammad's mother Amina had given birth to him. This stage relic, against which pilgrims could rub their cheeks for baraka, was identified by a green marble slab, framed in silver. We noted earlier (Figure 36) Muhy al-Din Lari's representation of the place of the Prophet's birth. Although Lari locates it outside of the house-mosque, this seems to be simply a techinique adopted by the illustrator to more clearly present the stage relic.

The site where Mohammad unfurled his battle flag was memorialized, and preserved as the Mosque of the Banner (masjid al-raya). It is mentioned in the sixteenth century, and stands today as a small unadorned mosque.[140] The earliest commemorative locations, however, were a camping spot at al-Batha' and the gorge leading to the Hajj site of Muzdalifa, which were visited by the early Muslim community specifically in memory of the Prophet.[141] Several such locations are listed in the later pilgrimage literature. These include the homes of the Prophet's companions and members of his family, as well as locations identified with episodes in the Qur'an, such as the valley of ants that Solomon spoke to, or the cave of blood in Damascus identified with Cain and Abel. These sites have not been included among our stage relics since they lack framing, which as we have seen above may take various forms, such as cupolas, plaques, or strategically placed black/dark stones. It is these marking and framing gestures that distinguish a stage relic and visually define it. The latter may be a mosque, a shrine, a natural topographical feature, etc. In a recent study of a series of curious round black stones, Barry Flood has illuminated one of these marking practices. The challenge to Flood was to explain the presence of these cut and decorated stones found in mihrabs in Medina, in the cave under the Sakhra, and in the Ka'ba. In light the devotional practices associated with these sites, it seems clear that these stones were commemorative markers, which identified the precise locations at which Muhammad had performed salat.[142] Accordingly, by our typology these round commemorative stones are the framing for stage relics.

In their aggregate, this presentation may seem to deal with a bewildering number of examples. My aim, however, has not been to make a quantitative argument, but rather substantiate my proposal for five categories of relics: the corporeal, the contact, the imprint, the animated, and stage relics. Building on this model, I argued that the medium's relationship to the image at some points determines the distinctions between the categories themselves. Beyond this, we also saw the peculiar meditations on death – the broken and defeated bodies – intertwined with the transformative experience of devotional love, all of which were negotiated between relics and their devotees. With this typology in place, I turn in the next chapter to set some of the most prominent of these relics within their geographical and political milieus.

FIVE

RELIGIOUS TOPOGRAPHY AND THE RELIC

In proposing the relic typology of Chapter 4, I have sought to do more than simply draw lines and propose categories. Just as importantly, this has been an exercise in the inspection, sorting, and thus the recovery, of relics. While alternative or additional categories may be proposed by subsequent research – which would be welcome responses to what I've done here – all such efforts contribute to increasingly nuanced engagements with these objects, and the religious cultures that frame them. With relics and their reception now in somewhat better focus, the following pages will explore the wider discourses, and the bodily engagements, through which relics negotiated their roles in political projects; projects that inextricably wove religion into the practices of power. Two prominent and often interrelated phenomena were the use of relics as markers of authority, and the attempts to engineer new religious landscapes through their strategic appropriation. The history of these symbolic claims to authority, along with the evolving topographies of pilgrimage, relied on the presence and power of relics.

To anchor the politics of a relic within a material field, we might usefully recall Catherine Bell's insights on performativity and ritual. Briefly, she points out that a ritual actor operates within the confines of a conceptual system, while never being fully determined by it. Bell's approach stresses the agency of actors, who at one level encounter their ritual objects immediately, while at another level, keep only a weak (though real) connection to the wider religious or political worlds in which they operate.[1] The virtue of this approach is that it avoids over determining the meaning of specific objects, i.e. conflating the entire system with a single act or object, as well as making explanatory room for a diversity of outcomes. That is to say, while each historical instance requires a framework (or "system" in Bell's words), such a framework will not instantiate identically in each case. I take this open-endedness to be same idea Sean Kelly is arguing for in his reading of Merleau-Ponty.[2] Here what Kelly calls the "background phenomena" is key. These are things like an artist's style in relation to an artwork – always there, but in each instance appearing differently – or the understanding of an observer, which must recede from view while continuing to function as a guide to what perceptions are possible. These are the frameworks that are at play in the variegated history of relics as players on the political stage. As we shall see, their "backgrounds," the theories of Islamic kingship, or the tenets of pilgrimage, are always in play, and yet do not guarantee one outcome over another.

The association of relics with religious leadership and kingship was clear to the earliest Muslim community. One Qur'anic passage makes this connection between relics and authority explicit. In their search to appoint a king from among their number, the Children of Israel consider Saul. To assuage their doubts, and to confirm Saul's divine right, they are told, "A sign of his kingship is that an Ark (*tabut*) will come to you in which are assurance (*sakina*) from your Lord, and the remnants (*baqiyya*) left by the families of Moses and Aaron, carried by angels." (Q. 2:248) From at least the first half of the second Islamic century, exegetes identified these remnants as contact relics, with various lists being proffered. Muqatil ibn Sulayman (d. 767) claimed these remnants included pieces of Moses' tablets, as well as his staff and turban, along with heavenly manna collected in a golden bowl. To this list al-Tabari (d. 923) added the staff of Aaron and the sandals of Moses. Qur'an commentators up into the medieval period, such as Ibn al-Jawzi (d. 1200), Fakhr al-Din al-Razi (d. 1210), and al-Baydawi (d. 1286), present variations on these lists.[3] In the late fifteenth century, the Egyptian exegete Jalal al-Din al-Suyuti also identified these remnants as relics, and added that the Ark contained images (*suwwar*) of the prophets, which had been sent down to Adam. He states that each prophet handed this collection down to his successor, until the Ark was lost to the Amalekites in battle. While the tradition of images of the prophets seems to have been rather peripheral, the association of relics with leadership and authority has deep roots.[4]

The association of authority with the relics of Muhammad seems to have mirrored these Qur'anic connections. While the Prophet's immediate successors, the caliphs, held few regal accoutrements to mark their authority, such as a crown or throne, they did carry objects handed down to them, which confirmed the favor of Muhammad. As we noted earlier, the conferring of swords was one mechanism by which such approval was made manifest. More systematically, however, and thus more convincing as a symbol of authority, was Muhammad's spear. Muhammad inherited if from the royal Negus of Ethiopia, by way of al-Zubayr ibn al-'Awwam. The Prophet had used this lance to demarcate his personal prayer space, and had it carried before him on festival days.[5] It was handed down to his immediate caliphal successors in Medina, who had it carried before them on official occasions. The governor and imams of Medina continued the practice until al-Mutawakkil had it brought to his court in Samarra in the ninth century.[6] Elsewhere, from the troubled time of the early caliphate, Muhammad's staff was directly associated with the authority to rule. One day, while leaning on a staff (*'asa*) preaching – the staff upon which Muhammad, Abu Bakr, and 'Umar used to lean– the caliph 'Uthman was accosted by an opponent, who seized the staff and broke it over his knee. After the altercation, the caliph had the staff repaired, bound back together with a strip of iron. His rule, like the broken staff, however, would never recover its former state. Humiliated, 'Uthman remained largely out of the public eye, and would be assassinated later that year.[7]

Later caliphs continued to rely on prophetic relics to signal their authority. The founder of the Umayyad dynasty, Mu'awiyya (d. 680), bought Muhammad's *burda* cloak from Ka'b ibn Zuhayr, who claimed to have received it directly from the Prophet himself. In his classic manual on the rule of the caliphate, *The Ordinances of Government*, al-Mawardi traces the *burda* through Umayyad rule, and its subsequent adoption by their Abbasid successors. Upon the death of the last Umayyad caliph, Abu al-'Abbas al-Saffah (d. 754) collected the *burda* from the royal treasury, upon which he would found his new dynasty.[8] Al-Mawardi makes it clear that these relics had served this purpose from the earliest days of the Prophet's successors, calling the staff and the *burda* the "signs of caliphal authority" (*min shi'ar al-khilafa*). Many relic objects came in and out of circulation, associated with the caliphs and their claims to inherit authority.[9] At least one caliph was incredulous, but continued to venerate Prophetic relics simply to reassure his public.[10] Precious and useful as they were, however, not every relic survived. We are told that Muhammad's signet ring was passed down to his immediate successors, the caliphs Abu Bakr, 'Umar, and 'Uthman, but that the latter lost it in a well.[11] The ring would reappear half a century later in an 'Abbasid transfer of the "signs of authority." Upon the death of the caliph Harun al-Rashid in 809, his trusted eunuch collected from among his estate the Prophet's *burda*, his staff and signet ring, and bestowed them upon Harun's son and successor al-Amin. It is not clear from the sources if this was considered to be the ring that 'Uthman had lost, or if this was a second ring. Regardless, this ring disappears, and is absent from the next list of relics. A brief civil war saw the defeat of al-Amin and the presentation of his severed head, along with the Prophet's *burda*, staff, and prayer rug, to his victorious brother al-Ma'mun (d. 833).[12]

The death of al-Husayn at Karbala would not only open a new chapter in Islamic religious practice – that of the Shi'ite public mourning rituals along with the passion play known as the *Ta'ziyya* – but also produce what is likely the most important relic in Islamic tradition, that of al-Husayn's head. The first location for the head was Damascus, capital of the Umayyads then under the caliph Yazid, who received the head of his enemy in a golden bowl. Parallels with the martyrdom of John the Baptist, who both Muslims and Christians shared as a figure of devotion in Damascus, are striking.[13] The early history of the relic in Damascus is contested, with perhaps the most prominent account claiming that one of Yazid's successors 'Abd al-Malik (d. 717) buried the head in a Muslim cemetery.[14] Subsequent veneration of the relic is unclear until 1176, at which point we know that an elaborate shrine was functioning in the eastern end of the great Umayyad mosque. Historians and travelers of the day remark on the beauty of the small hall, associated with the memory of not only al-Husayn, but also that of his father 'Ali, and of his son Zayn al-'Abidin.[15] There are, however, no bodies buried there. The shrine's central focus is instead the commemoration of the absent relic. In addition to an enclosure in one corner of the hall, marking the temporary resting place of the head, a silver casing is built into the wall to indicate where the relic was once displayed. Figure 40 shows the niche, which continues to attract visitors and devotional attention. The inscription in silver on a red background simply labels the relic as "Our lord, Husayn." The upper inscription begins with the *basmala*, followed by a Qur'an passage (17:33) evoking the tragedy of Karabala and the authority of the Shi'i imams: "And whoso is killed unjustly – We have given authority unto his heir." This silver framing contrasts with the unseen but imagined relic: The gruesome and messy decapitation stands out against the clean, sharp lines of the enclosure. The signs of violence and death, inscribed directly on the head itself, are powerfully contrasted by the framing. Additionally, this space, in its small dimensions in comparison to an adult human body, evokes the dismemberment that is such an important part of the relic. Husayn was a martyr, killed in the cause of righteousness, with the violence of that killing displayed upon his body. In addition to this inscribing of death, the relic is also celebrated by its association with the niche. The negative space not only evokes the distant body part, but recovers it as an object of devotion, framed by precious silver, as a reflection of the fallen hero's place in the affections of devotees.

Another head, that of John the Baptist, is also venerated at the great Umayyad mosque. Its presence is more central than al-Husayn's memorial, standing prominently within the ritual prayer space of the mosque. Figure 41 shows the domed shrine covering the spot where the caliph al-Walid (d. 715) found the head of Yahya ibn Zakariyya during renovations to transform the cathedral into a mosque. This discovery would not have come as a great

40 Silver niche in Husayn shrine: Damascus. Credit: Photo by Toushiro. Creative Commons.

surprise, since the site itself – known as the Cathedral of Saint John – had long
been dedicated to this holy man, who also appears in the Qur'an.[16] Medieval
sources describe the discovery, and note the miraculous signs that the skin and
hair remained intact.[17] As a site for pilgrimage, the head of the Muslim prophet
Yahya not only attracted pilgrims, but also served as a home for a group of
pious devotees (*fuqara'*) who lived as a Sufi group at the mosque, reciting the
Qur'an day and night near the relic. This group was active in the late twelfth

41 Tomb of John the Baptist in Umayyad Mosque.
Credit: Niday Picture Library/ Alamy Stock Photo

century, with various devotional groups gathering at the site well into the fourteenth century.[18] In a contesting narrative, the head of John the Baptist also lay, for a period, in Aleppo. It was discovered in Ba'albak in 1043, and transported in a strongbox to Aleppo's citadel.[19]

While the head of John served as an anchor, connecting the Umayyad mosque to its Christian antecedents, the head of al-Husayn had quite a different career. Moving across a devotional landscape extending from Karbala in Iraq, across Syria, and finally into Egypt, al-Husayn's head seeded a number of shrines thanks to the drops of blood that fell from the relic. In each city where the head was processed, it was met with a variety of responses, ranging from horror to triumphal jeering.[20] To the west of Kufa lies a shrine that marks a spot where the camel carrying the body of 'Ali knelt.[21] Ibn Jubayr notes local claims that that site was also 'Ali's burial place. The landscape is rich with sites referencing the tragic fate of the family. In Najaf, the mosque of the Weeper (al-Hannana) was built over a spot where Husayn's head lay. From Kufa the head traveled north to Takrit, and then Mosul, where the *mashhad ra's al-Husayn* (Shrine of the Head of Husayn) was subsequently built (Map 2). From here it went to Nusaybin, where shrines to both the head and to drops of its blood were established. It then moved to Raqqa, and then to Balis where a Shrine of the Stone marks the resting spot of the head. Near Aleppo, the head was placed in the Marat Maruta convent, a site that was soon abandoned by

42 Husayn blood relic: Aleppo. Credit: Photo by Toushiro. Creative Commons.

the Christians and developed into a significant Shia shrine. A *mashhad* shrine to al-Husayn was built outside the city on the slope of Mt. Jawshan, and embellished by Saladin – although its association with al-Husayn is historically tenuous.[22] Figures 42 and 43 show the blood relic on its stone, and the use of silver funerary grills to house and display the relic.[23] This site was seriously damaged some time after 2011. The fate of the blood relic is unclear, but recent local television reports available on YouTube, indicate the site is structurally sound and will be restored. From Aleppo, the head traveled south to Hama, establishing another shrine, then on to Sayzar, Homs, Ba'albak, and Damascus.[24] The head would eventually come to rest in Cairo, where it would anchor the al-Husayn mosque and shrine – the most prominent site of pilgrimage in the city. We shall revisit the career of this relic below, when we discuss the use of relics in the creation of sacred topographies.

The sources are unclear about when the head might have left Damascus, but some three centuries later it was rediscovered in Asqalon. According to one historian, the son of the powerful Fatimid vizier Badr al-Jamali, al-Afdal, entered Asqalon in 1098 and discovered the head, digging it out of a decrepit place (*makan daris*). Al-Afdal perfumed the relic, processed with it, and eventually built

43 Shrine of the drop of blood.
Credit: Photo by Daniel Demeter. Syria Photo Guide

a shrine complex to house it.[25] Another version of the story, likely the more accurate one, has Badr al-Jamali himself discovering the relic, and building a shrine for it in 1091. A lengthy inscription on the minbar records the event (Figure 44): "By a miracle the Mighty One has made manifest (*izharuhu*) the head of our lord the Imam Martyr 'Abd Allah al-Husayn ibn Abi Talib at Asqalon, out of a place the oppressors had concealed it, intent on obscuring its light! This light a sign that He had promised to make known." Badr al-Jamali, it

44 Minbar of Saladin in Hebron.
Credit: Photo by author

continues, "is divinely favored with veneration of the head, and the dignity of its spiritual station (*maqam*). He ordered that this minbar be made for the sanctuary he established, in the most honored place of which he buried the head as a qibla for the amir (caliph), and for the prayers of those accepted by God, and an intercessor for pilgrims and those who seek its/his intercession."[26]

However, this sanctuary in Asqalon was to serve only as a temporary home. Some 60 years later, as Crusader armies threatened it, the minbar was moved to the tomb of the Patriarchs in Hebron, where it stands today. The relic, however, took a different path, making its way to Cairo. Bereft of its relic and spectacular minbar, the shrine site nevertheless continued to thrive, with reports from the late twelfth century of an active site, even after the city's destruction by Saladin before the advancing Crusaders.[27] In the 1920s Tawfiq

45 Husayn Shrine in Asqalon.
Credit: Library of Congress Prints and Photographs Division, Washington, DC. Nitrate negative
4 × 5 in. Reproduction number LC-DIG-matpc-21686 (Call Number LC-M33–12761-A).
Matson Photo Service: Registers, vol. 2, [1940–1946]. Given by The Episcopal Home, 1978.

Canaan described a broken column, topped with a green head-dress and
wrapped in red cloth, marking the temporary burial spot of the head, and
noted the annual festival (*mawsim*) that continued to be observed at the site.[28]
A photograph from April 1943 (Figure 45) shows that festival crowds continued to gather in the courtyard of the shrine. This building was destroyed in
the 1950s as part of the campaign to erase the Arab-Islamic heritage of the
region – and a small commemorative platform was built in the 1980s.[29]

Having left Asqalon shortly before the city fell to the Crusaders, the head
moved through the Egyptian Delta, establishing shrines in its wake.[30] Witnesses claimed the relic still bled, and that rather than decaying, it gave off the
scent of musk. Not surprisingly, in 1153 when the head arrived in Cairo, it was
received with great ceremony.[31] A eunuch of the caliph's harem met the relic
and rode with it up the canal, disembarking in Kafur's garden, which he
crossed on foot, entering the Fatimid palace to deliver the relic to the caliph
al-Zafir.[32] The head was placed in a palace shrine, the Saffron Tomb (*Turbat
al-zafran*), which it shared with the remains of various departed Fatimid caliphs.
With the assassination of al-Zafir, the governor of Asyut province, Salih Tala'i
assumed the regency and effective rule over the empire. His ambition drove
him not only to construct a large mosque, still known by his name today,
across from the monumental Zuwayla Gate, but also to house within it the
head al-Husayn. The most likely location for the shrine would have been one

of the rooms to the left or right of the main entrance. Despite his audacity, resistance from the caliphal family dissuaded the ambitious regent, and the head was instead moved to the purpose-built Cupola of the Daylamites within the palace.[33] Al-Maqrizi notes that all who entered before the relic would kiss the ground, and that during the Fatimid observances of the mourning day of 'Ashura, it was the site of many tears and great lamentation over the death of Husayn. On this occasion, it was also the site for the sacrifice of camels, sheep, and cattle.[34] Caroline Williams has argued that the vizier Ma'mun al-Bata'ihi (d. 1125) also built the al-Aqmar mosque with an intention to house the head.[35]

The current home for the head is a shrine in the mosque of al-Husayn, situated in front of great Fatimid mosque-university of al-Azhar. The Husayn site was established in 1154 only 18 years before Saladin would overthrow the Shia rulers, and establish his own Sunni Ayyubid dynasty. In 1187, the traveler Ibn Jubayr described the site, with al-Husayn's head in a silver casket, over which a magnificent edifice had been built. The reliquary was covered with a variety of brocade, surrounded by white candles, large and small, set for the most part in pure silver or gold candelabras. "We saw men crowded around the blessed tomb, touching it, with great devotion smoothing with their hands the *kiswa* that hung upon it. In tears, this crowd circumambulated it, calling out their prayers, all so that they might benefit from the *baraka* of this holy grave."[36] Posterity would celebrate the figure of Saladin; the romantic European image presented him as the noble adversary of Richard the Lionheart, while for Sunni historians he was the champion and restorer of Sunnism.[37] While Saladin did bring his Egyptian and Syrian domains under the nominal rule of the caliph in Baghdad, and reoriented al-Azhar to Sunni practice, he continued to support veneration of the head. We know that Saladin not only embellished the tomb, but also expanded the mosque in which it was housed. The funerary inscriptions on the tomb continued to carry pro-Shia themes, even if some inscriptions seem to have been erased by the new pro-Sunni regime.[38]

We shall see further examples of relic patronage below that include both Sunni and Shia actors, making clear that the practice of relic veneration in this part of the Islamic world played across sectarian lines. This is not say, however, that there was never resistance to relic devotion. One of the most strident critics in this period, whom we met above, was the jurist Ibn Taymiyya. His objections to the head of al-Husayn were not based on a claim that this was a Shia rather than a Sunni practice, but rather that it might be considered an imitation of Christian and Jewish practices; the hadith he recalls, explicitly warns against copying the ways of the Christians and the Jews. Just as importantly, Ibn Taymiyya also took every opportunity to challenge the authenticity of such sites. He not only doubts that the head is actually in Cairo, but offers several alternative accounts of its final burial, with his own preference being for a story of its return to Medina and inhumation next to al-Husayn's relatives.[39] Despite his doubts and disapproval, Ibn Taymiyya does not reject relic veneration out of hand. It is not until the nineteenth century that significant shrine opposition becomes explicit in the public discourse.

While the head of al-Husayn certainly became the most prominent destination for pilgrims in Cairo, it was not the first head to appear on Egypt's devotional landscape. One of the earliest funerary monuments in Islamic history was a shrine for the head of Muhammad ibn Abi Bakr (d. 658). Son of the first caliph Abu Bakr, Muhammad served as governor of Egypt, was involved in the attacks upon the caliph 'Uthman, and was himself killed when 'Amr ibn al-'As seized Egypt under the caliph Mu'awiyya.[40] A shrine-mosque was built to house his head, stored in copper box filled with ashes, which sources variously locate in front of the mihrab or beneath the minaret. This site, however, never seems to have become a significant pilgrimage site.[41] Within a century, another head was enshrined, that of Zayd ibn Zayn al-'Abidin (d. 740). A descendant of 'Ali ibn Abi Talib, Zayd rose in Kufa against the Umayyads, but was crucified during the suppression of his revolt.[42] Egyptian sources describe his head being displayed in Cairo on the minbar of the mosque of 'Amr ibn al-'As. Apparently local sentiments were rather more sympathetic to Zayd, and the unspecified "people of Cairo" forcefully seized the disgraced head and enshrined it in the Muharras mosque, which seems to have been purpose-built to receive the head. The site was somehow lost, but al-Afdal, son of Badr al-Jamali, is recorded as having organized for its recovery, and subsequent veneration. It remains a destination for pilgrims today, but since at least the fourteenth century it has been known simply as the shrine (*mashhad*) of Zayn al-'Abidin.[43] The historian Gaston Wiet notes this site has undergone several major renovations, leaving nothing of the original structure.

Yet another head relic made its appearance in Cairo soon after. In an attempt to seize power for the Hasanid branch of the pro-Shia Alids, Ibrahim 'Abd Allah rebelled against the newly established 'Abbasid regime. This was a political project the Hasanids pursued under both the Umayyads and the Abbasids. Ibrahim was killed in 763, when his revolt failed in Iraq, crushed by the caliph al-Mansur.[44] Al-Maqrizi tells us that Ibrahim's head was sent to Cairo for display, but that again the "people of Cairo" seized it, and enshrined it in the mosque of the Well and Fig.[45]

The historical record of the construction of these shrines is incomplete, which makes the politics difficult to reconstruct. Yet taken together, veneration of the heads clearly resist any easy explanation that would reduce them to simple symbols of the authority of the reigning caliphs. Killing Muhammad, the son of the first of the "rightly guided caliphs," would not have been good for Mu'awiyya public image. The Sunni caliph was already dealing with criticism for his disastrous campaign against 'Ali ibn Abi Talib, which led to the death of many of the Prophet's immediate blood line. As Shi'ism developed, it would adopt an adversarial posture toward the first three Islamic caliphs (Abu Bakr, 'Umar, and 'Uthman), who it saw as usurpers of the 'Ali's divine right to rule. Being behind the death of Abu Bakr's son, could not have helped Mu'awiyya. The politics of the Zayd relic are also messy. The Sunni caliph of the day, Hisham ibn 'Abd al-Malik, sought to make an example of this Shia-identified rebel, circulating his head throughout the empire, and displaying it in the most prominent mosque of Egypt. Although we do not know who exactly the "people of Cairo" were in this report, the fact that the relic was not only taken down from its display on the minbar, but also set up in its own shrine, can only be seen as public rebuke to the caliph. The same lesson would appear to be at play around the head of Ibrahim.

In their quest for clear and causal connections behind the politics of relics, historians have often overemphasized the links between sovereigns, the population, and the religious landscape. Some have seen in the rise of the shrine of the Head of Husayn, an effort by the Shia Fatimids to stir up the devotional sensitivities of the population, in an effort to elicit support for their unpopular regime.[46] These theories fail to account fully for the such practices. As we saw earlier, when Saladin reasserted Sunni Islam as the official orientation of Egypt, he preserved the shrine of Husayn. If this site were simply an incitement to support Shi'ism and the Fatimid cause, it would have been rebranded as al-Azhar was, or simply destroyed. Instead, it received Saladin's patronage, and continued to expand well into the modern period. De Smet, like other scholars before him, also struggles to explain the rise of shrine cults in the Fatimid period. He notes that it was not the Fatimid caliphs themselves who were primarily behind these developments. Badr al-Jamali and his descendants, who occupied the vizierate, commanded great authority, and were paramount in the creation of the new religious landscape. De Smet recognizes that the head relics do not represent figures particularly central to the Isma'ili brand of Shiism, which raises a thorny question: Why would the Fatimid regime not instead champion the relics of pro-Isma'ili figures? If one wants to insist that cold political calculation is behind the construction of these devotional landscapes, then these choices look like lost opportunities, or even complete failures. De Smet offers an interesting, if convoluted answer. He suggests that in their choice of relics, the viziers were surreptitiously practicing a policy of de-Isma'ilization.[47] It is not clear from the evidence, however, what they were putting in its place though. It seems recovering a coherent and consistent policy on this matter is impossible. These viziers patronized patently Sunni figures, like Muhammad ibn Abi Bakr, as well as figures such as Husayn and Zayd ibn Zayn al-'Abdidin. Instead of being explained away as instantiations of the realpolitik of those in power, the history of these relics, and the topographies they helped to define, tell a much more complex story.

Sacred objects have played an important role in the many attempts to redraw the pilgrimage maps of Islam. Perhaps the most dramatic example, if the least understood, is that of the Isma'ili Shia Carmathians, who in 930 overran Mecca, seized the *kiswa* and the Black Stone. One source tells us, it was only thanks to the residents of Mecca hiding the *maqam Ibrahim* (the stone with Abraham's footprints) in a nearby valley, that that relic was not also taken. Despite their penchant for murder and thievery, the Carmathians were not simple marauders; their leader Abu Tahir al-Jannabi clearly had a plan. A popular report among the revolutionary and messianic elements of the day had 'Ali declaring that in the End times, the Black Stone of the Ka'ba will sit in the Great Mosque of Kufa.[48] In an effort to hasten this apocalypse, and in the process develop their own economic resources as a shrine center, the Carmathians resolved to undermine the Meccan Hajj, and to redirect it to their stronghold of Kufa. Abu Tahir's attacks on the Hajj caravans continued for several seasons. After the raid on Mecca, a later source recalls, the Black Stone was taken to Kufa and hung from the seventh column of its Great Mosque. Eventually, the experiment was deemed a failure, and with the movement waning, the Black Stone was returned to Mecca some 20 years later, after a significant ransom was paid.[49] In another of Kufa's mosques, the Masjid al-Sahla, a green stone was preserved, which according to Shia sources, was inscribed with the portraits of all prophets. The stone is lost, and the site did not survive into the sixteenth century.[50] In this early period of Shia history, its sacred topography was still very much in flux. Although Kufa and the nearby center of Najaf would continue to play important roles, several other important Shia shrine cities would develop, relegating Kufa to being only one among many sacred centers.

Earlier, we traced the impact that the head of Husayn had across the religious landscape of the Fertile Crescent. We also saw that the relic made an important contribution to the development of the great Umayyad mosque. Within this context of religious topography, we should also recall the role of another relic at the site, that of the head of Saint John, which figures prominently in the layout of the site. The caliph al-Walid is celebrated for his discovery of the head, during work to transform the basilica into a mosque. The hagiographical details supplied along with the narrative of al-Walid's discovery – the head was found lying in a basket, with its hair and skin miraculously intact – were clearly intended to authenticate the relic, and to encourage pilgrimage to the shrine. The political context for this, and his building of the al-Aqsa Mosque across from the Dome of the Rock, was one in which the newly emerged Umayyad dynasty was reorienting the caliphate away from Medina and toward Syria. Mu'awiyya, the founder of the Umayyad dynasty, some forty years earlier had made a failed bid to have the Prophet's pulpit moved from Medina to Syria – surely in an effort to reconfigure the sacred topography of the day.[51]

In these efforts, al-Walid was essentially continuing his father's political program. 'Abd al-Malik (d. 705) had only a few years earlier built the dome over the Sakhra Rock, recalling this as the site of the Prophet's heavenly ascension, as well as the apocalyptic claim that this would be the place where humanity would be gathered at the End of days. While never made explicit, the implications were that Jerusalem could rival Mecca and Medina as ritual center of Islam. The wider political context seemed to support this. At the time, two branches of the Umayyad ruling family vied for control of the caliphate, with 'Abd al-Malik in control of greater Syria, and his rival Ibn al-Zubayr in possession of Mecca and Medina. Some of the more polemical historians of later centuries would claim explicitly that 'Abd al-Malik's intention had been to divert the Hajj to Jerusalem, where the Rock and its Dome would be circumambulated in place of the Ka'ba. While this site would of course remain a prominent destination for pilgrims, the theory of its intended purpose as an alternate Hajj would remain unproven, since 'Abd al-Malik soon overcame Ibn al-Zubayr, and seized Arabia for himself.[52]

In Islamic Egypt, relics were also important in efforts to reorganize the religious landscape. Despite their Isma'ili Shia identity, which ensured then minority status among the wider subject Sunni population, the Fatimid dynasty in Egypt (969–1171) was clearly seeking to establish its Islamic credentials. As we noted earlier, the program of shrine building associated with Badr al-Jamali, seemed to be designed to champion a Fatimid rule that was not stridently Isma'ili, but rather one that reflected a wider devotional vision of the Islamic tradition centered loosely on the descendants of Muhammad. The Fatimid caliphs' ancestral lineage could be traced back to Fatima and 'Ali. When al-Mu'izz triumphantly entered Cairo in 972, leaving behind the dynasty's North African capital at al-Mahdiyya, the center of gravity of the Isma'ili movement was clearly shifting eastward. Not surprisingly then, al-Mu'izz arrived in Egypt with the coffins (*tawabit*) of his ancestors and those of the previous three caliphs, al-Mahdi, al-Qa'im, and al-Mansur, among the royal baggage.[53]

Two generations later, the Fatimid caliphate was headed by al-Hakim (d. 1021), inheriting his position at the age of eleven. Despite the many threats against Fatimid rule from the 'Abbasids and the Carmathians, which persisted throughout his reign, al-Hakim sought nothing less than to recenter the Islamic landscape around his capital Cairo. The first leg of this project involved the relics of one of the most important Shia imams, Ja'far al-Sadiq, who died in Medina in 765. The caliph al-Hakim charged one of his most trusted missionaries with the task of opening Ja'far al-Sadiq's home, which had been sealed since his death, and bringing any relics he found there back to Cairo. The list of objects recovered was perhaps surprisingly short: a Qur'an, a wooden cup, a bamboo shield, a lance, a prayer mat, and a bed. The prayer mat would be particularly valued by the Fatimids, and would be ceremoniously brought out of the royal treasury each year for the breaking of the Ramadan fast.[54]

The second leg of al-Hakim's endeavor consisted of nothing less than the theft of the bodies of Muhammad and the caliphs Abu Bakr and 'Umar from Medina, and their transfer to new shrines in Cairo. The historical sources around this event are somewhat confusing, with a number of divergent narratives in circulation. In brief, the stories describe a plot in which a group of Egyptian agents began to dig a tunnel from an adjoining house into the mosque-house of the Prophet, with the intention of surreptitiously gaining access to the graves and the bodies. One report has the plot, thanks to the divine intervention by way of a dream, being uncovered and stopped by people of Medina. In another version, the Fatimid agent tasked with the theft had made significant progress, but a devastating hurricane, which toppled pack animals and killed several people, demonstrated a divine disapproval that caused the agent to lose confidence, and abandon his project.[55] Despite the equivocal nature of the written sources, there is material evidence that al-Hakim did prepare shrines to receive these relics. Yusuf Raghib's study of three Cairene monuments, all of which have curious origins and shifting identities, seems to have located the intended home for the stolen Medina relics.[56] If successful, al-Hakim's project would have reconfigured a significant portion the Hajj – bearing in mind the importance of the Prophet's grave and the sanctity of Medina, which prevailed up into the middle of the twentieth century.

On a less ambitious scale than al-Hakim's efforts, relics could also play a foundational role in the creation of religious institutions. In one example from thirteenth-century Damascus, the relic of Muhammad's shoe became a uniquely effective bridge between believers and the Prophet. We noted in the previous chapter that when the Ayyubid prince, al-Malik al-Ashraf (d. 1237) established his new school and library, the Ashrafiyya, for the study of hadith near the citadel of Damascus, he made its centerpiece a sandal that had belonged to Muhammad. The prince left little doubt as to his own devotion to the object, and by implication the piety of the entire institution. He had first come into contact with the relic thanks to Ibn al-Hadid – from a Damascene family well-known for trading in relics – who ceremonially introduced the relic to Ashraf, at which point the prince bared his head, and in joyful tears began to kiss the precious object and rub it against his cheeks.[57] There were two niches on the qibla wall of his madrasa. The one to the right of the mihrab contained copies of the Qur'an, while the one to the left housed the noble sandal. To shelter the relic, a small door, clad in yellow copper resembling gold, had been installed. Additionally, there were three veils hanging over the niche, one green, one red, and one yellow. The sandal rested upon a stand, and its outline would be engraved upon an ebony tablet, which could be sprinkled with perfume and transferred to any devotee who kissed the outline of the sandal. Devotees visited the site on Mondays and Thursdays, when the relic was displayed and tracings could be made.[58]

Although it did not survive the onslaught of Tamerlane at the turn of the fourteenth century, the power of this relic was substantial, ensuring it a high-profile career in public protests. In 1312, when the merchants of Damascus were joined by the religious class in public demonstrations against the oppressive local governor, the Prophet's shoe was brought out of the Ashrafiyya college. A mass of protestors assembled, and lead by the preacher of the Umayyad mosque, Jalal al-Din al-Qaziruni, along with the flags of the mosque, the 'Uthmanic Qur'an, and the sandal, they marched together to confront the governor. Their protest, however, was not well received. Jalal al-Din was violently arrested and dragged to the governor's palace, while the sandal and the codex were thrown to the ground. News of this unrest alone was probably enough to get the governor dismissed, but for Muhammad ibn Qalawun, the Sultan back in Cairo, the insult to the codex and the sandal was unforgiveable, and he had the governor publicly humiliated and thrown in jail.[59]

As a miraculous relic, the sandal could be enlisted to help with personal afflictions, beyond the political. An individual in crisis of course would have been the typical pilgrim visiting the Ashrafiyya sandal. But significantly, a rendering of the sandal could perform essentially the same services. Stylized representations were copied from each other in the thirteenth century, handed down along with their chains of transmitters, to guarantee their authenticity much as hadith reports from the Prophet and his companions were.[60] The great hadith commentator, al-Qastallani (d. 1517) related claims that tracings of the sandal would bring blessings to its owners, safeguard them from sedition, the machinations of their enemies, and the malevolencies of every devil and jealous evil eye.[61] Ibn 'Asakir describes a tracing of the sandal being placed upon a suffering woman, resulting in a miraculous cure.[62] These traced relics proliferated within Islamic book culture, appearing alongside poems and devotional descriptions of Muhammad and his virtues, all the while serving as tangible sites of relic interaction for their readers. Thus, these illustrations themselves became active relics. One modern scholar has noted how the tracing of the sandal in a manuscript copy of Ibn 'Asakir's work, is clearly warn from readers touching the image.[63] As we noted earlier, the Qadiri example (Figure 34), is typical, showing an embellished outline, along with the two stylized leather straps. Often the straps are indicated simply by two circles, representing the holes made to hold them, which Muhammad used to secure his sandals to his feet.[64] Despite the embellishments, and stylized appearance, the precise dimensions of the tracing are crucial. As long as the dimensions are preserved, a limitless number of true copies can be generated. A tracing made in 1848 – reproduced here by the Damascene scholar Issam Eido in Figure 46 – consists of a thin double line. The contents of the book make clear that despite its stylized reduction, the relic fully retains its power to deter misfortune. In an echo of this process of copying and reproduction, it seems appropriate that our tracing appears in an eighteenth-century commentary on a seventeenth-century commentary on the famous panegyric poem *Dala'il al-khayrat* by the fifteenth-century Sufi poet al-Jazuli. In this example, the line of reproductions spans from the fifteenth to the twenty-first centuries. In a 1901 printed copy, Yusuf al-Nabahani guarantees the accuracy of his image by reassuring his reader that it has been photographically reproduced from an earlier seventeenth-century rendering in a book by al-Maqqari. Although al-Nabahani's relic/tracing is mass produced, its miraculous and curative efficacy is sustained.[65]

Importantly, here the relic extends itself far beyond the confines of the hadith school library in which it was lovingly stored. We noted in Chapter 2 of this book, the appearance of the *mahmal* in various provincial centers of Egypt, and what I called a "scattering of the *mahmal*." In those examples, versions of the original object appeared in new but closely related religious contexts – i.e. local Hajj rituals and Sufi saint days. With the sandal relic, we encounter another scattering, but in this case, one that occurs through the practice of tracing. Thus, the outline of the relic is far more than a shorthand or a symbol. Rather than being a lesser copy of an original, the tracings are also fully the relic, and they wield the *baraka* that the sandal does. In this, such renderings resist our prevailing concepts of a sign and signified, or simulation. Although al-Malik al-Ashraf may not have intended it, through copying practices the relic extends its presence and is scattered infinitely – something he would have surely pointed to as proof of his relic's miraculous power.

While the history of the relics of Cairo does not include simulacra like the sandal tracings, their story is nevertheless a dynamic one. In addition to providing a home for al-Husayn's peripatetic head, Egypt was marked by a rich landscape that housed, displayed, and even paraded holy relics. In the previous chapter, we saw the themes of love and death evoked in various ways as individuals interacted with relics; the topography that the relics of Cairo were to engineer was built upon and imbued with such experiences. The starting point for much of this story is the Convent of the Relics of the Prophet (*ribat athar al-nabi*), which we encountered earlier in our discussion of imprint relics. This site (Map 3) became both a gathering and a departure point for much of the history of the relics of Cairo. Arising from this site, and circulating around the city, relics appeared as part of ritual events, which included prayers

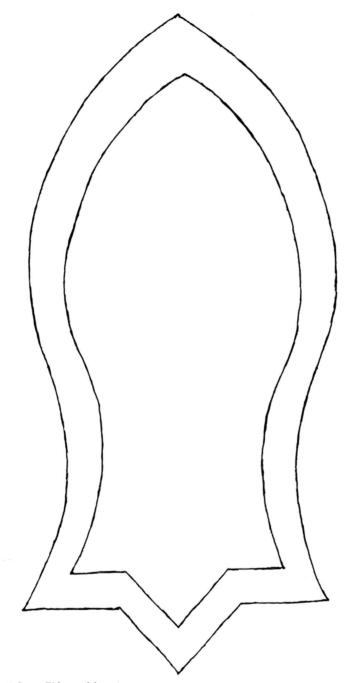

46 Issam Eido sandal tracing.
Credit: From tracing by Abd al-Qadir Habbal (fl 1848) in Sulayman ibn 'Umar Jamal, *Kitab al-minah al-ilahiyya bi-sharh Dala'il al-khayrat* ms 130 fols, 170 × 120 mm, 27 lines. Held by University of Michigan. Digital copy, Hathi Trust: https://catalog.hathitrust.org/Record/006782286

for the rise of the Nile, for rain, and on occasion as elaborate processions that celebrated the foundation of new shrines.

While the Ribat played a key role in the history of relics, it is a rather peculiar religious intuition. In our survey of the various types of Islamic relics, we saw the great variety of places in which they may be found; and as the head of al-Husayn approached Cairo, we noted that several sites were prepared to house it. The Convent of the Relics of the Prophet is notable in that it was conceived primarily as a shrine for relics. Its origin goes back to the early 1300s, when over several decades, it was built by a powerful family of viziers from the Banu Hinna family, with the *waqf* resources from a nearby garden to be devoted to its upkeep in perpetuity. Taj al-Din ibn Hinna (d. 1303) had purportedly purchased the relics from the Hijaz. With the fall of Baghdad in 1258 and the relocation of what remained of the ʿAbbasid caliphate to Cairo, the religious profile of the city was steadily rising. In the wake of this development, several members of the Hinna family – who were also admirers of al-Busiri's poem on the Mantle of the Prophet, which we discussed earlier – endowed religious and educational institutions around thirteenth-century Cairo, in addition to the Ribat.[66] The site underwent a number of improvements and expansions in the late fourteenth century; a college for training in Shafiʿi law was added by Sultan al-Ashraf Shaʿban (d. 1377), and al-Zahir Barquq (d. 1399) built a quay into the Nile to accommodate visitors arriving by boat. Barquq's son Faraj al-Din was also a patron of the shrine. The fourth Mamluk sultan we know to have endowed the Convent was Qansuh al-Ghawri (d. 1516), although his beneficence was tempered with imperiousness – as we shall see, he later appropriated several of the Convent's relics for his own funerary complex.[67]

A source from about 40 years later offers an inventory of the relics, describing a number of curtains hanging over a wooden strongbox, in which was found a smaller box holding pieces of the Prophet's bowl, a copper kohl applicator stick, a shoe awl, and tweezers.[68] From about the same period, Ibn Kathir and al-Qalqashandi add an iron comb and parts of a staff to this list.[69] One source claims the Ribat's relics were available to the public on Wednesday each week.[70] We noted earlier some of the rituals these relics participated in, particularly having to do with the Nile. In the thirteenth and fourteenth centuries, anxieties around the yearly life-giving flood of the Nile led to elaborate supplications being organized. When water levels were lower than expected in 1450, Sultan Jaqmaq ordered the caliph to distribute alms at the Ribat and to petition the Prophet there.[71]

In the seventeenth century, the Ribat was rebuilt. An inscription at the site dates the work to 1663, under the rule of the Ottoman Sultan Mehmet IV. The more immediate patron, however, was the Sultan's governor in Egypt, Melek Ibrahim Pasha, who "built this mosque above the footprint" – and in another inscription, "who renovated this shrine (*maqam*) over the footprint."[72] It is not clear exactly when the imprint relic appeared in the Ribat; it is not mentioned in the earlier sources, nor is the precise nomenclature for the building complex itself fixed. Ibrahim Pasha's inscriptions clearly distinguish between sections of the site, calling one a masjid and one a *maqam*; al-Sahkawi called the building simply the site (*mahall*) of the relics. It is perhaps unsurprising that over its seven-century history, nomenclature has shifted, and relics have come and gone.

Shortly after the Ottoman rebuilding, Evlia Celebi paid a visit and described a further function and identity for the site – a center for the practice of Sufism. Celebi tells us that the Ribat provided permanent housing for 100 married Sufis of the Khalwatiyya order.[73] With such a large number to support on a day-to-day basis, it seems likely that Ibrahim Pasha would have had to set aside significant resources to sustain the institution, signaling the scale of his investment in a revitalized Ribat. Al-Nabulusi visited the site in 1694, and as we noted earlier, described the central position of the footprints and the use of rosewater in devotional rituals. This focus on the footprints is important, as it seems the Ribat lost some, if not all, of its contact relics to the maneuverings of Sultan Qansuh al-Ghawri, at the turn of the sixteenth century. Like any good Mamluk sultan, Al-Ghawri invested tremendously in building his own mausoleum, which was intended not only represent him to posterity, but also be the final resting place for several of his immediate family and descendants.[74] In this case, the Sultan's tomb lay within a group of buildings that would include a mosque, minaret, and madrasa for the teaching of law, and an elaborate hall for Sufi meetings. While al-Ghawri renovated the Convent of the Relics of the Prophet, he more importantly removed several of its relics to his future tomb complex, which was located near al-Azhar and across the street from the shrine of al-Husayn. This 1504 translation of relics, however, was not a surreptitious exercise; on the contrary, it was marked by a public procession of great ceremony. The historian Ibn Iyas notes what a remarkable occasion this procession was, led by the head judges of the four schools of law along with the military and religious elite of the day. The heads of the major Sufi orders participated, leading their followers, who carried banners and recited the litanies of their orders. Al-Ghawri also transferred a magnificent Qur'an, allegedly in the hand of the caliph 'Uthman and formerly kept in the Baktumuriyya *khanqah* of the Qarafa, to his funerary complex. While Ibn Iyas was suitably impressed, even writing a few lines of poetry to celebrate the occasion, he does register his unease around the apparent violations to Convent's original foundation *waqf* stipulations.[75]

An interesting connection arises with regard to the founding of this relic shrine and that of Qaytbay, which we met earlier. In what is likely a mirroring of the long-established role of eunuchs at the Prophet's grave in Medina, both

Qaytbay and al-Ghawri stipulated explicitly that eunuchs should be employed in perpetuity at their mausoleum shrines to welcome visiting pilgrims and to serve the relics.[76] Earlier, we also noted the role of eunuchs in relation to the relics of Harun al-Rashid, and in the official reception ritual for the head of al-Husayn in Fatimid Cairo.

Although we are not told which objects al-Ghawri paraded, we do have details regarding another regal procession of relics, one that took place almost four centuries later. Held in 1888, this event represented perhaps the last chapter in a long a history of relic veneration and shrine building. We shall return to this procession, but note must first be made of a series of initial movements of the relics around Cairo. In 1788, it seems that the relics in al-Ghawri's mausoleum had fallen into obscurity, and were languishing at that location. When the Chief Military Adjutant (*qadi 'askar*) of the time was told of their sorry condition, he mobilized his significant resources to build stands and a strongbox to protect them, and organized a procession that included himself, several legal associates, and judges parading with the relics while calling blessings down upon the Prophet. The footprints are not mentioned, but rather three contact relics are listed: pieces of a shirt and staff, and a kohl applicator.[77] The next occasion the relics appear in procession, is some 70 years later. Details are few, but one source records that these relics – again, no mention of the footprints – were moved from al-Ghawri's funerary complex to the mosque-shrine of Sayyida Zaynab. In the same year, 1858, however, they were again moved, but this time with great ceremony, to the State Treasury in the Citadel. It seems the stop at Sayyida Zaynab was never intended to be permanent. About 30 years later, the relics were transferred to the Ministry of Pious Endowments, and one year later, in 1888, they found another temporary home in the Abdin Palace, the official residence of the Khedive of Egypt.[78]

An elaborate scene unfolded at the Abdin palace, in which the Khedive Tawfiq Pasha, accompanied by his brother Husayn Kamil Pasha, and three prominent ministers in Tawfiq's administration, emerged from the residence, each of them carrying one of the sacred relics, wrapped in green silk with golden embroidery. They were met by the chief judge of Egypt, the shaykh of al-Azhar, and the Grand Mufti, along with the heads of the two leading Sufi families, the Wafa's and the Bakris. The head of the Bakri Sufi family received the Khedive's relic, and processed with it through the streets, with two relics carried by their bearers, walking on each side. Their three-hour procession to the shrine-mosque of Husayn, eventually included some 30,000 people, with another 200,000 gathered to watch – if the reports of the newspapers of the day are to be believed.[79] (Map 4) The procession was led by mounted police, followed by heads of the Sufi orders, a squadron of soldiers, the leading scholars of the day, followed by university students, and 20 pages with braziers

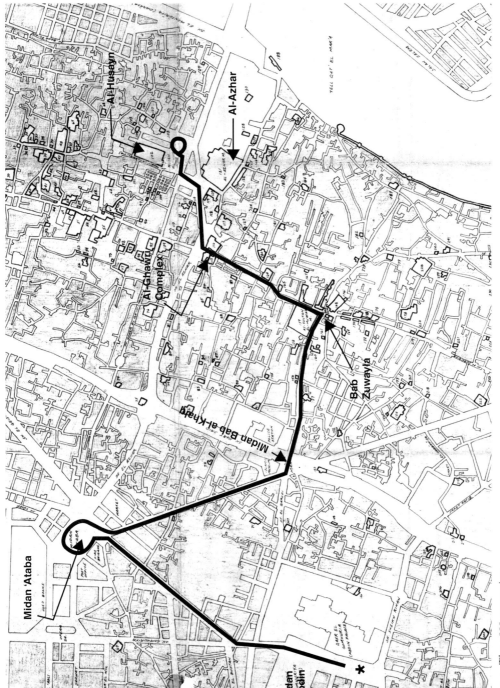

MAP 4   The 1888 procession

and bottles of perfume. When the procession reached the Husayn shrine-mosque, the relics were placed in a treasury, along with a copy of the Qur'an in the hand of the caliph 'Uthman. The keys were presented to the surveyor of endowments, passages from the Qur'an were recited, and a sermon was delivered by the shaykh of the mosque of the Citadel, in which he lauded the relics, and called down blessings upon the Sultan and his representative the Khedive.[80] This procession not only supported the development of the shrine of al-Husayn as a center for pilgrimage and relics, but it also put the relics themselves into the public eye. Even if we concede some exaggeration on the estimates of participants and viewers, the processions nevertheless put the relics before the public in a dynamic performance of authority and religiosity – political leaders assumed the mantle of propagators of the faith, and the relics reasserted themselves as preeminent sites of religiosity and public piety.

Khedive Tawfiq's successor, 'Abbas Hilmi, continued to develop this location as a relic site. In 1893, 'Abbas commissioned a special room to be built for the relics, which opened onto both the tomb of al-Husayn, and the wider mosque prayer space. The relics on display at this location include a kohl container and applicator, a piece of the Prophet's shirt and staff, two hairs of Muhammad's beard, and one of his swords. Taymur also notes that some objects have gone missing: pieces of a spear and staff, a basket, tweezers, and the Prophet's comb.

Our survey has followed relics across regions and eras. We have seen that from the earliest accounts of religious authority, objects associated with the Prophet have been put into play. This visual culture encompassed both worldly sovereignty and religious authority, with relics negotiating their place within an often contested political landscape. Relics were precious guarantors of power, but they were also vulnerable, and their damage or loss could have dire consequences. Relics also offered power to those who sought to appropriate them in projects to redraw the pilgrimage landscape. Beyond the power struggles of caliphs and amirs, we also saw relics in motion. The sandal of the Prophet could move itself through time and space thanks to the multiplier effect of its tracing. Copies can be reproduced infinitely, with no reduction to the relic's power. The head relics, and particularly that of al-Husayn, also multiplied themselves. A single relic could, by traveling across the landscape or being seized by an urban mob, multiply its presence by spawning commemorative shrines, or transform itself from a display of violent wrath to an object of intimate devotion. The multiplication of presence continued through the parades transferring relics across the urban landscape.

SIX

DEFACING AND DISPLACING

In 1022, a violent and apparently demented pilgrim entered the *haram*, the sacred space around the Ka'ba, with a sword in one hand and a mace in the other. It was the festival of Immolation, marking the end of the Hajj, the busiest and most crowded point of the pilgrimage. His target, however, was not any of his fellow Hajjis, although most of them were Sunnis, and he was a minority Shia. It was the Ka'ba, and in particular the Black Stone lodged in its eastern corner. The iconoclast began his assault, striking the Stone three times with his mace. In his rage the Egyptian cried out, "How long will this black stone be worshipped? Neither Muhammad nor 'Ali would object to what I do here – I shall demolish this shrine!" The pilgrims around him recoiled in horror, and fell back helpless, until one among them plucked up his courage, and struck the man with a dagger. In their indignation and anger, the crowd swarmed and tore the attacker to bits, then burned what was left of his body. A group of conspirators nearby was identified, and the 20 or so who could not escape were killed by the angry mob. The situation escalated, and soon all Egyptians and North Africans on the Hajj became targets of looting and pillage. The following day, the damage to the precious stone was assessed. The attacker, it seems, had only managed to knock a few shavings off of the Black Stone, which the Meccans quickly repaired.[1]

The Black Stone, of course, is a central focus of the ritual circumambulation of the Ka'ba. The prophet Muhammad had often touched it, and even kissed it, while completing the rite. Thus, the pilgrims' horror at the attempted iconoclasm is understandable. And yet, the iconoclast claimed to be working within the bounds of a properly Islamic rationale; in his own words, "Neither Muhammad nor ʿAli would object. . ." The whole issue, then, is not as settled as one might think. Skepticism toward this official litholatry, it turns out, did have roots within the tradition. The hadith literature preserves a clear objection to this veneration, which we met briefly in chapter one above. The canonical collections relate an episode in which the caliph ʿUmar objects to kissing the stone. His stated reason, recalling the rejection of idol worship, was that stones are inanimate objects, and incapable of responding to humans. Despite his misgivings, ʿUmar completes the ritual, ironically registering his objections by speaking to the Stone itself: "Truly, I know that you are but a stone, and can neither benefit nor harm anyone. Had I not seen God's Apostle kissing you, I would not have kissed you."[2] Another important companion, and future caliph, voiced something of the same objection. ʿAli asked Muhammad, "How does this Black Stone deserve our veneration?" At which point the Prophet reminded ʿAli of its celestial origins.[3] Pointing out that the Stone came from Paradise might seem to miss the concerns raised about venerating stones, implying that some are indeed of divine origin. Such veneration, however, was a tradition well established in Arabia, as it was in the wider Near East. Together these attitudes represent the range of positions that sit together, if uncomfortably, within Islamic tradition. The following pages will explore this Arabian litholatry, with an eye to the responses it evoked, many of which were forms of iconoclasm. We will subsequently turn to the afterlives of another set of stones, the Pharaonic spolia of medieval Egypt, to trace the rise and fall of an Islamic landscape that embraced such objects.

But let us not leave ʿUmar's and Ali's objections too quickly, since they capture something of the complexities at play as an object negotiates with the forces that would deface and displace it. I would like here to underline not the obvious dissonance within the tradition, which venerates a stone that owes its identity in part to the attacks on other stones, the idols of the Kaʿba; but rather the complex negotiation within and around the object, between its inhering presence and its denotive significations. These irreducible and yet connected dimensions of inhering and denoting are at play in ʿUmar's objections. The Black Stone is a visual focal point for all Hajj pilgrims. Its framing from the medieval period onward, by a silver collar, could not present more of an eye-catching contrast. The Stone was touched by the devout, as part of their circumambulation. On his final pilgrimage, tradition tells us that Muhammad needed the help of a camel mount, and a long stick, to circulate and touch the Stone. While the numbers of pilgrims involved in the modern Hajj makes such ritual contact impractical, the Black Stone continues to sit fully and intensely at the center of every pilgrim's experience of the Hajj. Its presence within the experience of the Hajj persists, despite its convoluted denotive significance.

After all, even the skeptical Companion 'Umar, who wondered how kissing the Stone could be squared with the divine injunction against the worship of idols, in the end gave it the proper salute.

To bring these object-centered practices into sharper focus, I must first briefly address the wider issue of the image in Islam. Much of the attitudes and censorship that have traditionally been associated with images, also appear in relation to iconoclasm. We shall encounter several examples in the chapter below. The first thing to be said about image prohibition is a caveat against over determination. That is to say, rather than tracing out the logic of Islamic law in relation to the image, and taking that as the normative Muslim practice, a more fulsome investigation will reveal several distinct tendencies at play, awkwardly sharing the religious landscape with one another.

Recent studies show the complex nature of this question. The highpoint for such debates was a 50-year period, ending in 725. Relevant proof texts from the hadith are many, and they reveal a variety of assumptions about the impact of images, as well as their denotive mechanisms. In one set of traditions, the objection hinges on the assumption that images deceive their viewers; they make a claim on the viewer that they have a spirit, which in truth they do not. We are warned that, "Those who make (or possess) images will be punished on the Day of Resurrection. It will be said to them 'Bring to life what you have created'" – in contrast to the prophet Jesus, who did fashion birds out of clay, and blew life into them (Q. 5:110). The accusation is that all artworks are lifeless imitations, which make false claims upon their beholders. Sculpted or carved forms are also deceptive in the same way. Allah Himself tells us that, "The worst of people are those who set out to create, like I do. Let them but create a kernel of corn, an ant-egg, or a barley-corn."[4] The deception here is the tension between the viewer's experience of an object, and the object's "true" status. The objection is one that operates with a collapsed sense of the denoted and the inhering. That is to say, the viewer cannot distinguish between an original and its representation, and will be duped into conflating the two. The accursed image-makers will be exposed for their deception, when in the after-life they fail before God's challenge to blow life into the "creatures" they have made. The theological anxiety is clear, seeking to reserve the act of creation for the Creator exclusively.

Another series of hadith recounts how the angel Gabriel ordered the Prophet to rid his house of all images. Muhammad is given options; he can cut the heads off of all images, so as to render them lifeless, without spirit (*ruh*) – more specifically, so they, "become like trees." Later iconoclasts would go through manuscript libraries looking for renderings of humans in order to symbolically decapitate them by drawing a line across their necks. Another alternative for the Prophet was to turn curtains decorated with animal images into cushions and pillows.[5] The latter repurposing would serve the same iconoclastic function as decapitation, symbolically killing them, by relegating the images to degrading locations, where they would lie on the ground and be sat upon. Gabriel was not the only one to object to images. Muhammad himself ordered his wife Aisha to take away a curtain decorated with bird or winged horse images, because it distracted him during his prayers.[6] The tension between the image itself, and what it represents, arises again. In this instance, it seems the Prophet is not objecting to the presumptuous denotations behind the images on the curtain – that is, that an artisan is impersonating the creator God. Instead, it is the immediate experience of the images themselves in that historical instant – too realistic to be ignored – that Muhammad is responding too.

For our proposes, I'll underline two key points from this discussion. The first is that no simple description of Islamic aniconism, or hostility to images, is possible. Going back to the earliest sources, the life of Muhammad, the picture gets increasingly complex. Clearly, there were theological issues at stake (i.e. the nature of creation and its Creator), as well as bodily practices and viewing culture at play. It should not surprise us then to find that images actually persist in Islamic visual culture. In the Prophet's own house, Aisha's flying horses did not go extinct, but rather, they lived on in a carefully considered new frame. Dolls and other toys were exempt.[7] The images in texts often persisted. Decapitation, after all, generates a spectacle. Depriving an image of its spirit leaves another image, that of a corpse, to negotiate a new place in the visual field. We will see that this theme of the persistent return of objects resonates with our case studies below.

From this consideration of images, we must turn to a related practice, that of iconoclasm. Let us begin by pointing out that the complex picture around image prohibition, confirms what historians have been documenting more widely. Barry Flood has made the important observation that assumptions of a monolithic Muslim response to images not only blinds us to the complexity of those responses, but it also precludes those specific iconoclastic "moments" in history that might illuminate that complexity for us.[8] What Flood says for the study of image prohibition generally, plays out at the regional level too. In the medieval Egyptian context, Nasser Rabbat cautions against an overemphasis on image prohibition. When written with such leanings, he warns, social history is incapable of engaging the popular arts or the philosophical discourses, which demonstrated at times a lively engagement with images and objects – as examples in the remainder of this chapter will confirm.[9] The same can be said for Islam in South Asia, where scholarship has recently forced a nuancing of the one-dimensional portrait of Muslims as image haters, blind to the aesthetics of the religious cultures around them.[10]

These assumptions also needed to be reconsidered in another cross-cultural setting, that between the Islamic heartlands and Christian Byzantium. When the lines between iconoclasts and iconodules were first drawn in the eighth century, the influence of Islamic image prohibition was often invoked. Recent scholarship has, however, largely rejected this connection, pointing out that explicit Islamic policies of image prohibition were in fact rare (e.g. Yazid II's edict of 723 against Christian display of icons, was reversed by his successor Hisham), and that the Islamic influence on Byzantine culture and intellectual life was far more nuanced and complex than being simply the origin of iconophobia.[11]

This nuancing, around both the engagements with images and their socio-political contexts, should also be extended to our definitions of iconoclasm and reuse. Some received categories, inherent within those paradigms, do not stand up under closer inspection. Dario Gamboni troubles the distinction between damaging and destroying, when he notes that removing an artwork from the location in which it was made, or where it was intended to sit, can destroy it.[12] The artwork ceases to be what it was – and in that sense, is destroyed. This is an important insight, but it is certainly not the last word. When image prohibition did take place, several outcomes were possible. Rather than signaling the utter erasure of an image, iconoclastic events often left behind broken, mutilated, and displaced, objects. As we shall see below, this is far from erasure – instead, it was a crisis that forced a renegotiation of an object's meaning. In his attempt to describe the afterlife of reuse in Indian mosque architecture, Barry Flood proposes to refocus on the sites as "total artworks." This is not to downplay the loss suffered by the iconoclastic actions that made such compositions possible, but rather his intent is to provide an alternative to a reductive search for a pristine and original object. Instances of reuse, he argues, can be read as attempts to recode the object's meaning within its current context, that is, within its "new iconographic and aesthetic conventions."[13] I would like to embrace this as a starting point, but will propose a greater burden to be borne by the objects of reuse. My suggestion is that a significant component of the objects' renegotiations is the ability, indeed the necessity, to preserve and display the violence of those extractions upon their surfaces. Here I am inspired by Walter Benjamin's characterization of Baroque art as bearing the, "imprint of the progression of history."[14] In our case, I will argue by carrying the record of their dispossession, Pharaonic spolia open new possibilities in which to negotiate their future.

This marking upon the object, leaving a trace of the transformative encounter, is in some ways as important as the original violent act itself. Jean-Luc Nancy's reflections on iconoclasm weaves the act and the object together intimately. He claims that, "violence. . . always completes itself in an image. . . The violent person wants to see the mark he makes on the thing or being he assaults, and violence consists precisely in imprinting such a mark."[15] The scratching out of faces, the symbolic decapitation by drawing a line across

the neck, along with the pulling of heiroglyph-incsribed stones out of their
original settings, leaves an image altered for posterity, forever carrying this
supplement. The instances of reuse that we will explore below, carry these
violent markers, displaying them in various ways. Here iconoclasm has become
formative to the new life of the object – what in speaking of texts, Jacques
Rancière has called an essential "self-display," the condition of the object
communicating both the ostensible message (he calls this the "body") and
the force that made this body possible (the "idea of the idea").[16] In the case of
our Pharaonic objects of reuse, we shall note both of these dimensions at play.
They are at once reworked, re-presented, even domesticated through their
new Islamic framing, and by their isolated out-of-place and scarred faces, they
are both accessible and distant. J.-L. Nancy builds upon Walter Benjamin's
analysis of aura, as the immediately accessible image that nevertheless maintains
a distance within it. Yet Nancy claims all images perform a version of this
double standing, in which they cross the distance of the withdrawal, even
while maintaining that essential distance.[17] All of this is to say, rather than
treating the Pharaonic objects reused in Islamic visual culture as passive or inert
casualties, we should instead make room for their presence; a presence that
itself operates with a depth preserving the otherness of the iconoclastic violence, while negotiating its immediate standing as an image.

Islamic confrontations with images and idols have their roots in the religious
culture of Arabia. The Qur'an, the hadith, as well as the earliest histories of the
community, all variously mention the idols, gods, and shrines of Muhammad's
day. It should not surprise us to learn that pre-Islamic Arabia – the period
Islamic sources call the Age of Ignorance, or *al-jahiliyya* – did not develop in
isolation, but was in fact part of the wider Near Eastern cultural landscape.
Arabia reflected much of the diversity of the region, with Judaism, Christianity, and Zoroastrianism, all present, in addition to temples to ancient Egyptian
gods. The southern peninsula, including the Yemen, had been an agricultural
center for many centuries, while the region of the Hejaz, with the small urban
centers of Mecca and Yathrib/Medina, was based on oasis and nomadic
culture, relying heavily on caravan trade. The visual culture of pre-Islamic
religion was reflective of the wider Hellenistic traditions of the Near East,
representing its various gods in sculpture and painting.[18] Modern archeological
surveys in Arabia are limited in number, yet they reveal the degree to which
pre-Islamic art was influenced by the Hellenistic world around it.[19]

Out of Muslim sources, beginning with the Qur'an, some of this sacred
topography emerges. In two places the scripture mentions Arabian gods. The
enemies of Noah advise, "By no means should you abandon your gods; leave
not Wadd, Suwa', or Yaghuth, neither Ya'uq nor Nasr" (Q. 71:23), and an
apparent rejection of Allah having angelic daughters: "Have you considered
al-Lat and al-'Uzza? And Manat, the third? Is the male for you, and to Him the

female?" (Q. 53:19–21). In his *Book of Idols,* Ibn al-Kalbi (d. 768) describes a pantheon of some 25 different gods from across Arabia. Many were versions of popular Near Eastern gods, but some seem to have been particularly Arabian. Ibn al-Kalbi provides rather sparse descriptions, but some details are intriguing. The idol al-Lat, he tells us, was located in al-Ta'if, and was a cube-shaped rock. She belonged by the 'Attab ibn Malik tribe, who had built a shrine for her. Al-'Uzza's shrine was in the valley of Nakhla, north of Mecca. The Quraysh tribe held her to be the highest of this pantheon of idols, and they used to sacrifice to her, and seek her favors. Three sacred trees marked al-'Uzza's location, but it is not clear what form of stone, if any, was enshrined there. Ibn al-Kalbi tells us that al-Manat was venerated by all Arabs, particularly those of the Aws and Khazraj tribes. She was to be found on the Red Sea coast, between Mecca and Medina, although no details of her form have come down to us.[20]

In the Islamic sources, there are several accounts of the origins of idols and idolatry. Together, they display a nuanced position toward such practices. Idols are at once declared errant, yet due to their association with early monotheistic practices, their stories are preserved. The children of Seth used to visit the grave of Adam, to offer prayers for his soul. One of the children of Cain observed them, and complained to his kin that their line and descendants had no such rituals. As a solution, one of their number carved an idol for them to circumambulate in devotion.[21] In another report, the five idols of the people of Noah had originally been the five pious sons of Adam. When one of them died, Satan visited his grieving brothers, offering to put up an image of the departed in the *qibla* niche, at the front of their mosque. The brothers rejected the offer, noting it would encroach upon God's exclusive right to be worshipped, but they agreed to allow the image to be mounted as a memorial, in the rear of their mosque. Here the theme of decline and the fall from an originary purity – behind much of the Islamic revelation's self-image in relation to rival monotheistic traditions – begins to surface. As the brothers each passed away, their representations accumulated in the mosque, until the good character of those men, and the noble initial intentions behind the images, were forgotten. It was then only a small step to the practice of idolatry.[22] Ibn al-Kalbi adds to this narrative the detail that during the Great Flood, these images/idols floated about, eventually coming to ground in the land of Judah, where they were covered by shifting sands – to be retrieved by 'Amr ibn Luhayy, upon direction from an oracle, and taken back to Tihama in Arabia, and there set up for worship.[23]

Another version of the origin of idolatry preserves the abominable practice's noble origins. We are told that in pre-Islamic Arabian history, once Mecca had become too small for its inhabitants, and some set out in search of new lands, each left with a small stone from the Sacred Precinct of the Ka'ba, as a tribute to the great shrine. Wherever they settled, they set these stones up for veneration, and as had been their practice around the Ka'ba, circumambulated them. Over time, these Arabs became attached to their stones, which had become their idols, and adopted new practices that had been unknown to the religion of Abraham and Ishmael. Litholators, they nevertheless retained some of the original practices of religion, such as honoring the Ka'ba, attending to the stages of the Hajj and 'Umra, and witnessing God's oneness. In this religious confusion, the Quraysh and the Kinana tribes introduced their idols into the Meccan sanctuary, albeit subordinating their pantheon to the one lord of the Ka'ba.[24]

The Qur'an relates a long pre-Islamic history of ancient peoples and the prophets who were sent to them. Accounts of idol worship extend beyond the story of the people of Noah. In post-Qur'anic literature, the story of the Arab nation of Thamud is the backdrop for more of this type of narrative. In one account, the Thamud set up a large stone idol, which bore the face of a man, the neck of a mule, with hands and feet like horse's hooves, crowned and plated with gold. The prophet Salih's father served as custodian to the idol's shrine, but once it became clear that he would father a divine messenger, the demon that had been hiding within the idol confessed its deception; the idol then toppled onto its face, in a self-inflicted act of iconoclasm. In another instance, Satan approaches the nation of Thamud, which was mourning the loss of its recently departed king. The devil promises to lead the Thamud and sets a likeness of the king on his empty throne. The idol, in the form of the noble king, is inhabited by a demon, who commands the Thamud to take him as a god, besides Allah.[25]

While the genealogical connections to a noble origin serve to domesticate the loathsome act of idolatry, rendering it a perversion of Abrahamic mono-theism, some origins are rather more ignoble than others. Ibn al-Kalbi tells the story of the genesis of the idols Isaf and Na'ila, who originally had been a man and a woman from Yemen, who undertook the pilgrimage to Mecca. Once at the Ka'ba, and with no one watching, they entered, and there indulged their carnal urges. Divine punishment was swift, and the two were turned to stone. As a warning to others to avoid such offences, they were displayed, one on hill of Safa and the other at Marwa. In time, however, the lesson was forgotten, and people began worshipping the images, and the Quraysh moved them into the pantheon of idols ranged around the Ka'ba.[26]

As Muslims and others reflected on these idols, the distinctions we made above between the denotive and inhering, come easily to hand. In the early eleventh century, the Persian polymath al-Biruni identified these distinctions, and even gave them a sociological framework. The uneducated classes, he said, are unable to properly distinguish between material representations and the truths they represent. Thus, the "natural" preference for the palpable (*mahsus*) over the abstract (*ma'qul*) is found unconditionally among those of lower social standing, while the learned have no need or affinity for images. This, al-Biruni concludes, has led Christians, Jews, Manicheans, and Hindus to worship idols, and to incorporate images in their worship. The common Muslim is also similarly flawed, and would venerate images of the Prophet, of Mecca, and the Ka'ba, when presented with them. Al-Biruni then describes some of the same responses we saw earlier in our discussion of relics: kissing, rubbing the object against one's cheek, and rolling on the ground before it.[27] In a recent comparative study of ancient Mesopotamian idol fashioning, scholars have pointed out this tension between the palpable and the abstract, and investigated strategies to reconcile them. Of particular interest is the case of the god Shamash, around whom rituals were practiced that erased the division between the human intervention that created the object, and the object itself. To this end, the ancient Mesopotamian craftsmen who fashioned the idol Shamash, are recorded in inscriptions as throwing their tools into a river, with priests symbolically cutting off their hands with wooden swords. The point was to conflate as fully as possible the presence of the carved figure with the god him/herself. In this case, it was the attempt to cross the divide between the god Shamash, who stood at a distance, watching over the rites, and Shamash the idol, who in his newly fashioned stone body was somehow equally present.[28]

However useful and ubiquitous it may be, this binary of the palpable and the abstract does not stand up well in every instance. Complications arise when we consider examples of figural and non-figural representation among idols. The tradition of betyls, non-figural standing-stones, is both ancient and surprisingly persistent. Examples from early history are numerous, with Jacob's pillar perhaps the best known (Gen. 28:18–22). What bears noting, however, is that figural and non-figural litholatry appear to have been largely interchangeable, comfortably sharing devotional landscapes. In fact, the written sources on ancient Arabian idols rarely specify whether they are referring to shaped objects, or stones left in their natural form. The question of representation, then, does not seem to hinge completely on similitude. Freedberg made a similar point for Greco-Roman practices, when he noted that the archaeological record makes any assumption of an evolution from crude found objects toward increasingly anthropomorphic ones, untenable.[29]

The idols of Arabia, whether figural or not, were subject to iconoclastic violence. Indeed, the "smashing of idols" became a key theme in the story of Islamic origins. The Qur'anic revelation itself operated with much the same rationale in relation to the religious systems it encountered. While recognizing the validity of earlier Jewish and Christian revelations, the Qur'an unequivocally dismisses them as corrupted, and puts itself in their place. The origin of idolatry stories, as we saw earlier, resonates with a similar theme of decline from a noble origin. The visual culture around idols mirrored the wider Islamic message of recovery and restoration – and in this register a key instrument was iconoclasm. The narrative arc of the prophet Muhammad's mission reaches its climax not with the taking of Mecca, but rather in the breaking of the idols that were found in the precincts around the Kaʻba. Iconoclasm is so central to the Islamic story of origins, that it tells us much more about later Muslim polemics than it ever could about the pre-Islamic religions of Arabia.[30] As becomes quickly apparent, these objects resist linear narrative; as the "other" is more a ghost than a real opponent, the idols of iconoclasm tell an ongoing story in an Islamic voice.

When Muhammad took Mecca in 630, one of his first acts was to enter the Sacred Precinct and circumambulate the Kaʻba, extending his staff in order to touch the Black Stone. He then called for the key to the Kaʻba. Upon entering it, Muhammad found a dove made of wood, which he broke with his bare hands. In another report, he found pictures the Quraysh had placed in the Kaʻba – the images of Abraham he destroyed, but the two of Jesus and Mary were spared.[31] The Sacred Precinct held 360 idols that day, and when Muhammad pointed at them with his staff, declaring "Truth has come, and falsehood is gone. Truly, falsehood is bound to perish." (Q. 17:81) they fell over backwards.[32] It is worth noting that the hadith literature often takes passages out of their Qur'anic context, with the aim of illuminating them and re-contextualizing scripture. This passage, which in the Qur'an is not clearly associated with this idol episode, is a case in point. Prominent in this pantheon was Hubal, an idol made of red agate, standing over a well pit. Al-Azraqi locates this pit, or likely a dried up well, in the "interior" (*batn*) of the Kaʻba. At times, it functioned as a depository for the precious objects donated to the shrine.[33] In addition to being associated with the practice of divining arrows, al-Azraqi notes explicitly that Hubal was in the form of a person, but its original right hand had broken off and been replaced with another in gold.[34]

The attack on images was not restricted to Mecca. In an extension of the iconoclastic interventions in Mecca, shrines around the region were also attacked. Ibn al-Kalbi notes the existence of other Kaʻbas.[35] Of the first, the Kaʻba of Najran, in Southern Arabia, we are given almost no information. In fact, Ibn al-Kalbi's brief description seems to contradict itself, saying that the Banu Harith venerated this Kaʻba, but in the next sentence suggests that this was not a site used for ritual worship. The second report is also very brief, and self-contradictory. We are told that in Sindad, in the region between Kufa and Basra, a Kaʻba had been erected. The report stipulates that this Kaʻba was not a place of worship, but then cites one ʻAhd al-Dar ibn Hudayb, entreating his people to join him in building a shrine that would rival the Kaʻba, and divert the Arab pilgrimage traffic to their region. Despite his initial statement to the contrary, Ibn al-Kalbi notes that this petition fell upon deaf ears, the implication being that the Kaʻba of Sindad was in fact never built.[36]

More substantial accounts, however, survive of the attacks on other shrines. Although the sources are somewhat confused, with more than one location being supplied for the idol, Dhu al-Khalasa figures prominently in the tradition.[37] Sources describe one Khalasa idol located in Mecca, decorated with necklaces and ostrich eggs, and receiving offerings of barley and wheat.[38] The second location was known as the "Yemenite Ka'ba," because of its location between Mecca and San'a. Its success made it a rival to that of Mecca. The shrine lay under the protection of the Khath'am tribe, who threatened to revive the site after the death of the Prophet.[39] Ibn al-Kalbi describes Dhu al-Khalasa as a carved piece of white quartz wearing the semblance of a crown. The idol was toppled, and became the threshold of the gate of the congregational mosque of Tabala, but not before the Khath'am and their allies lost some three hundred fighters defending her.[40]

Another site closer to Mecca, to the north, in the valley of Nakhla, was the location of al-'Uzza – yet here also, the details are somewhat confused.[41] A brief report notes that in the course of the skirmishes during the expedition of Uhud, Abu Sufyan carried al-'Uzza along with "al-Lata" into battle against the Muslims.[42] Ibn al-Kalbi relates that when the Prophet seized Mecca, he sent Khalid ibn al-Walid to destroy the sacred grove associated with al-'Uzza. Khalid was there confronted by an Abyssinian woman with disheveled hair, hands on her shoulders, and gnashing her teeth. After cutting down the last tree, Khalid killed the custodian Dubayya and al-'Uzza, who turned immediately into ashes. A later report adds that before she died, al-'Uzza fired sparks at her attacker, in an effort to set him ablaze. Khalid returned to the Prophet and related his exploits – to which the Prophet replied, "That was al-'Uzza. But she is no more. The Arabs shall have none after her. Verily, she shall never be worshipped again."[43] Elsewhere, Ibn al-Kalbi notes explicitly that al-'Uzza was an idol, who occupied a shrine, in which people would receive oracular communications.[44] The earlier *Sira* literature, adds detail to the story, but presents al-'Uzza as an inanimate idol. Here we are told that as Khalid approached the shrine, Dubayya hung a sword on her, that she might protect herself. The custodian climbed a nearby hill, and recited the following lines: "O al-'Uzza, you must cut this Khalid to pieces. Throw off your veil and tuck up your dress! O al-'Uzza, if you can't kill this mortal Khalid, then take your punishment, give in, and become a Muslim/Christian."[45]

The figure of al-'Uzza presents us with a puzzle. As we saw in the *Sira* report, she is an idol, very likely of worked stone. However, in parts of Ibn al-Kalbi's account, al-'Uzza takes the form of an Abyssinian woman. It is not clear whether this woman is the goddess herself or a demon who had inhabited the idol – a common trope in the literature – or the idol come to life. What we do know, is that in his answer to Khalid, Muhammad recognized her explicitly in this human form. For answers, we might consider a similar example from the episode of the cleansing of the Ka'ba. The historian al-Waqidi (d. 823) adds an interesting detail to the story of the lovers Isaf and Na'ila, who were transformed into stone and eventually became idols. When Muhammad broke these idols, "there came out from one of these two stones a gray-haired woman, who was tearing at her face with her nails, naked, pulling at her hair, and crying out in woe. Asked about that, the Prophet said, 'This is Na'ila who has abandoned hope that she will ever be worshipped in your land again.'"[46] Since this gray-haired woman is described as coming out of the broken idol, she is clearly to be taken as the demon that had given it life. The demons who inhabited such objects, however, are not usually presented as desiring worship, except as a ruse to misguide humans. That is to say, Na'ila here bemoans the loss of worship – as a god or goddess would presumably do – not the fact that her ruse at misdirecting gullible worshipers has been put to an end. But more importantly, some of the wider implications of these inconsistencies are worth considering.

As we noted earlier, in the rite of the ancient Mesopotamian idol makers, the god Shamash was the idol itself as well as the deity overseeing the idol-making ritual. The status of the goddesses al-'Uzza and Na'ila, whether they are inhabiting the objects, or are themselves the objects, remains ambiguous. Whether an object is a betyl (*nasab*), idol (*sanam*), or image (*wathan*) is often unclear, and apparently beside the point. As with Shamash, there is here an unstable sense of subjecthood for the image. In other words, the resistance of objects to interpretive reduction – to recall the overarching theme of this book – here plays out as the idol being both itself and outside itself.

If we imagine the cases of the goddesses in a synchronic structure, in which they are simultaneously present in more than one place, it should be no surprise that we can trace a similar process on a diachronic scale. Despite their initial fate at the hands of various early Muslim iconoclasts, several of these figures reappear on the Arabian landscape. Despite her ignominious end as a threshold in the gate of the mosque at Tabala, the idol Dhu al-Khalasa is also reported to have been destroyed in the eighteenth century. The editor of Al-Azraqi's *Akhbar Makka* records the event of November 1925, in which sons of the House of Sa'ud destroyed Dhu al-Khalasa – no details are provided, but it was likely a betyl.[47] Ibn 'Abd al-Wahhab himself had been an iconoclast, having arranged in 1743 for the destruction of the tomb of the Companion Zayd ibn al-Khattab, and the cutting of a venerated grove, known as the "Trees of the Companions."[48] Travelogues from the nineteenth century identify a number of idols in the city of Ta'if. These are described in the *Book of Idols* by Ibn al-Kalbi, but he locates them elsewhere.[49] One of these travelers left a detailed description from 1878. Charles Doughty describes three stone idols, or "bethels." Al-'Uzza was some 20 feet long, with an impression taken to be her mouth, at one end identified as her head (*maqam al-ra's*). Nearby lies

47 Idols and Gods al-Hubal, al-Lata, and al-Uzza.
Credit: Charles Doughty, *Travels in Arabia Deserta*, 2 volumes (London: Cape, 1926), originally
published in 1888

the small broken stone called al-Hubal, about five feet in length – it was cut in
two by the heroic iconoclast 'Ali ibn Abi Talib.[50] A third betyl was found in
the same neighborhood, that of al-Lat. Like al-'Uzza, she was of unworked
granite, and an indented section is identified as her "head" (Figure 47). Local
practice included the sick rubbing themselves against the stones, in hopes of
relief from their illnesses. It seems these idols not only embody a shifting and
scattering of subjecthood, as we noted earlier, but in more concrete terms,
with the bodily references used in relation to the betyls' heads and mouths, the
boundary between figural idols and non-figural also begins to break down.

Another version of this scattering subjectivity reappears in Islamic Egypt,
centered around that quintessentially Pharaonic object, the pyramid. Medieval
Muslim theories about the purpose and origins of the pyramids, as we shall see
below, were varied and often fanciful, but in an echo of the Arabian betyls and
idols, the pyramids were often animated by spectral figures. Al-Suyuti tells us
that a frightening spirit in the form of a naked woman, with hair down to the
ground, was known to patrol the seaward pyramid (presumably Khufu's) at
Giza. The spirits of the neighboring pyramids took the form of a young man,
naked and tawny, and an old man holding a censer and dressed as a monk,
both of whom haunt their monuments after sundown.[51] Stories of the inhabiting spirits of pyramids abound in the sources.[52]

In its relations with the visual and material culture of the Pharaonic period,
Islamic Egypt developed a variety of perspectives, building in part upon what
had developed in Arabia. Unlike the context of early Muslim communities in
Arabia, which had access to the non-Islamic cultures around them – the
so-called Arab pagans, the Jews, and Christian Arabs – the Islamic perspectives
on Pharaonic culture were limited to the objects, architecture, and images that

survived from the ancient period – roughly 2700 BCE up to the Roman invasion of 30 BCE. The Muslim armies and their allies took Egypt from the Byzantines in 640 CE. In the interim, the rise of Christianity in Egypt, and the development of Coptic language, albeit an inheritance from ancient Egypt, marked a widening gap that pushed the Egypt of the Pharaohs ever further back into the mists of time. Nevertheless, Islamic interaction with these artifacts offers a complex portrait of images and objects, as they negotiate their way into new Islamic horizons.

While instances of iconoclasm were commonplace – as we shall see shortly – there were also a number of voices raised in defense of the surviving objects and monuments of the Pharaonic past. Sayf al-Din ibn Jubra's words elegantly reflect the depth of the aesthetic judgment that could be occasioned by these objects:

> By God! What a strange and wonderful (spectacle)
>   Is presented by the structure of the Pyramids to (men's) hearts!
> They conceal from the hearing (of men) the story of their people,
>   But strip all veils from their (own) wonders.[53]

Ibn Jubra's posture toward Pharaonic material culture is receptive to both the denoted dimensions, what he calls the "story" of the sciences and wisdom of the makers, and the connoted, inherent, and immediate impact that is made upon the senses, or in his words, the "unveiling" of the pyramids' wonders. A few centuries earlier, the astronomer Muhammad ibn Umail Tamimi not only described the images he encountered, but also offered his aesthetic interpretations. Upon entering either a pyramid or a temple – the term *birba* here is ambiguous – Tamimi notes the statue of a seated female "idol," and on the walls pictures of men wearing colorful costumes, which he calls the most perfect and beautiful of compositions. Tamimi describes another nearby painting of two birds, facing each other, biting each other's tails. The overall composition is circular, and gives the sense of one bird wanting to raise the other up, while the other seeks to constrain his companion.[54] The medieval Muslim admirers and defenders of Pharaonic objects drew on a variety of concepts and rationales in decrying both wanton and principled, iconoclasm. As Ibn Jubra and Muhammad Tamimi begin to show us, the scope of Muslim response ran the full range of aesthetic critique.

Although ancient Egyptian writing could not be read by medievals, the admirers of the ancient images could appeal to the inherent beauty of the writing and objects. In his description of the temple of Akhmim, the twelfth-century traveler Ibn Jubayr, celebrates the artistic achievement of the site:

> The ceiling of this temple (*haykal*) consists of stone slabs so well fitted together that they appear to be a single continuous covering. This ceiling is covered with images in wondrous colors, so vivid that the viewer takes

it to be a wooden ceiling. A series of images cover each slab. Some portray birds so strikingly it seems they are about to take flight. There are also pictures of humans (*adamiyya*), in marvelous forms (*ra'i'a al-shakl*), of striking appearance, each one in its own pose. They hold various objects in their hands, such as statues, weapons, or birds. Some are making gestures towards others with their hands. A full description would be beyond words! Inside and out, from the floor to ceiling, the temple also displays gigantic pictures. These non-human forms are a terrible warning, and strike fear in every heart. There isn't a place that is not covered by a mix of pictures, engravings, or texts. These texts, however, cannot be deciphered.[55]

Ibn Jubayr is clearly impressed with the design, composition, and scale of the images and text displayed on the wall of the temple. He makes no pretense to being able to decipher the images or writing, a fact that does not stop him from celebrating their aesthetic achievement.

Admirers often referred to symmetry when extoling Pharaonic objects. In his discussion of the great Sphinx at Giza, al-Maqrizi attributes its beauty to its proportions. In his day, the Sphinx's face still bore its red paint, and the sands had blown up to its neck covering its lion-shaped body. Maqrizi and others assumed the statue was of a man standing, and thus estimated his height to be about 35 m. We don't know what Maqrizi would have thought of the full Sphinx if he had seen it, but he does tell his readers, "The figure is beautiful, and its features full of charm and grace. He seems to be smiling!"[56] He quotes an "eminent man" on the topic, to the effect that the Sphinx's proportions are as perfect as any found in nature, and that this is all the more incredible because the Pharaonic artists preserved the proportions despite the enormity of the statue.

During his time in Egypt, the physician and polymath 'Abd al-Latif al-Baghdadi (d. 1231) recorded many of his reactions to Pharaonic objects. His comments often echo the language that earlier writers like Galen and Aristotle had used around the theory of beauty. Galen had argued that beauty in the human body is found in proper proportions, which generate pleasure in those who see them. Perfect proportions are to be found in the correlation between structure and purpose – whether by the intention of an artist or craftsman, or as found in nature.[57] Standing before a Pharaonic colossus, al-Baghdadi remarks, "Assuredly, nothing can be more marvelous than the sight of such minute proportions with respect to the different parts of the body preserved in a statue of this colossal magnitude. . . From these dimensions and these relative proportions result the beauty and elegance of the whole figure (*yahsulu husnu al-hay'a wa malah al-sura*)."[58]

Different versions of this theory of beauty based on proportion and balance had been in circulation for some time. The popular ninth-century writer al-Jahiz had explained physical beauty as consisting of completeness (*tamam*), moderation or symmetry (*i'tidal*), and proper measure (*wazn*), with beautiful objects of all kinds manifesting "proper measure" through balance in form and composition.[59] The great commentator on Aristotle, Ibn Sina, whom al-Baghdadi read carefully, had defined beauty in similar terms: order (*nazm*), composition (*ta'lif*), and symmetry (*i'tidal*).[60]

After a visit to the nearby ruins of Memphis, al-Baghdadi comments on the skill and perfect proportions on display in the scattered objects. He writes, "As for the idols found among these ruins, whether their great number or their extraordinary size be considered, they surpass description (*yafutu al-wasf*): nor can even a conception of them be formed: but most worthy of admiration is the nicety observed in their forms, their exact proportions, and their resemblance to nature."[61] Al-Baghdadi finds the objects beautiful thanks to their proportions, but he also registers his awe at their size and number, which he feels defy description. His experience is sublime: There seems to be no end to the objects and to the impressions they make on the viewer. He tells us, "The more the collection (of ruins) is considered, the greater the admiration it inspires; and every additional glance at the ruins is a source of fresh delight. Scarcely do they give birth in the mind of the beholder to one idea, than another originates, still more admirable. One moment he prides himself on his perfect comprehension of them, and again, another instant, his pride is lowered by the staring conviction of the inadequacy of his conceptions."[62]

According to al-Baghdadi, the visual import of these objects had significant influence on the Jews and Christians of the region. We are told that the People of Israel acquired their damnable weakness for graven images through the time spent in Egypt, living among peoples who worshipped these impressive monuments. The Copts and Sabeans too, al-Baghdadi tells us, were greatly affected by the Pharaonic objects of devotion left behind by their Egyptian ancestors. The upshot was the incorporation of images into their churches and temples as part of their rituals of worship. The influence of these venerated objects was all the more powerful, due to their parallels with the Christian doctrine of divinity incarnated in the body and person of Christ.[63]

Beyond the immediate aesthetic claims Pharaonic monuments and art made on their Muslim viewers, there were other reasons, perhaps more practical ones, to oppose their destruction. Al-Baghdadi does not mince words on the matter; he declares Saladin's general, who tore down the ancient columns of Alexandria, to be as mindless as a child who can't tell right from wrong. The greedy treasure hunters of his day who, among other outrages, destroyed the Green Chapel (naos) by tunneling under it, are simply, "ignorant and stupid."[64] These objects and images, al-Baghdadi tells us, were not simply for pleasure or decoration, but rather intended to preserve important information for posterity. They are there as an archive, by which later generations and peoples can discern the "sciences, history, and genius" of those who built them.[65] Al-Suyuti provides an oft-repeated story of the mythical King Sawrid, to whom the building of the pyramids is attributed. We are told he ruled some three centuries before the great flood, and that following a warning in a dream, he built the Eastern Pyramid (of Khufu), within which he inscribed maps of the celestial spheres and stars.[66] In his treatment of the pyramids, al-Maqrizi is impressed by the monuments, and what they can teach us. He speaks of a perfect execution of construction, and claims that, "If you consider them closely, you will see that the noblest minds were at work, subtle intelligences were exhausted in the effort, and luminous souls applied themselves fully... (The pyramids) tell their story, extoling their abilities. They inform us of their lives, pronounce on their great knowledge and intellects, and tell their history."[67] In the thirteenth century, the geographer al-Idisi warned that much wisdom would be lost if the Pharaonic monuments of Egypt were to be destroyed. They were erected by wise builders of "pure spirit" (arwah tahira).[68] The content to be transmitted, however, remained elusive. Various interpretations were proffered – we shall see below some claims to decoding mystical Sufi secrets from hieroglyphs – however, the most sustained engagements with ancient Egyptian symbols were to be found in the Hermetic tradition, based on alchemy and theurgy. The pyramids were popularly held to be built by ancient kings to protect them and their wealth from the Great Flood, or erected by Hermes to hide his books of wisdom.[69]

While the specific lessons to be learned from the monuments and the hieroglyphic inscriptions might have been difficult to decipher, another argument in their defense was perhaps clearer. This was the appeal to the precedent set by earlier generations of Muslims, who saw in these monuments a confirmation of the historical accuracy of the Qur'an. Al-Suyuti tells us that in his day, the consensus among the "shaykhs of Egypt" was that the pyramids had been built by Shaddad, the son 'Ad, the progenitor of the people of 'Ad, mentioned in the Qur'an (Q. 11:50). Additionally, several sites have been identified as Joseph's prison, mentioned in Qur'an 12:36.[70] Al-Baghdadi notes that although past Muslim rulers of Egypt rejected the polytheism that inspired the ancient Egyptians, they preserved these relics of antiquity. These wise Muslim rulers, he continues, saw the monuments as archives of the sciences of the past, as well as "witnesses to the truth of the books of revelation... Thus, the sight of what remains of them adds the testimony of proof to that of authority and confirms the verity of (Islamic) tradition."[71]

The geographer al-Idrisi echoes this perspective, and takes it further, when he points to the fact that various Companions of the Prophet lived in Egypt, and were buried virtually in the shadow of the pyramids. Their presence among the objects of the Pharaonic inheritance, al-Idrisi concludes, sanctified the land of Egypt. We are told that, "These valiant holy warriors, the Companions, never raised a hand against the pyramids." Rather, they left them intact as a warning to all humanity. Al-Idrisi seeks to bring Egypt fully into the Islamic landscape – Giza thus becomes a holy land (*ard muqaddasa*), as it is the resting place of both Biblical prophets and the Companions of Muhammad. In a rather awkward reinterpretation, al-Idrisi claims Moses's invitation to his people to, "enter the holy land" (Q. 5:21), is directing them to the "land of the mastabas and pyramids, where the hooves of the horses of the Companions touched the ground."[72] In the following century, another defender, al-Rashidi (d. 1400), condemned Muslim iconoclasts, noting that the earliest and most pious Muslim rulers of Egypt had left the ancient monuments intact for the benefit of posterity.[73]

Another reason to preserve Pharaonic monuments was the wide-spread belief in their power as talismans. For example, the Sphinx at Giza was held to be a particularly powerful protector of the city of Cairo. Its lion body, however, was unknown to Egyptians until excavations in the nineteenth century. The common belief was that this statue deterred the drifting sands, and prevented the western desert from invading the cultivated lands of Giza.[74]

Hieroglyphs themselves were held to have a magical ability to avert misfortune. Thus, the reuse of blocks of stone inscribed with hieroglyphs was believed to keep insects and birds out of mosques. The Copts were, of course, aware of this and incorporated Pharaonic thresholds into their sacred spaces: An inscribed black granite slab supposedly kept the birds out of the church of Saint Onuphris. Significant reuse can be found, for example, in the monastery of Apa Jeremias, built on the edge of Saqqara.[75] Barry Flood has noted that figural apotropaia were a shared phenomenon among the mosques and churches of Syria.[76] In his pilgrimage manual, al-Harawi mentions that the central mosque of Saha (i.e. Kafr al-Shaykh, in the Egyptian delta north of Tanta) has as its lintel a black stone inscribed with hieroglyphs, beyond which birds refuse to pass.[77] The identification of ancient monuments as talismans was widespread. When rebuilding the Great Mosque of Damascus under the caliph al-Walid (d. 715), a cave was discovered, which contained a stone statue of a man on horseback. In one hand the statue held a pearl, which the caliph placed in the mihrab of the mosque. The other hand was broken open, and in it were found one grain of barley and one of wheat. The caliph was told that if this statue's hand had been preserved, Damascus would never see its stores of grain infested by weevils.[78] As speculative as it might have been, the belief in the apotropaic functions of both statues and hieroglyphic writing, had fortuitous implications – namely, helping to incorporate spolia that otherwise might have been lost, preserving them in the medieval Islamic landscape.

In spite of their eloquent defenders, Pharaonic objects and images remained vulnerable to attack. Some of the most dramatic assaults have come down to us in the historical record. A Sufi resident of the Sa'id al-Su'ada convent, by the name of Muhammad of the Constant Fast (Sa'im al-Dahr), took it upon himself to rid the city of a number of artifacts that offended his religious sensibilities. Despite his penchant for fasting, this Sufi was an energetic iconoclast, not only toward Pharaonic images, but also those of Islamic origin. One day in 1379, Sa'im al-Dahr turned on the ranks of heraldic lions that Sultan Baybars' had carved into his "Bridge of Lions." This bridge has not survived, but it is unlikely this was the cause of its demise. Muhammad of the Constant Fast then attacked the Sphinx, claiming it was his moral duty to blot out the statue's face. The chronicler al-Maqrizi tells us that these attacks broke the Sphinx's nose and ears – details presented in haste, since the Sphinx still has its ears today.[79] Al-Maqrizi laments that this sabotage weakened the Sphinx's apotropaic ability to hold back the sands of the desert, which subsequently encroached upon the city from the west. Another account claims the attack left Egypt open to invasion by the Crusaders, while Evlia Celebi's account from the seventeenth century disapproves even more harshly, and describes the Sufi iconoclast being lynched by a mob at Giza, and interred ignominiously at the foot of the Sphinx.[80]

The iconoclastic impulse, however, could also appear in much more thoughtful and creative ways. In his thirteenth-century pilgrimage guide book, al-Harawi describes in detail his own encounter with a colossal statue in Luxor. Wielding the tools of writer, in his case a pen cut from a palm frond, al-Harawi scribbled verses from the Qur'an across the statue's chest: "Have they not traveled through the land, and seen how was the end of those who came before them, who had been stronger, tilled the land and built more upon it than they? When messengers came to them with clear proofs – surely it was not God who wronged them, but they wronged themselves." (Q. 30:9) With their emphasis on the fleeting nature of human endeavor, these passages must have reflected al-Harawi's indignation and anxiety before these impressive monuments. He then adds the following, "Where have the mighty gone? The king Khusrows of the past? They are gone, along with the treasures they amassed. Many found the battlefields too small to contain their vast armies, yet now they themselves are confined to their sarcophagi. May God have mercy on those who reflect and understand."[81]

Al-Harawi's anxiety is clearly not that of Muhammad of the Constant Fast – the former is responding to what he sees as human audacity, while the latter was policing the landscape to purify it of offending images. Yet another motivation can be detected. It was at play perhaps most clearly behind the iconoclastic acts of the mystic Dhu al-Nun al-Misri (d. 859). This enigmatic figure, a Sufi and an alchemist, recorded several of his visionary experiences, which took place in the temples of his home town Akhmim, in Upper Egypt. Some believed his accomplished spiritual status allowed him to read the hieroglyphs, transmitting their ancient wisdom into the Islamic era. After "deeply contemplating" one series of hieroglyphs, its meaning emerged, which he translated as: "Destiny commands, and fate laughs" – another inscription ran, "He who examines the stars knows nothing; but the Lord of the stars does as He likes."[82] Dhu al-Nun not only took the Pharaonic monuments as archives of knowledge – they also provoked his anxiety. We are told that in the great Temple of Akhmim, Dhu al-Nun would read the remarkable images, absorbing their great wisdom (*hikmatan 'azimatan*), and then destroy them.[83]

While quite distinct from each other, the attacks on the Sphinx and the colossus in Luxor do share one important characteristic: They both preserve their target objects, which rather than being obliterated, are turned into frames or displays for the iconoclasm visited upon them. Although its assailant would have liked to reduce it to rubble, the Sphinx still stands, bearing clearly the marks of the attack; and al-Harawi's vandalized colossus would continue to stand, turned now into a marker of its own derision. We might call the outcome of such disfiguring a "sign of both the power and the powerlessness" of the object,[84] a phrase that captures the complex and scattered nature of these objects as they move through history. In much the same way, the temple images that Dhu al-Nun destroyed came to embody this scattered signification: in the hands of the mystic, they were somehow both revelatory and forbidden. Just as there was no single Muslim attitude toward ancient images, when subjected to iconoclastic violence, the objects demonstrated a plurality of signification. The openings represented by the objects' responses to violence, make manifest what earlier in this book I characterized as a resistance to reduction. As we shall see below, Pharaonic objects would continue such negotiated resistance within Islamic architecture, and beyond.

There seems to be no limit to the possible reuses of Pharaonic materials in the medieval built environment. They appear as pillars, sills, capitals, blocks in the foundations of walls and bridges; the greatest number perhaps acting as lintels and thresholds. Monumental buildings such as palaces and defensive fortifications, include significant amounts of reuse material, but mosques, shrines, and mausolea are more numerous and prominent sites.[85] While it is impossible to account for all of the unmarked materials reused in medieval constructions – inscribed objects, bearing plant and animal motifs, hieroglyphic writing, images of gods, kings, and others, are readily identifiable. Yet even this subset is vast, with new examples appearing regularly, as Islamic archeological and restoration projects continue to unearth materials. A doctoral dissertation from the early 1990s has begun to study this material, beginning with 118 inscribed Pharaonic pieces, which have been incorporated into the Islamic architecture of medieval Cairo.[86] While some Pharaonic temples and pyramids were dismantled by medieval builders, a recent study has concluded that the vast majority of Pharaonic spolia came by way of reused Roman and Byzantine buildings in Egypt that had earlier pillaged Pharaonic sites. The authors point out that many of the reuse stones that appeared in Islamic buildings came from demolished Byzantine structures, which had themselves been constructed using Roman materials.[87] Since we can rarely track the earlier lives of the Pharaonic spolia we will be looking at below, we should bear in mind that our current accounts of their reuse are only the latest chapters in the life stories of these objects.

Scholars have made several attempts to enumerate the motivations behind the reuse of *spolia*, with the three most prominent being the pragmatic need for building materials, the aesthetic impulse to create pleasing or impressive structures, and the ideological desire to represent symbolically the overcoming of an enemy culture, religion, or civilization. While hewing essentially to this threefold typology, Michael Geenlagh has identified 17 sub-categories for reuse, found among European, Byzantine, and Islamic practices – with the "pragmatic economic" being most common, and the ideological the least prevalent.[88] By contrast, the historian of the Crusades, Carol Hillenbrand, also identified the categories of the practical and the aesthetic, but put more emphasis on the third, which consists of displays of the spoils of victory.[89] In a more recent study, Richard McClary surveys the Islamic appropriations of Byzantine spolia, and offers a more flexible paradigm. He concludes, "There was a shifting and imprecise sliding scale of overlapping motivations, with clearly symbolic reuse in some cases, and in others more overly prosaic, practical reasons for the reuse of elements from a different, earlier and largely subjugated tradition of lithic architectural expression."[90] McClary's attention to the "sliding scale" of motivations, seems a useful turn in allowing for the complexity and indeterminacy that prevail around specific objects and actors. Yet a note of caution is in order – in light of the almost complete absence of information on individual objects and actors, Greenlagh warns against the desire to find meaning behind every reused stone: "... just where a certain block stops being apotropaic and becomes either decorative or inconsequential, we (historians) usually cannot say."[91]

While caution in presuming to determine iconoclasts' and builders' motives is prudent, we may engage more usefully with reused materials, using more nuanced categories. Surveying European traditions, Anthony Cutler has proposed distinguishing between reuse driven by the immediate material needs of builders, and reuse with an eye on the past, which constitutes a gesture to history.[92] The historical consciousness Cutler sees in some spolia may include the ideological or triumphal uses we mentioned earlier, but framing out a wider category helps to avoid over determining motives, which are often unavailable to us by direct textual evidence. This wider category is also more amenable to the important conceptual turn, one that seeks to step away from the prevailing predilection in the history of art to privileging origins of objects.

In other words, attention to the historical gestures that were integral to the reuse of objects, will allow a richer and more complex story to be told. Earlier in this chapter we met Barry Flood's idea of a "total artwork," which proposed to see reused objects within their new material and aesthetic contexts. While such an approach does not efface the original significations of spolia, such details (inasmuch as they survive) are renegotiated within the new complex in which the objects are displayed. A similar paradigm has been proposed within the study of Buddhist iconoclasm. In an effort to move beyond the simple binary of destruction or preservation, iconoclasm can often be seen not as the erasure of cultural and religious meaning, but rather as a form of cultural activity.[93]

When a reuse, in Cutler's words, has opened an "eye to the past," it begins to generate new significance, an insight that Kopytoff also made within what he called the cultural redefinition and reuse of "alien objects."[94] In a similar effort, Richard Davis has traced the movement of Hindu icons from their religious contexts to their display in modern museums. These peregrinations occur within a single cultural zone, that of Hindu identified India, but the move from temple to gallery is only possible with a complete transformation in the "communities of response."[95] A better description, however, is Avinoam Shalem's "traveling artifacts," which describes Islamic objects that have crossed boundaries of time, culture, and religion, to make new homes in the material culture of European Christendom.[96] This framework has the virtue of focusing on the history of the objects, while making room for their redefinition of significance and meaning. Shalem's traveling artifacts, however, usefully disturb our predominating sense of object; these are artworks that are so shifting in their histories, that they do not have fixed meanings we can describe and trace out. He identifies a "hybride Ästhetik," at play around the artistic combining of objects, some altered, others not. Importantly, the earlier identities that inhered in the spolia are put into play, being either lost or reworked as part of an imagined history, which becomes woven into the identity of the new hybrid object.[97]

These observations illuminate many of the Pharaonic spolia under consideration in our study. The reimagining of the history of such materials, played out either within the context of religious anxiety, or the quest for lost knowledge, or as we shall see, a modern sense of cultural purity, overturns any simple story of their essence. This decentering of the object's essence is what Didi-Huberman was pointing to when he claimed the diachronic and synchronic dimensions of objects are utterly entwined: ". . . one must understand that in each historical object, all times encounter one another, collide, or base themselves plastically on one another, bifurcate, or even become entangled with one another."[98] It is within the context of this entangling, that we can hear the broken, displaced, and reused objects speak in a new way. More precisely, we encounter spolia resisting reduction to both their immediate surroundings, and any fixed origins. As Dale Kinney nicely puts it, spolia are, "survivors of violence, about which they might be mute (if they bear no visible signs of it) or eloquent."[99]

The survivors under consideration here are the many Pharaonic spolia that were preserved in Islamic religious architecture. The creation of this hybrid regional style can be dated roughly to the Mamluk and early Ottoman periods of Egypt – mid-thirteenth to seventeenth centuries CE. However, this land-scape, as we shall see, has largely been effaced by the physical interventions of a combination of puritanical religious ideology, and a modern colonial vision of cultural and stylistic purity.

Mosques are the most common contexts for the display of spolia, with lintels and steps being particularly prominent. In the town of Fuwa, in the Delta north of Disuq, the Nasr Allah mosque contains a hieroglyphic inscribed block, as one of the steps to its entrance. Also in the Delta, the Qinawi mosque incorporates a threshold block decorated with an inscribed plant motif, in addition to a pillar decorated with figures in a fertility procession.[100] In the same region, the mosque of Abu al-Makarim also contains a Pharaonic pillar, and the Kuraniyya mosque has incorporated into its well a block with undetermined figures carrying offerings on plates. The anthropologist Georg Stauth was unable to substantiate the claims he heard in 2006 at these sites that government officials had moved a number of blocks with hieroglyph inscriptions to Cairo.[101]

Many mosques in medieval Cairo have incorporated spolia. The erratic Fatimid caliph, al-Hakim (r. 996–1021) built a grand mosque, which incorporated at least three large blocks identifiable as coming from a temple of Akhenaten. The stones, showing sections of human legs, bowing figures, a partial gateway, figures bending over sacks (perhaps offerings), and a gazell, are all found incorporated into the north minaret.[102]

Thanks largely to the dense stone used, Pharaonic spolia were often used for lintels and thresholds; heavy foot traffic in mosques made this building material a good choice. The mosque of Sayyidi al-Bulqini, probably built around 1389 contained spolia in its threshold. The block, originally from the nearby city and religious center of Heliopolis, contained hieroglyphic texts relating to the Pharaoh Ramesses VI.[103] The proximity of Heliopolis to what became Islamic Cairo, would make it a convenient site for pillaging materials for medieval buildings. In the vast mosque-madrasa of Sultan Hasan, completed in 1359, a granite threshold was installed in the south side of the main hall that opened onto the *iwans* (open porticos) for the teaching of Islamic law. This was the largest vaulted hall of the medieval Muslim world.[104] The block, installed in the transition to the Maliki school's *iwan*, shows a partial royal cartouche of Amose, along with the image of a king, in offering posture, holding a vase, likely as part of a purification ritual. In the modern period, the block was taken out of the site, and moved to the Cairo museum.[105] A large grey granite sarcophagus, dating to the 26th dynasty (cir. 600 BCE), was used in the Ibn Tulun mosque as a ritual bathtub. The exterior is decorated with images including that of the gods Isis and Nefthys. It now rests in the British Museum.[106]

The threshold spolia in the mosque of Amir Lajin (d. 1299) was also removed from its Islamic context, to be preserved in the Egyptian Museum at Cairo. This was a stela fragment from the Ptolemaic period, of the third century BCE. The stone measures 195 × 40 cm, and is inscribed with a decree of Canopus, which like the Rosetta Stone, displays a single text in Hieroglyphs, Demotic, and Greek.[107] The mosque-mausoleum of Aslam al-Baha'i al-Silahdar, from the mid-fourteenth century, lost its engraved door jamb, which seems to have come from Heliopolis, to the Egyptian Museum.[108] Built a decade earlier, the mosque of al-Maridani bore above its main entrance a lintel inscribed with a winged disc, and a mirrored double rendering of Rameses II. The piece is now also in the Egyptian Museum.[109] The mosque-mausoleum of Kharybak, built shortly after 1502, includes a threshold block with mummiform Osiris and winged insect inscriptions.[110] This stone has remained *in situ*, continuing to serve as a front step to the mosque. The adjacent fourteenth-century mosque of Amir Aqsunqur also has an inscribed but heavily warn threshold in place.

Columns were also important building materials, which needed to bear heavy structural loads. One column of the Maridani mosque, completed in 1340, includes a section of red granite block from the sixteenth century BCE reign of Amenhotep.[111] Far more prominent columns, however, were those that some five years later were hauled from the temple at Ashmunain (Hermopolis), up to al-Nasir Muhammad's new mosque in the Cairo Citadel. Due to their size and weight, the 300 km trip from central Egypt was an epic undertaking. Al-Dawadari tells us that, "These columns were crafted by devils and jinn – humans being unable to produce such objects." Recalling the story of Solomon's control over an army of jinn slaves, he claims that ancient, "Priests. . . employed rebellious jinn in the construction of all their (Pharaonic) monuments." The two columns required thousands of laborers to move them along the streets of the city.[112]

Along with the pillars were obelisks that had stood in the temple complex of Hermopolis. Only the first 250–274 cm of the obelisks survive, but enough of the inscription is visible to establish they were dedicated to the god Thoth by the pharaoh Nectanebo II.[113] Despite the great effort it would have taken to get the obelisks up to the Citadel, this would not be their final resting place. During the French occupation of Egypt (1798–1801), Napoleon's *mission scientifique* had amassed a large collection of antiquities, including the Rosetta Stone discovered in 1799, along with the two obelisks torn from Nasir Muhammad's mosque and added to the horde bound for Europe. After the defeat of the French however, in 1800, General Menou was forced to relinquish the treasures to General Hely-Hutchinson, who forwarded them to the British Museum.[114] This was not the only treasure of Nectanebo II's to be recovered for the British Museum. The pharaoh's sarcophagus, which had been installed as an ablutions tank in the Attarin mosque of Alexandria – originally built as the church of St Athanasius – was transferred to London as part of the same haul.[115]

The mosque of Sultan Barsbay (d. 1438) once held part of a black basalt sarcophagus, bearing the figure of a high priest of Isis. How it was incorporated into the mosque's architecture is unknown, but the object is currently housed in the Cairo Museum.[116] Completed in 1349, the mosque of Amir Shaykhu once had an impressive stela (185 × 118 cm) in a section of its foundations, depicting four provincial satrap officials beneath a winged sun, along with substantial text running below. It is also now to be found in the Cairo Museum.[117] Records indicate that this black granite stela was "found" in 1870 by Muhammad Effendi Kourshid, a surveyor for the museum.[118] The threshold of the mid-eighteenth century mosque of al-Kikhya, is formed from a section of a black granite lid of a sarcophagus. The block – which bears hieroglyphic text from the Book of the Dead, along with the name of the departed, noting he had accompanied Alexander the Great in the conquest of Egypt – remains in place.[119]

In addition to mosques, several Sufi convents (*zawiyas* and *khanqahs*) incorporated Pharaonic spolia. The entrance to the Khanqah of Shaykhu consists of a fine Pharaonic-era lintel, sitting beneath the foundation inscription, under an iron grid opening onto the vestibule. Figure 48 shows the dark green granite lintel, 300 × 60 cm, with its finely carved bevel sloping downwards to a band

48 Pharaonic lintel over door of Shaykhu's Sufi convent.
Credit: Photo by author

of hieroglyphic text. There is clearly a thoughtful design behind this reuse, which incorporates the sloping angle of the lintel as a transition between the door frame and the Arabic inscription panel above. The hieroglyphs serve as a decorative feature across the top of the door frame. The piece was originally made for the Pharaoh Amasis (or Ahmose) I, and was known to medieval Arabs as the Green Chapel of Memphis.[120] Sources tell us that around 1349 Amir Shaykhu broke the Chapel into pieces, and reused parts of it for his *khanqah*, which was completed in 1355. The chronicler al-Qalqashandi adds that Shaykhu's initial intention was to move the entire naos (*bayt*) to Cairo, but he abandoned his plan once the construction cracked. This seems unlikely, however, since there would be no clear purpose for such an object in city, while spolia, as we have seen, were already a common sight.[121] Attacks on these small buildings continued at least in to the mid-nineteenth century. In his description of the Cairo Museum, Gaston Maspero describes pieces of "une chapelle monlithe," datable to the thirtieth dynasty, recently destroyed by a "high Egyptian functionary." Maspero hoped to locate the remaining pieces, and reconstruct the naos.[122]

A marble lintel, inscribed with a scene of priests petitioning the fertility goddess Astarte-Hathor, was incorporated into the *khanqah* of Sa'd al-Din Ibn al-Ghurab. The convent was completed in 1406, but lost its lintel to the Egyptian Museum in the modern period.[123] Parts of a black granite sarcophagus, from Saqqara, found their way into the foundation construction of the shrine of Husayn. These large blocks, engraved with images of birds, dogs, and a winged deity, were removed to the Egyptian Museum.[124] In the mid-sixteenth century two blocks of inscribed quartzite from Heliopolis were installed as lintels for the *zawiya* of Ahmad ibn Sha'ban, located near al-Azhar. Both are currently in place.[125] The *zawiya* and shrine of Ahmad Dardir (d. 1786) contained part of an offering table of Ramesses II (37 × 180 cm), as well as a block (36 × 125 cm) with representations of deities and a falcon. Both were moved to the Cairo Museum sometime in the nineteenth century, with no record left of their function in the Sufi building.[126]

Within Islamic funerary architecture – including shrines to saints, and mausolea for sultans and amirs – several examples of reuse are found. Figure 49 shows the threshold to the mosque of Sultan Faraj ibn Barquq's funerary complex, built in the Northern cemetery in 1411. It shows the large block bearing a rendering of a leg and foot.[127] There would seem to be little aesthetic impulse at play in this display, beyond an association of feet and legs with the threshold of a building. In the mausoleum complex of another sultan, Baybars al-Jashnakir (d. 1310), a basalt libation table was integrated into the prayer niche, but has been removed to the Cairo Museum.[128] At the same complex, a large Pharaonic sandstone, originally a door jamb, has been employed as a threshold. Three scenes are depicted, including pharaoh Rameses IX offering

49   Pharaonic threshold at Faraj ibn Barquq complex.
Credit: Photo by author

50   Pharaonic threshold at Baybars Jashnakir mausoleum.
Credit: Photo by author

wine-jars, and the pharaoh kneeling, as can be seen in Figure 50.[129] This image also encapsulates the historical layering at play in the monument: with the medieval marble flooring anchoring the Pharaonic spolia, upon which sit a pair of sandals kicked off by a worshipper in 2012. Other royal mausolea have preserved Pharaonic spolia. These include the mausoleum of Najm al-Din Ayyub (d. 1249) with its granite threshold displaying the lower half of three standing figures on its upper face.[130]

Several spolia incorporated into other sultanic mausolea have been removed to the Egyptian Museum. A two-meter high green schist panel, which

Pharaoh Nectanebo II had dedicated to the god Onuris, stood in the Qalawun (d. 1290) complex.[131] Sultan Qalawun's successor, his son Salah al-Din Khalil, would also reuse ancient materials such as sarcophagi, in his renovations of the mausoleum of the Prophet's companion Abu Hurayra, in Yibna, Palestine.[132] Part of a sarcophagus, bearing the cartouche of Ptolemy VI, was spolia integrated into the mausoleum of Sultan Inal (d. 1461). The other part of this sarcophagus appeared some 50 years later, in the mausoleum of Amir Qurq-mas. In 1983, the Qurqmas mausoleum was moved from its original location, next to the mosque of al-Hakim, and rebuilt in the northern cemetery. The move was undertaken in the context of Bohra Isma'ili Shia restorations of al-Hakim, and was likely the occasion for the removal of the sarcophagus reuse.[133]

A sandstone block with snake-headed and frog-headed deities once stood within the tomb of the Abbasid caliphs, in the Qarafa cemetery, but is now housed in the Cairo Museum.[134] A large block of red quartzite, attributed to Ramesses II, incorporated into the Mevlevi Sufi mausoleum, may still be found *in situ*.[135] The mausoleum of Salar (Sangar), dated to 1322 contained part of the black granite sarcophagus of Nectanebo. The object is now found in the Cairo Museum.[136]

While high-profile religious buildings erected in Cairo after the eighteenth century rarely included spolia, as the examples we noted earlier from the Delta suggest, this design and building practice has nevertheless continued into the modern period. In 1909, Massignon identified a pharaonic threshold bearing the name of Pharaoh Seti II, used in the recent construction of the Sufi saint Jalal al-Dashnawi's tomb in Dashna, some 100 km down the Nile from Luxor.[137] Further research, both on the ground and in the many arch-aeological reports published over the last century and a half, would surely locate more examples of Pharaonic spolia reused in medieval Muslim architec-ture. Further digging into the reports of the Comité de Conservation des Monuments de l'Art Arabe, might provide more details on where spolia were found. The "Comité" was established in 1881 and dominated by prominent Europeans such as J. Franz and Max Herz. In Chapter 2, we saw that Herz was instrumental in establishing of the Museum of Arab Art. Europeans directed the work of the Comité, which included making a list of the Islamic monu-ments that should be protected, as well as overseeing restorations of endan-gered buildings. A number of Egyptians were allowed significant roles in the work of the Comité, the most famous being 'Ali Pasha Mubarak (d. 1893), but full control was only assumed in 1952, when the Comité was replaced by the Egyptian Antiquities Organization, within the Egyptian Ministry of Cul-ture.[138] Antiquities looted by the French and the British had fed the European craze of Egyptomania, but just as importantly for the story of our spolia, Victorian England became fascinated with medieval Cairo, which it saw as the "authentic" Egypt, threatened by modernizing initiatives by both colonial rule and reform minded-Egyptians.[139] The colonial presence in Egypt, from Napoleon's invasion at the start of the nineteenth century to the departure of the British and the Free Officers' coup in 1952, had forged the modern understanding of Egyptian history, as well as intervening directly to preserve and organize the artifacts on the ground that supported that vision. As Donald Reid has put it, "Europe was staking its claim not only to the pharaonic, biblical, and classical pasts, but to the Arab and Islamic past as well."[140] In justification of their programs of acquisition of artifacts for both museums and private collections, the colonial powers claimed they were saving Pharaonic monuments from the modern iconoclastic Muslims of modern Egypt.[141]

The reordering of the Islamic landscape – the movement of Pharaonic spolia out of medieval buildings, and into museums – reflected the imposition of boundaries drawn according to a modern European and colonial perspective. Lives of real communities and real objects, however, were rarely so neatly segregated, and often violated the "modern" typology – being an inconvenience, if not an affront, to the European quest to map and organize the world. The divisions between Ancient, Coptic, and Arab-Islamic Egypt, were framed by colonial powers, but such a vision had to be violently forced upon the Egyptian landscape. Seeking to purify this medieval landscape, to identify and clean up its Islamic architecture, as well as isolating the ancient materials safely and securely in the colonial museum, the Comité and its inheritors, in fact swept away a chapter of Egyptian history. The denotive agenda the spolia evoked to the colonial eye was a confusion of categories and epochs, and provoked a vast material intervention, which largely obliterated a centuries old tradition of positive reception of Pharaonic material culture. The ostensible project of preservation in fact entailed significant destruction. More than simply a regional style of Arab or Islamic art and design, the positions that these spolia had negotiated for themselves constituted a unique aesthetic topography that had for centuries been the expression and experience of Islamic religious life in Egypt.

EPILOGUE

The challenge of what this book has been calling the devotional object is not a new one. The solutions I've developed, such as the "resisting" object, or the "scattered subject" that violates material and temporal boundaries, might sound novel, but the paradigm and its challenges were recognized long ago in medieval Islam. One elegant and provocative statement on the matter came from the mystical philosopher Ibn 'Arabi, who in the late twelfth century traveled from Islamic Spain, through Egypt, and settled permanently in Damascus. Despite his prodigious literary output, his lifelong obsession was the puzzle of the one and the many, or in more Islamic terms, the paradox of creation emanating from God, yet somehow remaining substantively independent. For Muslim mystics who came after him, Ibn 'Arabi's vast reflections on this paradox were a fertile place to explore issues such as the relation of the self to truth and to God. When the issue has been framed around the problem of an existence shared between the Creator and creation, the boundaries between knowing the self and knowing God seem to falter. Dancing across borders, Ibn 'Arabi also turns toward the challenge of the devotional object. In his discussion of the prophet Elijah, Ibn 'Arabi emphasizes the dual nature of truth, which extends beyond the transcendental to include the immanent. Employing a provocative technique, which remains controversial today because it does not shy away from pointing out the faults of some of God's prophets, he focuses on the limitations of Elijah's mission. After returning from his mystical vision, Ibn 'Arabi tells us Elijah had lost his ability to lust, retaining only his intellect. Rather than taking this as the perfection of the prophet's soul, finally having risen above the lower human appetites, Ibn 'Arabi claims that complete wisdom is now impossible for the prophet. The fullest realization includes not only the intellect, but also the mute knowledge of the passions, which Ibn 'Arabi at one point calls becoming "pure animal." Building beyond the Aristotelian identification of a rational faculty peculiar to humans, the provocative lesson for us is to seek the wider embrace of all "things in (both) principle and in form" (bi-usuliha wa suwariha).[1]

What Ibn 'Arabi pointed to as the unspeaking knowledge of forms has also drawn the attention of modern scholars of religion. Reflecting on research trajectories ahead for the field, Amy Hollywood identifies the challenge in the gap between the texts that have come down to us, and the objects that seem to stand silently before us. She calls for an evolution in our methodology, which will provide traction on the forms of religion "hitherto visible only indirectly" – the liturgies, manuals, guidebooks, images, and objects about which textual explanations have not survived.[2] In his reflections on efforts to give voice to the objects of religion, Avinoam Shalem has distinguished between two approaches in the field. The first sought an account of the historical contexts in which objects operated, while the second and more recent has focused on the biographies or the "traces of the object's adventures."[3] Here the proposal leads forward, he tells us, with attention to alteration, adjustment, modification, and displacement. His answer to Hollywood's challenge is to read the textual sources while viewing the objects, which together will tell the story of these "adventures." In essence, his advice is to pivot away from the construction of static frames, and their supposed explanatory power, turning toward objects as catalysts for action and behavior – thus giving indirect voice to artifacts.

Another perspective seeking to recover these voices is adopted by Jacques Rancière. Trying to escape the division between the representation and the autonomy of the artwork, he examines aesthetic practices in conjunction with the discourses that establish the conditions by which these are perceived *as* artistic and literary practices. For Rancière, the question at play is one of category formation itself. If we are to avoid the stagnant empiricism that would describe religion in isolation, as well as reductions of artworks to ideal and ideological universals – we must engage with the objects as they actively arose along with the discourses around what they are.[4] In other words, the theory of what an object was is historically inextricable from our fulsome understanding of that object now. The devotional object of religion thus emerges for us woven together with the evolving and negotiated understandings of what religion is.

In recent discussions, Richard King has widened this focus. Rancière warned us to take seriously the theorizing that plays out in the gap between the object and the world around it, and now King points to developments in the study of religion that have pushed us to acknowledge how the object is bounded by our acts of examination.[5] While Rancière shines a light on the theorizing that evolved along with the object in history, and King wants to us to include ourselves as the last chapter in that unfolding history of theory, the examinations offered in this book have laid bare some of those spaces and processes that both tradition and scholarship have occluded. The examinations offered in the above chapters not only constitute their object of study against the marginalizing gestures of a modern political form of Islam, but also against the erasures of Islamic visual culture imposed by various colonial administrations. The insights of Rancière, King, and others – among them the many aesthetics and visual culture studies I have enlisted in this book project – produce each in their own way small vehicles for reading against these dominant and controlling narratives.

In the register of this book's object-centered narrative, we have seen that Rancière's gap, far from being a negative space, is filled with pulsing, fluttering, bouncing and breaking objects. However, objects are in those spaces precisely as their boundaries blur, and their meanings are put into question. We saw the *mahmal* palanquin and *kiswa* coverings resisting the boundaries that would otherwise separate the devotional from the political; the objects themselves engaged the discourses of the medieval and modern periods in ways that resisted such simple binaries. The dressed Ka'ba played with the subjecthood of the pilgrim, collapsing the human–object divide, imitating, and yet completing, the Hajj in its own ritual clothing, asserting a monumental adornment, which overwhelmed and dwarfed the pilgrim. Likewise, the *mahmal* resisted easy reduction. Emerging from murky origins in the thirteenth century, the Hajj *mahmal* set out to determine its own origins. What the *mahmal* is – a virtual pilgrim on the Hajj, a symbol of projected political authority, a relic of the Prophet's tomb in Medina, a simulacrum of a saint shrine, or an artwork – is forever put into play. The *mahmal* puts space itself into flux, by collapsing vast distances; one could stand in Damascus or Cairo and commune with Muhammad's tomb, or touch the dress of the Ka'ba as it passed by on parade. The mobility of the object showed that the boundaries between prophets and saints are easily elided, with names, rituals, and forms, continually evolving. The modern boundary between the religious and the secular – itself largely an articulation of Islamist discourses – would be put into flux around contested sites and public rituals. Further, the colonial institution of the national museum remains an unsettled and ill-defined space, functioning to alienate the *mahmal*, re-deploying the category "secular" as a weapon to marginalize, all in the cause of Islamic reform.

In our discussion of banners and parading, we also saw objects that sat uneasily within their typically assigned boundaries. Inscribed religious banners float somewhere between "text" and "artwork." They serve as texts, making claims, declaring pious sentiments, and identifying the human actors associated with them, while their aesthetic power is generated by their decorative composition, along with their display within the framework of public spectacles. As texts, one peculiar dimension is their unreadability, or at least resistance to reading. Whether due to the difficulty of deciphering Arabic calligraphy, or the layered and rippling fabric media upon which they sit, these texts communicate at various levels simultaneously, not least of which is that of a performative object. These text/artworks are brought to their full significance when they are integrated into their related religious performances, with all of the indeterminacy and constructedness that any performance wagers with its audience. In the examples surveyed in Chapter 3, the texts resisted easy reading, requiring a technique based on glancing, which tends toward the visual force of an image, rather than decoding, as we usually understand the process of reading to work.

Boundaries were also resisted by the dynamic sacred relics in Chapters 4 and 5. While the typology of such objects remains a useful descriptor, it became clear that individually they would not easily lend themselves to such control. A sense that the materiality of relics unfolds almost endlessly, quickly arose. Historically, corporeal relics appeared, circulated, multiplied, and often easily disappeared. The sandal relic of Muhammad stands in several instantiations as a touchable object, yet from the twelfth century it gave rise to equally powerful relics which were tracings – precise, and yet stylized – of an original, or just as powerfully, tracings of earlier tracings. We noted the essential role that certain visual practices played in the constitution of relics – in particular, the devotional reflections on love and death. The relic is thus an object which rather than recalling a lost or distant beloved, violates the function of images, foreclosing on the absent, and imposing its own material presence. These viewing practices engage with an aesthetic that tilts toward the material presence of the relic, which rather than evoking the absent beloved, or symbolizing the divine, make immediate the finitude and vulnerability of every human body. These practices, which were described in terms of touching, clearly meant to evoke the intimacy of direct human contact, recalling experiences of love, and thus of infinite openings to the devotional self.

The final chapter began with an exploration of the traditions of Arabian idols and betyls. Although these objects were subject to significant description in the Islamic sources, they were also repeatedly singled out for attack and destruction. The objects seem to resist their own boundaries, both by reappearing in various historical periods and in assuming various forms. An idol may appear as an unworked stone, an anthropomorphic sculpture, or transform into a demonic individual when threatened by an iconoclast. The object under attack may also take on an afterlife for itself. That is to say, iconoclastic acts were not simply erasures of image and identity, but the victim object could resist, and bearing the violent signs of disruption upon it, negotiate new aesthetic and visual paradigms for its future. The Islamic reuse of Pharaonic spolia in Egypt illustrated this procedure in several ways. We noted that resistance was never static, and changes in the political and religious culture of Egypt in the modern era altered the range of possibilities. While the Islamist campaigns against the *mahmal* had relegated the sacred object to the museum, the Western interventions into Islamic visual culture – in particular the "preservation" of medieval Islamic heritage – led to a purging of Pharaonic spolia from their medieval contexts, and their relegation to Antiquities museums.

Throughout this book, a story has emerged around the objects of religion that troubles any fixed or necessary reduction of meaning. That is to say, attention to the histories of religious objects shows them to be uncooperative agents, resistant to any final determination by the discursive environments in which they found themselves. From the beginning, I have been characterizing this as the objects' resistance to the various determinations facing them at each historical turn. Objects and images are certainly connected to the theologies, philosophies, mythologies, and other cultural constructs that surround them. We have seen how these connections are essential to meaning-making, and yet our case studies have also shown that these are not rigid or automatic. My claim has been that the object is best understood to be negotiating its meaning – engaging with various concepts and ideas, resonating with some while resisting others.

In a recent study of material "vitality" and its implications for political theory, Jane Bennett reflects on the ethical stakes of such research. Her claim is that by cultivating a "a bit of anthropomorphism" this approach will serve as a corrective to the violent narcissism that has characterized our human dominance of the modern world. Her previous work on environmental values is clearly somewhere behind this claim, but I believe it holds for what I've been trying to do here. With its object-centered approach, this study frustrates the triumphalist and totalizing narratives that so often characterize religious discourse, and are echoed in the study of religion. Place is instead made for hybridity, negotiation, compromise, resilience, scattering, and survival. Rancière and King earlier underlined the importance of boundary formation, contestation, and change. This book has traced out the object's negotiations as resistance to overarching narratives and abstracted starting points, pushing back against concepts like purity, origin, and certitude. This recovery of the devotional object has seen the crossing of both cultural and physical borders, along with the negotiation of identity that such disruption entails, all of which make space for the mute voices of objects and images floating seductively somewhere out in the margins of Islamic history.

TABLE I: *Timeline of Middle East Empires*

395–1453	Byzantine Empire
632	Death of the Prophet Muhammad
632–661	Rule of the Rightly Guided (*Rashidun*) Caliphs
661–750	Umayyad Caliphate
750–1258	Abbasid Caliphate
909–1171	Fatimid Caliphate (North Africa, Egypt, Syria)
1171–1260	Saladin's Ayyubid Sultanate
1260–1517	Mamluk Sultanate
1300 –1923	Ottoman Empire
1453	Byzantium falls, and Ottomans establish Constantinople
1744	First Sa'udi state established (defeated by Muhammad 'Ali Pasha in 1818)
1798	Napoleon's campaign in Eygpt and Syria
1805–1849	Muhammad 'Ali, Pasha of Egypt
1926	Sa'udi kingdom established in Arabia
1882–1952	British Occupation of Egypt
1952	Republic of Egypt
1945	Syrian Republic

NOTES

PREFACE

1 Caroline Walker Bynum, *Christian Materiality: An Essay on Religion in Late Medieval Europe* (New York: Zone Books, 2011); David Morgan, *The Embodied Eye: Religious Visual Culture and the Social Life of Feeling* (Berkeley: University of California Press, 2012); Manuel Vásquez, *More Than Belief: A Materialist Theory of Religion* (New York: Oxford University Press, 2011); David Chidester, *Religion: Material Dynamics* (Berkeley: University of California Press, 2018). See bibliography for many more studies in this area.

2 I am drawing on Jacques Rancière's description of "optical machines." See his *Aisthesis: Scenes from the Aesthetic Regime of Art* (London: Verso, 2013), xi. See now also Charles Hirschkind, "Prayer Machine: An Introduction" *Material Religion* 12.1 (2016), 97–98.

INTRODUCTION

1 Finbarr Barry Flood, *Objects of Translation: Material Culture and Medieval "Hindu–Muslim" Encounter* (Princeton, NJ: Princeton University Press, 2009), 14.

2 Russell T. McCutcheon, *Critics Not Caretakers: Redescribing the Public Study of Religion* (Albany: State University of New York Press, 2001), 10.

3 Mircea Eliade, *The Sacred and The Profane: The Nature of Religion*, trans. Willard Trask (New York: Harcourt, 1987), 12.

4 Mircea Eliade, *Patterns in Comparative Religion*, trans. Rosemary Sheed (Cleveland, OH: World Publishing, 1963), xiii.

5 Henry Corbin, *En Islam iranien; Aspects spirituels et philosophiques*, 4 vols. (Paris: Gallimard, 1971–1972), xxvii–xxviii.

6 Clifford Geertz, *The Interpretation of Cultures* (New York: Basic Books, 1973), 127.

7 Talal Asad, *Genealogies of Religion; Discipline and Reasons of Power in Christianity and Islam* (Baltimore, MD: Johns Hopkins University Press, 1993), 199.

8 Asad, *Genealogies of Religion*, 29, and his "Reflections on Blasphemy and Secular Criticism," in Hent de Vries (ed.) *Religion: Beyond a Concept* (New York: Fordham University Press, 2008), 581.

9 Russell T. McCutcheon, *Manufacturing Religion: the Discourse on Sui Generis Religion and the Politics of Nostalgia* (New York: Oxford University Press, 1997), 136.

10 McCutcheon, *Critics not Caretakers*, x. For a similar insight on Eliade see Gavin Flood, *Beyond Phenomenology: Rethinking the Study of Religion* (New York: Continuum, 1999), 71.

11 Wayne Proudfoot, *Religious Experience* (Berkeley: University of California Press, 1985), 196.

12 Robert Segal, "In Defense of Reductionism," *Journal of the American Academy of Religion* 51, 1 (1983), 109.

13 Arthur Danto, *The Philosophical Disenfranchisement of Art* (New York: Columbia University Press, 2005), 16, and Arthur Danto, *The Abuse of Beauty: Aesthetics and the Concept of Art* (Chicago: Open Court, 2006), 9–15.

14 Grant H. Kester, "Aesthetics After the End of Art: an Interview with Susan Buck-Morss," *Art Journal* 56, 1 (1997): 39. For a description of religious aesthetics see Birgit Meyer and Jojada Verrips, "Aesthetics," in David Morgan (ed.) *Key Words in Religion, Media, and Culture*, (New York: Routledge, 2008), 27.

15 Asad, *Genealogies of Religion*, 31, and Webb Keane, "The Evidence of The Senses and The Materiality of Religion," *Journal of the Royal Anthropological Institute* 14, 1, (2008): 117–124.

16 Theodor W. Adorno, *Aesthetic Theory*, trans. Robert Hullot-Kentor (Minneapolis: University of Minnesota Press, 1997), 348.

17   Ted Cohen and Paul Guyer, *Essays in Kant's Aesthetics* (Chicago: University of Chicago Press, 1982), 12; Christian H. Wenzel, *An Introduction to Kant's Aesthetics: Core Concepts and Problems* (Malden, MA: Blackwell, 2005), 31–35; Nick Zangwill, "Unkantian Notions of Disinterest," *British Journal of Aesthetics*, 32, 2, (1992): 149.

18   Theodor Adorno, *Aesthetic Theory*, 333–343.

19   Meyer, "Aesthetics," 21–22.

20   Terry Eagleton, *The Ideology of the Aesthetic* (Oxford: Blackwell, 1990), 15–16.

21   Immanuel Kant, *The Critique of Judgment*, trans. J. H. Bernard (New York: Prometheus, 2000), 92.

22   Susan Buck-Morss, "Aesthetics and Anaesthetics: Walter Benjamin's Artwork Essay Reconsidered," *October* 62 (1992): 9.

23   Eagleton, *Ideology*, 21.

24   Birgit Meyer, "Powerful Pictures: Popular Christian Aesthetics in Southern Ghana," *Journal of the American Academy of Religion* 76.1 (2008): 97.

25   Meyer and Verrips, "Aesthetics," 27, and David Morgan, *Visual Piety: A History and Theory of Popular Religious Images* (Berkeley: University of California Press, 2006) 25–8.

26   Kant, *Critique of Judgment*, 110; and Zangwill, "Unkantian Notions of Disinterest," 149.

27   Eagleton, *Ideology*, 94.

28   Kester, "Aesthetics after the End of Art," 39. This point also made by Christopher Pinney, "Four Types of Visual Culture," in Christopher Tilley *et al.* (eds.) *Handbook of Material Culture*, (London: Sage, 2006), 131.

29   Igor Kopytoff, "The Cultural Biography of Things: Commoditization as Process," in Arjun Appadurai (ed.) *The Social Life of Things: Commodities in Cultural Perspective* (New York: Cambridge University Press, 1986), 66–68.

30   Adorno, *Aesthetic Theory*, 6.

31   Eagleton, *Ideology of the Aesthetic*, 21.

32   Adorno, *Aesthetic Theory*, 2–5.

33   Kester, "Aesthetics after the End of Art," 40.

34   Gülru Necipolu, *The Topakpi Scroll – Geometry and Ornament in Islamic Architecture* (New York: Oxford University Press, 1996), 83. See also Oleg Grabar, *The Mediation of Ornament* (Princeton, NJ: Princeton University Press, 1992), 152 and Ernst Gombrich, *The Sense of Order: A Study in the Psychology of Decorative Art*, 2nd edn. (New York: Phaidon, 1984), 225.

35   Eagleton, *Ideology*, 20. See also S. Brent Plate, *Walter Benjamin, Religion, and Aesthetics* (New York: Routledge, 2005), 2.

36   Clifford Geertz, *Islam Observed: Religious Development in Morocco and Indonesia* (Chicago: University of Chicago Press, 1968), 56.

CHAPTER 1

1   Edward William Lane, *Manners and Customs of the Modern Egyptians* (Cairo: Livres de France, 1989), 480.

2   At chapter 2, verse 125, the Qur'an identifies Abraham and Isma'il directly with the Ka'ba. God commands them to keep the site pure, to facilitate the pilgrim's worship. Various early reports have it that the *hijr* is the burial place of many prophets. Uri Rubin, "The Ka'ba: Aspects of Its Ritual Functions and Position in Pre-Islamic and Early Islamic Times," *Jerusalem Studies in Arabic and Islam* 8, 1 (1986): 111.

3   Maurice Gaudefroy-Demombynes, *Le Pèlerinage à la Mekke: étude d'histoire religieuse* (Paris: Geunther, 1977), 28, 38. Rubin, "The Ka'ba," 109–111.

4   Al-Azraqi, *Akhbar Makka wa ma ja'a fi-ha min al-athar*, 2 vols. (Mecca: Dar al-Thaqafa, 2001), 1:166–173. Al-Tabari, *The History of al-Tabari*, 40 vols., trans. vol. 21 Michael Fishbein (New York: State University of New York, 1989–2007), 21:231.

5   Al-Azraqi, *Akhbar Makka*, 1:322.

6   Ibid., 1:321–322.

7   See al-Ghazali, *Ihya 'ulum al-din*, 4 vols. (Cairo: Dar al-Taqwa, 2000) 1:373ff for more such hadith, and Gaudefroy-Demombines *Le pèlerinage*, 45.

8   Yohanan Friedman, "'Kufa is better': The Sanctity of Kufa in Early Islam and Shi'ism in Particular," *Le muséon* 126, 1–2 (2013): 226.

9   Al-Jarim, Muhammad N. *Adyan al-Arab fi al-Jahiliyya* (Cairo: Matba'a al-Sa'ada, 1923), 127–167.

10   Rubin "The Ka'ba," 106.

11   Al-Tha'labi, *'Ara'is al-majalis fi Qisas al-Anbiya or "Lives of the Prophets,"* trans. William Brinner (Leiden: Brill, 2002), 496.

12   Ibn Ishaq, *The Life of Muhammad*, trans. Alfred Guillaume (New York: Oxford University Press, 1967), 552.

13   Azraqi, *Akhbar Makka*, 1:164, 166.

14   The story of the earliest community, and its identity as distinctly Muslim, is rather less clear

than the sources and our modern conceptions of religious identity have presumed. It is not at all evident that Muhammad and the Qur'anic text drew such clear lines of differentiation between Muslims, Jews, and Christians. Especially early in his career, his message sounded like that of a Jewish reformer or the leader of a cross-communal group of "believers." See F. Donner, *Muhammad and the Believers* (Cambridge, MA: Belknap of Harvard University Press, 2010).

15 Tha'labi, *'Ara'is al-majalis*, 60.

16 Ibid., 148.

17 Ibid., 99.

18 Ibid., 149. Muhammad Ibn 'Abd Allah al-Kisa'i, *Tales of the Prophets,* trans. William M. Thackston, Jr. (Chicago: Kazi, 1997), 154.

19 Tha'labi, *'Ara'is al-majalis*, 140.

20 Muhammad I. Al-Bukhari, *Sahih al-Bukhari,* 9 vols. (Beirut: Dar al-Fikr, 1994), 4:141. Muhammad Shafi', "A Description of the Two Sanctuaries of Islam by Ibn 'Abd Rabbihi (d. 940)," in Thomas W. Arnold, and Reynold A. Nicholson (eds.) *A Volume of Oriental Studies Presented to Edward G. Browne* (Cambridge: Cambridge University Press, 1922), 428.

21 Nasir Khusraw, *Nasir-i Khusraw's Book of Travels [Safarnama]: A Parallel Persian-English Text,* trans. William M. Thackston, Jr. (Costa Mesa, CA: Mazda Publishers, 2001), 201–205.

22 See my forthcoming translation of Ibn Ishaq, *Selections from Ibn Ishaq's Biography of Muhammad* (Hackett Publishing) under "Tiban abu Karib's Campaign"; and 'Imad al-Din Ibn Kathir, *Tafsir al-Qur'an al-'azim,* 4 vols. (Cairo: Dar al-Taqwa, 2002), 4:164; Brannon M. Wheeler, *Mecca and Eden: Ritual, Relics, and Territory in Islam* (Chicago: University of Chicago Press, 2006), 26.

23 Azraqi, *Akhbar Makka,* 1:37.

24 Shafi', "A Description," 427.

25 William C. Young, "The Ka'ba, Gender, and the Rites of Pilgrimage," *International Journal of Middle East Studies* 25, 2 (1993): 293.

26 Azraqi, *Akhbar Makka,* 1:253.

27 Muhammad al-Batanuni, *al-Rihla al-Hijaziyya: li-Wali al-Ni'am al-Hajj 'Abbas Hilmi Basha al-Thani Khadiw Misr bi-qalam Muhammad Labib al-Batanuni,* 2nd edn. (Cairo: Matba'at al-Jamaliyya 1911), 108.

28 Richard Burton, *Personal Narrative of a Pilgrimage to al-Madinah and Meccah,* 2 vols. (London: George Bell and Sons, 1906), 2:212.

29 Gaudefroy-Demombines, *Le pèlerinage,* 50.

30 'Abd al-Rahman Ulaymi, *Uns al-Jalil bi-Ta'rikh al-Quds wa al-Khalil* (n.d., n.p.), 209.

31 Ibrahim Hilmi, *al-Mahmal: rihla sha'biyya fi wijan al-umma* (Cairo: Maktabat al-Turath al-Islami, 1993), 6.

32 Henri Lammens, "Culte de Bétyles et des processions chez les Arabes préislamites," *Bulletin de l'Institut Français d'Archéologie Orientale* 17 (1920): 42, and Richard Ettinghausen, "Notes on the Lusterware of Spain," *Ars Orientalis* 1 (1954): 137. Examples run from 'Aisha at the Battle of the Camel in 656, up to conflicts with the Sa'udis in the early 1900s.

33 Ettinghausen, "Notes on the Lusterware of Spain," 141. See Ibn Sa'd, *Kitab al-tabaqat al-kabir,* 9 vols. (Leiden: Brill, 1905–1940) vol. 1, pt. 2, sec. 1, p. 88, lines 24–25.

34 Ettinghausen, "Notes on the Lusterware of Spain," 145.

35 Ibid., also makes the connection between the empty qubba and the empty throne of Roman and Near Eastern political cultures. This use of emptiness is also at play in the Ka'ba itself, which at least after the first centuries of Islamic history has lain empty. Early in the Islamic period the Ka'ba served as a kind of storehouse for relics and treasures. See Avinoam Shalem, "Made for Show: The Medieval Treasury of the Ka'ba in Mecca," in Bernar O'Kane (ed.) *The Iconography of Islamic Art: Studies in Honor of Robert Hillenbrand* (Edinburgh: Edinburgh University Press, 2005): 276.

36 Jacques Jomier, "Le *Mahmal* de Sultan Qansuh al-Ghuri (début XVI siècle)," *Annales Islamologiques* 11 (1972): 184–186.

37 Jacques Jomier, *Le Mahmal et la caravane Égyptienne des pèlerins de la Mecque (XIII–XX siècles)* (Cairo: Presses de Institut Français d'Achéologie Orientale, 1953), 16.

38 Hilmi, *al-Mahmal,* 117. On page 119, Hilmi notes the brass finial plate at the front, followed by the year 1292/1875, and concludes that the *mahmal* frame has been reused, with a new cover. I confirmed this on a visit in November 2019.

39 Henry Maundrell, *A Journey from Aleppo to Jerusalem, at Easter, A.D. 1697* (Oxford: printed at the Theater, 1703), 127.

40 Edward W. Lane, and Stanley Lane-Poole, *Cairo Fifty Years Ago* (London: J. Murray, 1896), 163, Frederick Hasselquist, *Voyages and*

Travels in the Levant; In the Years 1749, 50, 51, 52, trans. Charles Linnæus (London: L. Davis and C. Reymers, 1766) 80.

41 Muhammad Ibn Fahd, *Ithaf al-wara bi-akhbar Umm al-qura*, 5 vols. (Mecca: Matba'a Jami'at Umm al-Qura, 1983), 4:644.

42 Jomier, *Le Mahmal*, 47; Francis E. Peters, *The Hajj: A Muslim Pilgrimage to Mecca* (Princeton, NJ: Princeton University Press, 1994), 348.

43 Malika Dekkiche, "New Source, New Debate: Re-evaluation of the Mamluk-Timurid Struggle for Religious Supremacy in the Hijaz," *Mamluk Studies Review* 18 (2014–2015): 260. In 1319 the Mamluks stopped the Ilkhanid sultan Abu Sa'id from hanging a *kiswa*. The following year, four *mahmals* entered Mecca in a priority of succession: first the Egyptian, then the Syrian, then the Ilkhanid, followed by the Yemeni. Ann Broadbridge, *Kingship and Ideology in the Islamic and Mongol Worlds* (New York: Cambridge University Press, 2008), 103.

44 'Abdallah 'Anqawi, "Kiswa al-Ka'ba fi al-'asr al-Mamluki," *Majallat Kulliyat al-Adab wa'l-'Ulum al-Insaniyya* 5 (1985): 17–18, and Dekkiche "New Source," 254–255, who also mentions *mahmals* coming from Shiraz four times in the fourteenth century.

45 Richard T. Mortel, "The Kiswa: Its Origins and Development from Pre-Islamic Times until the End of the Mamluk Period," *al-'Usûr* 3, 2 (1988): 36.

46 Sami S. 'Abd al-Malik, "Qit'a nadira min al-kiswa al-dakhiliyya li'l-ka'ba al-musharrafa bi'sm al-sultan al-Nasir Hasan bin Muhammad bin Qalawun tu'arrakh bi-sanat 791 AH / 1359–1360 m." *Annales Islamologiques* 38 (2004): 58. On pages 62–63, al-Malik provides the inscriptions, which include Q. 3:18 and 112:4. Pieces of this inner *kiswa* have been preserved at the Topakpi museum (13/1689).

47 Dekkiche, "New Source," 261–262.

48 Ibn Fahd, *Ithaf al-wara*, 3:170.

49 Jomier, *Le Mahmal*, 51.

50 Gilles Veinstein, "Holy Cities of the Hijaz under the Ottomans," in A. I. Al-Ghabban (ed.) *Roads of Arabia: Archaeology and History of the Kingdom of Saudi Arabia* (Paris: Somogy Art Publishers, 2010), 527.

51 Hilmi, *al-Mahmal*, 14.

52 René Tresse, *Le Pèlerinage Syrien aux Vlles Saintes de l'Islam* (Paris: Imprimerie Chaumette, 1937), 89.

53 Jomier, *Le Mahmal,* 55.

54 See also Burton, *Personal Narrative*, 2:187 on the station of the *mahmals* at Mount 'Arafat.

55 Tresse, *Le Pèlerinage Syrien,* 89.

56 For a study of a series of *mahmals* from this period see, Richard McGregor, "The *Mahmal* as Event and Actor," in Qaisra Khan (ed.) *The Hajj and the Arts of Pilgrimage* (forthcoming from the Khalili Trust).

57 Jomier, *Le Mahmal,* 144.

58 In addition to stifling *mahmal* pilgrimage, this conservative movement would reorganize the topographies of Mecca and Medina – as we shall see in chapters below. Salafism, Wahabbism, and related movements such as the Muslim Brotherhood are interrelated yet complex phenomena beyond the scope of the current discussion. For a brief overview see Abdullah Saeed, "Salafiya, Modernism, and Revival," in John L. Esposito and Emad El-Din Shahin (eds.) *The Oxford Handbook of Islam and Politics* (New York: Oxford University Press, 2013), 27–41. See also Natana J. DeLong-Bas, *Wahhabi Islam: From Revival and Reform to Global Jihad* (New York: Oxford University Press, 2008), 7–40, Henri Lauzière, *The Making of Salafism: Islamic Reform in the Twentieth Century* (New York: Columbia University Press, 2016), and John Calvert, *Sayyid Qutb and the Origins of Radical Islamism* (New York: Columbia University Press, 2010).

59 Al-Batanuni, *al-Rihla al-Hijaziyya*, 134–137; Burton, *Personal Narrative*, 2:215.

60 Venetia Porter, "Textiles of Mecca and Medina," in Venetia Porter (ed.) *Hajj: Journey to the Heart of Islam* (London: British Museum Press, 2012), 258.

61 Mortel, "The Kiswa," 32–33.

62 Ibid., 34, 36. The Prophet's wife Aisha was said to cut up old *kiswas* for distribution among the Muslims; Azraqi, *Akhbar Makka*, 42. This seems unlikely, however, in light of the fact that the earlier *kiswas* were not routinely removed in that period. We have another account of this kind of usage early in Islamic history: "Ibn al-Qasim (d. 191/806), a disciple of Malik ibn Anas, reported that his master showed him a copy of the Qur'an that had belonged to the latter's grandfather, which was embellished with silver and bound with a cover made of cloth of the Ka'ba." Abdelouahad Jahdani, "Du fiqh à la

codicology: quelques opinions de Malik (m. 179/796) sur le Coran-codex," *Mélanges de l'Université Saint-Joseph* 59 (2006): 274.

63 Taqi al-Din al-Maqrizi, *al-Mawa'iz wa al-i'tibar fi dhirk al-khitat wa al-athar*, 5 vols. (London: Al-Furqan Islamic Heritage Foundation, 2013) 1:612, 489–490. Marcel Cohen, *et al.*, eds. *Répertoire chronologique d'épigraphie arabe* (Cairo: Presses de l'Insitute Français d'Archéologie Orientale, 1931), 80, and see also 44, for a *kiswa* text from 776.

64 *Répertoire chronologique d'épigraphie arabe* 1, 101, (815) Kiswa. Al-Tabari, *The History of al-Tabari*, 32:29.

65 Robert B. Serjeant, "Material for a History of Islamic Textiles up to the Mongol Conquest," *Ars Islamica*, 9 (1942): 54–92; and 10 (1943): 71–104; and 11/12 (1946): 98–145; and 13 (1948): 75–117. Al-Qalqashandi tells us, *Subh al-a'sha*, 14 vols. (Cairo: Dar al-Kutub al-Misriyya, 1922) 4:281, that Caliph al-Ma'mun or al-Mutawakkil (d. 861), would send three veils each year. The first linked the hajj to the Ka'ba by arriving on the day of watering (*tarwiyya*) the 10th Dhu al-Hijja. The second, in Egyptian silk, arrived at the first moon of Rajab, linked to the old 'Umra practice. The third arrived the 27th of Ramadan, in supposed evocation of one of the Prophet's 'Umras. The lower white garment arrived at another 'Umra, the 10th of Muharram – this date was also becoming important for the Shia commemoration of Karbala. In the modern period, this covering, which was often torn by pilgrims, is missing, and the *kiswa* is simply raised beyond their reach.

66 Mortel, "The Kiswa," 36.

67 Taj al-Din Ibn Muyassar, *Akhbar Misr* (Cairo: Presses de l'Insitut Français d'Archéologie Orientale, 1981), 161–162. Heinz Halm interprets the *shamsa* as a crown, "Al-Shamsa. Hängekronen als Herrshaftszeichen der Abbasiden und Fatimiden," in Urbain Vermeulen and Daniel De Smet (eds.) *Egypt and Syria in the Fatimid, Ayyubid and Mamluk Eras* (Leuven: Peeters, 1995), 126–138.

68 Taqi al-Din al-Maqrizi *Itti'âz al-hunafa' bi akhbar al-a'immat al-fatimiyyin al-khulafa'*, 3 vols. (Cairo: Lajnat Ihya al-Turath al-Islami, 1967–1973), 1:140–142, and quoted in Jonathan Bloom, "The Mosque of al-Hakim in Cairo," *Muqarnas* 1 (1983): 27.

69 *Nasir-i Khusraw's Book of Travels*, 100. The original Persian text clearly describes

"mihrabs" and not "medallions" as Thackston has it. Charles Schefer's translation, *Safer Nameh: Relation du Voyage de Nassiri Khosrau en Syrie, en Palestine, en Égypte, en Arabie et en Perse pendant les années de l'Hégire 437–444 (1035–1042)* (Paris: Ernest Leroux, 1881), 204 has it right.

70 Finbarr Barry Flood, "The Iconography of Light in the Monuments of Mamluk Cairo," in Emily Lyle (ed.) *Sacred Architecture in the Traditions of India, China, Judaism, and Islam* (Edinburgh: Edinburgh University Press, 1992), 169–193. Nuha Khoury, "The Mihrab Image: Commemorative Themes in Medieval Islamic Architecture," *Muqarnas* 9 (1992): 16.

71 Mortel, "The Kiswa," 38.

72 Muhammad ibn Ahmad Ibn Jubayr, *Rihla* (Beirut: Dar Sadir, 1964), 157–158, and Ibn Jubayr, *The Travels of Ibn Jubayr*, trans. Roland Broadhurst (London: Goodword, 2016), 185.

73 Mortel, "The Kiswa," 42.

74 Al-Qalqashandi, *Subh al-a'sha*, 4:57.

75 Ibid., 4:281.

76 Ibid., 4:282.

77 Mortel, "The Kiswa," 42–43.

78 Al-Qalqashandi, *Subh al-a'sha*, 4:57.

79 Nasser Rabbat, *The Citadel of Cairo: A New Interpretation of Royal Mamluk Architecture* (New York: Brill, 1995), 153.

80 Hülya Tezkan, "Ka'ba Covers from the Topkapi Palace Collection and their Inscriptions," in Fahmida Suleman (ed.) *Word of God, Art of Man. The Qur'an and it Creative Expressions* (New York: Oxford University Press, 1997), 237.

81 Nassar, Nahla "Dar al-Kiswa al-Sharifa: Administration and Production," in Venetia Porter (ed.) *The Hajj: Collected Essays*(London: British Museum Press, 2013), 175–176.

82 Qutb al-Din al-Yunini, *Dhayl Mir'at al-Zaman*, 4 vols. (Haydarabad: Matba'at Majlis Da'irat al-'Uthmaniyya, 1954–1961), 1:534, and Taqi al-Din al-Maqrizi, *Al-Suluk li-ma'rifa duwwal al-muluk*, 8 vols. (Beirut: Dar al-Kutub al-'Ilmiyya, 1997), 1:562.

83 Al-Maqrizi, *Suluk*, 2:32; Jomier, *Le Mahmal*, 27, 35, 36.

84 Al-Maqrizi, *Suluk*, 2:163.

85 'Abdallah Ibn Battuta, *Rihla Ibn Battuta*, 2 vols. (Cairo: al-Maktaba al-Tijariyya al-Kubra, 1958), 1:59.

86   Jomier, *Le Mahmal*, 37; John Maloy, "Celebrating the *Mahmal*; the Rajab Festival in Fifteenth Century Cairo," in Judith Pfeiffer and Sholeh Quinn (eds.) *History and Historiography of Post Mongol Central Asia and the Middle East: Studies in Honor of John E. Woods* (Wiesbaden: Harrassowitz, 2006), 412. Public feasting for this event was also a well-established practice in Damascus. See Richard van Leeuwen, *Waqfs and Urban Structures: The Case of Ottoman Damascus* (Leiden: Brill, 1999), 104.

87   Maloy, "Celebrating the *Mahmal*," 419.

88   Hasselquist, *Voyages and Travels in the Levant*, 80.

89   Sophia Lane Poole, *The Englishwoman in Egypt: Letters from Cairo* (Philadelphia: G.B. Zieber & Co., 1845), 77.

90   Maloy, "Celebrating the *Mahmal*," 405.

91   Poole, *The Englishwoman in Egypt*, 58–59.

92   Amelia Edwards, *A Thousand Miles Up the Nile* (London: Longmans, Green, 1877), 26.

93   Under the modern centralization of the orders, the Bakris even established an official sequence in public processions. See Frederick de Jong, *Turuq and Turuq-Linked Institutions in Nineteenth Century Egypt* (Leiden: Brill, 1978), 67.

94   Isabel Burton, *The Inner Life of Syria, Palestine, and the Holy Land*, 2 vols. (London: H. S. King & Co., 1875) 1:57–58.

95   'Abd al-Rahman al-Jabarti, *'Aja'ib al-athar*, 4 vols. (Cairo: al-Matba'a Dar al-Kutub al-Misriyya, 1998), 3:83–84, and 'Abd al-Rahman al-Jabarti, *'Abd al-Rahman al-Jabarti's History of Egypt*, trans. and eds. Thomas Philipp, Moshe Pearlmann, *et al.*, 4 vols. (Stuttgart: Steiner, 1994) 3:77. For a European engraving of the *Mahmal*'s departure, from 1744, see Robert Irwin, "Journey to Mecca: A History (part 2)," in Porter (ed.) *Hajj: Journey to the Heart of Islam*, 145.

96   Al-Batanuni, *al-Rihla al-Hijaziyya*, 141.

97   Ibrahim Rif'at, *Mir'at al-Haramayn*, 2 vols. (Cairo: Matba'a Dar al-Kutub al-Misriyya, 1925), 2:150. We shall return to this covering in chapter 2.

98   Jomier, *Le Mahmal*, 66; Rif'at, *Mir'at al-Haramayn*, 2:152.

99   Mortel, "The Kiswa," 34.

100   Azraqi, *Akhbar Makka*, 1:255, and al-Qalqashandi, *Subh*, 4:279.

101   Jomier, *Le Mahmal*, 63.

102   Hasselquist, *Voyages and Travels in the Levant*, 81.

103   Edwards, *A Thousand Miles Up the Nile*, 26.

104   *Al-Jabarti's History of Egypt*, 3:308–309; Al-Jabarti, *'Aja'ib al-athar*, 3:320–321.

105   *Al-Jabarti's History of Egypt*, 3:227.

106   Muhammad 'Abd al-Fattah, "Ba'd al-mulahazat 'ala al-'ilaqa bayna murur al-mawakib wa wad'al-mabani al-athariyya fi shawari'madinat al-Qahira," *Annales Islamologiques* 25 (1991): 3.

107   Jomier, *Le Mahmal*, 64–65.

108   "li-yazuruhu man yurid al-tabarruk" al-Batanuni, *al-Rihla al-Hijaziyya*, 141. Leeder described a group of women (perhaps pictured) who have travelled from Upper Egypt to sit with the *mahmal* at Abbasiyya. Simon H. Leeder, *Veiled Mysteries of Egypt* (New York: C. Scribner's Sons, 1913), 207–208.

109   Jomier, *Le Mahmal*, 61.

110   Rif'at, *Mir'at al-Haramayn*, 1:142. Another Egyptian functionary, Muhammad Sadiq Basha, describes a similar ritual for the year 1880. See his *Rihla mish'al al-mahmal* (Beirut: Dar al-'Arabiyya li'l-Mawsu'at, 2014), 206.

111   Faroqhi, Suraya. *Pilgrims and Sultans: the Hajj under the Ottomans, 1517–1683* (New York: Tauris, 1994), 38–39.

112   Rif'at, *Mir'at al-Haramayn*, 1:13. For a similar account, but from 1911, see Leeder, *Veiled Mysteries*, 214.

CHAPTER 2

1   Hilmi, *al-Mahmal*, 4.

2   For an overview, see Lisa Golombek, "The Draped Universe of Islam," in Richard Ettinghausen and Priscilla Soucek (eds.) *Content and Context of Visual Arts in the Islamic World* (University Park: Pennsylvania State University Press, 1988), 25–50.

3   *Al-Jabarti's History of Egypt*, 3:308–309, Al-Jabarti, *'Aja'ib al-athar*, 3:320–321. Topkapi Palace Museum in Istanbul holds what is likely the oldest surviving example, dated to 1682. See Venetia Porter, *The Art of Hajj* (London: British Museum Press, 2012), 71.

4   Leeder provides a photograph also, but mistakenly calls it a covering for the tomb of Abraham. See Leeder, *Veiled Mysteries of Egypt*, 205. For another example, see Rif'at, *Mir'at al-Haramayn*, vol. 1, fig. 53.

5   Maurice Gaudefroy-Demombynes, "Notes sur la Mekke et Médine," *Revue de l'histoire des religions* 39 (1918): 337.

6   Gerald, R. Hawting, "The Origins of the Muslim Sanctuary in Mecca," in Gauthier H. A. Juynboll (ed.) *Studies on the First Century of Islamic Society* (Carbondale: Southern Illinois University Press, 1982), 39.

7   Khalil Ibn Shahin, *La Zubda Kachf al-Mamalik de Khalil al-Zahiri*, trans. Jean Gaulmier (Beirut: Presses de l'Institut Français de Damas, 1950), 14, and Francis E. Peters, *Jerusalem: the Holy City in the Eyes of Chroniclers, Visitors, Pilgrims, and Prophets* (Princeton, NJ: Princeton University Press, 1985), 197.

8   'Ali ibn 'Abdallah al-Samhudi, *Wafa al-wafa bi akhbar dar al-Mustafa*, 5 vols. (London: al-Furqan, 2001), 2:137. For an early twentieth-century hanging for the pulpit see Rif'at, *Mir'at al-Haramayn*, vol. 1, fig. 98.

9   Thomas H. R. Munt, *The Holy City of Medina: Sacred Space in Early Islamic Arabia* (New York: Cambridge University Press, 2014), 23–27, 65–93.

10   Munt, *Holy City*, 129–133. The great medieval jurist Taqi al-Din al-Subki (d. 1355) wrote *Shifa al-saqam fi ziyarat khair al-anam* (A Cure for All Ills in Visiting the Best of Humanity) in defense of the practice.

11   Munt, *Holy City*, 135–140.

12   'Ali ibn 'Abdallah al-Samhudi, *Khulasat al-wafa bi akhbar dar al-Mustafa* (Medina: al-Maktaba al-'Imiyya, 1972), 298.

13   For a Fatimid *kiswa* presented in 1123 on the occasion of Nawruz, see Boaz Shoshan, *Popular Culture in Medieval Cairo* (New York: Cambridge University Press, 1993), 42.

14   Muhammad H. al-Mojan, "The Textiles Made for the Prophet's Mosque at Medina," (trans. Liana Saif) in Ventia Porter and Liana Saif (eds.) *The Hajj: Collected Essays* (London: British Museum Press, 2013), 185.

15   M. Al-Mojan, "The Textiles," 188. The mother of Harun al-Rashid, al-Khayzuran, was likely the first to commission a covering for the Prophet's chamber. Ibid., p. 184. In Chapter 4 we shall see that al-Khayzuran would also play a central role in preserving other early Islamic devotional sites.

16   Al-Samhudi, *Khulasat al-wafa*, 317–318.

17   Musa al-Yunini, *Early Mamluk Syrian Historiography: Al-Yunini's Dhayl Mir'at al-zaman*, 2 vols., ed. and trans. Li Guo (Leiden: Brill: 1998), 2:215.

18   Muhammad Amin, *al-Awqaf wa al-hayat al-ijtima'iyya fi Misr* (Cairo: Dar al-Nahda al-'Arabiyya, 1980), 105; and al-Samhudi, *Khulasat al-wafa*, 299.

19   Geoffrey R. D. King, *The Traditional Architecture of Saudi Arabia* (London: Tauris, 1998), 50.

20   Peters, *The Hajj*, 94; and Tresse, *Le Pèlerinage Syrien*, 176.

21   Tezkan, "Ka'ba Covers," 230.

22   Ibid., 232. Note that the *kiswa* Tezkan lists in figure 14.9, p. 234, contains the Qur'anic verse 9:33, "He sent His messenger with guidance and the religion of truth…" not Qur'an 2:144 as is stated in the caption.

23   Rif'at, *Mir'at al-Haramayn*, 1:12.

24   Al-Batanuni, *al-Rihla al-Hijaziyya*, 141.

25   Peter W. Schienerl, "Kameldarstellungen im ägyptischen Schmuck – und Amulettwesen," *Archiv fur Völkerkunde* 33 (1979): 146, 149, 152.

26   Al-Jabarti, *'Aja'ib al-athar*, 4:311; *Al-Jabarti's History of Egypt*, 4:276.

27   Muhammad Ibn al-Hajj, *al-Madkhal*, 4 vols. (Cairo: al-Matba'a al-Misriyya, 1929), 1:272.

28   Shoshan, *Popular Culture*, 131.

29   Juan Campo, *The Other Side of Paradise: Explorations into the Religious Meanings of Domestic Space in Islam* (Columbia: University of South Carolina Press, 1991), 182.

30   *Rihla ibn Jubayr*, 19–20, and *Travels of Ibn Jubayr*, 37.

31   Lane and Lane-Poole, *Cairo Fifty Years Ago*, 85.

32   Al-Jabarti, *'Aja'ib al-athar*, 3:300–301.

33   Maurice Gaudefroy-Demombynes, "Le Voile de la Ka'ba," *Studia Islamica* 2 (1954): 18.

34   Al-Jabarti, *'Aja'ib al-athar*, 1:193; *Al-Jabarti's History of Egypt*, 1:178.

35   Hilmi, *al-Mahmal*, 197.

36   Ibid., 20.

37   Josef W. Meri, *The Cult of the Saints Among Muslims and Jews in Medieval Syria* (New York: Oxford University Press, 2002), 259–260.

38   Muhammad Ibn Iyas, *Bada'i' al-zuhur fi waqa'i' al-duhur*, 5 vols. (Cairo: Al-Hay'a al-Misriyya al-'Amma li al-Kitab, 1982–1985), 4:337, and Carl Petry, *Protectors or Praetorians?: The Last Mamluk Sultans and Egypt's Waning as a Great Power* (Albany: State University of New York Press, 1994), 162.

39   Maria Sardi, "Weaving for the Hajj under the Mamluks," in Porter, *The Hajj: Collected essays*, 171.

40   Nazami al-Ju'beh, "Kiswa (tomb cover) for the Prophet of God, Ibrahim (Abraham)" in "Discover Islamic Art: Museum with No Frontiers," 2019 (online). I read "غ-ا-ر" in

the first panel, and thus "cavern/cave" instead of Al-Ju'beh's reading of "protector." The images available online do not show the Qur'anic texts Al-Ju'beh refers to.

41 David Samuel Margoliouth, "Sa'diya," *Shorter Encyclopaedia of Islam* (New York: Brill, 1991).

42 Burton, *Personal Narrative*, 2:215.

43 Al-Batanuni, *al-Rihla al-Hijaziyya*, 143.

44 For the text, see al-Maqrizi, *Khitat*, 4:790.

45 'Ali Basha Mubarak, *Khitat al-jadida*, 20 volumes in 4 (Cairo, Buqlaq: al-Matba'a al-Kubra al-Amiriyya, 1888), 6:52. Some scholars argue that the dome over the Sa'di shrine in Cairo dates back to the Fatimid-era, being that of Badr al-Jamali, Amir al-Juyush under caliph Al-Mustansir (r. 1036–1094); Yusuf Raghib, "Le mausolée de Yunus al-Sa'di, est-il celui de Badr al-Jamali?" *Arabica* 20, 3 (1973): 307.

46 Poole, *The Englishwoman in Egypt*, 56; Lane and Lane-Poole, *Cairo Fifty Years Ago*, 481.

47 Jomier, *Le Mahmal*, 19.

48 Muhammad A. Bakhit, *The Ottoman Province of Damascus in the Sixteenth Century* (Beirut: Librairie du Liban, 1982), 113.

49 On this figure see Safi al-Din Mansur, *La Risala de Safi al-Din ibn Abi al-Mansur ibn Zafir: biographies des maîtres spirituels connus par un cheikh égyptien du VIIe/XIIIe siècle,* ed. and trans. Denis Gril (Cairo: Presses de l'Insitut Français d'Archéologie Orientale, 1986), 215.

50 *For Those Who Sail to Heaven,* directed by Elizabeth Wickett (Icarus Films, c. 1990) VHS.

51 Georges Legrain, *Louqsor sans les Pharaons; Légendes et Chansons de la Haute Égypte* (Brussels: Vromant & Co., 1914), 87.

52 Rudolf Kriss, and Hubert Kriss-Heinrich, *Volksglaube in Bereich des Islam,* 2 vols. (Wiesbaden: O. Harrassowitz, 1960–1962), 2:104–105.

53 *Tabut* can also mean box or chest. At 2:248, the Qur'an uses *tabut* as the "ark" of the Ark of the Covenant. The word is also used for the basket that carried baby Moses on the Nile. Videos of some of the *mulid* processions of Abu al-Hajjaj (or al-Haggag) can be found on YouTube.

54 Legrain, *Louqsor sans les Pharaons*, 89.

55 Ibid., 90.

56 Karl B. Klunzinger, *Upper Egypt: Its People and Its Products* (London: Blackie & Son, 1878), 181–182.

57 Joseph W. McPherson, *Moulids of Egypt* (New York: Kegan Paul, 1990), 132, 134, which includes photos of the saint's "tub," and its circumambulation around the tombs.

58 Joska S. Schielke, *The Perils of Joy: Contesting Mulid Festivals in Contemporary Egypt* (Syracuse, NY: Syracuse University Press, 2012), 184–187. Abu 'Amra, the thirteenth-century patron saint of Jirja (north of Qina) is honored each year with a procession of his tomb covering. See Rachida Chih, *Sufism in Ottoman Egypt: Circulation, Renewal, and Authority in the Seventeenth and Eighteenth Centuries* (London: Routledge, 2019), 20.

59 B. L. Austin Kennett, "The Sacred Litter (Mahmal) of Kharga Oasis," *Man* 25 (August 1926): 134, 135. On the heraldic symbol of the cup see Leo A. Mayer, *Saracenic Heraldry, A Survey* (New York: Oxford University Press, 1999), 10.

60 M. Milwright, "The Cup of the Saqi: Origins of an Emblem of the Mamluk khassakiyya," *ARAM* 9–10 (1997–1998): 241–256. Cairo's Museum of Islamic Art preserves an extensive collection of Mamluk blazons on fabric and ceramics.

61 *Al-Liwa al-Islami,* May 17, 1990.

62 *Al-Ahli,* May 5, 1990.

63 Klunzinger, *Upper Egypt*, 103–104.

64 Nicolaas H. Biegman, *Egypt: Moulids, Saints and Sufis* (New York: Kegan Paul, 1990), 32, 35.

65 Burton, *Inner life of Syria*, 1:63–64.

66 Jomier, *Le Mahmal*, 68.

67 Hilmi, *al-Mahmal*, 242.

68 Jomier, *Le Mahmal*, 69–71.

69 Nassar, "Dar al-Kiswa al-Sharifa," 182.

70 Shoshan, *Popular Culture*, 68, 131.

71 Ibn al-Hajj, *al-Madkhal*, 1:272–275.

72 *Al-Manar,* juz' 8, 1905, 839–840; and juz' 27, 1926, 501.

73 *Al-Manar,* juz' 6, 1903, 876.

74 *Al-Manar,* 1926, 503.

75 Ibid., 501.

76 *Al-Ahram,* November 17, 1950, 4. Western newsreels from the period depicting Hajj parades are available, but to my eye at least, they are not obviously hostile or patronizing portrayals – see British Pathé reels from 1938 and 1946.

77 Jomier, *Le Mahmal*, 72.

78 The Sufis were from the Ahmadiyya order at this point, and not the Sa'diyya. See De Jong,

Turuq, 15, 67, on the Marzuqiyya branch of the Ahmadiyya dominating this procession from the eighteenth century onward.

79 Hilmi, *al-Mahmal*, 4, 201–202.

80 *Al-Liwa al-Islami*, May 17, 1990.

81 Ibid.

82 Donald Reid, "Cultural Imperialism and Nationalism: The Struggle to Define and Control the Heritage of Arab Art in Egypt," *International Journal of Middle East Studies* 24, 1 (1992): 58.

83 Elliott H. Colla, *Conflicted Antiquities: Egyptology, Egyptomania, Egyptian Modernity* (Durham, NC: Duke University Press, 2007), 117–120; and Donald Reid, *Whose Pharaohs? Archaeology, Museums, and Egyptian National Identity from Napoleon to World War I* (Cairo: American University in Cairo Press, 2002), 58.

84 Azra Dawood, "Failure to Engage: The Breasted-Rockefeller Gift of a New Egyptian Museum and Research Institute at Cairo (1926)" (MA thesis. Massachusetts Institute of Technology, Cambridge, MA, 2010), 15–40, DSpace@MIT.

85 Silvia Naef, "Peindre pour être moderne?" in Bernard Heyberger and Silvia Naef (eds.) *La multiplication des images en pays d'Islam* (Würtzburg: Ergon in Kommission, 2003), 196.

86 István Ormos, *Max Herz Pasha: 1856–1919; His Life and Career*, 2 vols. (Cairo: Presses de l'Institut Français d'Archéologie Orientale, 2009), 2:313–326. Faruq 'Askar, ed. Min dhakirat Mathaf al-Fann al-Islami, 1881m-2010m: mujallad watha'iqi tidhkari: al-'id al-mi'awi (Cairo: Wizarat al-Thaqafa, al-Majlis al-A'la li'l-Athar, 2010) 39–76.

87 Nasser Rabbat, "The Formation of the Neo-Mamluk Style in Modern Egypt," in Martha Pollak (ed.) *The Education of the Architect: Historiography, Urbanism, and the Growth of Architectural Knowledge: Essays Presented to Stanford Anderson*, (Cambridge, MA: MIT Press, 1997), 363–386.

88 Reid, *Whose Pharaohs?* 237–238.

89 Reid, "Cultural Imperialism," 65; *Whose Pharaohs?*, 245.

90 Ibid., 72.

91 Donald Reid, "The Egyptian Geographical Society: From Foreign Laymen's Society to Indigenous Professional Association," *Poetics Today* 14, 3 (1993): 539–544.

92 Heba Bizzari, "The National Geographic Society Museum," *Tour Egypt*, March 2, 2019, www.touregypt.net/featurestories/geographic.htm

93 Henri Lauzière, "Rashid Rida's Rehabilitation of the Wahhabis and Its Consequences," ch. 2 of his *The Making of Salafism*, 60–94.

94 Wendy Shaw, *Possessors and Possessed: Museums, Archaeology, and the Visualization of History in the Late Ottoman Empire* (Berkeley: University of California Press, 2003), 29.

95 Édouard Brémond, *Le Hédjaz dans la Guerre Mondiale* (Paris: Payot 1931), 53.

96 Carol Duncan, "Art Museums and the Ritual of Citizenship," in Ivan Karp *Exhibiting Cultures: The Poetics and Politics of Museum Display* (Washington: Smithsonian Press, 1991), 90–101. See also Carol Duncan, *Civilizing Rituals: Indside Public Art Museums* (New York: Routledge, 1995), 7–20.

97 Ibid. For a series of reflections on this theme, see Robert Nelson, R. *The Spirit of Secular Art: A History of the Sacramental Roots of Contemporary Artistic Values* (Melbourne: Monash University Press: 2007).

98 Philip Fisher, *Making and Effacing Art: Modern American Art in a Culture of Museums* (New York: Oxford University Press, 1991), 442.

99 Fisher, *Making and Effacing Art*, 348.

100 Roger Silverstone, "The Medium is the Museum: on objects and the logics in time and spaces," in Roger Miles and Lauro Zalvala (eds.) *Towards the Museum of the Future: New European Perspectives* (New York: Routledge, 1994), 165.

101 Fisher, *Making and Effacing Art*, 437.

CHAPTER 3

1 Franz Rosenthal, "Abu Haiyan al-Tawhidi on Penmanship," *Ars Islamica* 13 (1948): 14, 25 (translation with changes).

2 Plate, *Walter Benjamin*, 59, quoting from Benjamin's *Origin of German Tragic Drama*.

3 Irene A. Bierman, "The Art of the Public Text: Medieval Islamic Rule," in Irving Lavin (ed.) *World Art: Themes of Unity in Diversity*, 3 vols. (University Park: Pennsylvania State University Press, 1989), 2:283–290, and Irene A. Bierman, *Writing Signs: The Fatimid Public Text* (Berkeley and Los Angeles: University of California Press, 1998); Yasser Tabbaa, "The Transformation of Arabic Writing: pt. 2, the Public Text," *Ars Orientalis* 24 (1994): 121, 139. Tabbaa perhaps overstates these connections. See Yasser Tabbaa, *The Transformation of*

Islamic Art during the Sunni Revival (Seattle: University of Washington Press, 2001), 71, and Erica Cruikshank Dodd and Shereen Khairallah, *The Image of the Word: A Study of Quranic Verses in Islamic Architecture*, 2 vols. (Beirut: American University of Beirut, 1981), regarding Qur'an inscriptions on buildings, particularly 1:32, where they distinguish between text that is clearly polemical, for example the Dome of Rock, and text that is primarily in response to the architectural setting, e.g. the Nilometer.

4   Sheila Blair, "Floriated Kufic and the Fatimids," in Marianne Barrucand (ed.) *L'Égypte fatimide: son art et son histoiree* (Paris: Presses de l'Univerité de Paris-Sorbonne, 1999), 109.

5   Stephennie Mulder, "The Mausoleum of Imam al-Shafiʻi," *Muqarnas* 23 (2006): 19.

6   Tabbaa briefly mentions the positioning and coloration of inscriptions in the Nur al-D mosque. Yasser Tabbaa, "The Mosque of Nur al-Din in Mosul 1170–1171," *Annales Islamologiques* 36 (2002): 352. Bernard O'Kane, "Medium and Message in the Monumental Epigraphy of Medieval Cairo," in Mohammad Gharipour and Irvin Cemil Schick (eds.) *Calligraphy and Islamic Architecture in the Muslim World* (Edinburgh: Edinburgh University Press, 2013), 417, reminds us that inscriptions were often painted, which would have made them much more readable than they are today.

7   Grabar, *Mediation of Ornament*, 113–118. See also Richard Ettinghausen, "Arabic Epigraphy: Communication or Symbolic Affirmation," in Dickran Kouymjian (ed.) *Near Eastern Numismatics, Iconography, Epigraphy, and History: Studies in Honor of George C. Miles* (Beirut: American University of Beirut, 1974), 307.

8   Priscilla Soucek, "Material Culture and the Qur'an," *Encyclopaedia of the Qur'an* (Leiden: Brill, 2012) quoting Robert Hillenbrand, "Qur'anic epigraphy in Medieval Islamic Architecture," in *Revue des Études Islamiques* 54 (1986), 171–187. On the great variety of Qur'anic quotations that appeared in various periods, as well as the wide range of iconographic usage in mosques, see Dina Montasser, "Modes of Utilizing Qur'anic Inscriptions on Cairene Mamluk Religious Monuments," in Bernard O'Kane (ed.) *Creswell Photographs Re-examined: New Perspectives on Islamic Architecture* (Cairo: American University in Cairo, 2009), 191, 197. For a remarkable thirteenth-century inscription celebrating the Sufi occupants of a convent in Aleppo see Yasser Tabbaa, *Constructions of Power and Piety in Medieval Aleppo* (University Park, PA: Penn State University Press, 1997), 173–174. While less common than Qur'anic inscriptions, devotional poetry can be found in some Sufi buildings. For an example from Cairo see Richard McGregor, "Is this the End of Medieval Sufism?" in Rachida Chih, Catherine Mayeur-Jaouen, *et al.* (eds.) *Sufism in the Ottoman Era (16th–18th C.)*(Cairo: Presses de l'Institut Français d'Archéologie Orientale, 2010) 90. For a wide survey of examples see Bernard O'Kane's online datebase *The Monumental Insriptions of Historic Cairo*, https://islamicinscriptions.cultnat.org

9   ʻAbd al-Fattah, "Baʻd al-mulahazat," 1, 2, 5.

10   Paula Sanders, *Ritual, Politics, and the City in Fatimid Cairo* (New York: State University of New York Press, 1994), 32, 87.

11   Doris Behrens-Abouseif, "The Citadel of Cairo: stage for Mamluk Ceremonial," *Annales Islamologiques* 24 (1988), 30.

12   Rachida Chapoutot-Remadi, "Liens et relations au sein de l'élite mamluke sous les premiers sultans bahrides: 648/1250–741/1340" (PhD diss., Université de Provence, Aix-en-Provence, 1993), 504ff, and Jo Van Steenbergen, "Ritual, Politics, and the City in Mamluk Cairo: The Bayna l-Qasrayn as a Mamluk "lieu de mémoire', 1250–1382," in Alexander D. Beihammer *et al.* (eds.) *Court Ceremonies and Rituals of Power in Byzantium and the Medieval Mediterranean: Comparative Perspectives* (Leiden: Brill, 2013), 233, 265.

13   Henri Bresc, "Les entrées royales des Mamluks: Essai d'approche comparative," in École française de Rome (ed.) *Genèse de l'État moderne en Méditerranée: approches historique et anthropologique des pratiques et des représentations* (Rome: École française de Rome, 1993), 88; Chapoutot-Remadi, "Liens et relations," 85, 94; Bloom, "The Mosque of al-Hakim in Cairo," 15–36; Dominique Sourdel, "Questions de ceremonial "abbaside'," *Revue des Études Islamiques* 28 (1960): 121–148, and for Damascus see Tresse, *Le pèlerinage syrien*, 163. For a larger list of parade routes see ʻAbd al-Fattah, "Baʻd al-mulahazat," 3–5.

14   Al-Maqrizi, *Suluk*, 1:557 for 661 AH/1263 CE, 2:207 for 687 AH/1288 CE, 5:167 for 786 AH / 1384 CE.

15 Nasser Rabbat, *Staging the City: or How Mamluk Architecture Coopted the Streets of Cairo* (Berlin: EB-Verlag, 2014), 37–39, and 'Abd al-Fattah, "Ba'd al-mulahazat," 10.

16 Several women among the Mamluk elite are noted for their elaborate Hajj parades. See Doris Behrens-Abouseif, "The *Mahmal* Legend and the Pilgrimage of the Ladies of the Mamluk Court," *Mamluk Studies Review* 1 (1997): 87–96.

17 Abu al-Mahasin Yusuf Ibn Taghribirdi, *al-Nujum al-zahira fi muluk Misr wa al-Qahira.* Cairo: al-Mu'assasa al-Misriyya al-'Amma li'l-Ta'lif wa'l-Tarjama: 1963–1972 (16 vols.) 7:41.

18 Al-Qalqashandi, *Subh*, 4:6–9.

19 Ibn Taghribirdi, *Nujum* 16:57–58. In addition to his royal robes, Inal paraded under a large parasol, topped with bird-shaped finial.

20 Chapoutot-Remadi, "Liens et relations," 46, and Mustafa Banister, "'Naught Remains to the Caliph but his Title': Revisiting Abbasid Authority in Mamluk Cairo," *Mamluk Studies Review* 18 (2014–2015): 219–245.

21 Bresc, "Les entrées royales des Mamluks," 86.

22 Ibn Iyas, *Bada'i' al-zuhur*, 5:38–45.

23 Muhammad Ibn Iyas, *Journal d'un bourgeois du Caire: chronique d'Ibn Iyas*, trans. Gaston Wiet, 2 vols. (Paris: Armond Colin, 1955–1960) 2:36–42. William M. Brinner, "The significance of the Harafish and their sultan," *Journal of the Economic and Social History of the Orient* 6 (1963): 190–215.

24 Ibn Iyas, *Journal d'un bourgeois*, 2:65–73.

25 Al-Maqrizi, *Suluk*, 5:168, Ibn Taghribirdi, *Nujum*, 14:26.

26 Abu al-Mahasin Yusuf Ibn Taghribirdi, in William Popper (ed.) *Muntakhabat min hawadith al-duhur fi mada al-ayyam wa-shuhur*, 4 vols. (Berkeley: University of California Press, 1930–1942), 3:541.
Doris Behrens-Abouseif, "Qaytbay's Investments in the City of Cairo: Waqf and Power," *Annales Islamologiques* 32 (1998): 29–40.

27 Bresc, "Les entrées royales des Mamluks," 93. See further examples of the display of executed rebels in Carl Petry, *Twilight of Majesty: The Reigns of the Mamluk Sultans al-Ashraf Qaytbay and Qansuh al-Ghawri in Egypt* (Seattle: University of Washington Press, 1993), 57–72. See also Christian Lange, "Legal and Cultural Aspects of Ignominious Parading (*Tashhir*) in Islam," *Islamic Law and Society* 14, 1 (2007): 81–108.

28 Al-Yunini, *Dhayl mir'at al-zaman* as discussed by Donald Little, "The Fall of 'Akka in 690/1291: the Muslim Version," in Moshe Sharon (ed.) *Studies in Islamic History and Civilization in Honor of Professor David Ayalon* (Leiden: Brill, 1986), 179.

29 Michael W. Dols, *Black Death in the Middle East* (Princeton, NJ: Princeton University Press, 1977), 236–253, 305.

30 Taghribirdi, *Nujum*, 14:78f; Al-Maqrizi, *Suluk*, 6:496.

31 Taghribirdi, *Nujum*, 14:97; Al-Maqrizi, *Suluk*, 7:13.

32 Al-Jabarti, *'Aja'ib al-athar*, 3:83–84; *Al-Jabarti's History of Egypt*, 3:77. Aesthetic appreciation of the harmonious balance of a variety of properties within one compostion was a long-held idea. Ibn al-Haytham restates this ancient idea. Ibn Haytham, *The Optics of Ibn al-Haytham*, 2 vols. A. I. Sabra trans. (London: Warburg Institute, 1989), 1:204–206. We shall return to this and related theories of harmony and beauty in Chapter 6.

33 Chapoutot-Remadi, "Liens et relations," 94; Al-Maqrizi, *Suluk* 1:153.

34 Ira Lapidus, *Muslim Cities in the Latter Middle Ages* (Cambridge, MA: Harvard University Press, 1967), 176.

35 Adam Sabra, "From Artisan to Courtier: Sufism and Social Mobility in Fifteenth-Century Egypt," in Roxani E. Margariti, Adam Sabra, and Petra M. Sijpesteijn (eds.) *Histories of the Middle East: Studies in Middle Eastern Society, Economy and Law in Honor of A. L. Udovitch* (Leiden: Brill, 2011), 221–222.

36 *Al-Jabarti's History of Egypt*, 3:291.

37 'Abd al-Ghani al-Nabulusi, *Hadra al-unsiyya fi al-rihla al-Qudsiyya* (Beirut: Al-Masadir, 1990), 40, as cited in Samer Akkach, "The Poetics of Concealment: Al-Nabulusi's Encounter with the Dome of the Rock," *Muqarnas* 22 (2005): 110.

38 *Al-Jabarti's History of Egypt*, 3:482.

39 Ibid., 4:90.

40 Muhammad al-Sakhawi, *al-Daw' al-lami' fi a'yan al-qarn al-tasi'* (Beirut: Dar al-Jil, n.d.) 3:238.

41 Evliya Celebi, *Siyahatnameh Misr*, trans. Muhammad 'Awni (Cairo: Dar al-Kutub wa al-Watha'iq al-Qawmiyya, 2003), 560–562.

42 Richard McGregor, "Ansari, Zakariyya," *Encyclopaedia of Islam*, 3rd edn. (Leiden: Brill, 2007).

43   Al-Maqrizi, *Khitat*, 4/2:727–732, 829.

44   Muhammad Tawfiq al-Bakri, *Bayt al-Sadat al-Wafa'iyya bi'l-diyar al-Misriyya* Published as the introduction to Muhammad Wafa', *Sha 'a'ir al-'irfan fi alwah al-kitman* (Beirut: Dar al-Kutub al-'Ilmiyya, 2006), 49.

45   Al-Shawbari, *al-Tarjama al-Wafa'iyya* ms in Leiden University, Or. 14.437, fol. 11a. For further accounts of Abu al-Takhsis's rituals see Celebi, *Siyahatname Misr*, 591.

46   Jean de Thévenot, *The Travels of Monsieur de Thevenot into the Levant*, trans. R. L'Estrange (London: H. Clark, 1687) Part I, pages 149–150.

47   Vanselb, in Jomier, *Le Mahmal*, 66.

48   Hasselquist, *Voyages and Travels in the Levant*, 80, reporting on the year 1750.

49   *Al-Jabarti's History of Egypt*, 2:162.

50   Frederick de Jong, *Turuq and Turuq-linked*, 67. Under this centralization, Sufi orders were required to secure permits from the Ministry of Religious Endowments for all parades and *mawlid* events. See Frederick de Jong, "Turuq and Turuq-Opposition in 20th-Century Egypt," in Frederick de Jong (ed.) *Sufi Orders in Ottoman and Post-Ottoman Egypt and the Middle East* (Istanbul: Isis, 1994), 195. The appointing of shaykhs of the Orders also came under state control in this period.

51   Jomier, *Le Mahmal*, 71.

52   Yusuf Ibn Taghribirdi, *History of Egypt 1382–1469 AD, Part I, 1382–1399 AD*, trans. William Popper (Berkeley: University of California Press, 1954), 112.

53   Bresc, "Les entrées royales des Mamluks," 90.

54   Al-Maqrizi, *Khitat*, 1:716–717.

55   Catherine Mayeur-Jaouen, "Les processions pèlerines en Égypte: pratiques carnavalesques et intinéraires politiques, les inventions successives d'une tradition," in Sylvia Chiffoleau and Anna Madoeuf (eds.) *Les pèlerinages au Maghreb et au Moyen-Orient: espaces publics, espaces du public*. (Damascus: Presses de l'Institut français du proche orient, 2005), 227.

56   Al-Maqrizi, *Khitat*, 2:418 and 4:387.

57   Devin J. Stewart, "Popular Shiism in Medieval Egypt," *Studia Islamica* 84 (1996): 35–66.

58   McPherson, *Moulids*, 223.

59   Donald Preziosi, *Rethinking Art History: Meditations on a Coy Science* (New Haven, CT: Yale University Press, 1989), 169.

60   Shoshan, *Popular Culture*, 16. For more on this feud see Julian Johansen, *Sufism and Islamic Reform in Egypt: the Battle for Islamic Tradition* (Oxford: Clarendon, 1996), 103–114.

61   For a wider assessment of Sufism and its detractors, see the studies in Alexander Knysh, *Ibn 'Arabi in the Later Islamic Tradition: The Making of a Polemical Image in Medieval Islam* (New York: State University of New York Press, 1999).

62   *Al-Jabarti's History of Egypt*, 1:82.

63   Ibn Kathir in Meri, *Cult of the Saints*, 116–117.

64   Amina Elbendary, *Between Riots and Negotiations: Urban Protest in Late Medieval Egypt and Syria* (Berlin: EB-Verlag, 2012), 7, 28.

65   Tamer el-Leithy, "Sufis, Copts and the Politics of Piety: Moral Regulation in Fourteenth-century Upper Egypt," in Richard McGregor and Adam Sabra (eds.) *The Development of Sufism in Mamluk Egypt* (Cairo: Presses de l'Institut français d'archéologie orientale, 2006), 75, and Boaz Shoshan, "Grain Riots and the 'Moral Economy': Cairo, 1350–1517," *Journal of Interdisciplinary History* 10, 3 (1980): 459–478.

66   Elbendary, *Between Riots and Negotiations*, 29.

67   Al-Maqrizi, *Suluk*, 3:415.

68   Shoshana Felman, *The Scandal of the Speaking Body* (Stanford, CA: Stanford University Press, 2003), xiv, 55–56.

69   Judith Butler, *Gender Trouble: Feminism and the Subversion of Identity* (New York: Routledge, 1999), xxiv, and *Bodies that Matter: On the Discursive Limits of Sex* (New York: Routledge, 1993), 124–125. For further refinements see Saba Mahmood, *Politics of Piety: the Islamic Revival and the Feminist Subject* (Princeton, NJ: Princeton University Press, 2005).

70   Al-Maqrizi, *Suluk*, 3:45; and Ibn Taghribirdi, *al-Nujum*, 9:72.

71   Al-Maqrizi, *Suluk*, 7:447.

72   Fumihiko Hasebe, "Popular Movements and Jaqmaq, the Less Paternalistic Sultan: Some Aspects of Conflict in the Egyptian Cities, 1449–52," *Annals of Japan Association for Middle East Studies* 20, 2 (2005): 38; Muhammad Sakhawi, *al-Tibr al-masbuk fi dhayl al-muluk*, 4 vols. (Cairo: Dar al-Kutub wa'l-Watha'iq al-Qawmiyya, 2002–2007), 3:47–49.

73   Plate, *Walter Benjamin*, 59.

74   Belting, *Florence and Baghdad: Renaissance Art and Arab Science*, trans. Deborah Lucas Schneider (Cambridge, MA: Belknap Press, 2011), 113; Muhammad Ibn Haytham, *The Optics of Ibn al-Haytham*, 2 vols., trans. Abdelhamid

I. Sabra (London: Warburg Institute, 1989), 1:217, 223.

75 Khalil Athamina, "The Black Banners and the Socio-Political Significance of Flags and Solgans in Medieval Islam," *Arabica* 36, 3 (1989): 317. A commemorative shrine would be built over the place Muhammad was believed to have unfurled his banner just outside Mecca, the day he took the city. See Azraqi, *Akhbar Makka*, 2:201.

76 Martin Hinds, "The Banners and Battle cries of the Arabs at Siffin (AD 657)," in Martin Hinds *et al.* (eds.) *Studies in Early Islamic History* (Princeton, NJ: Darwin Press, 1996), 104–108.

77 Athamina, "The Black Banners," 316.

78 Leon Ary Mayer, *Mamluk Costume; A Survey* (Geneva: Albert Kundig, 1952), 13, and Al-Maqrizi, *Khitat*, 3:782.

79 Mayer, *Mamluk Costume*, 49.

80 Husain Efendi and Stanford Shaw, *Ottoman Egypt in the Age of the French Revolution* (Cambridge, MA: Harvard University Press, 1966), 101; Mayeur-Jaouen, "Les processions pèlerines en Égypte," 223–225.

81 Ibn al-Haytham notes the natural appeal of colors to the viewer. Ibn Haytham, *The Optics*, 1:200. Najm al-Din Kubra (d. 1220), who at one point studied mysticism in Egypt, developed an elaborate visionary approach to religious knowledge and experience. Henry Corbin, *The Man of Light in Iranian Sufism*, trans. Nancy Pearson (Boulder, CO: Shambhala, 1978), 64–79. Jamal Elias, *The Throne Carrier of God: The Life and Thought of 'Ala ad-Dawla as-Simnani* (Albany: State University of New York Press, 1995), 135–140. William Chittick, *Divine Love: Islamic Literature and the Path to God* (New Haven: Yale University Press, 2013), 432–436. Annemarie Schimmel, *And Muhammad is His Messenger: the Veneration of the Prophet in Islamic Piety* (Chapel Hill: University of North Carolina Press, 1985), 39. The development of color theory in Eygptian Sufism remains to be explored. In his *'Uyun al-haqa'iq* (Cairo: Dar al-Kutub al-Misriyya, ms Tasawwuf Taymur 180) fols 53a, 44b, Ibn Bahkhila (d. 1332) explores the "Muhammadan shadow," which marks the end of eras; and 'Ali Wafa' (d. 1405) identifies "black light" as the source and lord of all light. See his *Wasaya Sayyidi 'Ali Wafa'* (Paris: Bibliothèque Nationale, ms 1359) fol 88a. Helena

Hallenberg, *Ibrahim al-Dasuqi (1255–1296). A Saint Invented* (Helsinki: Finnish Academy of Sciences and Letters, 2005), 198–203.

82 Mayer, *Saracenic Heraldry*, 10–13, and Milwright, "The Cup of the Saqi," 241–265.

83 Sheila Blair and Jonathan Bloom, "Inscriptions in Art and Architecture," in Jane D. McAuliffe (ed.) *The Cambridge Companion to the Qur'an* (New York: Cambridge University Press, 2006), 174, and her *Islamic Inscriptions* (New York: New York University Press, 1998), 215.

84 Examples from eighth century are preserved: Dominique Sourdel, "Robes of Honor in 'Abbasid Baghdad During the Eighth to Eleventh Centuries," in Stuart Gordon (ed.) *Robes of Honor: the Medieval World of Investiture* (New York: Palgrave, 2001), 145, fn. 28. For examples from the thirteenth and fourteenth centuries, see Yedida K. Stillman, *Arab Dress, a Short History*, ed. Norman Stillman (London: Brill, 2003), plates 22, 23, and pages 12–136. The Textiles Museum in Cairo holds several examples from the Fatimid period, as does the Museum of Islamic Art. For Mamluk era examples, see Muhammad 'Abbas (ed.) *Manarat al-funun wa al-hadara al-Islamiyya* (Cairo: Mathaf al-Fann al-Islami, 2010), 56, 57.

85 Ahmad al-Baladhuri, *Futuh al-buldan* (Beirut: Dar al-Kutub al-'Ilmiyya, 2014), 48: (The term *al-hulal washy* could also be translated as embroidered clothing). On the developments of script on *tiraz* fabric during the Fatimid period, see Clause-Peter Haase, "Some Aspects of Fatimid Calligraphy on Textiles," in Marianne Barrucand (ed.) *L'Égypte fatimide: son art et son historie* (Paris: Presses de l'Univerité de Paris-Sorbonne, 1999), 343, and Sheila Blair, "Inscriptions on Medieval Islamic Textiles," in Muhammad Salim (ed.) *Islamische Textilkunst des Mittelalters: aktuelle Probleme* (Riggisberg [Switzerland]: Abegg-Stiftung, 1997), 95–104.

86 Athamina, "The Black Banners," 317.

87 Ibid., 318.

88 Sourdel, "Robes of Honor," 143. On the legitimacy of Saladin's rule see Yaacov Lev, *Saladin in Egypt*, 105–107.

89 Al-Qalqashandi, *Subh al-'asha* 3:276.

90 Marshall Hodgson, *The Venture of Islam*, 3 vols. (Chicago: University of Chicago Press, 1977), 2:13.

91 Robert Irwin, *The Middle East in the Middle Ages: The Early Mamluk Sultanate 1250–1382*

(Carbondale: Southern Illinois University Press, 1986), 43, and Jonathan Berkey, "Mamluk Religious Policy," *Mamluk Studies Review* 13, 2 (2009): 11–12, and Banister, "'Naught Remains'," 225–226, 243–244.

92   Bresc, "Les entrées royales des Mamluks," 83. quoting from Ibn Abi al-Fada'il's *al-Nahj al-sadid*.

93   Ibn Iyas, *Bada'i' al-zuhur*, 4:3.

94   Chapoutot-Remadi, "Liens et relations," 102.

95   For more on this intertwined symbolism, note discussion of the black and yellow banners that accompanied Qalawun's wife Tughay on her hajj in 1321: Behrens-Abouseif, "The Mahmal Legend," 92–93.

96   Linda Northrup, *From Slave to Sultan: the career of al-Mansur Qalawun and the Consolidation of Mamluk Rule in Egypt and Syria (678–689/ 1279–1290)* (Stuttgart: Franz Steiner, 1998), 176.

97   Walter B. Denny, "A Group of Silk Islamic Banners," *Textile Museum Journal* 4 (1974): 71, fig 6.

98   Sadiq, *Rihla mish'al al-mahmal*, 206.

99   Jomier, *Le Mahmal*, 17.

100 Suraiya Faroqhi, *Herrscher über Mekka: die Geschichte der Pilgerfahrt* (Munich: Artemis, 1990), 52.

101 Tresse, *Le pélerinage syrien*, 92, 170–171, and Burton, *Inner Life of Syria*, 57–58.

102 For an overview of this history see A. H. de Groot, "Sandjak-i Sherif," *Encyclopaedia of Islam*, 2nd edn. (Leiden: Brill, 2012).

103 Although parts of the inscription remain unreadable, my translation here corrects and adds to that of W. Thackston, as presented in Denny, "A Group of Silk Islamic Banners," 79. My thanks to Tony K. Stewart who provided technical assistance with imaging the banner texts.

104 Poole, *The Englishwoman in Egypt*, 77–78.

105 Winifred S. Blackman, *The Fellahin of Upper Egypt. Their religious, social and industrial life to-day with special reference to survivals from ancient times* (London: George G. Haarap & Co., 1927), 252–255.

106 Tawfiq Canann, *Mohammedan Saints and Sanctuaries in Palestine* (London: Luzac & Co., 1927), 199–212; and Amnon Cohen, "An Ottoman Festival (*mawsim*) Resurrected?" in David J. Wasserstein and Ami Ayalon (eds.) *Mamluks and Ottomans: Studies in Honour of Michael Winter* (New York: Routledge, 2006), 39.

107 Emma Aubin-Boltanski, "Le mawsim de Nabî Mûsâ: processions, espace en miettes et mémoire blessée: Territoires palestiniens (1998–2000)," in Sylvia Chiffoleau and Anna Madoeuf (eds.) *Les Pèlerinages au Maghreb et au Moyen-Orient* (Damascus: Institut Français du Proche-Orient, 2005), 60–61. On the 1947 parade with Sufis and banners at the shrine of Husayn in Asqalon, see Daniella Talmon-Heller, "Vicissitudes of a Holy Place: Construction, Destruction and Commemoration of Mashhad Husayn in Ascalon." *Der Islam* 93(1) (2016): 204–205.

108 The photograph appears as a frontispiece in Michel Gilsenan, *Saint and Sufi in Modern Egypt: An Essay in the Sociology of Religion* (Oxford: Clarendon Press, 1973). For an illustration of Mamluk architectural cresting, see Caroline Williams, *Islamic Monuments in Cairo: A Practical Guide* 4th edn. (Cairo: American University in Cairo Press, 1993), 32.

109 Pierre-Jean Luizard, "Un mawlid particulier," *Étypte-monde arabe* 14 (1993): 82.

CHAPTER 4

1   Ahmad Taymur Basha, *al-Athar al-nabawiyya* (Cairo: Matba'a Dar al-Kutub al-'Arabiyya, 1951), 34.

2   Richard McGregor, "Grave visitation," *Encyclopaedia of Islam*, 3rd edn. (Leiden: Brill, 2007–).

3   The classic Arabic dictionary, Ibn Manzur, *Lisan al-Arab*, 'Abdallah al-Kabir et al. (eds), 6 + 3 vols. (Cairo: Dar al-Ma 'arif, 1986) defines *athar* as simply, "The remainder of a thing." On the connection between oral reports and relics as artifacts, see Eerik Dickinson, "Ibn Shahrazuri and the Isnad," *Journal of the American Oriental Society*, 122, 3 (Jul.–Sep. 2002): 484.

4   Kevin Trainor, "*Pars pro toto*: On Comparing Relic Practices," *Numen* 57 (2010): 271. For a survey of footprints in Iran, with special attention to their Buddhist precedents, see Mostafa Vaziri, *Buddhism in Iran: An Anthropological Approach to Traces and Influences* (New York: Palgrave Macmillan, 2012), 67–80.

5   Muhy al-Din Ibn 'Arabi, *al-Futuhat al-makkiyya*, 8 vols. (Beirut: Dar al-Fikr, 1994) 1:285–286, and Carl W. Ernst, "An Indo-Persian Guide to Sufi Shrine Pilgrimage," in

Grace M. Smith and Carl W. Ernst (eds.) *Manifestations of Sainthood in Islam* (Istanbul: Isis Press 1993), 60. Ibn Jubayr describes mosques closely associated with certain saints, as imprinted or stamped (*mawsum*) with their *baraka*. *Rihla ibn Jubayr*, 36, and *Travels of Ibn Jubayr*, 53.

6 Hans Belting, *An Anthropology of Images: Picture, Medium, Body*, trans. Thomas Dunlap (Princeton, NJ: Princeton University Press, 2011), 16.

7 Robert Sharf, "On the Allure of Buddhist Relics," *Representations* 66 (Spring 1999): 85.

8 Hans Belting "Image, Medium, Body: A New Approach to Iconology," *Critical Inquiry* 31 (Winter 2005): 312.

9 Recently, Josef Meri has proposed a "Typology of relics," which is a useful list of objects grouped under the individuals with whom they are associated. See his "Relics of Piety and Power in Medieval Islam," *Past and Present*, supp. 5 (2010): 119.

10 Brannon M. Wheeler, "Collecting the Dead Body of Muhammad: Hair, Nails, Sweat and Spit," in Christianne Gruber and Avinoam Shalem (eds.) *The Image of the Prophet Between Ideal and Ideology: A Scholarly Investigation* (Berlin: Walter de Gruyter, 2014), 45, 61, and Brannon M. Wheeler, "Gift of the Body," *Numen* 57 (2010): 344, 372.

11 Abu 'Uthman al-Jahiz, *al-Bayan wa al-tabyin*, 4 vols. in 2 (Cairo: Maktabat al-Khanji, 1998), book 2: section 1: 81–82.

12 Terry Eagleton, *After Theory* (New York: Basic Books, 2003), 161.

13 Theories of the sublime have often focused on the experiences of fear and pleasure. A typical concern has been with the violent powers of nature, or of imposing buildings, which threaten to overwhelm the viewer. Kant, *Critique of Judgment*, 123–150. In contrast, we shall see below that relics particularly in their brokenness and incompleteness are not sublime.

14 Jean-Luc Nancy, *The Inoperative Community* (Minneapolis: University of Minnesota Press, 1991), 87.

15 'Umar ibn al-Farid, *'Umar ibn al-Farid: Sufi Verse, Saintly Life*, trans. Th. Emil Homerin (New York: Paulist Press, 2001) 133.

16 Muhammad Wafa', *Sha'a'ir al- 'irfan fi alwah al-kitman* (Beirut: Dar al-Kutub al-'Ilmiyya, 2006), 92. The Sufi conception of annihilation of self in the divine was often tied to the idea of passionate consuming love (*'ishq*). For an overview see the classic eleventh-century Sufi manual, *Al-Qushayri's Epistle on Sufism*, trans. Alexander Knysh (Reading: Garnet, 2007), 325–335. Theologians also worked out elaborate models of love, and its degrees. See for example, Joseph Norment Bell, *Love Theory in Later Hanbalite Islam* (Albany: State University of New York, 1979), 156–160.

17 Margaret R. Miles, "Image," in Mark C. Taylor (ed.) *Critical Terms for Religious Studies*, (Chicago: University of Chicago Press, 1998), 169.

18 Maurice Merleau-Ponty, *The Visible and the Invisible*, trans. Alphonso Lingis (Evanston, IL: Northwest University Press, 1968), 130–138.

19 Schimmel, *And Muhammad is His Messenger*, 32.

20 Muhammad ibn 'Isa al-Tirmidhi, *al-Shama'il al-Muhammadiyya*, 2 vols. (Beirut: Dar al-Hadith, 1988), 1:7–8.

21 J. M. Rogers, *Empire of the Sultans: Ottoman Art from the Khalili Collection* (Alexandra Virginia: Art Services International, 2000), 270–275. Jamal Elias, *Aisha's Cushion: Religious Art, Perception, and Practice in Islam* (Cambridge MA.: Harvard University Press, 2012), 272–274.

22 Jonathan G. Katz, "Dreams and Their Interpretation in Sufi Thought and Practice," in Özgen Felek and Alexander Knysh (eds.) *Dreams and Visions in Islamic Societies* (Albany: State University of New York Press, 2013), 190.

23 Pierre Lory, "L'interprétation des rêves de portée religieuse chez Ibn Shahin," in Richard McGregor and Adam Sabra (eds.) *The Development of Sufism in Mamluk Egypt*(Cairo: Presses de l'Institut français d'archéologie orientale, 2006), 260, fn. 5; Éric Geoffroy, *Le Soufisme en Égypte et en Syrie sous les derniers mamelouks et les premiers ottomans: orientations spirituelles et enjeux culturels* (Damascus: Presses de l'institut français du proche orient: 1996), 435, 479.

24 Valery J. Hoffman, "Annihilation in the Messenger of God: the Development of a Sufi Practice," *International Journal of Middle East Studies* 31 (1999): 356.

25 'Abd al-Wahhab al-Sha'rani, *Lata'if al-minan wa al-akhlaq fi wujub al-tahadduth bi-ni'mat Allah 'ala al-itlaq: al-ma'ruf bi al-Minan al-kubra* (Cairo: 'Alam al-Fikr, 1976), 365.

26   Ibid.

27   Ibn Faris Abu al-Lata'if, *al-Minah al-Ilahiyya min manaqib al-sadat al-Wafa'iyya*, published as an appendix to Muhammad Wafa', *al-Masami'* (Beirut: Dar al-Kutub al-'Ilmiyya, 2007), 11.

28   John C. Lamoreaux, *The Early Muslim Tradition of Dream Interpretation* (Albany: State University of New York, 2002); Jonathan G. Katz, *Dreams, Sufism, and Sainthood: the Visionary Career of Muhammad al-Zawawi* (Leiden: Brill 1996). For modern Egyptian debates around interpretation see Amira Mittermaier, *Dreams that Matter: Egyptian Landscapes of the Imagination* (Berkeley: University of California Press, 2011).

29   Suzanne P. Stetkevych, *The Mantle Odes: Arabic Praise Poems to the Prophet Muhammad* (Bloomington: Indiana University Press, 2010), 82.

30   Soucek, "Material Culture and the Qur'an," in *Encyclopaedia of the Qur'an*; Travis Zadeh, "Drops of Blood: Charisma and Political Legitimacy in the Translatio of the Uthmanic Codex of al-Andalus," *Journal of Arabic Literature* 39 (2008): 331–332.

31   Josef W. Meri, "A Late Medieval Syrian Pilgrimage Guide: Ibn al-Hawrani's *Al-Isharat ila Amakin al-Ziyarat (Guide to Pilgrimage Places)*" *Medieval Encounters* 7, 1 (2001): 73–74.

32   Meri, "A Late Medieval Syrian Pilgrimage Guide," 35; and Nancy Khaleq, *Damascus after the Muslim Conquest: Text and Image in Early Islam* (New York: Cambridge University Press, 2011), 125. In surah Yusuf (Q. 12:96) Joseph's shirt is placed over his father Jacob's face to cure his blindness.

33   Al-Bukhari, *Sahih* "Book of Clothing," 77, hadith 5859, 5896; Wheeler, *Mecca and Eden*, 72; Gauthier H. A. Juynboll, *Encyclopedia of Canonical Hadith* (Leiden: Brill, 2007), 573; Muhammad Ibn Sa'd, *al-Tabaqat*, 11 vols. (Cairo: Maktabat al-Khanji, 2001) 1:371.

34   Taymur, *al-Athar al-nabawiyya*, 93.

35   Rudolf Kriss and Hubert Kriss-Heinrich, *Volksglaube in Bereigh des Islam*, 2 vols. (Wiesbaden: O. Harassowitz, 1960–1962), 1:330–331; Taymur, *al-Athar*, 92; Thierry Zarcone, "Pilgrimage to the 'Second Meccas' and 'Ka'bas' of Central Asia," in Alexandre Papas, Thomas Welsford, and Thierry Zarcone (eds.) *Central Asian Pilgrims: Hajj Routes and Pious Visits between Central Asia and the Hijaz* (Berlin: K. Schwarz, 2012), 252.

36   Canaan, *Mohammedan Saints*, 82.

37   Rachel Milstein, "Futuh-i Haramayn: Sixteenth-century Illustrations of the Hajj Route," in David J. Wasserstein and Ami Ayalon (eds.) *Mamluks and Ottomans: Studies in Honor of Michael Winter* (New York: Routledge, 2006), 177, and Hilmi Aydin, *Pavilion of the Sacred Relics, The Sacred Trusts, Topkapi Palace Museum, Istanbul* (Clifton, NJ: Tughra Books, 2014), 102–113, 138.

38   John Alden Williams, "The Khanqah of Siryaqus; a Mamluk Royal Religious Foundation," in Arnold H. Green (ed.) *In Quest of an Islamic Humanism: Arabic and Islamic Studies in Memory of Mohamed al-Nowaihi*,(Cairo: American University in Cairo Press, 1984), 118.

39   Wheeler, "Collecting," 53.

40   Th. Emil Homerin, "Saving Muslim Souls: The *Khanqah* and the Sufi Duty in Mamluk Lands," *Mamluk Studies Review* 3 (1999): 69–70.

41   David C. Lindberg, *Theories of Vision from al-Kindi to Kepler* (Chicago: University of Chicago Press, 1976), 9–44.

42   Muhy al-Din Ibn 'Arabi, *Fusus al-hikam* (Beirut: Dar al-Kutub al-'Arabi, 1946), 173.

43   Fatima Z. A. Langhi, "'Ajami Mysteries of Sitt 'Ajam bint al-Nafis," *Journal of the Muhyiddin Ibn 'Arabi Society* 46 (2009), access online http://www.ibnarabisociety.org/articles/sitt-ajam.html#note5 (January 2019).

44   Carlmela Baffioni, "From Sense Perception to the Vision of God: A Path Towards Knowledge According to the Ikhwan al-Safa," *Arabic Sciences and Philosophy* 8 (1998): 226; and Elizabeth Alexandrin, "Witnessing the Lights of the Heavenly Dominion: Dreams, Visions and the Mystical Exegesis of Shams al-Din al-Daylami," in Özgen Felek and Alexander Knysh (eds.) *Dreams and Visions in Islamic Societies* (Albany: State University of New York Press, 2013), 225.

45   Roland Betancourt, "Tempted to Touch: Tactility, Ritual, and Mediation in Byzantine Visuality," *Speculum* 91, 3 (2016): 661.

46   'Ali al-Harawi, *Guide des lieux de pèlerinage* trans. Janine Sourdel-Thomine (Damascus: Damascus: Presses de l'Institut français de Damas, 1957), 40; reference is also made to Khalid's sword. See Finbarr Barry Flood, *The Great Mosque of Damascus: Studies on the Makings of an Umayyad Visual Culture* (Leiden: Brill, 2001), 106–107. Muhammad's lance may have also been displayed

devotionally within a mihrab in the first Islamic century. See Finbarr Barry Flood, "Light in Stone: The Commemoration of the Prophet in Umayyad Architecture," in Jeremy Johns (ed.) *Bayt al-Maqdis: Jerusalem and Early Islam* (New York: Oxford University Press, 1999), 355.

47 Ibn al-Kalbi, *Book of Idols Being a Translation from the Arabic of the Kitab al-asnam*, trans. Nabih Amin Faris (Princeton, NJ: Princeton University Press, 2015), 13–14.

48 See Francesca Bellino, "Dhu l-Faqar," *Encyclopaedia of Islam*, 3rd edn. (Leiden: Brill, 2007–). For a more fulsome account of these swords see Wheeler, *Mecca and Eden*, 32–43.

49 Bloom, "Mosque of al-Hakim," 27.

50 Taymur, *al-Athar al-nabawiyya*, 26.

51 Aydin, *Pavilion of the Sacred Relics*, 268–335.

52 Qutb al-Din al-Yunini, *Dhayl mir'at al-zaman*, 2:46, and mentioned in Meri, *Cult of the Saints*, 110.

53 See, for example, Ahmad al-Maqarri, *Wasf na'l al-nabi al-musamma bi-fath al-muta'al fi madih al-na'al* (Cairo: Dar al-Qadi 'Ayyad, 1997).

54 Jean-Michel Mouton, "De quelques reliques conservées à Damas au Moyen-Âge," *Annales Islamologiques* 27 (1993): 252, as recorded by Sibt ibn al-Jawzi.

55 Al-Asqalani as quoted in Taymur, *al-Athar al-nabawiyya*, 107.

56 Aydin, *Pavilion of the Sacred Relics*, 39.

57 Taymur, *al-Athar al-nabawiyya*, 46. At one point, the Syrian town of Adhruh, associated with the conflict between 'Ali and Mu'awiyya, held a cloak. Daniella Talmon-Heller, *Islamic Piety in Medieval Syria: Mosques, Cemeteries and Sermons under the Zangids and Ayyubids (1146–1260)* (Leiden: Brill, 2007), 203.

58 Al-Maqrizi, *Khitat*, 4/2:514–522.

59 Aydin, *Pavilion of the Sacred Relics*, 210–226.

60 'Imad al-Din Ibn Kathir, *al-Bidaya wa-l-nihaya*, 8 vols. (Cairo: Dar al-Rayyan li'l-Turath, 1988), 4:143.

61 Michael Lecker, "Idol Worship in Pre-Islamic Yamama," unpublished paper available on academia.edu (January 2018).

62 Flood, "Light in Stone," 319. Polished black stones can also be found today in Cairo, in the mosques of al-Husayn and Shaykhu.

63 Michael Jan De Goeje, *Mémoire sur les Carmates du Bahraïn et les Fatimides* (Leiden: Brill, 1886), 107. On the history of the ram's horn see Nasser Rabbat, "The Dome of the Rock Revisited: Some Remarks on al-Wasiti's Accounts," *Muqarnas* 10 (1993): 8.

64 Daniel De Smet, "Le calife fatimide al-Hakim (996–1021) a-t-il voulu s'emparer des reliques du Prophète Muhammad?," in Phillipe Borgeaud and Youri Volokhine (eds.) *Les objets de la mémoire: pour une approche comparatiste des reliques et de leur culte* (New York: Peter Lang, 2005), 252.

65 Al-Maqrizi, *Khitat*, 4/2:801–802.

66 Sibt ibn al-Jawzi quoted in Mouton, "De quelques reliques," 251, and Talmon-Heller, *Islamic Piety*, 57. Daniella Talmon-Heller. "Scriptures as Holy Objects: Preliminary Comparative Remarks on the Qur'an and the Torah in the Medieval Middle East." *Intellectual History of the Islamicate World* 4 (2016): 232–238.

67 *Rihla ibn Jubayr*, 80, and *Travels of Ibn Jubayr*, 99.

68 Ibn Ishaq, *The Life of Muhammad*, 653–658.

69 Aydin, *Pavilion of the Sacred Relics*, 96–100.

70 *Rihla ibn Jubayr*, 170 and *Travels of Ibn Jubayr*, 200; al-Bukhari, *Sahih* "Kitab al-manaqib," hadith 3584, 3585. Several reports are collected in the *Shifa'* of Qadi 'Iyad. See Qadi 'Iyad, *Muhammad Messenger of Allah*, trans. Aysha Bewley (Inverness: Madinah Press, 1991), 168. Shafi', "Description of the Two Sanctuaries," 433.

71 *Rihla ibn Jubayr*, 170; Jean Sauvaget, *La mosquée omeyyade de Médine* (Institut français de Damas, 1947), 85–88.

72 *Nasir-i Khusraw's Book of Travels*, 99.

73 'Abd al-Wahhab al-Sha'rani, *al-Tabaqat al-kubra*, 2 vols., 2:43, Richard McGregor, *Sanctity and Mysticism in Medieval Egypt: The Wafa' Sufi Order and the Legacy of Ibn 'Arabi* (Albany: State University of New York, 2004), 144.

74 'Abd al-Ghani al-Nabulusi, *al-Haqiqa wa al-majaz fi al-rihla ila bilad al-Sham wa Misr wa al-Hijaz* (Cairo: al-Hay'a al-Misriyya al-'Amma li-l-Kitab, 1986), 240.

75 *Rihla ibn Jubayr*, 141, and *Travels of Ibn Jubayr*, 166.

76 Azraqi, *Akhbar Makka*, 2:199. Fatima Mernissi, *The Forgotten Queens of Islam* (Minneapolis: University of Minnesota Press, 1993), 60–67.

77 Rachel Milstein, "Shawq Nama – An Illustrated Tour of Holy Arabia," *Jerusalem Studies in Arabic and Islam* 25 (2001): 298, quoting Eyüb Sabri Pasha's *Mir'at al-Haramayn*.

78 'Abd al-Wahhab Abu Sulaiman, *al-Amakin al-ma'thura al-mutawattara fi Makka al-mukarrama* (London: Al-Furqan, 2009), 76–77, 249–251.

79 *The History of al-Tabari* 39:47.
80 *Rihla ibn Jubayr*, 145, and *Travels of Ibn Jubayr*, 171.
81 Nadia Abbott, *Two Queens of Baghdad; Mother and Wife of Harun al-Rashid* (Chicago: University of Chicago Press, 1946), 119.
82 Muhammad Husayn Haykal, *Fi manzil al-wahy* (Cairo: Maktaba al-Nahda al-Misriyya, 1939), 219–220.
83 Ahmad Zaki Yamani, *The House of Khadijah bin Khuwaylid*, trans. ʿAbdallah Abdel-Haleem (London: al-Furqan, 2014), 55–58.
84 *Rihla ibn Jubayr*, 91–92, 141–142. This site is represented as the small construction at the top of a pilgrimage manual (Figure 43), written in the second half of the tenth/sixteenth century, in Mecca. The structure, with two roofs, one a pyramid shape and the other a dome, is labeled as Fatima's house, and the birthplace of al-Hasan and al-Husayn. Most sources, however, have al-Hasan and al-Husayn being born in Medina, two years after the Hijra. Al-Samhudi, *Khulasat al-wafa*, 297. In 1671, however, one report describes this site as the place al-Hasan and al-Husayn recited the Qurʾan, and where the boys' seats had been preserved. See Evliya Celebi, *al-Rihla al-Hijaziyya*, trans. Al-Safsafi Ahmad al-Mursi (Cairo: Dar al-Afaq al-ʾArabi, 1999), 257. The site of ʿAli's birth was also associated with this neighborhood. Milstein, "*Shawq-Nama*," 276 and Milstein, "Futuh-i Haramayn," 174.
85 See Nicolaas J. G. Kaptein, "Mawlid," *Encyclopaedia of Islam*, 2nd edn. (Leiden: Brill, 2012).
86 Abu Sulaiman, *al-Amakin al-maʾthura*, 249.
87 Yamani, *House of Khadijah*, 113–162.
88 Taymur, *al-Athar al-nabawiyya*, 59–61.
89 Al-Harawi, *Guide des lieux de pèlerinage*, 18.
90 Julia Gonnella, *The Citadel of Aleppo; Description, History, Site Plan, and Visitor Tour* (Geneva: Aga Khan Trust for Culture, 2008), 38, and Tabbaa, *Constructions of Power*, 102, 107.
91 Al-Harawi, *Guide des lieux de pèlerinage*, 81. This might be the same site al-Nabulusi would later associate with a foot imprint attributed to the prophet Elija. Al-Nabulusi, *Al-Haqiqa wa al-majaz*, 279. This edition seems to have misprinted Ilyas as Ilyar.
92 Al-Harawi, *Guide des lieux de pèlerinage*, 99.
93 Ibid., 146, 172, 173.
94 George Makdisi, "The Topography of Eleventh Century Baghdad: Materials and Notes (II)" *Arabica* 6, 3 (1959): 289.
95 *Nasir-i Khusraw's Book of Travels* p. 40.
96 Guy Le Strange, *Palestine Under the Moslems: A Description of Syria and the Holy Land from A.D. 650 to 1500* (London: Committee of the Palestinian Exploration Fund, 1890), 132.
97 Le Strange, *Palestine Under the Moslems*, 136.
98 Canaan, *Mohammedan Saints*, 81. See also Qurʾan 19:57.
99 Finbarr Barry Flood, "An Ambiguous Aesthetic: Crusader *Spolia* in Ayyubid Jerusalem," in Sylvia Auld and Robert Hillenbrand (eds.) *Ayyubid Jerusalem: The Holy City in Context, 1187–1250* (London: Al-Tajir Trust, 2009), 203–205, and Canaan, *Mohammedan Saints*, 81.
100 Taymur, *al-Athar al-nabawiyya*, 63, from al-Nabulusi's *al-Hadrat al-uns*. Al-Nabulusi also notes the angels' fingerprints left on the Rock, when they restrained it as it tried to rise up and follow Muhammad in his ascent. A novel interpretation proposed by al-Nabulusi is that God made the Rock float in order to accustom Muhammad to the weightlessness he would himself experience during his ascension. Akkach, "The Poetics of Concealment," 124.
101 Gülru Necipoglu, "The Dome of the Rock as Palimpsest: ʿAbd al-Malik's Grand Narrative and Sultan Süleyman's Glosses," *Muqarnas*, 25 (2008): 29. Ibn Kathir also notes disapprovingly that figural representations of the footprint were painted as a kind of religious advertisement outside, on the gates to the mount.
102 Al-Nabulusi, *al-Haqiqa wa al-majaz*, 116, and Elizabeth Sirriyyah, "The Journeys of ʿAbd al-Ghani al-Nabulusi in Palestine (1101/1690 and 1105/1693)," *Journal of Semitic Studies* 24, 1 (1979), 65.
103 Milstein, "Kitab Shawq-Nama," 292.
104 *Rihla ibn Jubayr*, 59–60, and *Travels of Ibn Jubayr*, 80.
105 *Nasir-i Khusraw's Book of Travels*, 94.
106 Al-Nabulusi, *al-Haqiqa wa al-majaz*, 251, 293.
107 Abu Salim al-ʿAyyashi (d. 1679) quoted in Taymur, *al-Athar al-nabawiyya*, 59.
108 Taymur, *al-Athar al-nabawiyya*, 53.
109 Ibid., 54–58.
110 Ibid., 51.
111 Ibn Iyas, *Badaʾiʿ al-zuhur*, 2:124.
112 Ibn Iyas quoted in Jean-Charles Ducène, "Rites religieux et crue du Nil en Egypte médiévale," *Acta orientalia belgica* 23 (2010): 71.

113 Celebi as cited in Iman Abdulfattah, "Relics of the Prophet and Practices of His Veneration in Medieval Cairo," *Journal of Islamic Archaeology* 1.1 (2014): 90.

114 Al-Nabulusi, *al-Haqiqah wa al-majaz*, 239.

115 'Abd al-Samad Misri as quoted in Taymur, *al-Athar al-nabawiyya*, 61.

116 Ibid.

117 Janine Sourdel-Thomine, "Les anciens lieux de pélerinage," *Bulletin d'Etudes Orientales* 14 (1951): 73.

118 Burton, *Inner Life of Syria*, 1:65.

119 Ibn Kathir's *Bidaya* as quoted in Henri Laoust, "La biographie d'Ibn Taimiya d'après Ibn Kathir," *Bulletin d'études orientales* 9 (1942): 133.

120 Le Strange, *Palestine Under the Moslems*, 162–171 quotes from Ibn Faqih and Ibn 'Abd Rabbihi. See also Amikam Elad, *Medieval Jerusalem and Islamic Worship: Holy Places, Ceremonies, Pilgrimage* (Leiden: Brill, 1995), 72.

121 Said Nuseibeh, *The Dome of the Rock* (New York: Rizzoli International Publications, 1998), 68.

122 *Travels of Ibn Jubayr*, 51.

123 Burton, *Inner Life of Syria*, 60. She also makes a passing reference to a hoof-print in the Great Mosque.

124 Michael Meinecke, *Patterns of Stylistic Changes in Islamic Architecture: Local Traditions Versus Migrating Artists* (New York: New York University Press, 1996), 37; *Rihla Ibn Battuta*, 1:67.

125 Ibn Ahmad al-Hamdani, *The Antiquities of South Arabia* Faris, trans. Nabih A. Faris (Princeton, NJ: Princeton University Press, 1938), 48.

126 Al-Harawi, *Guide des lieux de pèlerinage*, 14.

127 *The Travels of Ibn Battuta*, 44.

128 Milstein, "Kitab Shawq-nama," 299; Milstein, "Futuh-i Haramayn," 174.

129 Burton, *Personal Narrative*, II: 254.

130 *Nasir-i Khusraw's Book of Travels*, 34.

131 Ibn al-Hawrani, "A Late Medieval Syrian Pilgrimage Guide," 51; The tools with which Noah built his ark hung as contact relics from the ceiling of the Mosque of Kufa. Al-Harawi, *Guide des lieux de pèlerinage*, 178, and see also M. J. Kister, "Sanctity Joint and Divided," *Jerusalem Studies in Arabic and Islam* 20 (1996): 32.

132 Al-Harawi, *Guide des lieux de pèlerinage*, 200, and Azraqi, *Akhbar Makka*, 2:202.

133 Mulder, S. *The Shrines of the 'Alids in Medieval Syria: Sunnis, Shi'is and the Architecture of Coexistence* (Edinburgh: Edinburgh University Press, 2014), 254, 263.

134 Muhammad ibn Ahmad al-Muqaddasi, *Ahsan al-Taqasim fi ma'rifat al-aqalim* (Leiden: Brill, 1906), 151.

135 *Rihla ibn Jubayr*, 175, and *Travels of Ibn Jubayr*, 205.

136 *Rihla ibn Jubayr*, 241, and *Travels of Ibn Jubayr*, 278.

137 Milstein, "Kitab Shawq-nama," 283.

138 Q. 3:46, 5:110, 19:16, 19:29. Necipoglu, "Dome of the Rock as Palimpsest," 34; Elad, *Medieval Jerusalem*, 93–97.

139 Azraqi, *Akhbar Makka,* 2:199.

140 'Ali Muhammad al-Nahrawani, *Kitab al-i'lam bi-a'lam bayt Allah al-haram* (Mecca: al-Maktaba al-Tijariyya, 1996), 42.

141 Miklos Muranyi, "The Emergence of Holy Places in Islam," *Jerusalem Studies in Arabic and Islam* 39 (2012): 166, 170.

142 Flood, "Light in Stone," 320–321. Flood dates these stones to the early eighth century, with the stone in Medina being removed in 1301. A similar stone placed in the Shahristan mosque in Fars is explained as an "inspired memorial" to the more historically accurate markings in the Haramayn and Jerusalem. To Flood's study, we should add the nineteenth-century report, which describes a hexagonal stone with diamond shaped embellishments, placed in the mihrab of the room in the House of Khadija, where Muhammad received revelation. See Eyüp Sabri Pasha, *Mawsu'a Mir'at al-Haramayn al-Sharifayn wa Jazirat al-'Arab*, 2 vols. (Cairo: Dar al-Afaq al-'Arabiyya, 2004), 2:864. For a 1989 description of the niche, see Yamani, *House of Khadija*, 104, 142.

CHAPTER 5

1 Catherine Bell, "Performance," in Charles Taylor (ed.) *Critical Terms for Religious Studies* (Chicago: University of Chicago Press, 1998), 216.

2 Sean D. Kelly, "Seeing Things in Merleau-Ponty," in Taylor Carman (ed.) *The Cambridge Companion to Merleau-Ponty* (Cambridge: Cambridge University Press, 2005), 75–76.

3 For quick comparison see www.al-tafsir.com. Al-Tabari deals with the Ark at some length in his *History of Al-Tabari*, 3:125–128, 131–134.

4   Oleg Grabar, "The Story of Portraits of the Prophet Muhammad," *Studia Islamica* 96 (2003): 19–38. In the Jewish sources, however, the association with kingship is largely absent. See, for example, Louis Ginzberg, *The Legends of the Jews*, trans. Paul Radin, 7 vols (Baltimore, MD: The Johns Hopkins University Press, 1998), 3:156–161, 2:34.

5   *The History of al-Tabari*, 7:26, 34:152.

6   Estelle Whelan, "Origins of the Mihrab Mujawwaf: A Reinterpretation," *International Journal of Middle East Studies* 18, 2 (1986): 214, 222 fn 71.

7   *The History of al-Tabari*, 15:183.

8   Al-Mawardi, *al-Ahkam al-sultaniyya*, 222.

9   Hilal al-Sabi, *The Rules and Regulations of the 'Abbasid Court*, trans. Elie Salem (Beirut: American University of Beirut, 1977), 73.

10 Dickinson, "Ibn Shahrazuri and the Isnad," 482.

11 Al-Mawardi, *al-Ahkam*, 223.

12 *The History of al-Tabari*, 31:11, 196–199.

13 Khalid Sindawi, "The Head of Husayn Ibn 'Ali: From Decapitation to Burial, Its Various Places of Burial, and the Miracles That It Performed," *Journal of Ancient Near Eastern Studies* 40 (2003): 246.

14 Daniel De Smet, "La Translation du Ra's al-Husayn au Caire Fatimide," in Urbain Vermulen (ed.) *Egypt and Syria in the Fatimid, Ayyubid, and Mamluk Eras*, 2 vols. (Leiden: Peeters, 1998), 2:32.

15 Descriptions from Ibn 'Asakir, Ibn Jubayr, and al-Harawi, are presented in Mulder, *Shrines of the 'Alids*, 202–208.

16 Flood, *Great Mosque of Damascus* 1–3, 108. De Smet "La Translation," 34 fn 24–25, claims there is no pre-Islamic Christian tradition of veneration of the head.

17 Meri, "A Late Medieval Syrian Pilgrimage Guide," 23.

18 Janine Sourdel-Thomine, *et al.* ."La découverte d'un culte de *nabi* Zakariyya à la grande mosquée de Damas à l'époque ayyoubide," *Der Islam* 90, 2 (2013): 435–439.

19 Al-Harawi, *Guide des lieux de pèlerinage*, 7.

20 Sindawi, "Head of Husayn," 246.

21 *Rihla ibn Jubayr*, 187 and *Travels of Ibn Jubayr*, 220.

22 Sauvaget, "Deux sanctuaires," 225–26, and Jean Sauvaget, *Alep: essai sur le développement d'une grande ville syrienne, des origines au milieu du XIXe siècle* (Paris: P. Guenther, 1941),

124–125; Mulder, *The Shrines of the 'Alids*, 82–98; and Tabbaa, *Constructions of Power*, 110–121.

23 Jean Sauvaget, "Deux sanctuaires chiites d'Alep," *Syria* 9, 3 (1928): 226. In an interesting parallel, a local tradition in the Nile Delta grew up around a series of shrine-mosques dedicated to the prominent early Jewish convert to Islam 'Abdallah Ibn Salam (d. 633). It is believed that upon his death, angels carried his body to its final resting place, with drops of his blood falling to the ground at various locations at which shrines would later be built. On this figure generally, see Muhammad Ibn Sa'd, 11 vols. *Kitab al-Tabaqat al-kabir* (Cairo: Maktaba al-Khanji, 2001), 5:377–386. On the drops of blood and the shrines see Muhammad 'Abd al-Nabi, *Sidi 'Abdallah ibn Salam* (Mansoura, Egypt: n.p., n.d.) discussed in Georg Stauth, "'Abdallah b. Salam: Egypt, Late Antiquity and Islamic Sainthood," in Johann P. Arnason, Armando Salvatore, and Georg Stauth (eds.) *Islam in Process: Historical and Civilizational Perspectives* (Piscataway, NJ: Transaction, 2006), 158–189.

24 De Smet "La Translation," 35, and Mulder, *The Shrines of the 'Alids*, 256.

25 Al-Maqrizi, *Khitat*, 1:406; De Smet, "La Translation," 37–38. It should come as no surprise that in medieval dream interpretation, the discovery of the bones of a prophet signaled the preservation and revival of religion. See Pierre Lory, "La vision du prophète en rêve dans l'onirocritique musulmane," in Éric Chaumont *et al.* (eds.) *Autour du regard: mélanges Gimaret* (Louvain: Peeters, 2003), 204. Al-Afdal himself was an avid relic hunter. Later in Cairo, he would discover two more heads of members of the Prophet's family, those of Zayd ibn 'Ali Zayn al-'Abidin, and Ibrahim ibn 'Abd Allah. Caroline Williams, "The Cult of the Alid Saints in the Fatimid Monuments of Cairo. Part I: The Mosque of al-Aqmar," *Muqarnas* 1 (1983): 38–42.

26 Moshe Sharon, *Corpus Inscriptionum Arabicarum Palaestinae*, 6 vols. (Leiden: Brill, 1997) 1:156–157. My translation. For more detail on the head at Asqalon, see Talmon-Heller, "Vicissitudes of a Holy Place," 186–191.

27 De Smet, "La Translation," 39.

28 Canaan, *Mohammedan Saints*, 151, 215.

29 Meron Rappoport, "History Erased," *Haaretz* 5, July 2007, https://www.haaretz.com/

1.4950011. For the shrine, Rappoport refers to the work of Meron Benvenisti, but I have been unable to locate the source in any of Benvenisti's published work. For story of the Isma'ili construction of the platform and prayer space, see Talmon-Heller, "Vicissitudes of a Holy Place," 208–214.

30 Al-Harawi, *Guide des lieux de pèlerinage*, 108–109.

31 Al-Maqrizi, *Khitat*, 1:408.

32 De Smet, "La translation," 40.

33 Al-Maqrizi, *Khitat*, 1:408, De Smet "La translation," 40, Sanders, *Ritual, Politics, and the City in Fatimid Cairo*, 131.

34 Al-Maqrizi, *Khitat*, 1:408.

35 Williams, "The Cult of the 'Alid Saints," 41.

36 *Rihla Ibn Jubayr*, 20; Talmon-Heller, *Islamic Piety*, 57. The seventeenth-century writer, al-Nabulusi, visited the shrine and notes the devotional prayers of *dhikr* and *sama'* taking place adjacent to the shrine. See his *al-Haqiqa wa al-majaz*, 245.

37 Anne-Marie Eddé, "Bilad al-Sham, from the Fatimid conquest to the fall of the Ayyubids (359–658/970–1260)," in Maribel Fierro (ed. vol. 2) *The New Cambridge History of Islam*, 6 vols. (Cambridge: Cambridge University Press, 2010), 183–185.

38 Caroline Williams, "The Qur'anic Inscriptions on the Tabut of al-Husayn in Cairo," *Islamic Art* 2 (1987):10.

39 Taqi al-Din Ahmad Ibn Taymiyya, *Makan ra's al-Husayn: Hal mashhad ra's al-Husayn bi-l-Qahira aw 'Asqalan?* (Beirut: Dar al-Jil, 1997), 9, 12. Text from Ibn Taymiyya's *Majmu' Fatawa Shaykh al-Islam Ibn Taymiyya*, 37 vols. (Medina: Wizarat al-Shu'un al-Islamiyya, 2004), 27:450–490. For a survey of the eight locations claimed by various historians, see Suad Mahir Muhammad, *Mukhallafat al-Rasul fi al-masjid al-Husayn* (Cairo, Dar al-Nashr, 1989), 26–38. A century later, al-Samhudi would also claim that al-Husayn's head had been taken to Medina and buried in his mother's grave. 'Ali ibn 'Abdallah al-Samhudi, *Khulasat al-wafa bi-akhbar dar al-Mustafa* (Medina: al-Maktaba al-'Ilmiyya, 1972), 427.

40 Al-Maqrizi, *Khitat*, 2:44, 4:376–378.

41 Muwaffaq al-Din Ibn 'Uthman, *Murshid al-zuwwar ila qubur al-abrar* (Cairo: Al-Dar al-Misriyya al-Lubnaniyya, 1995), 200–201; Yusuf Raghib, "Les premiers monuments funéraires de l'Islam," *Annales Islamologiques* 9 (1970):

23–24. A small mosque in Old Cairo is dedicated to Muhammad ibn Abi Bakr, but a new shrine was built in Mitt Damsis, about 25 km east of Tanta, in 1950. The head, along with supporting documentation, was found in the course of renovations to an earlier mosque.

42 *The History of al-Tabari*, 39:234.

43 Al-Maqrizi, *Khitat*, 2:436; Gaston Wiet, *Matériaux pour un corpus inscriptionum arabicum (Première partie Égypte; tome deuxième – Égypte)* (Cairo: Presses de Institut Français d'Achéologie Orientale, 1894–1903), 214–216.

44 *The History of al-Tabari*, 28:289–290; Laura Veccia Vaglieri, "Ibrahim 'Abd Allah," *Encyclopaedia of Islam*, 2nd edn. (Leiden: Brill, 2012); Farhad Daftary, *The Isma'ilis: Their History and Doctrines* (Cambridge: Cambridge University Press, 1990), 83.

45 Al-Maqrizi, *Khitat*, 4/1:383. For Maqrizi's account of the later construction of the Tibr mosque over this site, see his *Khitat*, 2:72.

46 De Smet, "La translation," 41, where he characterizes the positions of Caroline Williams and Paula Sanders.

47 De Smet, "La translation," 42–43.

48 Friedman, "Kufa Is Better," 217.

49 Wilfred Madelung, "Karmati," *Encyclopaedia of Islam*, 2nd edn. (Leiden: Brill, 2012); Francis E. Peters, *Mecca: A Literary History of the Muslim Holy Land* (Princeton, NJ: Princeton University Press, 1994), 124–126. Claims for the special status of the Kufa mosque were well established, including one that the prophet Abraham had prayed at the fifth column of the mosque. Kister, "Sanctity Joint and Divided," 32.

50 Friedman, "Kufa is Better," 218–220.

51 *The History of al-Tabari*, 18:101.

52 Oleg Grabar, "Kubbat al-Sakhra," *Encyclopaedia of Islam*, 2nd edn. (Leiden: Brill, 2012); Elad, *Medieval Jerusalem and Islamic Worship*, 147–173; Necipoglu, "The Dome of the Rock as Palimpsest," 28, 36–37.

53 Al-Maqrizi, *Itti'az*, 1:134.

54 Yusuf Raghib, "Un épisode obscure d'histoire fatimide," *Studia Islamica* 43 (1978): 129. This is not to say that Medina was without relics. The corpses of some of the Prophet's wives were transported to their graves on Muhammad's bed. Leor Halevi, *Muhammad's Grave: Death Rites and the Making of Islamic Society* (New York: Columbia University Press, 2007), 153.

55 Raghib, "Un épisode obscure d'histoire fati-mide," 127–128.

56 Yusuf Raghib, "Les mausolées fatimides du quartier d'al-Mashahid," *Annales Islamologiques* 17 (1981): 3. It is significant to note that this Fatimid project would have included the veneration of the relics of Abu Bakr and 'Uthman, figures who often elicited resentment from the Shia perspective.

57 Ibn al-Jawzi quoted in Stephen Humphreys, *From Saladin to the Mongols: The Ayyubids of Damascus, 1193–1260* (Albany: State University of New York Press, 1977), 212–213, and Dickinson, "Ibn Shahrazuri and the Isnad," 482.

58 Ibn Rushayd al-Sibti (d. 1321) as quoted in Taymur, *al-Athar al-nabawiyya*, 113. See also al-Maqqari, *Wasf na'l al-nabi*, 516–517. Meri, "Relics of Piety," 110, reads this passage, from another edition of al-Maqqari's *Fath*, as describing a box with an opening on its upper side through which the relic could be accessed.

59 Taymur, *al-Athar al-nabawiyya*, 115–116.

60 Dickinson, "Ibn Shahrazuri and the Isnad," 484.

61 Al-Qastallani's *al-Mawahib* quoted in Meri, "Relics of Piety," 110.

62 Meri, "Relics of Piety," 109. See also al-Maqqari, *Wasf na'l al-nabi*, 352, 404.

63 Meri, "Relics of Piety," 110, fn. 52.

64 Al-Tirmidhi, *al-Shama'il al-Muhammadiyya*, 1:40–43, provides details on the Prophet's sandals from hadith and other early sources.

65 Anastase Marie de St. Elie, "Le culte rendu par les Musulmans aux sandales de Mahomet," *Anthropos* 5, 2 (1910): 365.

66 Abdulfattah, "Relics," 84–85.

67 Behrens-Abouseif, *Cairo of the Mamluks*, 295–296, Abdulfattah, "Relics," 87.

68 Burhan al-Din al-Halabi (d. 1438) quoted in Taymur, *al-Athar al-nabawiyya*, 33.

69 Taymur, *al-Athar al-nabawiyya*, 32.

70 Ibn Iyas, *Bada'i' al-zuhur* 4:69; *Journal d'un bourgeois du Caire* 1:66.

71 Al-Sakhawi, *al-Tibr al-masbuk*, 3:28.

72 Abdulfattah, "Relics," 89, Taymur, *al-Athar al-nabawiyya*, 50.

73 Abdulfattah, "Relics," 90.

74 For an attempt to track the politics of such regal building practices, see Julien Loiseau, "Le tombeau des sultans: Constructions monumentales et stratégies funéraires dans les sultanats mamelouk et ottoman," *Turcica* 41 (2009): 305–340.

75 Ibn Iyas, *Bada'i' al-zuhur*, 4:68–69; *Journal d'un bourgeois du Caire* 1:66; Behrens-Abouseif, "Sultan al-Ghawri and the Arts," 83–84.

76 Behrens-Abouseif, "Sultan al-Ghawri and the Arts," 84, and Shaun Marmon, *Eunuchs and Sacred Boundaries in Islamic Society* (New York: Oxford University Press, 1995), 53.

77 Al-Jabarti, *'Aja'ib al-athar*, 2:268, and *Al-Jabarti's History of Egypt*, 2:287.

78 Taymur, *al-Athar al-nabawiyya*, 43, quoting from Muhammad al-Bilbawi's *al-Tarikh al-Husayni*. Al-Bilbawi was an important religious functionary at this time, and likely an eyewitness to at least some of these events. I have not been able to consult this work.

79 *Al-Waqa'i al-Misriyya* as quoted in Taymur, *al-Athar al-nabawiyya*, 44.

80 Taymur, *al-Athar al-nabawiyya*, 44–46. The author would have been 17 years of age when this event took place.

CHAPTER 6

1 'Izz al-Din Ibn al-Athir, *al-Kamil fi al-tarikh*, 11 vols. (Beirut: Dar al-Kutub al-'Ilmiyya, 1987) 8: 141, and reproduced by Jalal al-Din al-Suyuti, in his *Husn al-muhadara fi akhbar Misr wa al-Qahira*, 2 vols. (Beirut: Dar al-Kutub al-'Ilmiyya, 1997), 2:244, and al-Maqrizi, *Itti'az al-hunafa'* 2:131. The iconoclast was identified as an agent of the Fatimid caliph.

2 *Sahih Muslim* "The Book of Pilgrimage," *Sahih Bukhari* "The Book of Pilgrimage" vol. 2, book 26, number 667.

3 Al-Zahiri, *La Zubda kachf al-mamâlik*, 12.

4 Daan Van Reenen, "The Bilderverbot; a New Survey," *Der Islam* 67 (1990), 46.

5 Van Reenen, "The Bilderverbot," 33, 42, 53.

6 Ibid., 43.

7 Ibid., 54.

8 Finbarr Barry Flood, "Between Cult and Culture: Bamyan, Islamic Iconoclasm, and the Museum," *The Art Bulletin* 84, 4 (2002): 641.

9 Nasser Rabbat, "'Aj'ib and Gharib: Artistic Perception in Medieval Arabic Sources," *The Medieval History Journal* 9, 1 (2006): 104, 110.

10 Elias, *Aisha's Cushion*, 136.

11 Oleg Grabar, "Islam and Iconoclasm" in Anthony Bryer and Judith Herrin (eds.) *Iconoclasm: Papers Given at the Ninth Spring Syposium of Byzantine Studies, University of Birmingham, March 1975* (Birmingham: Center for Byzantine

Studies, 1977), 45–52; Geoffrey R. D. King, "Islam, Iconoclasm, and the Declaration of Doctrine" *Bulletin of the School of Oriental and African Studies* 48, 2 (1985): 267, 276; Elias, *Aisha's Cushion*, 68–69; Daniel J. Sahas, "Iconoclasm" in *Encyclopaedia of the Qur'an* (Leiden: Brill, 2012).

12 Dario Gamboni, *The Destruction of Art: Iconoclasm and Vandalism since the French Revolution* (New Haven, CT: Yale University Press, 1977), 20.

13 Finbarr Barry Flood, "Refiguring Iconoclasm in the Early Indian Mosque" in Anne McClanan and Jeffrey (eds.) *Negating the Image: Case Studies in Iconoclasm*Johnson (New York: Ashgate, 2005), 22, 28.

14 Plate, *Walter Benjamin, Religion, and Aesthetics*, 69.

15 Jean-Luc Nancy, *The Ground of the Image*, trans. Jeff Fort (New York: Fordham University Press, 2005), 20.

16 Jacques Rancière, *Mute Speech: Literature, Critical Theory, and Politics* trans. J. Swenson (New York: Columbia University Press, 2011), 142.

17 Nancy, *Ground of the Image*, 3–5.

18 Toufic Fahd, *Le Panthéon de l'Arabie centrale à la veille de l'Hégire* (Paris: Librarie Orientaliste Paul Geuthner, 1968), 249–253.

19 'Abd al-Rahman al-Ansari, *Qaryat al-Fau: A Portrait of Pre-Islamic Civilisation in Saudi Arabia* (London: Croom Helm, 1981), 28–29; Barbara Finster, "The Material Culture of Pre-and Early Islamic Arabia," in Finbarr Barry Flood and Gülru Necipoglu (eds.) *A Companion to Islamic Art and Architecture*, 2 vols. (New York: John Wiley & Sons, 2017), 69.

20 Ibn al-Kalbi, *Book of Idols*, 13–34. In his *The Idea of Idolatry and the Emergence of Islam: From Polemic to History* (Cambridge: Cambridge University Press, 2006), 91–92, Gerald R. Hawting casts doubt on the authorship of this book, as well as pointing out that only a shortened version of the original has come down to us.

21 Ibn al-Kalbi, *Book of Idols*, 44.

22 Michael Lecker, "Wadd, the Weaponed Idol of Dumat al-Jandal and the *Qussas*," in *Dieu et déesses d'Arabie: images et représentations*, ed. Isabelle Sachet (Paris: De Boccard, 2012), 124–125.

23 Ibn al-Kalbi, *Book of Idols*, 44–47.

24 Ibn Ishaq, *The Life of Muhammad*, 35–36.

25 Al-Kisa'i, *Tales of the Prophets*, 118, 127.

26 Hawting, *The Idea of Idolatry*, 102; Geoffrey R. D. King, "The Sculptures of the Pre-Isalmic Haram at Mecca" in Warwick Ball, Leonard Harrow, and Ralph Pinder-Wilson (eds.) *Cairo to Kabul: Afghan and Islamic Studies Presented to Ralph Pinder-Wilson* (London: Melisende, 2002), 145. Fahd sees the story as a warning against the practice of temple prostitution, known in ancient Syria. Fahd, *Panthéon de l'Arabie*, 104.

27 Muhammad ibn Ahmad al-Biruni, *Kitab al-Biruni fi tahqiq ma li'l-Hind* (Andhra Pradesh: Osmania, 1958), 84–85; Muhammad ibn Ahmad al-Biruni, *AlBeruni's India: an Account of the Religion, Philosophy, Literature, Geography, Chronology, Astronomy, Customs, Laws and Astrology of India About A.D. 1030*, 2 vols., trans. Eduard Sachau (London: Kegan Paul, 1914) 1:111.

28 Josh Ellenbogen, and Aaron Tugenhaft, "Introduction," in *Idol Anxiety*, ed. Josh Ellenbogen (Palo Alto, CA: Stanford University Press, 2011), 1–6.

29 David Freedberg, *The Power of Images: Studies in the History and Theory of Response* (Chicago: University of Chicago Press, 1989), 68.

30 See the bibliography for the works of Hawting, King, Lecker.

31 On the various accounts of the images and their fate, see "The Bilderverbot," 37, 40, and Azraqi, *Akhbar Makka*, I:164, 166, as mentioned above in chapter One.

32 Azraqi, *Akhbar Makka*, 1:120; al-Kisa'i, *Tales of the Prophets*, 352.

33 Shalem, "Made for Show," 276; Azraqi, *Akhbar Makka* 1:117; King, "Sculptures of the Pre-Isalmic Haram," 146.

34 Azraqi, *Akhbar Makka*, 1:117.

35 For a survey of Ka'bas and related architecture, see Hashim Mohammad Al-Tawil, "Early Arab Icons: Literary and Archaelogical Evidence for the Cult of Religious Images in Pre-Islamic Arabia" (Ph.D diss., University of Iowa, Iowa City, 1993), 255–272, University Microfilms International.

36 Ibn al-Kalbi, *Book of Idols*, 38-40.

37 Hawting, *Idea of Idolatry*, 124–125. A shrine named Buss, set up as a rival to the Ka'ba, was destroyed in the Prophet's day by non-Muslim Arabs of Mecca. M. J. Kister, "Mecca and the Tribes of Arabia: Some Notes on Their Relations" in Moshe Sharon (ed.)

Studies in Islamic History and Civilization in Honor of Professor David Ayalon (Leiden: Brill, 1997), 43.

38 Fahd, *Panthéon de l'Arabie*, 67, cites al-Azraqi and Ibn Hisham as sources, and notes that the Mecca-based Khalasa is absent in Ibn al-Kalbi.

39 Michael Lecker, "Was Arabian Idol Worship Declining on the Eve of Islam?" in Michael Lecker (ed.) *People, Tribes and Society in Arabia Around the Time of Muhammad* (London: Routledge, 2005), 22. Ibn Kathir's commentary on Q. 53:19 provides further details.

40 Ibn al-Kalbi, *Book of Idols*, 31; Hawting, *Idea of Idolatry*, 92. At Tabala, the goddess was represented in both betyl and anthropomorphic forms. See Fahd, *Panthéon de l'Arabie*, 65.

41 Hawting, *Idea of Idolatry*, 139–140.

42 *The History of al-Tabari* 7:114. Earlier in their careers as Near Eastern goddesses, al-Lat and al-'Uzza may have simply represented different manifestations of the same deity. John F. Healey, *The Religion of the Nabataeans* (Leiden: Brill, 2001), 108, 114. Complicating the picture further, the biography of Muhammad mentions the goddess al-'Uzza standing within or near the Ka'ba: Muhammad Ibn Ishaq, *al-Sira al-Nabwiyya* (Beirut: Dar al-Kutub al-'Ilmiyya, 2004), 94.

43 Ibn al-Kalbi, *Book of Idols*, 22; and al-Jahiz as cited in Hawting, *Idea of Idolatry*, 109, fn. 67.

44 Ibn al-Kalbi, *Book of Idols*, 16; Hawting, *Idea of Idolatry*, 139. In pre-Islamic Nabatean religion, al-'Uzza could be found in a number of shrines, with at least one case in which she appears to be in the unworked form of a betyl. Healey, *Religion of the Nabataeans*, 115–116.

45 Ibn Ishaq, *The Life of Muhammad*, 565.

46 Hawting, *Idea of Idolatry*, 68–69.

47 *Akhbar Makka* 1:381–382, 388. The phenomenon of ancient Arabian cultural survivals persisting into the modern era is an intriguing one, which has only recently begun to be explored. Majeed Khan has noted practices of rock carving spanning millenia, continuing to the present era. Majeed Khan, "Rock Art of Saudi Arabia," *Arts* 2 (2013): 448, 455.

48 Samer Traboulsi, "An Early Refutation of Muhammad ibn Abd al-Wahhab's Reformist Views," *Die Welt des Islams* 43 (2002): 376.

49 Hawting, *Idea of Idolatry*, 92.

50 Charles Montagu Doughty, *Travels in Arabia Deserta*, 2 vols. (Cambridge: Cambridge University Press, 1888) 2:511, 515.

51 Jalal al-Din al-Suyuti, "The Treatise on the Egyptian Pyramids *(Tuhfat al-kiram fi khabar al-ahram)*," trans. Leon Nemoy, *Isis* 30 (1939): 31–32.

52 Martyn Smith, "Pyramids in Medieval Islamic Landscape: Perceptions and Narratives," *Journal of the American Research Center in Egypt* 43 (2007): 1–14, p. 12; Murtada ibn al-'Afif, *L'Égypte de Murtadi fils du Gaphiphe*, trans. Gaston Wiet (Frankfurt: Intstitute for the History of Arabic-Islamic Science at the Johann Wolfgang Goethe University, 2008), 64–66, 71, 109. For more on this work and its author see Yusur Raghib, "L'auteur de l'Égypte de Murtadi fils du Gaphiph" *Arabica* 21 (1974): 203–209.

53 Al-Suyuti, "Treatise on the Egyptian Pyramids," 37.

54 Murtada, *L'Égypte de Murtadi fils du Gaphiphe*, 101. Tamimi is probably at Abu Sir, or Busir, near Memphis. See *Ibid*, 100. The term birba came into Arabic from the Coptic perpe, which is from p3 r3-pr in ancient Egyptian. See Christian Cannuyer, "L'intérêt pour l'Égypte pharaonique à l'époque fatimide; étude sur *L'Abrégé des Merveilles (Mukhtasar al-'aja'ib),*" in *L'Égypte fatimide: son art et son historire*, ed. Marianne Barrucand (Paris: Presses de l'Univerité de Paris-Sorbonne, 1999), 490.

55 *Rihla ibn Jubayr*, 36–37 (my translation), *Travels of Ibn Jubayr*, 54.

56 Al-Maqrizi, *Khitat*, 1:331–334.

57 Galen, *On the Usefulness of the Parts of the Body*, trans. Margaret T. May (Ithaca, NY:Cornell University Press, 1968), 79, 529.

58 'Abd al-Latif al-Baghdadi, *The Eastern Key – Kitab al-ifada wa al-i'tibar*, trans. Ivy E. Zand, John A. Videan, and Kamal Hafuth (London: George Allen and Unwin, 1964), 143. On the intellectual formation of al-Baghdadi, see Shawkat M. Toorawa, "A Portrait of 'Abd al-Latif al-Baghdadi's Education and Instruction," in Joseph Lowry, Devin J. Stewart, and Shawkat M. Toorawa (eds.) *Law and Education in Medieval Islam: Studies in Memory of Professor George Makdisi* (Cambridge: E. J. W. Gibb Memorial Trust, 2004), 91–109. Elsewhere al-Baghdadi says, "The beauty (*husn*) and

countenance of these statues, and their just proportions, are the complete acme of excellence in the art of sculpture, and as perfect as can be experienced in stone" Al-Baghdadi, *Eastern Key*, 147.

59 Abu 'Uthman al-Jahiz, *The Epistle on Singing-Girls*, trans. Alfred Felix Landon Beaston (Warminster: Aris & Phillips, 1980), 12–13 Arabic, 25 English trans.

60 Cecilia Martini Bonadeo, *The Stanford Encyclopedia of Philosophy*, s.v. "'Abd al-Latif al-Baghdadi" (Fall 2015 Edition) https://plato.stanford.edu/archives/fall2015/entries/al-baghdadi/; Deborah L. Black, "Aesthetics in Islam," in Edward Craig (ed.) *Routledge Encyclopedia of Philosophy* (London: Routledge, 1998), 75–79 and Ibn Sina, *A Treatise on Love by Ibn Sina*, trans. Emil Ludwig Fakhenheim, *Mediaeval Studies* 7.1 (1945): 221; Aphrodite Alexandrakis and Nicholas Moutafakis (eds.) *Neoplatonism and Western Aesthetics* (Albany: State University of New York, 2002). Remarking on the beauty of the Sphinx, al-Baghdadi says it is "remarkably handsome, and the mouth expresses much grace and beauty: one might fancy it smiling gracefully." One of the most impressive things he saw during his time in Egypt, he continues, was the "The proportions (*tanasub*) of the face of the Sphinx," the parts of which – the nose, the eyes, the ears – are in similar proportion to those found in nature (al-Baghdadi, *Eastern Key*, 125).

61 Al-Baghdadi, *Eastern Key*, 141.

62 Ibid., 137.

63 Ibid., 155–157.

64 Ibid., 131, 140, 161.

65 Ibid., 139, 113.

66 Al-Suyuti, "Treatise on the Egyptian Pyramids," 23.

67 Al-Maqrizi, *Khitat*, 1:326.

68 Ulrich Haarmann, "Regional Sentiment in Medieval Islamic Egypt," *Bulletin of the School of Oriental and African Studies* 43 (1980): 61.

69 Alexander Fodor, "The Origins of the Arabic Legends of the Pyramids," *Acta Orientalia Academiae Scientiarum Hungaricae* 23, 3 (1970): 339. Murtada ibn al-'Afif, *L'Égypte de Murtadi*, 83. On the disputed history and parameters of Hermeticism, see Darrell Dykstra, "Pyramids, Prophets, and Progress: Ancient Egypt in the

Writings of 'Ali Mubarak" *Journal of the American Oriental Society* 114, 1 (1994): 58. On this area more widely, see the further studies of Pierre Lory, Noah Gardiner, Shahzad Bashir, and Matthew Melvin-Koushki in the bibliography.

70 Haarmann, "Regional Sentiment," 57, fn. 13.

71 Al-Baghdadi, *Eastern Key*, 159.

72 Haarmann, "Regional Sentiment," 60–61, 64. Haarmann rightly characterizes al-Idrisi's work as an Islamicizing of ancient Egypt. See also Haarmann's "In Quest of the Spectacular: Noble and Learned Visitors to the Pyramids Around 1200 AD," in *Islamic Studies Presented to Charles J. Adams*, eds. Wael Hallaq and Donald Little (Leiden: Brill, 1991), 57–67.

73 Haarmann, "Regional Sentiment," 64.

74 Al-Maqrizi, *Khitat*, 1:331; Al-Suyuti cites claims of protective function to the Sphinx: *Husn al-muhadara*, 1:63, 68; and "Treatise on the Egyptian Pyramids," 29.

75 Abu Salih al-Armani, *The Churches and Monasteries of Egypt and Some Neighboring Countries, Attributed to Abu Salih, the Armenian*, trans. Basil T. A. Evetts (Oxford: Clarendon, 1895), 111–112. Myriam Wissa, "Sur quelques pratiques de remploi du marbre et du calcaire en Égypt: incursion au monastère copte de saint Jérémie à Saqqara," *Ancient West and East* 9 (2010): 228–231. The reuse of capitals for mosque columns was common, with Byzantine, Ptolemaic, and Pharaonic sources used – the latter being the least common. See Marianne Barrucand, "Remarks on the Iconography of the Medieval Capitals of Cairo: Form and Emplacement," in Bernard O'Kane (ed.) *The Iconography of Islamic Art: Studies in Honor of Robert Hillenbrand* (New York: American University in Cairo Press, 2005), 34, 38.

76 Finbarr Barry Flood, "Image Against Nature: Spolia as Apotropaia in Byzantium and the Dar al-Islam," *The Medieval History Journal* 9, 1 (2006): 151–152. See also Julia Gonnella, "Columns and Hieroglyphs: Magic Spolia in Medieval Islamic Architecture of Northern Syria," *Muqarnas* 27 (2010): 103–120.

77 Al-Harawi, *Guide des lieux de pèlerinage*, 108.

78 'Ali ibn al-Hassan Ibn 'Asakir, *La Description de Damas d'Ibn 'Asakir*, trans. Nikita Élisséeff

(Damascus: Institut français du proche orient, 2008), 69.

79 Al-Maqrizi, *Khitat*, 1:333. Some lions of Baybars have survived in the fortifications of the Citadel. See Doris Behrens-Abouseif, *Islamic Architecture of Cairo* (Leiden: Brill, 1989), 81.

80 Haarmann, "Regional Sentiment in Medieval Islamic Egypt," 64.

81 'Ali al-Harawi, *al-Isharat ila ma'rifat al-ziyarat* (Cairo: Maktabat al-Thaqafa al-Diniyya, 2002), 44; al-Harawi, *Guide des lieux de pèlerinage*, 104; al-Harawi, *A Lonely Wayfarer's Guide to Pilgrimage* trans. Joseph W. Meri (Princeton, NJ: Darwin Press, 2004), 110.

82 'Ali ibn Yusuf al-Qifti, *Ta'rikh al-hukama* (Leipzig: Dieterichsche Verlagsbuchhandlung, 1908), 185; Abu al-Hasan al-Mas'udi, *Les Prairies d'Or (Muruj al-dhahab)*, Arabic with French trans. by Charles Barbier de Meynard and Michel Pavet De Courteille, 9 vols. (Paris: L'Imprimerie Nationale, 1914), 2:401-402. For more reports on temples, see Ibn 'Asakir, *Ta'rikh madina Dimashq* 80 vols. (Beirut: Dar al-Fikr, 1995) 17:405, and Muhy al-Din Ibn 'Arabi, *al-Kawkab al-durri fi manaqib Dhi al-Nun al-Misri* (Beirut: Dar al-Kutub al-'Ilmiyya, 2005), 115. In a recent study, Michael Ebstein notes that Egyptian Hermetecists had been fond of the idea of discovering ancient books of wisdom and science, attributing such finds to many before Dhu al-Nun. See his "Dhu al-Nun al-Misri and Early Islamic Mysticism," *Arabica* 61, 5 (2014): 598.

83 Al-Maqrizi, *Khitat*, 1:82.

84 Fabio Rambelli and Eric R. Reinders, *Buddhism and Iconoclasm in East Asia: A History* (New York: Bloomsbury, 2012), 179.

85 The medieval "mining" of stone from Pharaonic sites was carried out on a significant scale. See Jean-Pierre Corteggiani, "The Site" in André Raymond (ed.) *Cairo: An Illustrated History* (New York: Rizzoi, 2001), 45-49.

86 Jane Jakeman, "Abstract Art and Communication in 'Mamluk' Architecture" (PhD diss., University of Oxford, Oxford, 1993) British Library, British Thesis Service. Her survey does not include the hundreds of blocks that were removed from the Nilometer, or objects from other parts of Egypt.

87 James A. Harrell, Lorenzo Lazzarini, Mathias Bruno, "Reuse of Roman Ornamental Stones in Medieval Cairo, Egypt," http://www.eeescience.utoledo.edu/faculty/harrell/egypt/mosques/ASMOSIA_VI_Text.htm (retrieved online August 3, 2016).

88 Michael Greenlagh, "Spolia: A Definition in Ruins," in Richard Brilliant (ed.) *Reuse Value: Spolia and Appropriation in Art and Architecture* (London: Taylor & Francis, 2016), 81, 88.

89 Carole Hillenbrand, *The Crusades, Islamic Perspectives* (Edinburgh: Edinburgh University Press, 2009), 384–385.

90 Richard Pian McClary, "The Re-use of Byzantine *Spolia* in Rum Saljuq Architecture," *bfo-Journal* 1 (2015): 19.

91 Greenlagh, "Spolia: A Definition in Ruins," 90, 75.

92 Anthony Cutler, "Reuse or Use? Theoretical and Practical Attitudes Toward Objects in the Early Middle Ages" in *Settimane di Studio del Centro Italiano di Studi sull'Alto Medioevo* 46 (1999): 1064–1065.

93 Rambelli, *Buddhism and Iconoclasm*, 171.

94 Kopytoff, "The Cultural Biography of Things," 67.

95 Richard H. Davis, *Lives of Indian Images* (Princeton, NJ: Princeton University Press, 1997), xi.

96 Avinoam Shalem, "Multivalent Paradigms of Interpretation and the Aura or Anima of the Object," in Benoît Junod *et al.* (eds.) *Islamic Art and the Museum: Approaches to Art and Archeology of the Muslim World in the Twentieth-Century* (London: Saqi, 2011), 103.

97 Avinoam Shalem, "Islamishe Objekte in Kirchenshätzen," in Christine van Eickels and Klaus van Eickels (eds.) *Das Bistum Bamberg in der Welt des Mittelalters* (Bamburg: University of Bamberg Press, 2007), 172–174. Shalem, "Multivalent Paradigms," 103.

98 Georges Didi-Huberman, "Has the Epistemological Transformation Taken Place?" in Michael F. Zimmerman (ed.) *The Art Historian: National Traditions and Institutional Practices* (Williamstown, MA: Sterling and Francine Clark Art Institute, 2003), 131.

99 Dale Kinney, "Introduction" in Richard Brilliant and Dale Kinney (eds.) *Reuse Value: Spolia and Appropriation in Art and Architecture from Constantine to Sherrie Levine* (Burlington: Ashgate Publishing, 2011), 4.

100 Georg Stauth, *Ägyptische heilige Orte II, zwischen den steinen des pharao und islamischer*

moderne (Bielefeld: Transcript-Verlag, 2015), 194, 201, 204.

101 Stauth, *Ägyptische heilige Orte II*, 198–201, 194.

102 Jakeman, "Abstract Art," 122–124. On the very unusual bastions al-Hakim added to his minarets, see Bloom, "Mosque of al-Hakim," 18. For the gazell carving, dated to the Amarna period, see Corteggiani, "The Site," 16.

103 Jakeman, "Abstract Art," 128; Nicholas Warner, *The Monuments of Historic Cairo: A Map and Descriptive Catalogue* (Cairo: American University in Cairo Press, 2004), 160, entry #481.

104 Behrens-Abouseif, *Islamic Architecture of Cairo*, 124.

105 Jakeman, "Abstract Art," 164; Bertha Porter and Rosalind L. B. Moss, *Topographical Bibliography of Ancient Egyptian Hieroglyphic Texts, Reliefs, and Paintings. Volume IV, Lower and Middle Egypt* microfiche edition (Oxford: Griffith Institute, 1981), 72.

106 Porter, *Topographical Bibliography*, 72.

107 Jakeman, "Abstract Art," 161.

108 Jakeman, "Abstract Art," 156. Warner, *Monuments*, 105, entry #112.

109 Jakeman, "Abstract Art," 156. Warner, *Monuments*, 108, entry #120.

110 Jakeman, "Abstract Art," 160. Warner, *Monuments*, 134, entry #248; Flood, "Image Against Nature," 156.

111 Jakeman, "Abstract Art," 57. Warner, *Monuments*, 108, entry #120.

112 Al-Dawadari, *Kanz al-durar wa jami' al-ghurar*, 9 vols. (Wiesbaden: Harrassowitz, 1961), 9:382–383.

113 Nigel Strudwick, *Masterpieces of Ancient Egypt* (Austin: University of Texas Press, 2006), 286.

114 Jakeman, "Abstract Art," 177, 179. Gaston Maspero, *Guide du visiteur au Musée de Boulaq* (Cairo: Musée d'Antiquités, 1883), 353.

115 Strudwick, *Masterpieces of Ancient Egypt*, 288.

116 Jakeman, "Abstract Art," 145.

117 Jakeman, "Abstract Art," 171; Porter, *Topographical Bibliography*, 73.

118 Maspero, *Guide du visiteur*, 55.

119 Jakeman, "Abstract Art," 140; Porter, *Topographical Bibliography*, 71.

120 Jakeman, "Abstract Art," 172; Bruno H. Stricker, "Le Naos Vert de Memphis" *Annales du Service des Antiquités de l'Égypte* 39 (1939), 219.

121 'Abd al-Latif al-Baghdadi, *Relation de l'Égypte*, trans. Antoine Isaac de Sacy (Paris: Imprimerie impériale, 1810), 249, fn 65; Al-Qalqashandi, *Subh al-a'sha*, 3:321.

122 Maspero, *Guide du visiteur*, 7.

123 Jakeman, "Abstract Art," 159; Warner, *Monuments*, 142, entry #312.

124 Jakeman, "Abstract Art," 147.

125 Jakeman, "Abstract Art," 150–151; Warner, *Monuments*, 104, entry #103.

126 Jakeman, "Abstract Art," 152. Porter, *Topographical Bibliography*, 72; Richard McGregor, "Ahmad Dardir," *Encyclopaedia of Islam,* 3rd edn. (Leiden: Brill, 2012).

127 Behrens-Abouseif, *Islamic Architecture of Cairo*, 144–146.

128 Jakeman, "Abstract Art," 132; Porter, *Topographical Bibliography*, 71.

129 Jakeman, "Abstract Art," 133; Keppel Archibald Cameron Creswell, *Muslim Architecture of Egypt*, 2 vols. (Oxford: Clarendon, 1952-1959) vol. 2, pl. 95d.

130 Jakeman, "Abstract Art," 136; Creswell, *Muslim Architecture of Egypt*, 2: 101.

131 Jakeman, "Abstract Art," 143; Warner, *Monuments*, 96, entry #43. On this object see the recent remarks by Iman Abudulfattah, "Theft, Plunder, and Loot," *Mamluk Studies Review* 20 (2017): 110–111, 131.

132 Yehoshua Frenkel, "Baybars and the Sacred Geography of Bilad al-Sham," *Jerusalem Studies in Arabic and Islam* 25 (2001), 168.

133 Jakeman, "Abstract Art," 135; Behrens-Abouseif, *Islamic Architecture of Cairo*, 143, 154–155. Warner, *Monuments*, 118, entry #170.

134 Jakeman, "Abstract Art," 181; Thomas Leisten, "Dynastic Tomb or Private Mausolea?" in Marianne Barucand (ed.) *L'Égypte fatimide: son art et son histoire* (Paris: Presses de l'Université de Paris-Sorbonne, 1999), 465-478.

135 Jakeman, "Abstract Art," 181; Luisa Bongrani-Fanfoni, "On a Re-employed Quartzite Block of the Pharaonic Age," *Göttinger Miszellen: Beiträge zur ägyptologischen Diskussion* 117/118 (1990): 143–152.

136 Jakeman, "Abstract Art," 163; Warner, *Monuments*, 136, entry #261; Porter, *Topographical Bibliography*, 72.

137 Louis Massignon, "Seconde note sur l'état d'avancement des études archéologiques arabes

en Égypte, hors du Caire," *Bulletin de l'institut français d'archéologie orientale* 9 (1909): 88.

138 Reid, *Whose Pharaohs?* 222–232; Caroline Williams, "Islamic Cairo: Endangered Legacy," *The Middle East Journal* 29 (1985): 235.

139 Caroline Williams, "The Victorian Invention of Medieval Cairo: A Case Study of Medievalism and the Construction of the East" *Middle East Studies Association Bulletin* 37.2 (2003): 186.

140 Reid, "Cultural Imperialism," 73.

141 Colla, *Conflicted Antiquities*, 72–115.

EPILOGUE

1   Ibn 'Arabi, *Fusus al-hikam*, 187.

2   Amy Hollywood, *Acute Melancholia and Other Essays* (New York: Columbia University Press, 2016), 115.

3   Shalem, "Multivalent Paradigms," 103.

4   Rockhill's introduction to Rancière, *Mute Speech*, 5–6.

5   Richard King, "The Copernican Turn in the Study of Religion," *Method and Theory in the Study of Religion* 25 (2013): 142.

BIBLIOGRAPHY

SECONDARY LITERATURE

'Abbas, Muhammad. *Manarat al-funun wa al-hadara al-Islamiyya* (Cairo: Mathaf al-Fann al-Islami, 2010).

Abbott, Nadia. *Two Queens of Baghdad; Mother and Wife of Harun al-Rashid* (Chicago: University of Chicago Press, 1946).

'Abd al-Fattah, Muhammad. "Ba'd al-mulahazat 'ala al-'ilaqa bayna murur al-mawakib wa wad'al-mabani al-athariyya fi shawari'madinat al-Qahira." *Annales Islamologiques* 25 (1991): 1–10.

'Abd al-Majid, Layla. "Al-Mahmal 'abr al-'usur al-tarikhiyya." *Majalla Kuliyyat al-Lughat wa't-Tarjama* 7(2) (2014): 156-302.

'Abd al-Malik, Sami S. "Qit'a nadira min al-kiswa al-dakhiliyya li'l-ka'ba al-musharrafa bi'sm al-sultan al-Nasir Hasan bin Muhammad bin Qalawun tu'arrakh bi-sanat 791 AH / 1359-1360 m." *Annales Islamologiques* 38 (2004): 57–68.

'Abd al-Wahhab, Hasan. "al-Athar al-manqula wa'l-muntahala fi'l-'imra al-Islamiyya." *Bulletin de l'Institut d'Égypte* 38 (1955–1956): 243–283.

Abu Sulaiman, 'Abd al-Wahhab. *Al-Amakin al-ma'thura al-mutawattara fi Makka al-mukarrama* (London: Al-Furqan, 2009).

Adorno, Theodor W. *Aesthetic Theory*. Translated by Robert Hullot-Kentor (Minneapolis: University of Minnesota Press, 1997).

Abdulfattah, Iman. "Relics of the Prophet and Practices of His Veneration in Medieval Cairo." *Journal of Islamic Archaeology* 1, 1 (2014): 75–104.

Abdulfattah, Iman. "Theft, Plunder, and Loot." *Mamluk Studies Review* 20 (2017): 93–132.

Akkach, Samer. "The Eye of Reflection: Al-Nabulusi's Spatial Interpretation of Ibn 'Arabi's Tomb." *Muqarnas* 32 (2015): 79–95.

Akkach, Samer. "The Poetics of Concealment: Al-Nabulusi's Encounter with the Dome of the Rock." *Muqarnas* 22 (2005): 110–127.

Aksoy, Sule and Rachel Milstein, "A Collection of Thirteenth-Century Illustrated Hajj Certificates." In Irvin Cemil Schick (ed.), *M. Ugur Derman Festschrift: Papers Presented on the Occasion of His Sixty-Fifth Birthday* (Istanbul: Sabanci Universitesi, 2000), 101–134.

Alexandrin, Elizabeth. "Witnessing the Lights of the Heavenly Dominion: Dreams, Visions and the Mystical Exegesis of Shams al-Din al-Daylami." In Özgen Felek and Alexander Knysh (eds.) *Dreams and Visions in Islamic Societies*, 215–232 (Albany: State University of New York Press, 2013).

Amin, Muhammad. *al-Awqaf wa al-haya al-ijtima'iyya fi Misr* (Cairo: Dar al-Nahda al-'Arabiyya, 1980).

Amirsoleimani, Soheila. "Clothing in the Early Ghaznavid Courts: Hierarchy and Mystification." *Studia Iranica* 32.2 (2003): 213–242

'Anqawi, 'Abdallah. "Kiswa al-Ka'ba fi al-'asr al-Mamluki." *Majallat Kulliyat al-Adab wa'l-'Ulum al-Insaniyya* 5 (1985): 1–23.

Al-Ansari, 'Abd al-Rahman. *Qaryat al-Fau: A Portrait of Pre-Islamic Civilisation in Saudi Arabia* (London: Croom Helm, 1981).

Arjana, Sophia R. *Pilgrimage in Islam: Traditional and Modern Practices* (London: Oneworld, 2017).

Al-'Arif, Yusuf Hasan. *Al-Rihla al-Hajjiyya: qira'at fi al-matn wa'l-madamin* (Beirut: Al-Intishar al-'Arabi, 2014).

Asad, Talal. *Genealogies of Religion; Discipline and Reasons of Power in Christianity and Islam* (Baltimore: Johns Hopkins University Press, 1993).

Asad, Talal. "Reflections on Blasphemy and Secular Criticism." In Hent de Vries (ed.) *Religion: Beyond a Concept*, 580–610 (New York: Fordham University Press, 2008).

Asif, Manan Ahmed. "A Demon with Ruby Eyes." *Medieval History Journal* 16, 2 (2013): 335–369.

'Askar, Faruq (ed.) *Min dhakirat Mathaf al-Fann al-Islami, 1881m-2010m: mujallad watha'iqi tidhkari: al-'id al-mi'awi* (Cairo: Wizarat al-Thaqafa, al-Majlis al-A'la li'l-Athar, 2010).

Athamina, Khalil. "The Black Banners and the Socio-Political Significance of Flags and Solgans in Medieval Islam." *Arabica* 36, 3 (1989): 307–326.

Aubin-Boltanski, Emma. "Le mawsim de Nabî Mûsâ: processions, espace en miettes et mémoire blessée: Territoires palestiniens (1998–2000)." In Sylvia Chiffoleau and Anna Madoeuf (eds.) *Les Pèlerinages au Maghreb et au Moyen-Orient*, 59–80 (Damascus: Presses de l'Institut français du proche orient, 2005).

Austin Kennett, B. L. "The Sacred Litter (Mahmal) of Kharga Oasis." *Man* 25 (August 1926): 133–136.

Ayada, Souâd. "L'islam, religion esthétique." *Esprit* 305, 6 (June 2004): 115–30.

Aydin, Hilmi. *Pavilion of the Sacred Relics, The Sacred Trusts, Topkapi Palace Museum, Istanbul* (Clifton, NJ: Tughra Books, 2014).

Al-Azmeh, Aziz. *The Emergence of Islam in Late Antiquity: Allah and His People* (New York: Cambridge University Press, 2014).

Al-Azmeh, Aziz. "Rhetoric for the Senses: A Consideration of Muslim Paradise Narratives." *Journal of Arabic Literature* 26,3 (1995): 215–231.

Baffioni, Carmela. "From Sense Perception to the Vision of God: A Path Towards Knowledge According to the Ikhwan al-Safa." *Arabic Sciences and Philosophy* 8 (1998): 213–231.

Bakhit, Muhammad A. *The Ottoman Province of Damascus in the Sixteenth Century* (Beirut: Librairie du Liban, 1982).

Bal, Meike. *Loving Yusuf: Conceptual Travels From Present to Past* (Chicago: University of Chicago Press, 2008).

Banister, Mustafa. "'Naught Remains to the Caliph but His Title': Revisiting Abbasid Authority in Mamluk Cairo." *Mamluk Studies Review* 18 (2014–2015): 219–245.

Bandyopadhay, Sibaji. *Aesthetics of Theft*. In Arindam Chakrabarti (ed.) *The Bloomsbury Research Handbook of Indian Aesthetics and the Philosophy of Art* (New York: Bloomsbury, 2016), 195–214.

Al-Barjawi, 'Abd al-Ra'uf. *Fusul fi 'ilm al-jamal* (Beirut: Dar al-Afaq al-Jadida, 1981).

Barrucand, Marianne. "Remarks on the Iconography of the Medieval Capitals of Cairo: Form and Emplacement." In Bernard O'Kane (ed.) *The Iconography of Islamic Art: Studies in Honor of Robert Hillenbrand* (New York: American University in Cairo Press, 2005), 23–44.

Bashir, Shahzad. *Messianic Hopes and Mystical Visions: Nurbakhshiyya Between Medieval and Modern Islam* (Columbia: University of South Carolina Press, 2003).

Bashir, Shahzad. *Sufi Bodies: Religion in Medieval Islam* (New York: Columbia University Press, 2011).

Bauden, Frédéric. "Mamluk Era Documentary Studies: The State of the Art." *Mamluk Studies Review* 9 (2005): 16–60.

Bauer, Thomas. "Toward an Aesthetics of Mamluk Literature." *Mamluk Studies Review* 17 (2013): 2–22.

Behrens-Abouseif, Doris. "Between Quarry and Magic: The Selective Approach to Spolia in the Islamic Monuments of Egypt." In Alina Payne (ed.) *Dalmatia and the Mediterranean: Portable Archeology and the Poetics of Influence* (Leiden: Brill, 2014), 402–425.

Behrens-Abouseif, Doris. "The Citadel of Cairo: Stage for Mamluk Ceremonial." *Annales Islamologiques* 24 (1988): 25–79.

Behrens-Abouseif, Doris. *Islamic Architecture of Cairo* (Leiden: Brill, 1989).

Behrens-Abouseif, Doris. "The Islamic History of the Lighthouse of Alexandria." *Muqarnas* 23 (2006): 1–14.

Behrens-Abouseif, Doris. "The *Mahmal* Legend and the Pilgrimage of the Ladies of the Mamluk Court." *Mamluk Studies Review* 1 (1997): 87–96.

Behrens-Abouseif, Doris. "Qaytbay's Investments in the City of Cairo: Waqf and Power." *Annales Islamologiques* 32 (1998): 29–40.

Bell, Catherine. "Performance." In Charles Taylor (ed.) *Critical Terms for Religious Studies* (Chicago: University of Chicago Press, 1998), 205–224.

Bell, Joseph Norment. *Love Theory in Later Hanbalite Islam* (Albany: State University of New York, 1979).

Bellino, Francesca. "Dhu l-Faqar." In *Encyclopaedia of Islam*. 3rd edn. (Leiden: Brill, 2007).

Belting, Hans. *An Anthropology of Images: Picture, Medium, Body*. Translated by Thomas Dunlap (Princeton, NJ: Princeton University Press, 2011).

Belting, Hans. *Florence and Baghdad: Renaissance Art and Arab Science*. Translated by Deborah Lucas Schneider (Cambridge: Belknap Press, 2011).

Belting, Hans. "Image, Medium, Body: A New Approach to Iconology." *Critical Inquiry* 31 (Winter 2005): 302–320.

Bennett, Jane. *Vibrant Matter: a Political Ecology of Things* (Durham, NC: Duke University Press, 2010).

Berkey, Jonathan. *The Transmission of Knowledge in Medieval Cairo: A Social History of Islamic Education* (Princeton, NJ: Princeton University Press, 1992).

Betancourt, Roland. "Tempted to Touch: Tactility, Ritual, and Mediation in Byzantine Visuality." *Speculum* 91, 3 (2016): 660–689.

Berkey, Jonathan. "Mamluk Religious Policy." *Mamluk Studies Review* 13, 2 (2009): 6–22.

Biegman, Nicolaas H. *Egypt: Moulids, Saints and Sufis* (New York: Kegan Paul, 1990).

Bierman, Irene A. "The Art of the Public Text: Medieval Islamic Rule." In Irving Lavin (ed.) *World Art: Themes of Unity in Diversity*, 3 vols. (University Park: Pennsylvania State University Press, 1989), 2:283–290.

Bierman, Irene A. *Writing Signs: The Fatimid Public Text* (Berkeley and Los Angeles: University of California Press, 1998).

Bizzari, Heba. "The National Geographic Society Museum." *Tour Egypt* (Cairo), March 2, 2019, www.touregypt.net/featurestories/geo graphic.htm

Blackman, Winifred S. *The Fellahin of Upper Egypt. Their Religious, Social and Industrial Life to-Day with Special Reference to Survivals from Ancient Times* (London: George G. Haarap & Co., 1927).

Blair, Sheila. "Floriated Kufic and the Fatimids." In Marianne Barrucand (ed.) *L'Égypte fatimide: son art et son histoire* (Paris: Presses de l'Univerité de Paris-Sorbonne, 1999), 107–116.

Blair, Sheila and Jonathan Bloom. "Inscriptions in Art and Architecture." In Jane D. McAuliffe (ed.) *The Cambridge Companion to the Qur'an* (Cambridge: Cambridge University Press, 2015), 181–210.

Blair, Sheila. "Inscriptions on Medieval Islamic Textiles." In Muhammad Salim (ed.) *Islamische Textilkunst des Mittelalters: aktuelle Probleme* (Riggisberg [Switzerland]: Abegg-Stiftung, 1997), 95–104.

Blair, Sheila. *Islamic Inscriptions* (New York: New York University Press, 1998).

Bloom, Jonathan. "The Mosque of al-Hakim in Cairo." *Muqarnas* 1 (1983): 15–36.

Bodman, Whitney S. *The Poetics of Iblis: Narrative Theology in the Qur'an* (CambridgeMA: Harvard University Press, 2011).

Bongrani-Fanfoni, Luisa. "On a Re-employed Quartzite Block of the Pharaonic Age." *Göttinger Miszellen: Beiträge zur ägyptologischen Diskussion* 117/118 (1990): 143–152.

Bourah, Bijoy H. "The Impersonal Subjectivity of Aesthetic Emotion." In Arindam Chakrabarti (ed.) *The Bloomsbury Research Handbook of Indian Aesthetics and the Philosophy of Art* (New York: Bloomsbury, 2016), 127–148.

Boustan, Ra'anan. "Jewish Veneration of the 'Special Dead' in Late Antiquity and Beyond." In Cynthia Hahn and Holger A. Klein (eds.) *Saints and Sacred Matter: the Cult of Relics in Byzantium and Beyond*, 61–80 (Washington, DC: Dumbarton Oaks Research Library and Collections, 2015).

Brémond, Édouard. *Le Hédjaz dans la Guerre Mondiale* (Paris: Payot 1931).

Bresc, Henri. "Les entrées royales des Mamluks: Essai d'approche comparative," in the École française de Rome (ed.) *Genèse de l'État moderne en Méditerranée: approches historique et anthropologique des pratiques et des représentations* (Rome: École française de Rome, 1993) 82–96.

Brinner, William M. "The significance of the Harafish and their sultan." *Journal of the Economic and Social History of the Orient* 6 (1963): 190–215.

Broadbridge, Ann. *Kingship and Ideology in the Islamic and Mongol Worlds* (New York: Cambridge University Press, 2008).

Brockopp, Jonathan E. "Interpreting Material Evidence: Religion at the 'Origins of Islam'." *History of Religions* 55, 2 (Nov. 2015): 121–147.

Brockopp, Jonathan E. *Muhammad's Heirs: the Rise of Muslim Scholarly Communities, 622–950* (Cambridge: Cambridge University Press, 2017).

Brown, Bill. "Thing Theory." *Critical Inquiry* 28, 1 (Autumn, 2001): 1–22.

Brown, Peter. "Images as a Substitute for Writing." In Evangelos Chrystos and Ian Wood (eds.) *Modes of Communication: Proceedings of the First Plenary Conference at Merida* (Leiden: Brill, 1999), 15–34.

Buck-Morss, Susan. "Aesthetics and Anaesthetics: Walter Benjamin's Artwork Essay Reconsidered." *October* 62 (1992): 3–41.

Burns, Ross. *Aleppo: A History* (New York: Routledge, 2017).

Burton, Isabel. *The Inner Life of Syria, Palestine, and the Holy Land.* 2 vols. (London: H.S. King & Co., 1875).

Burton, Richard. *Personal Narrative of a Pilgrimage to al-Madinah and Meccah.* 2 vols. (London: George Bell and Sons, 1906).

Butler, Beverly. "Museums and Museum Displays." In Charles Tilley et al., (eds.) *Handbook of Material Culture* (London: Sage, 2006), 480–499.

Butler, Judith. *Bodies that Matter: On the Discursive Limits of Sex* (New York: Routledge, 1993.

Butler, Judith. *Gender Trouble: Feminism and the Subversion of Identity* (New York: Routledge, 1999).

Bynum, Caroline Walker. *Christian Materiality: An Essay on Religion in Late Medieval Europe* (New York: Zone Books, 2011).

Calvert, John. *Sayyid Qutb and the Origins of Radical Islamism* (New York: Columbia University Press, 2010).

Campo, Juan. *The Other Side of Paradise: Explorations into the Religious Meanings of Domestic Space in Islam* (Columbia: University of South Carolina Press, 1991).

Canann, Tawfiq. *Mohammedan Saints and Sanctuaries in Palestine* (London: Luzac & Co., 1927).

Cannuyer, Christian. "L'intérêt pour l'Égypte pharaonique à l'époque fatimide; étude sur *L'Abrégé des Merveilles (Mukhtasar al-'aja'ib).*" In Marianne Barrucand (ed.) *L'Égypte fatimide: son art et son historire* (Paris: Presses de l'Univerité de Paris-Sorbonne, 1999), 483–496.

Çelik, Zeynep. *Displaying the Orient: Architecture of Islam at Nineteenth-Century World's Fairs* (Berkeley: University of California Press, 1992).

Chapoutot-Remadi, Mounira. "Symbolisme et formalisme de l'élite mamluke: la cérémonie de l'accession à l'émirat." In Henri Bresc (ed.) *Genèse de l'état moderne en Méditerranée* (Rome: École française de Rome, 1993), 61–79.

Chapoutot-Remadi, Rachida. "Liens et relations au sein de l'élite mamluke sous les premiers sultans bahrides: 648/1250–741/1340." PhD diss., Univeristé de Provence, Aix-en-Provence, 1993. Theses.fr

Chidester, David. *Religion: Material Dynamics* (Berkeley: University of California Press, 2018).

Chih, Rachida. *Sufism in Ottoman Egypt: Circulation, Renewal, and Authority in the Seventeenth and Eighteenth Centuries* (New York: Routledge, 2019).

Chih, R. "Un soufi réformiste, le shaykh Muhammad Hasanayn Makhluf (1861–1936)." *Revue des mondes musulmans et de la Méditerranée* 95–98 (avril 2002):189–204.

Chittick, William. *Divine Love: Islamic Literature and the Path to God* (New Haven, CT: Yale University Press, 2013).

Cobb, Paul. "Virtual Sacrality: Making Muslim Syria Sacred Before the Crusades," *Medieval Encounters* 8, 1 (2003): 35–55.

Cohen, Marcel. *et al.* (eds.) *Répertoire chronologique d'épigraphie arabe* (Cairo: Presses de l'Institut français d'archéologie orientale, 1931).

Cohen, Amnon. "An Ottoman Festival (*mawsim*) Resurrected?" In David J. Wasserstein and Ami Ayalon (eds.) *Mamluks and Ottomans: Studies in Honour of Michael Winter* (New York: Routledge, 2006) 34–44.

Cohen, Ted and Paul Guyer. *Essays in Kant's Aesthetics* (Chicago: University of Chicago Press, 1982).

Colla, Elliott H. *Conflicted Antiquities: Egyptology, Egyptomania, Egyptian Modernity* (Durham, NC: Duke University Press, 2007).

Cook, Michael. "Pharaonic History in Medieval Egypt." *Studia Islamica* 57 (1983): 67–103.

Cooperson, Michael. "Images Without Illustrations: the Visual Imagination in Classical Arabic Biography." *Interdisciplinary Journal of Middle Eastern Studies* 8 (2001): 7–20.

Corbin, Henry. *En Islam iranien; Aspects spirituels et philosophiques* 4 vols. (Paris: Gallimard, 1971–1972).

Corbin, Henry. *The Man of Light in Iranian Sufism.* Translated by Nancy Pearson (Boulder, CO: Shambhala, 1978).

Corteggiani, Jean-Pierre. "The Site." In André Raymond (ed.) *Cairo: An Illustrated History* (New York: Rizzoi, 2001), 15–55.

Creswell, Keppel Archibald Cameron. *Muslim Architecture of Egypt*, 2 vols. (Oxford: Clarendon, 1952–1959).

Crowther, Paul. *How Pictures Complete Us; The Beautiful, the Sublime, and the Divine* (Palo Alto, CA: Stanford University Press, 2016).

Cruikshank Dodd, Erica and Shereen Khairallah. *The Image of the Word: A Study of Quranic Verses in Islamic Architecture*, 2 vols. (Beirut: American University of Beirut, 1981).

Cutler, Anthony. "Reuse or Use? Theoretical and Practical Attitudes Toward Objects in the Early Middle Ages." *Settimane di Studio del Centro Italiano di Studi sull'Alto Medioevo* 46 (1999): 1055–1079.

Daftary, Farhad. *The Isma'ilis: Their History and Doctrines* (Cambridge: Cambridge University Press, 1990).

Danto, Arthur. *The Abuse of Beauty: Aesthetics and the Concept of Art* (Chicago: Open Court, 2006).

Danto, Arthur. *The Philosophical Disenfranchisement of Art* (New York: Columbia University Press, 2005).

Davis, Richard H. *The Lives of Indian Images* (Princeton, NJ: Princeton University Press, 1997).

Dawood, Azra. "Failure to Engage: The Breasted-Rockefeller Gift of a New Egyptian Museum and Research Institute at Cairo (1926)." MA thesis. Massachusetts Institute of Technology, Cambridge, MA, 2010. DSpace@MIT.

De Goeje, Michael Jan. *Mémoire sur les Carmates du Bahraïn et les Fatimides* (Leiden: Brill, 1886).

De Groot, A. H. "Sandjak-i Sherif." *Encyclopaedia of Islam*, 2nd edn. (Leiden: Brill, 2012).

De Jong, Frederick. *Turuq and Turuq-Linked Institutions in Nineteenth Century Egypt: a Historical Study in Organizational Dimensions of Islamic Mysticism* (Leiden: Brill, 1978).

De Jong, Frederick. "Turuq and Turuq-Opposition in 20th-Century Egypt." In Frederick de Jong (ed.) *Sufi Orders in Ottoman and Post-Ottoman Egypt and the Middle East* (Istanbul: Isis, 1994) 185–196.

De Smet, Daniel. "Le calife fatimide al-Hakim (996–1021) a-t-il voulu s'emparer des reliques du Prophète Muhammad?" In Phillipe Borgeaud and Youri Volokhine (eds.) *Les objets de la mémoire: pour une approche comparatiste des reliques et de leur culte* (New York: Peter Lang, 2005), 247–265.

De Smet, Daniel. "La Translation du Ra's al-Husayn au Caire Fatimide." In by Urbain Vermulen and Daniel De Smet (eds.) *Egypt and Syria in the Fatimid, Ayyubid, and Mamluk Eras II. Proceedings of the 4th and 5th International Colloquium organized at the Katholieke Universiteit Leuven in May 1995 and 1996*, 2 vols. (Leiden: Peeters, 1998) 2:29–44

De Thévenot, Jean. *The Travels of Monsieur de Thevenot into the Levant.* Translated by R. L'Estrange (London: H. Clark, 1687).

Dekkiche, Malika. "New Source, New Debate: Re-evaluation of the Mamluk-Timurid Struggle for Religious Supremacy in the

Hijaz." *Mamluk Studies Review* 18, (2014-2015): 246–271.

DeLong-Bas, Natana J. *Wahhabi Islam: From Revival and Reform to Global Jihad* (New York: Oxford University Press, 2008).

Denny, Walter B. "A Group of Silk Islamic Banners." *Textile Museum Journal* 4 (1974): 67–81.

Dickinson, Eerik. "Ibn Shahrazuri and the Isnad" *Journal of the American Oriental Society*, 122, 3 (Jul.–Sep. 2002): 481–505.

Didi-Huberman, Georges. "Has the Epistemological Transformation Taken Place?" In Michael F. Zimmerman (ed.) *The Art Historian: National Traditions and Institutional Practices* (Williamstown, MA: Sterling and Francine Clark Art Institute, 2003), 128–143.

Dols, Michael W. *Black Death in the Middle East* (Princeton, NJ: Princeton University Press, 1977).

Donner, Fred McGraw. *Muhammad and the Believers: At the Origins of Islam* (Cambridge, MA: Belknap of Harvard Univeristy Press, 2010).

Dorpmüller, Sabine, Jan Scholz, Max Stille, Ines Weinrich, (eds.) *Religion and Aesthetic Experience: Drama – Sermons – Literature* (Heidelberg: Heidelberg University Publishing, 2018).

Doughty, Charles Montagu. *Travels in Arabia Deserta*. 2 vols. (Cambridge: Cambridge University Press, 1888).

Ducène, Jean-Charles. "Rites religieux et crue du Nil en Egypte médiévale." *Acta orientalia belgica* 23 (2010): 63–76.

Duncan, Carol. "Art Museums and the Ritual of Citizenship." In Ivan Karp (ed.) *Exhibiting Cultures: The Poetics and Politics of Museum Display* (Washington: Smithsonian Press, 1991), 88–103.

Duncan, Carol. *Civilizing Rituals: Indside Public Art Museums* (New York: Routledge, 1995).

Dykstra, Darrell. "Pyramids, Prophets, and Progress: Ancient Egypt in the Writings of 'Ali Mubarak." *Journal of the American Oriental Society* 114, 1 (1994): 54–65.

Eagleton, Terry. *After Theory* (New York: Basic Books, 2003).

Eagleton, Terry. *The Ideology of the Aesthetic* (Oxford: Blackwell, 1990).

Ebers, Georg. *Egypt: Descriptive, Historical, and Picturesque*. 2 vols. Translated by C. Bell (London: Cassell and Co., 1898).

Ebstein, Michael. "Dhu al-Nun al-Misri and Early Islamic Mysticism." *Arabica* 61, 5 (2014): 559–612.

Eddé, Anne-Marie. "Bilad al-Sham, from the Fatimid conquest to the fall of the Ayyubids (359–658/970–1260)." In (6 vols., various editors). *The New Cambridge History of Islam*, vol. 2 (ed.) Maribel Fierro (Cambridge: Cambridge University Press, 2010), 2:159–200.

Efendi, Husain and Stanford Shaw. *Ottoman Egypt in the Age of the French Revolution* (Cambridge, MA: Harvard University Press, 1966).

El Rashidi, Seif and Sam Bowker. *The Tentmakers of Cairo: Egypt's Medieval and Modern Appliqué Craft* (Cairo: The American University in Cairo Press, 2018).

El-Bashir, Esam Ahmed. *Al-Jamal, Ru'ya Maqasidiyya* (London: al-Furqan, 2015).

El-Bizri, Nader. "Classical Optics and the Perspectival Traditions Leading to the Renaissance." In Charles Carman and John Hendrix (eds.), *Renaissance Theories of Vision* (Aldershot, UK: Ashgate, 2010), 11–30.

El-Bizri, Nader. "A Philosophical Perspective on Alhazen's *Optics*." *Arabic Sciences and Philosophy* 15 (2005): 189–218.

Elad, Amikam. *Medieval Jerusalem and Islamic Worship: Holy Places, Ceremonies, Pilgrimage* (Leiden: Brill, 1995).

Elbendary, Amina. *Between Riots and Negotiations: Urban Protest in Late Medieval Egypt and Syria* (Berlin: EBVerlag, 2012).

Eliade, Mircea. *The Sacred and The Profane: The Nature of Religion*. Translated by Willard Trask (New York: Harcourt, 1987).

Eliade, Mircea. *Patterns in Comparative Religion*. Translated by Rosemary Sheed (Cleveland, OH: World Publishing, 1963).

Elias, Jamal J. *Aisha's Cushion: Religious Art, Perception, and Practice in Islam* (Cambridge, MA: Harvard University Press, 2012).

Elias, Jamal J. *Alef is for Allah: Childhood, Emotion, and Visual Culture in Islamic Societies* (Oakland: University of California Press, 2018).

Elias, Jamal J. *The Throne Carrier of God: the Life and Thought of 'Ala ad-Dawla as-Simnani* (Albany: State University of New York Press, 1995).

Ellenbogen, Josh, and Aaron Tugenhaft, "Introduction." In Josh Ellenbogen (ed.) *Idol Anxiety* (Palo Alto, CA: Stanford University Press, 2011), 1–18.

Elsner, Jas. "Iconoclasm as Discourse: From Antiquity to Byzantium." *Art Bulletin* 94(2) (2002): 368–394.

Ephrat, Daphna. *Spiritual Wayfarers, Leaders in Piety: Sufis and the Dissemination of Islam in medieval Palestine* (Cambridge, MA: Harvard University Press, 2008).

Ephrat, Daphna. "Sufism and Sanctity: the genesis of the Wali Allah in Mamluk Jerusalem and Hebron." In David J. Wasserstein and Ami Ayalon (eds.) *Mamluks and Ottomans: Studies in Honour of Michael Winter* (New York: Routledge, 2006), 4–18.

Ernst, Carl W. "An Indo-Persian Guide to Sufi Shrine Pilgrimage." In Grace M. Smith and Carl W. Ernst (ed.) *Manifestations of Sainthood in Islam* (Istanbul: Isis Press 1993), 43–67.

Ernst, Carl W. *It's Not Just Academic!: Essays on Sufism and Islamic Studies* (Los Angeles: Sage, 2019).

El-Leithy, Tamer. "Sufis, Copts and the Politics of Piety: Moral Regulation in Fourteenth-century Upper Egypt." In Richard McGregor and Adam Sabra (eds.) *The Development of Sufism in Mamluk Egypt* (Cairo: Presses de l'Institut français d'archéologie orientale, 2006), 75–119.

Ettinghausen, Richard. "Arabic Epigraphy: Communication or Symbolic Affirmation." In Dickran Kouymjian (ed.) *Near Eastern Numismatics, Iconography, Epigraphy, and History: Studies in Honor of George C. Miles* (Beirut: American University of Beirut, 1974), 297–318.

Ettinghausen, Richard. "Notes on the Lusterware of Spain," *Ars Orientalis* 1 (1954): 133–156.

Fahd, Toufic. *Le Panthéon de l'Arabie centrale à la veille de l'Hégire* (Paris: Librarie Orientaliste Paul Geuthner, 1968).

Farihi, Fatima bint Muhammad. "Azmat al-mahmal wa ta'amul al-malik 'Abd al-'Aziz ma'a-ha 1344/1926." *Majalla Jami'a Umm al-Qura al-Sharifa* 59 (2013): 359–402.

Faroqhi, Suraiya. *Herrscher über Mekka: die Geschichte der Pilgerfahrt* (Munich: Artemis, 1990).

Faroqhi, Suraiya. *Pilgrims and Sultans: the Hajj under the Ottomans, 1517–1683* (New York: Tauris, 1994).

Felman, Shoshana. *The Scandal of the Speaking Body* (Palo Alto, CA: Stanford University Press, 2003).

Fernandes, Leonor. "The Foundation of Baybars al-Jashankir: Its Waqf, History, and Architecture. *Muqarnas* 4 (1987): 21–42.

Finster, Barbara. "The Material Culture of Pre-and Early Islamic Arabia." In Finbarr Barry Flood and Gülru Necipoglu (eds.) *A Companion to Islamic Art and Architecture*, 2 vols. (New York: John Wiley & Sons, 2017) 61–88.

Fisher, Philip. *Making and Effacing Art: Modern American Art in a Culture of Museums* (New York: Oxford University Press, 1991).

Flood, Finbarr Barry. "Between Cult and Culture: Bamyan, Islamic Iconoclasm, and the Museum." *The Art Bulletin* 84, 4 (2002): 641–659.

Flood, Finbarr Barry. "An Ambiguous Aesthetic: Crusader *Spolia* in Ayyubid Jerusalem." In Sylvia Auld and Robert Hillenbrand (eds.) *Ayyubid Jerusalem: The Holy City in Context, 1187–1250* (London: Al-Tajir Trust, 2009) 202–215.

Flood, Finbarr Barry. "From the Prophet to Postmodernism? New World Orders and the End of Islamic Art." In Elizabeth Mansfield (ed.) *Making Art History: A Changing Discipline and its Institutions* (New York: Routledge, 2007) 31–53.

Flood, Finbarr Barry. *The Great Mosque of Damascus: Studies on the Makings of an Umayyad Visual Culture* (Leiden: Brill, 2001).

Flood, Finbarr Barry. "The Iconography of Light in the Monuments of Mamluk Cairo." In Emily Lyle (ed.) *Sacred Architecture in the Traditions of India, China, Judaism, and Islam*

(Edinburgh: Edinburgh University Press, 1992)169–93.

Flood, Finbarr Barry. "Image Against Nature: Spolia as Apotropaia in Byzantium and the Dar al-Islam." *The Medieval History Journal* 9, 1 (2006): 143–166.

Flood, Finbarr Barry. "Light in Stone: The Commemoration of the Prophet in Umayyad Architecture." In Jeremy Johns (ed.) *Bayt al-Maqdis: Jerusalem and Early Islam* (New York: Oxford University Press, 1999), 311–359.

Flood, Finbarr Barry. *Objects of Translation: Material Culture and Medieval "Hindu-Muslim" Encounter* (Princeton, NJ: Princeton University Press, 2009).

Flood, Finbarr Barry. "Refiguring Iconoclasm in the Early Indian Mosque." In Anne McClanan and Jeffrey Johnson (eds.) *Negating the Image: Case Studies in Iconoclasm* (New York: Ashgate, 2005), 15–40.

Flood, Gavin. *Beyond Phenomenology: Rethinking the Study of Religion* (New York: Continuum, 1999).

Fodor, Alexander. "The Origins of the Arabic Legends of the Pyramids." *Acta Orientalia Academiae Scientiarum Hungaricae* 23, 3 (1970): 335–363.

Freedberg, David. *The Power of Images: Studies in the History and Theory of Response* (Chicago: University of Chicago Press, 1989).

Frenkel, Miriam. "Constructing the Sacred: Holy Shrines in Aleppo and Its Environs." In Urbain Vermulen and Kristof D'Hulster (eds.) *Egypt and Syria in the Fatimid, Ayyubid, and Mamluk Eras. VI. Proceedings of the 14th and 15th International Colloquium Organized at the Katholieke Universiteit Leuven in May 2005 and May 2006* (Leiden: Brill, 2010), 63–78.

Frenkel, Yehoshua. "Baybars and the Sacred Geography of Bilad al-Sham," *Jerusalem Studies in Arabic and Islam* 25 (2001): 153–170.

Friedman, Yohanan. "'Kufa is better': The sanctity of Kufa in early Islam and Shi'ism in particular" *Le muséon* 126, 1–2 (2013): 203–37.

Gallin, Pauli. "Mamluk Art Objects in Their Architectural Context." Ph.D diss., Boston College, 2017. ProQuest Dissertations & Theses Global.

Gamboni, Dario. *The Destruction of Art: Iconoclasm and Vandalism since the French Revolution* (New Haven, CT: Yale University Press, 1977).

Garcin, Jean-Claude. *Espaces, pouvoirs et idéologies de l'Égypte médiévale* (London: Variorum Reprints, 1987).

Gardiner, Noah. "Esotericist Reading Communities and the Early Circulation of the Sufi Occultist Ahamd al-Buni's Works." *Arabica* 64, 3–4 (2017): 405–441.

Gaudefroy-Demombynes, Maurice. *Le Pèlerinage à la Mekke: étude d'histoire religieuse* (Paris: Geunther 1977).

Gaudefroy-Demombynes, Maurice. "Notes sur la Mekke et Médine." *Revue de l'histoire des religions* 39 (1918): 316–344.

Gaudefroy-Demombynes, Maurice. "Le Voile de la Ka'ba." *Studia Islamica* 2 (1954):5–21.

Geertz, Clifford. *The Interpretation of Cultures* (New York: Basic Books, 1973).

Geertz, Clifford. *Islam Observed: Religious Development in Morocco and Indonesia* (Chicago: University of Chicago Press, 1968).

Geoffroy, Éric. *Le Soufisme en Égypte et en Syrie sous les derniers mamelouks et les premiers ottomans: orientations spirituelles et enjeux culturels* (Damascus: Presses de l'institut français du proche orient: 1996).

Gilsenan, Michel. *Saint and Sufi in Modern Egypt: An Essay in the Sociology of Religion* (Oxford: Clarendon Press, 1973).

Golombek, Lisa. "The Draped Universe of Islam." In Richard Ettinghausen and Priscilla Soucek (eds.) *Content and Context of Visual Arts in the Islamic World*. 25–50 (University Park, PA: Pennsylvania State University Press, 1988).

Gombrich, Ernst Hans Joseph. *The Sense of Order: A Study in the Psychology of Decorative Art*, 2nd edn. (New York: Phaidon, 1984).

Gonnella, Julia. *The Citadel of Aleppo; Description, History, Site Plan, and Visitor Tour* (Geneva: Aga Khan Trust for Culture, 2008).

Gonnella, Julia. "Columns and Hieroglyphs: Magic Spolia in Medieval Islamic

Architecture of Northern Syria." *Muqarnas* 27 (2010): 103–120.

Gonzalez, Valerie. *Beauty and Islam: Aesthetics in Islamic Art and Architecture* (New York: I. B. Tauris, 2001).

Grabar, Oleg. "Islam and Iconoclasm." In Anthony Bryer, and Judith Herrin (eds.) *Iconoclasm: Papers Given at the Ninth Spring Syposium of Byzantine Studies, University of Birmingham, March 1975* (Birmingham: Center for Byzantine Studies, 1977), 45–52.

Grabar, Oleg. "Kubbat al-Sakhra." *Encyclopaedia of Islam*. 2nd edn. (Leiden: Brill, 2012).

Grabar, Oleg. *The Mediation of Ornament* (Princeton, NJ: Princeton University Press, 1992).

Grabar, Oleg. "The Story of Portraits of the Prophet Muhammad." *Studia Islamica* 96, (2003): 19–38.

Greenlagh, Michael. "Spolia: A Definition in Ruins." In Richard Brilliant (ed.) *Reuse Value: Spolia and Appropriation in Art and Architecture* (London: Taylor & Francis, 2016), 79–95.

Griffith, Sidney H. "Theodore Abu Qurrah's Arabic Tract on the Christian Practice of Venerating Images." *Journal of the American Oriental Society* 105, 1, (Jan.–Mar. 1985): 53–73.

Gril, Denis. "Le corps du Prophète." *Revue des mondes musulmans et de la Méditerranée* 113–114 (2006): 37–57.

Gruber, Christiane. "In Defense and Devotion: Affective Practices in Early Modern Turco-Persian Manuscript Paintings." In Kishwar Rizvi (ed.) *New Studies in Ottoman, Safavid, and Mughal Art and Culture* (Leiden: Brill, 2018), 95–123.

Gruber, Christiane. *The Praiseworthy One: the Prophet Muhammad in Islamic Texts and Images* (Bloomington, IN: Indiana University Press, 2018).

Gruber, Christiane. "The Prophet Muhammad's Footprint." In Robert Hillenbrand, A. C. S. Peacock, Firuza Abdullaeva (eds.) *Ferdowsi, the Mongols, and the History of Iran*, 297–305 (New York: I.B. Tauris, 2013).

Haarmann, Ulrich. "In Quest of the Spectacular: Noble and Learned Visitors to the Pyramids Around 1200 AD." In Wael Hallaq and Donald P. Little (eds.) *Islamic Studies Presented to Charles J. Adams* (Leiden: Brill, 1991), 57–67.

Haarmann, Ulrich. "Regional Sentiment in Medieval Islamic Egypt." *Bulletin of the School of Oriental and African Studies* 43 (1980): 55–66.

Haase, Clause-Peter. "Some Aspects of Fatimid Calligraphy on Textiles." In Marianne Barrucand (ed.) *L'Égypte fatimide: son art et son historire* (Paris: Presses de l'Univerité de Paris-Sorbonne, 1999), 339–347.

Hahn, Cynthia, J. *Strange Beauty: Issues in the Making and Meaning of Reliquaries, 400-circa 1204* (University Park: Pennsylvania State University Press, 2012).

Hahn, Cynthia. J. "What Do Reliquaries Do for Relics?" *Numen* 57 (2010): 284–316.

Halevi, Leor. *Muhammad's Grave: Death Rites and the Making of Islamic Society* (New York: Columbia University Press, 2007).

Hallenberg, Helena. *Ibrahim al-Dasuqi (1255–1296). A Saint Invented* (Helsinki: Finnish Academy of Sciences and Letters, 2005).

Halm, Heinz. "Al-Shamsa. Hängekronen als Herrshaftszeichen der Abbasiden und Fatimiden," In Urbain Vermeulen and Daniel De Smet (eds.) *Egypt and Syria in the Fatimid, Ayyubid and Mamluk Eras* (Leuven: Peeters, 1995), 126–138.

Hampikian, Nairy. "Mu'ayyad Shaykh and the Landscape of Power." *Annales Islamologioques* 46 (2012): 195–214.

Hanna, Nelly. *An Urban History of Bulaq in the Mamluk and Ottoman Periods* (Cairo: Presses de Institut Français d'Achéologie Orientale, 1983).

Al-Harithy, Howayda. "The Concept of Space in Mamluk Architecture." *Muqarnas* 18 (2001): 73–93.

Harrell, James A. Lorenzo Lazzarini, Mathias Bruno. "Reuse of Roman Ornamental Stones in Medieval Cairo, Egypt/" www.eeescience.utoledo.edu/faculty/harrell/egypt/mosques/ASMOSIA_VI_Text.htm (retrieved online August 3, 2016).

Harris, Rachel and Rahliä Dawut, "Mazar Festivals of the Uyghurs: Music, Islam and the Chinese State." *British Journal of Ethnomusicology* 11, 1 (2002):101–118.

Hasan, Hebatallah Muhammad Fathi and Hamada Ahmad. Al-Mahmal al-Misri: dirasa tarikhiyya." *Majalla ithaf al-jami'at al-'arabiyya li-l-siyaha wa'l-diyafa* 6(2) (2009): 25–50.

Hassan, Mona. *Longing for the Lost Caliphate: A Transregional History* (Princeton, NJ: Princeton University Press, 2017).

Hassan, Mona. "Poetic Memories of the Prophet's Family: Ibn Hajar al-'Asqalani's Panegyrics for the 'Abbasid Sultan-Caliph of Cairo al-Musta'in." *Journal of Islamic Studies* 29, 1 (2018): 1–24.

Hasebe, Fumihiko. "Popular Movements and Jaqmaq, the Less Paternalistic Sultan: Some Aspects of Conflict in the Egyptian Cities, 1449–52." *Annals of Japan Association for Middle East Studies* 20, 2 (2005): 27–51.

Hawting, Gerald R. *The Idea of Idolatry and the Emergence of Islam: From Polemic to History* (Cambridge: Cambridge University Press, 2006).

Hawting, Gerald R. "The Origins of the Muslim Sanctuary in Mecca" in Gauthier H. A. Juynboll (ed.) *Studies on the First Century of Islamic Society* (Carbondale: Southern Illinois University Press, 1982), 23–47.

Haykal, Muhammad Husayn. *Fi manzil al-wahy* (Cairo: Maktaba al-Nahda al-Misriyya, 1939).

Healey, John F. *The Religion of the Nabataeans* (Leiden: Brill, 2001).

Heo, Angie. *The Political Lives of Saints: Christian-Muslim Mediation in Egypt* (Berkeley: University of California Press, 2018).

Hillenbrand, Carole. *The Crusades, Islamic Perspectives* (Edinburgh: Edinburgh University Press, 2009).

Hillenbrand, Robert. "Qur'anic epigraphy in medieval Islamic architecture." *Revue des Études Islamiques* 54 (1986): 171–187.

Hilmi, Ibrahim. *Al-Mahmal: rihla sha'biyya fi wijan al-umma* (Cairo: Maktabat al-Turath al-Islami, 1993).

Hinds, Martin. "The Banners and Battle cries of the Arabs at Siffin (AD 657)." In Martin Hinds et al., (eds.)*Studies in Early Islamic History* (Princeton, NJ: Darwin Press, 1996), 97–142.

Hirschler, Konrad. *Medieval Damascus: Plurality and Diversity in an Arabic Library: The Ashrafiya Library Catalogue* (Edinburgh: Edinburgh University Press, 2016).

Hirschler, Konrad. "The 'Pharaoh' Anecdote in Pre-Modern Arabic Historiography." *Journal of Arabic and Islamic Studies* 10 (2010): 24–44.

Hirschler, Konrad. *The Written Word in the Medieval Arabic Lands: a Social and Cultural History of Reading Practices* (Edinburgh: Edinburgh University Press, 2012).

Hirschkind, Charles. *The Ethical Soundscape: Cassette Sermons and Islamic Counterpublics* (New York: Columbia University Press, 2006).

Hirschkind, Charles. "Prayer Machine: An Introduction." *Material Religion* 12.1 (2016): 97–98.

Hodgson, Marshall G. S. *The Venture of Islam*, 3 vols. (Chicago: University of Chicago Press, 1977).

Hodgson, Marshall G. S. "Islam and Image." *History of Religions* 3, 2 (Winter, 1964): 220–260.

Hofer, Nathan. *The Popularization of Sufism in Ayyubid and Mamluk Egypt, 1173–1325* (Edinburgh: Edinburgh University Press).

Hoffman, Valery J. "Annihilation in the Messenger of God: the Development of a Sufi Practice." *International Journal of Middle East Studies* 31 (1999): 351–369.

Hollywood, Amy. *Acute Melancholia and Other Essays* (New York: Columbia University Press, 2016).

Homerin, Th. Emil. "Saving Muslim Souls: The *Khanqah* and the Sufi Duty in Mamluk Lands." *Mamluk Studies Review* 3 (1999): 59–81.

Humphreys, Stephen. *From Saladin to the Mongols: the Ayyubids of Damascus, 1193–1260* (Albany: State University of New York Press, 1977).

Humphreys, Stephen. "The Expressive Intent of the Mamluk Architecture of Cairo: A Preliminary Essay." *Studia Islamica* 35 (1972): 69–119.

Humphreys, Stephen. "Women as Patrons of Architecture in Ayyubid Damascus." *Muqarnas* 11 (1994): 35–54.

Al-Ibrashy, May. "The Life and Times of the Mamluk Turba: Processual Subversion of

Inceptual Intent" *Annales Islamologioques* 46 (2012): 145–166.

Irfan, Ahmed. "The Destruction of the Holy Sites in Mecca and Medina," *Islamica* 15 (2006): 71–74.

Irwin, Robert. "Journey to Mecca: A History (part 2)" in Venetia Porter (ed.) *Hajj: journey to the heart of Islam* (London: British Museum Press, 2012), 136–219.

Irwin, Robert. *The Middle East in the Middle Ages: The Early Mamluk Sultanate 1250–1382* (Carbondale: Southern Illinois University Press, 1986).

Jahdani, Abdelouahad. "Du fiqh à la codicology: quelques opinions de Malik (m. 179/796) sur le Coran-codex." *Mélanges de l'Université Saint-Joseph* 59 (2006): 269–279.

Jakeman, Jane. "Abstract Art and Communication in 'Mamluk' Architecture." PhD diss., University of Oxford, Oxford, 1993. British Library, British Thesis Service.

Al-Jarim, Muhammad N. *Adyan al-Arab fi al-Jahiliyya* (Cairo: Matba'a al-Sa'ada, 1923).

Jay, Martin. "Cultural Relavtivism and the Visual Turn." *Journal of Visual Culture* 1, 3 (2002): 267–278.

Johansen, Julian. *Sufism and Islamic Reform in Egypt: The Battle for Islamic Tradition* (Oxford: Clarendon, 1996).

Jomier, Jacques. "Le Mahmal de Sultan Qansuh al-Ghuri (début XVI siècle)." *Annales Islamologiques* 11, (1972): 183–188.

Jomier, Jacques. *Le Mahmal et la caravane Égyptienne des pèlerins de la Mecque (XIII-XX siècles)* (Cairo: Presses de Institut Français d'Achéologie Orientale, 1953).

Al-Ju'beh, Nazami. "Kiswa (tomb cover) for the Prophet of God, Ibrahim (Abraham)" in "Discover Islamic Art: Museum With No Frontiers" 2019 (online)

Kaptein, Nicolaas J. G. "Mawlid." In *Encyclopaedia of Islam*, 2nd edn. (Leiden: Brill, 2012).

Kant, Immanuel. *The Critique of Judgment*. Translated by J. Bernard (New York: Prometheus, 2000).

Karamustafa, Ahmet T. *God's Unruly Friends: Dervish Groups in the Later Islamic Middle Period* (Salt Lake City: University of Utah Press, 1994).

Karamustafa, Ahmet T. *Sufism: The Formative Period* (Edinburgh: Edinburgh University Press, 2007).

Katz, Jonathan G. *Dreams, Sufism, and Sainthood: The Visionary Career of Muhammad al-Zawawi* (Leiden: Brill 1996).

Katz, Jonathan G. "Dreams and Their Interpretation in Sufi Thought and Practice." In Özgen Felek and Alexander Knysh (eds.) *Dreams and Visions in Islamic Societies* (Albany: State University of New York Press, 2013), 181–198.

Keane, Webb. "The Evidence of The Senses and The Materiality of Religion." *Journal of the Royal Anthropological Institute* 14, 1, (2008): 110–127.

Kelly, Sean D. "Seeing Things in Merleau-Ponty." In Taylor Carman (ed.) *The Cambridge Companion to Merleau-Ponty* (Cambridge: Cambridge University Press, 2005), 74–110.

Kenney, Ellen. *Power and Patronage in Medieval Syria: The Architecture and Urban Works of Tankiz al-Nasiri* (Chicago: Middle East Documentation Center, 2009).

Kermani, Navid. *God is Beautiful: The Aesthetic Experience of the Quran*. Translated by Tony Crawford (Malden, MA: Polity, 2014).

Kester, Grant H. "Aesthetics after the End of Art: an interview with Susan Buck-Morss" *Art Journal* 56, 1 (1997): 38–45.

Al-Khadimi, Nur al-Din, "Al-funun al-khadima li'l-maqasid wa al-maqasid al-khadima li'l-funun." In Ibrahim al-Bayumi Ghanem (ed.) *Al-funun fi daw' maqasid al-shari'a al-Islamiyya* (London: al-Furqan, 2017).

Khaleq, Nancy. *Damascus after the Muslim Conquest: Text and Image in Early Islam* (New York: Cambridge University Press, 2011).

Khaleq, Nancy. "Medieval Muslim Martyrs to the Plague: Venerating the Companions of Muhammad in the Jordan Valley." In Cynthia Hahn and Holger A. Klein (eds.) *Saints and Sacred Matter: the Cult of Relics in Byzantium and Beyond* (Washington, DC: Dumbarton

Oaks Research Library and Collections, 2015), 83–98.

Khan, Majeed. "Rock Art of Saudi Arabia." *Arts* 2 (2013): 447–475.

Khosronejad, Pedram. *The Art and Material Culture of Iranian Shi'ism: Iconography and Religious Devotion in Shi'i Islam* (London: I.B. Tauris, 2014).

Khoury, Nuha N. "The Dome of the Rock, the Ka'ba, and Ghumdan: Arab Myths and Umayyad Monuments." *Muqarnas* 10 (1993): 57–66.

Khoury, Nuha N. "The Mihrab Image: Commemorative Themes in Medieval Islamic Architecture." *Muqarnas* 9 (1992): 11–28.

King, Geoffrey R. D. "Islam, Iconoclasm, and the Declaration of Doctrine." *Bulletin of the School of Oriental and African Studies* 48, 2 (1985): 267–277.

King, Geoffrey R. D. "The Sculptures of the Pre-Isalmic Haram at Mecca." In Warwick Ball, Leonard Harrow and Ralph Pinder-Wilson (eds.) *Cairo to Kabul: Afghan and Islamic Studies Presented to Ralph Pinder-Wilson* (London: Melisende, 2002), 144–150.

King, Geoffrey R. D. *The Traditional Architecture of Saudi Arabia* (London: Tauris, 1998).

King, Richard "The Copernican Turn in the Study of Religion." *Method and Theory in the Study of Religion* 25 (2013): 137–159.

Kinney, Dale. "Introduction." In Richard Brilliant and Dale Kinney (eds.) *Reuse Value: Spolia and Appropriation in Art and Architecture from Constantine to Sherrie Levine* (Burlington: Ashgate Publishing, 2011), 1–12.

Kister, M. J. "Maqam Ibrahim. A Stone with an Inscription." *Le Muséon* 84 (1971): 477–491.

Kister, M. J. "Mecca and the Tribes of Arabia: Some Notes on Their Relations." In Moshe Sharon (ed.) *Studies in Islamic History and Civilization in Honor of Professor David Ayalon* (Leiden: Brill, 1997), 33–58.

Kister, M. J. "Sanctity Joint and Divided." *Jerusalem Studies in Arabic and Islam* 20 (1996): 18–65.

Klunzinger, Karl B. *Upper Egypt: Its People and Its Products. A Descriptive Account of the Manners, Customs, Superstitions, and Occupations of the People of the Nile Valley, the Desert, and the Red Sea Coast, with Dketches of the Natural History and Geology* (London: Blackie & Son, 1878).

Knysh, Alexander. *Ibn 'Arabi in the Later Islamic Tradition: The Making of a Polemical Image in Medieval Islam* (New York: State University of New York Press, 1999).

Knysh, Alexander. *Sufism: A New History of Islamic Mysticism* (Princeton, NJ: Princeton University Press, 2017).

Kopytoff, Igor. "The Cultural Biography of Things: Commoditization as Process" in Arjun Appadurai (ed.) *The Social Life of Things: Commodities in Cultural Perspective* (New York: Cambridge University Press, 1986), 64–91.

Kriss, Rudolf and Hubert Kriss-Heinrich. *Volksglaube in Bereich des Islam.* 2 vols. (Wiesbaden: O. Harrassowitz, 1960–1962).

Kugle, Scott Alan. *Sufis and Saints' Bodies: Mysticism, Corporeality, and Sacred Power in Islam* (Chapel Hill: University of North Carolina Press, 2007).

Kukkonen, Taneli. "The Good, the Beautiful, and the True; Aesthetical Issues in Islamic Philosophy." *Studia Orientalia* 111 (2011): 95–111.

Lammens, Henri. "Culte de Bétyles et des processions chez les Arabes préislamites" *Bulletin de l'Institut Français d'Archéologie Orientale* 17 (1920): 39–101.

Lamoreaux, John C. *The Early Muslim Tradition of Dream Interpretation* (Albany: State University of New York, 2002).

Lane, Edward William and Stanley Lane-Poole, *Cairo Fifty Years Ago* (London: J. Murray, 1896).

Lane, Edward William. *Manners and Customs of the Modern Egyptians* (Cairo: Livres de France. 1989).

Lange, Christian. "Legal and Cultural Aspects of Ignominious Parading (*Tashhir*) in Islam." *Islamic Law and Society* 14, 1, (2007): 81–108.

Langhi, Fatima Z. A. "'Ajami Mysteries of Sitt 'Ajam bint al-Nafis." *Journal of the Muhyiddin Ibn 'Arabi Society* 46 (2009), access online www.ibnarabisociety.org/articles/sitt-ajam.html #note5 (January 2019).

Lapidus, Ira. *Muslim Cities in the Latter Middle Ages* (Cambridge, MA: Harvard University Press, 1967).

Laoust, Henri. "La biographie d'Ibn Taimiya d'après Ibn Kathir." *Bulletin d'études orientales* 9 (1942): 115–162.

Lauzière, Henri. *The Making of Salafism: Islamic Reform in the Twentieth Century* (New York: Columbia University Press, 2016).

Le Strange, Guy. *Palestine Under the Moslems: A Description of Syria and the Holy Land from A.D. 650 to 1500* (London: Committee of the Palestinian Exploration Fund, 1890).

Leaman, Oliver. *Islamic Aesthetics: An Introduction* (Edinburgh: Edinburgh University Press, 2004).

Lecker, Michael. "Idol Worship in Pre-Islamic Yamama" unpublished paper available on academia.edu (January 2018).

Lecker, Michael. "Wadd, the Weaponed Idol of Dumat al-Jandal and the *Qussas*." In Isabelle Sachet (ed.) *Dieux et déesses d'Arabie: images et représentations* (Paris: De Boccard, 2012), 123–130.

Lecker, Michael. "Was Arabian Idol Worship Declining on the Eve of Islam?" In Michael Lecker (ed.) *People, Tribes and Society in Arabia Around the Time of Muhammad* (London: Routledge, 2005), 2–43.

Leeder, Simon H. *Veiled Mysteries of Egypt* (New York: C. Scribner's Sons, 1913).

Legrain, Georges. *Louqsor sans les Pharaons; Légendes et Chansons de la Haute Égypte* (Brussels: Vromant & Co., 1914).

Leisten, Thomas. "Dynastic Tomb or Private Mausolea?" In Marianne Barucand (ed.) *L'Égypte fatimide: son art et son histoire*, (Paris: Presses de l'Université de Paris-Sorbonne, 1999), 465–478.

Lev, Yaacov. *Saladin in Egypt* (Leiden: Brill, 1998).

Levtzion, Nehemia. "Mamluk Egypt and Takrur (West Africa)" in Moshe Sharon (ed.) *Studies in Islamic History and Civilization in Honor of Professor David Ayalon* (Leiden: Brill, 1986), 183–208.

Lindberg, David C. *Theories of Vision from al-Kindi to Kepler* (Chicago: University of Chicago Press, 1976).

Little, Donald. "The Fall of 'Akka in 690/1291: the Muslim Version." In Moshe Sharon (ed.) *Studies in Islamic History and Civilization in Honor of Professor David Ayalon* (Leiden: Brill, 1986), 159–181.

Loiseau, Julien. *Les Mamelouks: XIIIe-XVIe siècle: une expérience du pouvoir dans l'islam médiéval* (Paris: Seuil, 2014).

Loiseau, Julien. "Le tombeau des sultans: Constructions monumentales et stratégies funéraires dans les sultanats mamelouk et ottoman." *Turcica* 41 (2009): 305–340.

Lorand, David. "A Block of Ramesses II Reused as a Threshold in the Wakala of Qawsun (Cairo)." *The Journal of Egyptian Archaeology* 99 (2013): 270–273.

Lory, Pierre. "L'interprétation des rêves de portée religieuse chez Ibn Shahin." In Richard McGregor and Adam Sabra (eds.) *The Development of Sufism in Mamluk Egypt* (Cairo: Presses de l'Institut français d'archéologie orientale, 2006), 259–266.

Lory, Pierre. "La vision du prophète en rêve dans l'onirocritique musulmane." In Éric Chaumont *et al.*, (eds.) *Autour du regard: mélanges Gimaret* (Louvain: Peeters, 2003), 181–212.

Luizard, Pierre-Jean. "Un mawlid particulier." *Égypte-monde arabe* 14 (1993): 79–102.

Mackie, Louise W. *Symbols of Power: Luxury Textiles from Islamic Lands, 7th–21st Century* (New Haven, CT: Yale University Press, 2015).

Madelung, Wilfred. "Karmati." *Encyclopaedia of Islam*. 2nd edn. (Leiden: Brill, 2012).

Maghen, Ze'ev. "See No Evil: Morality and Methodology in Ibn al-Qattan al-Fasi's *Ahkam al-nazar bi-hissat al-basar*." *Islamic Law and Society* 14.3 (2007) 342–390.

Mahmood, Saba. *Politics of Piety: the Islamic Revival and the Feminist Subject* (Princeton, NJ: Princeton University Press, 2005).

Majeed, Tehnyat. "The Char Muhammad Inscription, Shafa'a, and the Mamluk Qubbat al-Mansuriyya." In Sebastian Günther and Todd Lawson (eds.) *Roads to Paradise: Eschatology and Concepts of the Hereafter in Islam*, 2 vols. (Leiden: Brill, 2017), 1010–1032.

Makdisi, George. "The Topography of Eleventh Century Baghdad: Materials and Notes (II)." *Arabica* 6, = 3 (1959): 281–309.

Maloy, John. "Celebrating the Mahmal; the Rajab Festival in Fifteenth Century Cairo." In Judith Pfeiffer and Sholeh Quinn (eds.) *History and Historiography of Post Mongol Central Asia and the Middle East: Studies in Honor of John E. Woods* (Wiesbaden: Harrassowitz, 2006), 404–427.

Mandair, Arvind-Pal Sing. *Religion and the Specter of the West: Sikhism, India, Postcoloniality, and the Politics of Translation* (New York: Columbia University Press, 2009).

Mansur, Safi al-Din. *La Risala de Safi al-Din ibn Abi al-Mansur ibn Zafir: biographies des maîtres spirituels connus par un cheikh égyptien du VIIe/XIIIe siècle*. Edited and translated by Denis Gril (Cairo: Presses de l'Insitut Français d'Archéologie Orientale, 1986).

Margoliouth, David Samuel. "Sa'diya." In *Shorter Encyclopaedia of Islam* (New York: Brill, 1991).

Marmon, Shaun. *Eunuchs and Sacred Boundaries in Islamic Society* (New York: Oxford University Press, 1995).

Martini Bonadeo, Cecilia. *The Stanford Encyclopedia of Philosophy*, s.v. "'Abd al-Latif al-Baghdadi" (Fall 2015 Edition) https://plato.stanford.edu/archives/fall2015/entries/al-baghdadi/

Mas, Ruth. "Refiguring Translation in Religious Studies." *Method and Theory in the Study of Religion* 23, (2011): 143–159.

Massignon, Louis. "Seconde note sur l'état d'avancement des études archéologiques arabes en Égypte, hors du Caire." *Bulletin de l'institut français d'archéologie orientale* 9 (1909): 83–98.

Maundrell, Henry. *A Journey from Aleppo to Jerusalem, at Easter, A.D. 1697* (Oxford: printed at the Theater, 1703).

Mayer, Leo A. *Mamluk Costume; A Survey* (Geneva: Albert Ku).

Mayer, Leo A. *Saracenic Heraldry, A Survey* (Oxford: Clarendon Press, 1933).

Mayeur-Jaouen, Catherine. "Les processions pèlerines en Égypte: pratiques carnavalesques et intinéraires politiques, les inventions successives d'une tradition." In Sylvia Chiffoleau and Anna Madoeuf (eds.) *Les pèlerinages au Maghreb et au Moyen-Orient: espaces publics, espaces du public* (Damascus: Presses de l'Institut français du proche orient, 2005), 217–233.

McClary, Richard Pian. "The Re-use of Byzantine *Spolia* in Rum Saljuq Architecture." *bfo-Journal* 1 (2015):14–22

McCutcheon, Russell T. *Critics Not Caretakers: Redescribing the Public Study of Religion* (Albany: State University of New York Press, 2001).

McCutcheon, Russell T. *Manufacturing Religion: the Discourse on Sui Generis Religion and the Politics of Nostalgia* (New York: Oxford University Press, 1997).

McGregor, Richard. "Ansari, Zakariyya." In *Encyclopaedia of Islam*, 3rd edn. (Leiden: Brill, 2007).

McGregor, Richard. "Grave visitation." In *Encyclopaedia of Islam*, 3rd edn. (Leiden: Brill, 2007).

McGregor, Richard. "Is this the End of Medieval Sufism?" In Rachida Chih, Catherine Mayeur-Jaouen, *et al.*, (eds.) *Sufism in the Ottoman Era (16th–18ᵗʰ C.)*, C(airo: Presses de l'Institut Français d'Archéologie Orientale, 2010), 83–100.

McGregor, Richard. *Sanctity and Mysticism in Medieval Egypt: The Wafa' Sufi Order and the Legacy of Ibn 'Arabi* (Albany: State University of New York, 2004).

McPherson, Joseph W. *Moulids of Egypt* (New York: Kegan Paul, 1990).

Meinecke, Michael. *Patterns of Stylistic Changes in Islamic Architecture: Local Traditions Versus Migrating Artists* (New York: New York University Press, 1996).

Meinecke-Berg, Victoria. "Spolien in der mittelalterlichen Architektur von Kairo." In Paule Posener-Krieger *et al.* (eds.) *Ägypten, Dauer und Wandel: Symposium anlässlich des 75 Jährigen Bestehens des Deutschen archäologischen Instituts Kairo am 10. und 11. Oktober 1982* (Mainz: Ph. Von Zabern, 1985), 153–159.

Meloy, John. *Imperial Power and Maritime Trade: Mecca and Cairo in the Latter Middle Ages* (Chicago: University of Chicago Press, 2012).

Melvin-Koushki, Matthew, "How to Rule the World: Occult-Scientific Manuals of the Early Modern Persian Cosmopolis." *Journal of Persianate Studies* 11, 2 (2019): 140–154.

Melvin-Koushki, Matthew, "Introduction: De-orienting the Study of Islamicate Occultism." *Arabica* 64, 3–4 (2017): 287–295.

Meri, Josef W. "A Late Medieval Syrian Pilgrimage Guide: Ibn al-Hawrani's *Al-Isharat Ila Amakin Al-Ziyarat (Guide to Pilgrimage Places)*." *Medieval Encounters* 7, 1 (2001): 3–78.

Meri, Josef W. *The Cult of the Saints Among Muslims and Jews in Medieval Syria* (New York: Oxford University Press, 2002).

Meri, Josef W. "Relics of Piety and Power in Medieval Islam." *Past and Present* supp. 5 (2010): 97–120.

Merleau-Ponty, Maurice. *Phenomenology of Perception*. Translated by Colin Smith (London: Routledge, 1962).

Merleau-Ponty, Maurice. *The Visible and the Invisible*. Translated by Alphonso Lingis (Evanston, IL: Northwest University Press, 1968).

Mernissi, Fatima. *The Forgotten Queens of Islam* (Minneapolis: University of Minnesota Press, 1993).

Meyer, Birgit and Jojada Verrips, "Aesthetics." In David Morgan (ed.) *Key Words in Religion, Media, and Culture* (New York: Routledge, 2008), 20–30.

Meyer, Birgit. "Powerful Pictures: Popular Christian Aesthetics in Southern Ghana." *Journal of the American Academy of Religion* 76, 1 (2008): 82–110.

Michot, Jean. "Les fresques du pèlerinage au Caire." *AARP; Art and Archaeology Research Papers* 13 (1978): 7–21.

Miles, Margaret R. "Image." In Mark C. Taylor (ed). *Critical Terms for Religious Studies* (Chicago: University of Chicago Press, 1998), 160–172.

Milstein, Rachel. "Futuh-i Haramayn: Sixteenth-century Illustrations of the Hajj Route." In David J. Wasserstein and Ami Ayalon (eds.) *Mamluks and Ottomans: Studies in Honor of Michael Winter* (New York: Routledge, 2006), 166–194.

Milstein, Rachel. "Shawq Nama – An Illustrated Tour of Holy Arabia." *Jerusalem Studies in Arabic and Islam* 25 (2001): 275–345.

Milwright, M. "The Cup of the Saqi: Origins of an Emblem of the Mamluk khassakiyya" *ARAM*. 9–10 (1997–98): 241–56.

Mitchel, Timothy. *Rule of Experts: Egypt, Techno-Politics, Modernity* (Berkeley: University of California Press, 2002).

Mitchell, W. J. Thomas. *Picture Theory: Essays on Verbal and Visual Expression* (Chicago: University of Chicago Press, 1994).

Mitchell, W. J. Thomas. "Showing Seeing: A Critique of Visual Culture." In Michael Ann Holly and Keith Moxey (eds.) *Art History, Aesthetics, Visual Studies* (Williamstown, MA: Clark Art Institute, 2002), 231–250.

Mitchell, W. J. Thomas. *What Do Pictures Want? The Lives and Loves of Images* (Chicago: University of Chicago Press, 2005).

Mittermaier, Amira. *Dreams that Matter: Egyptian Landscapes of the Imagination* (Berkeley: University of California Press, 2011).

Moin, Azfar. *The Millenial Sovereign: Sacred Kingship and Sainthood in Islam* (New York: Columbia University Press, 2012).

Moin, Azfar. "Sovereign Violence: Temple Destruction in India and Shrine Desecration in Iran and Central Asia." *Comparative Studies in Society and History* 57.2 (2015): 467–496.

Al-Mojan, Muhammad H. "The Textiles Made for the Prophet's Mosque at Medina" (trans. Liana Saif). In Ventia Porter and Liana Saif (eds.) *The Hajj: Collected Essays* (London: British Museum Press, 2013), 184–194.

Montasser, Dina. "Modes of Utilizing Qur'anic Inscriptions on Cairene Mamluk Religious Monuments." In Bernard O'Kane (ed.) *Creswell Photographs Re-examined: New Perspectives on Islamic Architecture* (Cairo: American University in Cairo, 2009), 187–218.

Morgan, David. "The Ecology of Images: Seeing and the Study of Religion." *Religion and Society: Advances in Research* 5 (2014): 83–105.

Morgan, David. *The Embodied Eye: Religious Visual Culture and the Social Life of Feeling* (Berkeley: University of California Press, 2012).

Morgan, David. *Visual Piety: A History and Theory of Popular Religious Images* (Berkeley: University of California Press, 2006).

Mortel, Richard T. "The Kiswa: its origins and development from pre-Islamic times until the end of the Mamluk period." *al-'Usûr* 3, 2 (1988): 30–46.

Morris, James W. "Imagining Islam: Intellect and Imagination in Islamic Philosophy,

Poetry, and Painting." *Religion and the Arts* 12 (2008): 294–318.

Moser, Stephanie. *Wondrous Curiosities: Ancient Egypt at the British Museum* (Chicago: University of Chicago Press, 2006).

Mouton, Jean-Michel "De quelques reliques conservées à Damas au Moyen-Âge." *Annales Islamologiques* 27 (1993): 245–254.

Moxey, Keith. "Visual Studies and the Iconic Turn." *Journal of Visual Culture* 7 (2008): 131–146.

Mulder, Stephennie. "The Mausoleum of Imam al-Shafiʻi." *Muqarnas* 23 (2006): 15–46.

Mulder, Stephennie. *The Shrines of the ʻAlids in Medieval Syria: Sunnis, Shiʻis and the Architecture of Coexistence* (Edinburgh: Edinburgh University Press, 2014).

Munt, Thomas H. R. *The Holy City of Medina: Sacred Space in Early Islamic Arabia* (New York: Cambridge University Press, 2014).

Muranyi, Miklos "The Emergence of Holy Places in Islam." *Jerusalem Studies in Arabic and Islam* 39, (2012): 165–171

Murata, Kazuyo *Beauty in Sufism: the Teachings of Ruzbihan Baqli* (Albany: State University of New York Press, 2016).

Naef, Silvia. "Peindre pour être moderne?" In Bernard Heyberger and Silvia Naef (eds.) *La multiplication des images en pays d'Islam* (Würtzburg: Ergon in Kommission, 2003), 189–208.

Nancy, Jean-Luc. *The Ground of the Image*. Translated by Jeff Fort (New York: Fordham University Press, 2005).

Nancy, Jean-Luc. *The Inoperative Community* (Minneapolis: University of Minnesota Press, 1991).

Al-Naqar, ʻUmar ʻAbd al-Razzaq. *The Pilgrimage Tradition in West Africa: An Historical Study with special Reference to the Nineteenth Century* (Khartoum: Khartoum University Press, 1972).

Nassar, Nahla "Dar al-Kiswa al-Sharifa: Administration and Production." In Venetia Porter (ed.) *The Hajj: Collected Essays*, 175–183 (London: British M).

Navaro-Yashin, Yael. "Affective Spaces, Melancholic Objects: Ruination and Production of Anthropological Knowledge." *Journal of the Royal Anthropological Institute* 15 (2009): 1–18.

Necipoglu, Gülru. "The Dome of the Rock as Palimpsest: ʻAbd al-Malik's Grand Narrative and Sultan Süleyman's Glosses." *Muqarnas*, 25 (2008): 17–106.

Necipoglu, Gülru. *The Topakpi Scroll – Geometry and Ornament in Islamic Architecture* (New York: Oxford University Press, 1996).

Nelson, Robert. *The Spirit of Secular Art: A History of the Sacramental Roots of Contemporary Artistic Values* (Melbourne: Monash University Press: 2007).

Nevo, Yehuda D. and Judith Koren, "The Origins of the Muslim Descriptions of the Jahili Meccan Sanctuary." *Journal of Near Eastern Studies* 49 (Jan. 1990): 23–44.

Northrup, Linda. *From Slave to Sultan: the career of al-Mansur Qalawun and the Consolidation of Mamluk Rule in Egypt and Syria (678–689/1279–1290)* (Stuttgart: Franz Steiner, 1998).

Nuseibeh, Said. *The Dome of the Rock*. (New York: Rizzoli International Publications, 1998).

Ohtoshi, Tetsuya. "Cairene Cemeteris as Public Loci in Mamluk Egypt." *Mamluk Studies Review* 10, no. 1 (2006) 83–116.

O'Kane, Bernard. "Medium and Message in the Monumental Epigraphy of Medieval Cairo." In Mohammad Gharipour and Irvin Cemil Schick (eds.) *Calligraphy and Islamic Architecture in the Muslim World* (Edinburgh: Edinburgh University Press, 2013), 416–430.

O'Kane, Bernard. "Monumental Calligraphy in Fatimid Egypt: Epigraphy in Stone, Stucco, and Wood." In by Assadullah Souren Melikian-Chirvani (ed.) *The World of the Fatimids* (Toronto: Aga Khan Museum and Munich: Hirmer Verlag, 2018), 142–159.

O'Kane, Bernard. Online datebase, *The Monumental Insriptions of Historic Cairo* https://islamicinscriptions.cultnat.org

O'Meara, Simon. "Muslim Visuality and the Visibility of Paradise and the World." In Sebastian Günther and Todd Lawson (eds.) *Roads to Paradise: Eschatology and Concepts of the Hereafter in Islam*, 2 vols. (Leiden: Brill, 2017), 555–565.

Ormos, István. *Max Herz Pasha: 1856–1919; His Life and Career*. 2 vols. (Cairo: Presses de l'Institut Français d'Archéologie Orientale, 2009).

Pahlitzsch, Johannes. "The Development of the Commemoration of the Dead until the Time of the Mamluks." *Endowment Studies* 1.1 (2017): 96–125.

Parker, Ann and Avon Neal. *Hajj Paintings: Folk Art of the Great Pilgrimage* (Cairo: American University in Cairo Press, 2009).

Patel, Youshaa. "Their Fires shall not be Visible": The Sense of Muslim Difference." *Material Religion* 14.1 (2018): 1–29.

Patrizi, Luca. "Relics of the Prophet." In Coeli Fitzpatrick and Adam H. Walker (eds.) *Muhammad in History, Thought, and Culture: An Encyclopedia of the Prophet of God*, 2 vols. (Santa Barbara: ABC-CLIO, 2014), 2:517–520.

Peters, Francis E. *The Hajj: A Muslim Pilgrimage to Mecca* (Princeton, NJ: Princeton University Press, 1994).

Peters, Francis E. *Jerusalem: the Holy City in the Eyes of Chroniclers, Visitors, Pilgrims, and Prophets* (Princeton, NJ: Princeton University Press, 1985).

Peters, Francis E. *Mecca: A Literary History of the Muslim Holy Land* (Princeton, NJ: Princeton University Press, 1994).

Petry, Carl. *Protectors or Praetorians?: The Last Mamluk Sultans and Egypt's Waning as a Great Power* (Albany: State University of New York Press, 1994).

Petry, Carl. "Robing Ceremonials in Late Mamluk Egypt: Hallowed Traditions, Shifting Protocols." In Stewart Gordon (ed.) *Robes of Honor: The Medieval Worlds of Investiture* (New York: Palgrave, 2001), 353–377.

Petry, Carl. *Twilight of Majesty: the Reigns of the Mamluk Sultans al-Ashraf Qaytbay and Qansuh al-Ghawri in Egypt* (Seattle: University of Washington Press, 1993).

Pippin, Robert B. *After the Beautiful: Hegel and the Philosophy of Pictorial Modernism* (Chicago: University of Chicago Press, 2014).

Pinney, Christopher. "Four Types of Visual Culture," in Christopher Tilley *et al.* (eds.) *Handbook of Material Culture* (London: Sage, 2006), 131–145.

Plate, S. Brent. *Walter Benjamin, Religion, and Aesthetics* (New York: Routledge, 2005).

Porter, Bertha and Rosalind L. B. Moss. *Topographical Bibliography of Ancient Egyptian Hieroglyphic Texts, Reliefs, and Paintings. Volume IV, Lower and Middle Egypt*. Microfiche edition (Oxford: Griffith Institute, 1981).

Porter, Venetia. *The Art of Hajj* (London: British Museum Press, 2012).

Porter, Venetia. "Textiles of Mecca and Medina" in Venetia Porter Venetia Porter (ed.) *Hajj: journey to the heart of Islam* (London: British Museum Press, 2012), 256–265.

Preziosi, Donald. *Art, Religion, Amnesia: The Enchantments of Credulity* (New York: Routledge, 2014).

Preziosi, Donald. *Rethinking Art History: Meditations on a Coy Science* (New Haven, CT: Yale University Press, 1989).

Promey, Sally M. "Religion, Sensation, and Materiality: An Introduction." In Sally M. Promey (ed.) *Sensational Religion: Sensory Cultures in Medieval Practice* (New Haven: Yale University Press, 2014), 1–21.

Promey, Sally M. "Situating Visual Culture." In Karen Halttunen (ed.) *A Companion to American Cultural History* (Malden, MA: Blackwell, 2014), 279–294.

Proudfoot, Wayne. *Religious Experience* (Berkeley: University of California Press, 1985).

Puerta Vilchez, José Miguel. *Aesthetics in Arabic Thought: from Pre-Islamic Arabia Through al-Andalus*, tranlated by Consuelo Lopez-Morillas (Leiden: Brill, 2017).

Rabbat, Nasser. "*'Aj'ib* and *Gharib*: Artistic Perception in Medieval Arabic Sources." *The Medieval History Journal* 9, 1 (2006): 99–113.

Rabbat, Nasser. *The Citadel of Cairo: A New Interpretation of Royal Mamluk Architecture* (New York: Brill, 1995).

Rabbat, Nasser. "The Dome of the Rock Revisited: Some Remarks on al-Wasiti's Accounts." *Muqarnas* 10 (1993): 66–75.

Rabbat, Nasser. *Mamluk History Through Architecture: Monuments, Culture and Politics in Medieval Eygpt and Syria* (New York: I.B. Tauris, 2010).

Rabbat, Nasser. "The Formation of the Neo-Mamluk Style in Modern Egypt." In Martha Pollak (ed.) *The Education of the Architect:*

Historiography, Urbanism, and the Growth of Architectural Knowledge: Essays Presented to Stanford Anderson (Cambridge, MA: MIT Press, 1997), 363–386.

Rabbat, Nasser. *Staging the City: or How Mamluk Architecture Coopted the Streets of Cairo* (Berlin: EB-Verlag, 2014).

Raghib, Yusuf. "L'auteur de l'Égypte de Murtadi fils du Gaphiph" *Arabica* 21 (1974): 203–209.

Raghib, Yusuf. "Un épisode obscure d'histoire fatimide," *Studia Islamica* 43 (1978): 125–132.

Raghib, Yusuf. "Le mausolée de Yunus al-Sa'di, est-il celui de Badr al-Jamali?" *Arabica* 20, 3 (1973): 305–7.

Raghib, Yusuf. "Les mausolées fatimides du quartier d'al-Mashahid," *Annales Islamologiques* 17 (1981): 1–30.

Raghib, Yusuf. "Les premiers monuments funéraires de l'Islam," *Annales Islamologiques* 9 (1970): 21–36.

Rambelli, Fabio and Eric R. Reinders, *Buddhism and Iconoclasm in East Asia: A History* (New York: Bloomsbury, 2012).

Rancière, Jacques. *Aisthesis: Scenes from the Aesthetic Regime of Art* (London: Verso, 2013).

Rancière, Jacques. *Mute Speech: Literature, Critical Theory, and Politics*. Translated by James Swenson (New York: Columbia University Press, 2011).

Raymond, André. *Cairo: City of History*. Translated by Willard Wood (Cairo: American University in Cairo Press, 2001).

Reid, Donald M. "Cultural Imperialism and Nationalism: The Struggle to Define and Control the Heritage of Arab Art in Egypt." *International Journal of Middle East Studies* 24, 1 (1992): 57–76.

Reid, Donald M. "The Egyptian Geographical Society: From Foreign Laymen's Society to Indigenous Professional Association." *Poetics Today* 14, 3 (1993): 539–572.

Reid, Donald M. *Whose Pharaohs? Archaeology, Museums, and Egyptian National Identity from Napoleon to World War I* (Cairo: American University in Cairo Press, 2002).

Renard, John. "Review Essay: Religion and the Arts in Islamic Studies." *Religion and the Arts* 14 (2010): 297–317.

Robinson, Arthur E. "The Mahmal of the Moslem Pilgrimage." *Journal of the Royal Asiatic Society of Great Britain and Ireland* 1 (Jan. 1931): 117–127.

Rogers, J. M. *Empire of the Sultans: Ottoman Art from the Khalili Collection* (Alexandra, VA: Art Services International, 2000).

Rosenthal, Franz. "Abu Haiyan al-Tawhidi on Penmanship." *Ars Islamica* 13 (1948): 1–30.

Ross, Alison. *Walter Benjamin's Concept of the Image* (London: Routledge, 2016).

Rosser-Owen, Miriam. "Andalusi *Spolia* in Medieval Morocco: 'Architectural Politics, Political Architecture.'" *Medieval Encounters* 20 (2014): 152–198.

Roxburgh, David, *Writing the Word of God: Calligraphy and the Qur'an* (New Haven, CT: Yale University Press, 2008).

Ruffle, Karen G. "Presence in Absence: The Formation of Reliquary Shi'ism in Qutb Shahi Hyderabad." *Material Religion* 13.3 (2017): 329–535.

Rubin, Uri. "The Ka'ba: Aspects of Its Ritual Functions and Position in Pre-Islamic and Early Islamic Times." *Jerusalem Studies in Arabic and Islam* 8, 1 (1986): 97–131.

Sabra, Adam. "From Artisan to Courtier: Sufism and Social Mobility in Fifteenth-Century Egypt." In Roxani E. Margariti, Adam Sabra, and Petra M. Sijpesteijn (ed.) *Histories of the Middle East: Studies in Middle Eastern Society, Economy and Law in Honor of A. L. Udovitch* (Leiden: Brill, 2011), 213–232.

Saeed, Abdullah. "Salafiya, Modernism, and Revival." In John L. Esposito and Emad El-Din Shahin (eds.) *The Oxford Handbook of Islam and Politics* (New York: Oxford University Press, 2013), 27–41.

Sahas, Daniel J. "Iconoclasm." In *Encyclopaedia of the Qur'an* (Leiden: Brill, 2012).

Sardi, Maria. "Mamluk Textiles." In Margaret S. Graves (ed.) *Islamic Art, Architecture and Material Culture: New Perspectives* (Oxford: Archaeopress, 2012, 7–14.

Sardi, Maria. "Weaving for the Hajj under the Mamluks." In Ventia Porter and Liana Saif (eds.) *The Hajj: Collected Essays* (London: British Museum Press, 2013), 169–174.

Sanders, Paula. *Ritual, Politics, and the City in Fatimid Cairo* (New York: State University of New York, 1994).

Sauvaget, Jean. *Alep: essai sur le développement d'une grande ville syrienne, des origines au milieu du XIXe siècle* (Paris: P. Guenther, 1941).

Al-Sayyid, Muhammad 'Ali. *Min durub al-Hajj fi Misr* (Cairo: Al-Hay'a al-'Amma li-Qusur al-Thaqafa, 2010).

Sauvaget, Jean. "Deux sanctuaires chiites d'Alep." *Syria* 9, 3 (1928): 224–237.

Schielke, Joska S. *The Perils of Joy: Contesting Mulid Festivals in Contemporary Egypt* (Syracuse, NY: Syracuse University Press, 2012).

Schienerl, Peter W. "Kameldarstellungen im ägyptischen Schmuck – und Amulettwesen." *Archiv für Völkerkunde* 33 (1979): 137–156.

Schimmel, Annemarie. *And Muhammad is His Messenger: the Veneration of the Prophet in Islamic Piety* (Chapel Hill: University of North Carolina Press, 1985).

Sedgwick, Mark. *Muhammad Abduh* (Oxford: One World, 2010).

Segal, Robert. "In Defense of Reductionism." *Journal of the American Academy of Religion* 51, 1 (1983): 97–124.

Shafi', Muhammad. "A Description of the Two Sanctuaries of Islam by Ibn 'Abd Rabbihi (d. 940)" in Thomas W. Arnold, and Reynold A. Nicholson (eds.) *A Volume of Oriental Studies Presented to Edward G. Browne* (Cambridge: Cambridge University Press, 1922), 416–438.

Shalem, Avinoam. "Aesthetics of Resistance: The "Unbelievable" Idol, Its Life, and Its Dual Death." In Margit Kern and Klaus Krüger (eds.) *Transcultural Imaginations of the Sacred* (Leiden: Brill, 2019), 180–196.

Shalem, Avinoam. "Islamishe Objekte in Kirchenshätzen." In Christine van Eickels and Klaus van Eickels, (eds.) *Das Bistum Bamberg in der Welt des Mittelalters* (Bamburg: University of Bamberg Press, 2007), 163–176.

Shalem, Avinoam. "Made for Show: The Medieval Treasury of the Ka'ba in Mecca." In Bernard O'Kane (ed.) *The Iconography of Islamic Art: Studies in Honor of Robert Hillenbrand* (Edinburgh: Edinburgh University Press, 2005), 269–284.

Shalem, Avinoam. "Multivalent Paradigms of Interpretation and the Aura or Anima of the Object." In Benoît Junod, *et al.* (eds.) *Islamic Art and the Museum: Approaches to Art and Archeology of the Muslim World in the Twentieth-Century* (London: Saqi, 2011), 101–115.

Sharf, Robert. "On the Allure of Buddhist Relics." *Representations* 66 (Spring 1999): 75–99.

Sharon, Moshe. *Corpus Inscriptionum Arabicarum Palaestinae*, 6 vols. (Leiden: Brill, 1997).

Shaw, Wendy. *Possessors and Possessed: Museums, Archaeology, and the Visualization of History in the Late Ottoman Empire* (Berkeley: University of California Press, 2003).

Shehab, Bahia. "Fatimid Kufi Epigraphy on the Gates of Cairo: Between Royal Patronage and Civil Utility." In Mohammad Gharipour and Irvin Cemil Schick (eds.) *Calligraphy and Architecture in the Muslim World* (Edinburgh: Edinburgh University Press, 2013), 275–292.

Shoshan, Boaz. "Grain Riots and the 'Moral Economy': Cairo, 1350–1517." *Journal of Interdisciplinary History* 10, 3 (1980): 459–478.

Shoshan, Boaz. *Popular Culture in Medieval Cairo* (New York: Cambridge University Press, 1993).

Silverstone, Roger. "The Medium is the Museum: on objects and the logics in time and spaces." In Roger Miles and Lauro Zalvala (eds.) *Towards the Museum of the Future: New European Perspectives* (New York: Routledge, 1994), 161–176.

Sindawi, Khalid. "The Head of Husayn Ibn 'Ali: From Decapitation to Burial, Its Various Places of Burial, and the Miracles That It Performed." *Journal of Ancient Near Eastern Studies* 40 (2003): 245–258.

Sirriyyah, Elizabeth. "The Journeys of 'Abd al-Ghani al-Nabulusi in Palestine (1101/1690 and 1105/1693)." *Journal of Semitic Studies* 24, 1 (1979): 55–69.

Smith, Martyn. "Pyramids in Medieval Islamic Landscape: Perceptions and Narratives." *Journal of the American Research Center in Egypt* 43 (2007): 1–14.

Sokoly, Jochen. "Textiles and Identity." In Finbarr Barry Flood and Gülru Necipoglu (eds.) *A Companion to Islamic Art and*

Architecture, 2 vols. (New York: John Wiley & Sons, 2017) 275–299.

Soucek, Priscilla. "Material Culture and the Qur'an." *Encyclopaedia of the Qur'an* (Leiden: Brill, 2012).

Sourdel, Dominique. "Questions de ceremonial 'abbaside'." *Revue des Études Islamiques* 28 (1960): 121–48.

Sourdel, Dominique. "Robes of Honor in 'Abbasid Baghdad During the Eighth to Eleventh Centuries." In Stuart Gordon (ed.) *Robes of Honor: the Medieval World of Investiture* (New York: Palgrave, 2001), 137–146.

Sourdel-Thomine, Janine. "Les anciens lieux de pélerinage." *Bulletin d'Etudes Orientales* 14 (1951): 65–85.

Sourdel-Thomine, Janine, Dominique Sourdel, Jean-Michel Mouton, and Clément Moussé. "La découverte d'un culte de *nabi* Zakariyya à la grande mosquée de Damas à l'époque ayyoubide." *Der Islam* 90, 2 (2013): 412–444.

Sourdel-Thomine and Dominque Sourdel, "Certificats de pèlerinage par procuration à l'époque mamlouke." *Jerusalem Studies in Arabic and Islam* 25 (2001): 212–233.

Sperl, Stefan. "Crossing Enemy Boundaries: al-Buhturi's Ode on the Ruins of Ctesiphon re-read in the Light of Virgil and Wilfred Owen." *Bulleting of the School of Oriental and African Studies* 69 (2006): 365–379.

St. Elie, Anastase Marie de. "Le culte rendu par les Musulmans aux sandales de Mahomet." *Anthropos* 5, 2 (1910): 363–366.

Stauth, Georg. *Ägyptische heilige Orte II, zwischen den steinen des pharao und islamischer moderne* (Bielefeld: Transcript-Verlag, 2015).

Stauth, Georg. "Abdallah b. Salam: Egypt, Late Antiquity and Islamic Sainthood." In Johann P. Arnason, Armando Salvatore, Georg Stauth (eds.) *Islam in Process: Historical and Civilizational Perspectives* (Piscataway, NJ: Transaction, 2006), 158–189.

Stetkevych, Suzanne P. *The Mantle Odes: Arabic Praise Poems to the Prophet Muhammad* (Bloomington: Indiana University Press, 2010).

Stewart, Devin J. "Popular Shiism in Medieval Egypt." *Studia Islamica* 84 (1996): 35–66.

Stillman, Yedida K. *Arab Dress, a Short History*. Edited by Norman Stillman (London: Brill, 2003).

Stricker, Bruno H. "Le Naos Vert de Memphis." *Annales du Service des Antiquités de l'Égypte* 39 (1939): 215–226.

Strudwick, Nigel. *Masterpieces of Ancient Egypt* (Austin: University of Texas Press, 2006).

Sunbul, Sharif and Tarek Atia. *Mulid! Carnivals of Faith* (Cairo: American University in Cairo Press, 1999).

Tabbaa, Yasser. *Constructions of Power and Piety in Medieval Aleppo* (University Park: Pennsylvania University Press, 1997).

Tabbaa, Yasser. "The Mosque of Nur al-Din in Mosul 1170–1171." *Annales Islamologiques* 36 (2002): 339–360.

Tabbaa, Yasser. "The Transformation of Arabic Writing: pt. 2, the Public Text." *Ars Orientalis* 24 (1994): 119–147.

Tabbaa, Yasser. *The Transformation of Islamic Art during the Sunni Revival* (Seattle: University of Washington Press, 2001).

Talmon-Heller, Daniella. *Islamic Piety in Medieval Syria: Mosques, Cemeteries and Sermons under the Zangids and Ayyubids (1146–1260)* (Leiden: Brill, 2007).

Talmon-Heller, Daniella. "Scriptures as Holy Objects: Preliminary Comparative Remarks on the Qur'an and the Torah in the Medieval Middle East." *Intellectual History of the Islamicate World* 4 (2016): 210–244.

Talmon-Heller, Daniella and Benjamin Z. Kedar, Yitzhak Reiter. "Vicissitudes of a Holy Place: Construction, Destruction and Commemoration of Mashhad Husayn in Ascalon." *Der Islam* 93(1) (2016): 182–215.

Taneja. Anand V. *Jinnealogy: Time, Islam, and Ecological Thought in the Medieval Ruins of Delhi* (Palo Alto, CA: Stanford University Press, 2018).

Al-Tawil, Hashim Mohammad. "Early Arab Icons: Literary and Archaelogical Evidence for the Cult of Religious Images in Pre-Islamic Arabia" PhD diss., University of Iowa, Iowa City, 1993. University Microfilms International.

Taylor, Christopher. *In the Vicinity of the Right-eous: Ziyara and the Veneration of Muslim Saints in Late Medieval Egypt.* (Leiden: Brill, 1998).

Taymur Basha, Ahmad. *al-Athar al-nabawiyya* (Cairo: Matba'a Dar al-Kutub al-'Arabiyya, 1951).

Tezkan, Hülya. "Ka'ba Covers from the Top-kapi Palace Collection and their Inscriptions." In Fahmida Suleman (ed.) *Word of God, Art of Man. The Qur'an and it Creative Expressions* (New York: Oxford University Press, 1997), 227–238.

Tolmacheva, Marina. "Female Piety and Patron-age in the Medieval 'Hajj'." In Gavin R.G. Hambly (ed.) *Women in the Medieval Islamic World: Power, Patronage, and Piety* (New York: St. Martin's Press, 1998), 161–180.

Toorawa, Shawkat M. "A Portrait of 'Abd al-Latif al-Baghdadi's Education and Instruc-tion." in Joseph Lowry, Devin J. Stewart, and Shawkat M. Toorawa (eds.) *Law and Education in Medieval Islam: Studies in Memory of Professor George Makdisi* (Cambridge: E. J. W. Gibb Memorial Trust, 2004), 91–109.

Traboulsi, Samer "An Early Refutation of Muhammad ibn Abd al-Wahhab's Reformist Views," *Die Welt des Islams* 43 (2002): 373–415.

Trainor, Kevin. "*Pars pro toto*: On Comparing Relic Practices." *Numen* 57 (2010): 267–283.

Tresse, René. *Le pèlerinage syrien aux villes saintes de l'Islam* (Paris: Imprimerie Chaumette, 1937).

Van Bladel, Kevin. *The Arabic Hermes: From Pagan Sage to Prophet of Science* (New York: Oxford University Press, 2009).

Van Leeuwen, Richard. *Waqfs and Urban Struc-tures: The Case of Ottoman Damascus* (Leiden: Brill, 1999).

Van Reenen, Daan. "The Bilderverbot; a New Survey." *Der Islam* 67 (1990): 27–77.

Van Steenbergen, Jo. "Ritual, Politics, and the City in Mamluk Cairo: The Bayna l-Qasrayn as a Mamluk 'lieu de mémoire', 1250–1382." In Alexander D. Beihammer *et al.* (eds.) *Court Ceremonies and Rituals of Power in Byzantium and the Medieval Mediterranean: Comparative Perspec-tives*, edited by, 227–271 (Leiden: Brill, 2013).,

Vásquez, Manuel. *More Than Belief: A Materialist Theory of Religion* (New York: Oxford Uni-versity Press, 2011).

Vattimo, Gianni. *Art's Claim to Truth*, edited by Santiago Zabala. Translated by Luca D'Isanto (New York: Columbia University Press, 2010).

Vauchez, André. *Sainthood in the Later Middle Ages.* Translated by Jean Birrell (New York: Cambridge University Press, 1997).

Vaziri, Mostafa. *Buddhism in Iran: An Anthropo-logical Approach to Traces and Influences* (New York: Palgrave Macmillan, 2012).

Veccia Vaglieri, Laura. "Ibrahim 'Abd Allah." In *Encyclopaedia of Islam.* 2nd edn. (Leiden: Brill, 2012).

Veinstein, Gilles. "Holy Cities of the Hijaz under the Ottomans" In A. I. Al-Ghabban (ed.) *Roads of Arabia: Archaeology and History of the Kingdom of Saudi Arabia* (Paris: Somogy Art Publishers, 2010), 522–545.

Walker, Bthany J. "Commemorating the Sacred Spaces of the Past: The Mamluks and the Umayyad Mosque at Damascus." *Near Eastern Archaeology* 67.1 (Mar., 2004): 26–39.

Warner, Nicholas. *The Monuments of Historic Cairo: A Map and Descriptive Catalogue* (Cairo: American University in Cairo Press, 2004).

Weisman, Itzchak. *Taste of Modernity: Sufism, Salafiyya, and Arabism in Late Ottoman Damas-cus* (Leiden: Brill, 2001).

Wenzel, Christian H. *An Introduction to Kant's Aesthetics: Core Concepts and Problems* (Malden, MA: Blackwell, 2005).

Wheeler, Brannon M. "Collecting the Dead Body of Muhammad: Hair, Nails, Sweat and Spit." In Christianne Gruber and Avinoam Shalem (ed.) *The Image of the Prophet Between Ideal and Ideology: A Scholarly Investigation* (Berlin: Walter de Gruyter, 2014), 45–64.

Wheeler, Brannon M. "Gift of the Body." *Numen* 57 (2010): 341–388.

Wheeler, Brannon. M. *Mecca and Eden: Ritual, Relics, and Territory in Islam* (Chicago: Univer-sity of Chicago Press, 2006).

Whelan, Estelle. "Origins of the Mihrab Mujaw-waf: A Reinterpretation." *International Journal of Middle East Studies* 18, 2 (1986): 205–223.

Wickett, Elizabeth (dir.) *For Those Who Sail to Heaven*. Icarus Films, 200-? VHS.

Wiet, Gaston. *Catalogue général du Musée de l'art islamique du Caire. Inscriptions historiques sur pierre* (Cairo: Presses de l'Institut français d'archéologie orientale, 1971).

Wiet, Gaston. *Matériaux pour un corpus inscriptionum arabicum (Première partie Égypte; tome deuxième – Égypte)* (Cairo: Presses de Institut Français d'Achéologie Orientale, 1894–1903).

Wiet, Gaston. *Mohammed 'Ali et les beaux-arts* (Cairo: Dar al-Ma 'arif, 1959).

Williams, Caroline. "The Cult of the Alid Saints in the Fatimid Monuments of Cairo. Part I: The Mosque of al-Aqmar." *Muqarnas* 1 (1983): 37–52.

Williams, Caroline. "Islamic Cairo: Endangered Legacy." *The Middle East Journal* 29 (1985): 231–246.

Williams, Caroline. *Islamic Monuments in Cairo: A Practical Guide*. 4th edn. (Cairo: American University in Cairo Press, 1993).

Williams, Caroline. "The Qur'anic Inscriptions on the Tabut of al-Husayn in Cairo." *Islamic Art* 2 (1987): 3–14.

Williams, Caroline. "The Victorian Invention of Medieval Cairo: A Case Study of Medivalism and the Construction of the East." *Middle East Studies Association Bulletin* 37, 2 (2003): 179–198.

Williams, John Alden. "The Khanqah of Siryaqus; a Mamluk Royal Religious Foundation." In Arnold H. Green (ed.) *In Quest of an Islamic Humanism: Arabic and Islamic Studies in Memory of Mohamed al-Nowaihi* (Cairo: American University in Cairo Press, 1984), 110–119.

Wissa, Myriam. "Sur quelques pratiques de remploi du marbre et du calcaire en Égypt: incursion au monastère copte de saint Jérémie à Saqqara." *Ancient West and East* 9 (2010): 221–237.

Yamani, Ahmad Zaki. *The House of Khadijah bin Khuwaylid*, translated by 'Abdallah Abdel-Haleem (London: al-Furqan, 2014).

Young, William C. "The Ka'ba, Gender, and the Rites of Pilgrimage." *International Journal of Middle East Studies* 25, 2 (1993): 285–300.

Zadeh, Travis. "Drops of Blood: Charisma and Political Legitimacy in the Translatio of the Uthmanic Codex of al-Andalus." *Journal of Arabic Literature* 39 (2008): 321–346.

Zadeh, Travis. "Touching and Ingesting: Early Debates over the Material Qur'an." *Journal of the American Oriental Society* 129, 3 (2009): 443–466.

Zaki Pasha, Ahmed. "Notice sur les couleurs nationales de l'Égypte musulmane." *Bulletin de l'Institut d'Égypte* 2 (1919): 61–95.

Zangwill, Nick. "Unkantian Notions of Disinterest" *British Journal of Aesthetics*, 32, 2 (1992): 149–152.

Zarcone, Thierry. "Pilgrimage to the 'Second Meccas' and 'Ka'bas' of Central Asia." In Alexandre Papas, Thomas Welsford, and Theirry Zarcone (eds.) *Central Asian Pilgrims: Hajj Routes and Pious Visits between Central Asia and the Hijaz* (Berlin: K. Schwarz, 2012), 251–277.

Zargar, Ali Cyrus. *Sufi Aesthetics: Beauty, Love, and the Human Form in Ibn 'Arabi and 'Iraqi* (Columbia: University of South Carolina Press, 2011).

Zargar, Ali Cyrus. *The Polished Mirror: Storytelling and the Pursuit of Virtue in Islamic Philosophy and Sufism* (London: Oneworld, 2017).

SOURCES

Abu al-Lata'if, Ibn Faris. *Al-Minah al-Ilahiyya min manaqib al-sadat al-Wafa'iyya*, published as an appendix to Muhammad Wafa', *al-Masami'* (Beirut: Dar al-Kutub al-'Ilmiyya, 2007).

'Abd al-Nabi, Muhammad. *Sidi 'Abdallah ibn Salam*. Mansoura, Egypt: n.p., n.d.

Alexandrakis, Aphrodite and Nicholas Moutafakis (eds.). *Neoplatonism and Western Aesthetics* (Albany: State University of New York, 2002).

Al-Armani, Abu Salih. *The Churches and Monasteries of Egypt and Some Neighboring Countries, Attributed to Abu Salih, the Armenian*. Translated by Basil T. A. Evetts (Oxford: Clarendon, 1895).

Al-Azraqi, Muhammad ibn 'Abd Allah. *Akhbar Makka wa ma ja'a fi-ha min al-athar*. 2 vols. (Mecca: Dar al-Thaqafa, 2001).

Al-Baghdadi, 'Abd al-Latif. *The Eastern Key – Kitab al-ifada wa al-i'tibar*. Translated by Ivy E. Zand, John A. Videan, and Kamal Hafuth (London: George Allen & Unwin, 1964).

Al-Baghdadi, 'Abd al-Latif. *Relation de l'Égypte*. Translated by Antoine Isaac de Sacy (Paris: Imprimerie impériale, 1810).

Al-Baladhuri, Ahmad. *Futuh al-buldan* (Beirut: Dar al-Kutub al-'Ilmiyya, 2014).

Al-Batanuni, Muhammad. *Al-Rihla al-Hijaziyya: li-Wali al-Ni'am al-Hajj 'Abbas Hilmi Basha al-Thani Khadiw Misr bi-qalam Muhammad Labib al-Batanuni*. 2nd edn. (Cairo: Matba'at al-Jamaliyya 1911).

Al-Biruni, Muhammad ibn Ahmad. *AlBeruni's India: an Account of the Religion, Philosophy, Literature, Geography, Chronology, Astronomy, Customs, Laws and Astrology of India About A.D. 1030*, 2 vols., Translated by Eduard Sachau (London: Kegan Paul, 1914).

Al-Biruni, Muhammad ibn Ahmad. *Kitab al-Biruni fi tahqiq ma li'l-Hind* (Andhra Pradesh: Osmania, 1958).

Al-Bukhari, Muhammad ibn Isma'il. *Sahih al-Bukhari*. 9 vols. (Beirut: Dar al-Fikr, 1994).

Celebi, Evliya. *Al-Rihla al-Hijaziyya*. Translated by Al-Safsafi Ahmad al-Mursi (Cairo: Dar al-Afaq al-'Arabi, 1999).

Celebi, Evliya. *Siyahatnameh Misr*. Translated by Muhammad 'Awni (Cairo: Dar al-Kutub wa al-Watha'iq al-Qawmiyya, 2003).

Al-Dawadari, Abu Bakr. *Kanz al-durar wa jami'al-ghurar*. 9 vols. (Wiesbaden: Harrassowitz, 1961).

Edwards, Amelia. *A Thousand Miles Up the Nile* (London: Longmans, Green, 1877).

Galen. *On the Usefulness of the Parts of the Body*. Translated by Margaret T. May (Ithaca, NY: Cornell University Press, 1968).

Al-Ghazali, Muhammad. *Ihya 'ulum al-din*. 4 vols. (Cairo: Dar al-Taqwa, 2000).

Ginzberg, Louis. *The Legends of the Jews*. Translated by Paul Radin. 7 vols. (Baltimore: The Johns Hopkins University Press, 1998).

Al-Hamdani, Ibn Ahmad. *The Antiquities of South Arabia*. Translated by Nabih A. Faris (Princeton, NJ: Princeton University Press, 1938).

Al-Harawi, 'Ali. *Guide des lieux de pèlerinage*. Translated by Janine Sourdel-Thomine (Damascus: Presses de l'Institut français de Damas, 1957).

Al-Harawi, 'Ali. *al-Isharat ila ma'rifat al-ziyarat* (Cairo: Maktabat al-Thaqafa al-Diniyya, 2002).

Al-Harawi, 'Ali. *A Lonely Wayfarer's Guide to Pilgrimage*. Translated by Joseph W. Meri (Princeton, NJ: Darwin Press, 2004).

Hasselquist, Frederick. *Voyages and Travels in the Levant; In the Years 1749, 50, 51, 52*. Translated by Charles Linnæus (London: L. Davis and C. Reymers, 1766).

Ibn 'Arabi, Muhy al-Din. *Fusus al-hikam* (Beirut: Dar al-Kutub al-'Arabi, 1946).

Ibn 'Arabi, Muhy al-Din. *Al-Futuhat al-makkiyya*. 8 vols. (Beirut: Dar al-Fikr, 1994).

Ibn 'Arabi, Muhy al-Din. *Al-Kawkab al-durri fi manaqib Dhi al-Nun al-Misri* (Beirut: Dar al-Kutub al-'Ilmiyya, 2005).

Ibn 'Asakir, 'Ali ibn al-Hasan. *La Description de Damas d'Ibn 'Asakir, historien mort à Damas en 571/1176*. Translated by Nikita Élisséeff (Damascus: Institut français du proche orient, 2008).

Ibn 'Asakir, 'Ali ibn al-Hasan. *Ta'rikh madina Dimashq* 80 vols. (Beirut: Dar al-Fikr, 1995).

Ibn al-Athir, 'Izz al-Din. *Al-Kamil fi al-tarikh*. 11 vols. (Beirut: Dar al-Kutub al-'Ilmiyya, 1987).

Ibn Bahkhila, *'Uyun al-haqa'iq* Cairo: Dar al-Kutub al-Misriyya, ms Tasawwuf Taymur 180.

Ibn Battuta, 'Abdallah. *Rihla* (Cairo: al-Maktaba al-Tijariyya al-Kubra, 1958).

Ibn Fahd, Muhammad. *Ithaf al-wara bi-akhbar Umm al-qura*. 5 vols. (Mecca: Matba'a Jami'at Umm al-Qura, 1983).

Ibn al-Farid, 'Umar. *'Umar ibn al-Farid: Sufi Verse, Saintly Life*. trans Th. Emil Homerin (New York: Paulist Press, 2001).

Ibn al-Hajj, Muhammad. *al-Madkhal*. 4 vols. (Cairo: al-Matba'a al-Misriyya, 1929).

Ibn Haytham, Muhammad. *The Optics of Ibn al-Haytham* 2 vols. Translated by Abdelhamid I. Sabra (London: Warburg Institute, 1989).

Ibn Ishaq, Muhammad. *The Life of Muhammad*. Translated by Alfred Guillaume (New York: Oxford University Press, 1967).

Ibn Ishaq, Muhammad. *al-Sira al-Nabwiyya* (Beirut: Dar al-Kutub al-'Ilmiyya, 2004).

Ibn Iyas, Muhammad *Bada'i 'al-zuhur fi waqa'i'- al-duhur*. 5 vols. (Cairo: Al-Hay'a al-Misriyya al-'Amma li'l-Kitab, 1982–1985).

Ibn Iyas, Muhammad. *Journal d'un bourgeois du Caire: chronique d'Ibn Iyas*. Translated by Gaston Wiet. 2 vols. (Paris: Armond Colin, 1955–1960).

Ibn Jubayr, Muhammad ibn Ahmad. *Rihla Ibn Jubayr* (Beirut: Dar Sadir, 1964).

Ibn Jubayr, Muhammad ibn Ahmad. *The Travels of Ibn Jubayr*. Translated by Roland Broadhurst (London: Goodword, 2016).

Ibn al-Kalbi. *Book of Idols Being a Translation from the Arabic of the Kitab al-asnam*. Translated by Nabih Amin Faris (Princeton, NJ: Princeton University Press, 2015).

Ibn Kathir, 'Imad al-Din. *Al-Bidaya wa-l-nihaya*. 8 vols. (Cairo: Dar al-Rayyan li'l-Turath, 1988).

Ibn Kathir, 'Imad al-Din. *Tafsir al-Qur'an al-'azim*. 4 vols. Cairo: Dar al-Taqwa, 2002).

Ibn Manzur. *Lisan al-Arab*. Edited by 'Abdallah al-Kabir et al., 6 + 3 vols. (Cairo: Dar al-Ma 'arif, 1986).

Ibn Muyassar, Taj al-Din. *Akhbar Misr* (Cairo: Presses de l'Insitute Français d'Archéologie Orientale, 1981).

Ibn Sa'd, Muhammad. *Kitab al-tabaqat al-kabir*. 9 vols. (Leiden: Brill, 1905–1940).

Ibn Sa'd, Muhammad. *al-Tabaqat*, 11 vols. (Cairo: Maktabat al-Khanji, 2001).

Ibn Shahin, Khalil. *La Zubda Kachf al-Mamalik de Khalil al-Zahiri*. Translated by Jean Gaulmier (Beirut: Presses de l'Institut Français de Damas, 1950).

Ibn Sina, *A Treatise on Love by Ibn Sina*. Translated by Emil Ludwig Fakhenheim. *Medieval Studies* 7, 1 (1945): 208–228.

Ibn Taghribirdi, Yusuf. *Muntakhabat min hawadith al-duhur fi mada al-ayyam wa al-shuhur* William Popper (ed.) 4 vols. (Berkeley: University of California Press, 1930–1942**).**

Ibn Taghribirdi, Yusuf. *History of Egypt 1382–1469 AD, Part I, 1382–1399 AD*. Translated by William Popper (Berkeley: University of California.

Ibn Taghribirdi, Yusuf. *Al-Manhal al-Safi wa al-mustawifa ba'd al-wafi*. 8 vols.) (Cairo: al-Hay'a al-Misriyya al-'Amma lil-Kitab, 1984).

Ibn Taghribirdi, Yusuf. *Al-Nujum al-Zahira fi muluk Misr wa al-Qahira* 8 vols.) (Cairo: Matba'at Dar al-Kutub: 2005).

Ibn Taymiyya, Taqi al-Din Ahmad. *Majmu 'Fatawa Shaykh al-Islam Ibn Taymiyya*. 37 vols. (Madina: Wizarat al-Shu'un al-Islamiyya, 2004).

Ibn Taymiyya, Taqi al-Din Ahmad. *Makan ra's al-Husayn: Hal mashhad ra's al-Husayn bi-l-Qahira aw 'Asqalan?* (Beirut: Dar al-Jil, 1997).

Ibn 'Uthman, Muwaffaq al-Din. *Murshid al-zuwwar ila qubur al-abrar* (Cairo: Al-Dar al-Misriyya al-Lubnaniyya, 1995).

'Iraqi, Fakhr al-Din. *Fakhr al-Din 'Iraqi: Divine Flashes*. Translated by William Chittick and Peter Lambton (New York: Paulist Press, 1982).

Al-Jabarti, 'Abd al-Rahman. *'Aja'ib al-athar fi tarajim al-akhbar*. 4 vols. (Cairo: al-Matba'a Dar al-Kutub al-Misriyya, 1998).

Al-Jabarti, 'Abd al-Rahman. *'Abd al-Rahman al-Jabarti's History of Egypt*. Translated and edited by Thomas Philipp, Moshe Pearlmann, et al., 4 vols. (Stuttgart: Steiner, 1994).

Al-Jahiz, Abu 'Uthman. *al-Bayan wa al-tabyin*. 4 vols. in 2 (Cairo: Maktabat al-Khanji, 1998).

Al-Jahiz, Abu 'Uthman. *The Epistle on Singing-Girls*. Translated by Alfred Felix Landon Beaston (Warminster: Aris & Phillips, 1980).

Jawad, 'Ali. *Al-Mufassal fi tarikh al-'Arab qabl al-Islam*. 10 vols. (Beirut: Dar al-'Ilm li'l-Malayin, 1968–1973).

Al-Kisa'i, Muhammad ibn 'Abdallah. *Tales of the Prophets*. Translated by Wheeler Thackston, Jr. (Chicago: Kazi, 1997).

Khusraw, Nasir. *Nasir-i Khusraw's Book of Travels [Safarnama]: A Parallel Persian-English Text*. Translated by William M. Thackston, Jr. (Costa Mesa, CA: Mazda Publishers, 2001).

Khusraw, Nasir. *Safer Nameh: Relation du Voyage de Nassiri Khosrau en Syrie, en Palestine, en Égypte, en Arabie et en Perse pendant les années de l'hégire 437–444 (1035–1042)* (Paris: Ernest Leroux, 1881).

Al-Maqqari, Ahmad. *Wasf na'l al-nabi al-musamma bi-fath al-muta'al fi madih al-na'al* (Cairo: Dar al-Qadi 'Ayyad, 1997).

Al-Maqrizi, Taqi al-Din. *Itti'âz al-hunafa' bi akhbar al-a'immat al-fatimiyyin al-khulafa'*. 3 vols. (Cairo: Lajnat Ihya al-Turath al-Islami, 1967–1973).

Al-Maqrizi, Taqi al-Din. *Al-Mawa'iz wa al-i'tibar fi dhirk al-khitat wa al-athar*. 5 vols. (London: Al-Furqan Islamic Heritage Foundation, 2013).

Al-Maqrizi, Taqi al-Din. *Al-Suluk li-ma'rifa duwwal al-muluk*. 8 vols. (Beirut: Dar al-Kutub al-'Ilmiyya, 1997).

Al-Maqrizi, Taqi al-Din. *Al-Dhahab al-masbuk fi dhikr man hajja min al-khulafa' wa'l-muluk* (Cairo: Maktabat al-Khanji, 1955).

Al-Mas'udi, Abu al-Hasan. *Les Prairies d'Or (Muruj al-dhahab)*. Arabic with French translation by Charles Barbier de Meynard and Michel Pavet De Courteille. 9 vols. (Paris: L'Imprimerie Nationale, 1914).

Al-Mawardi, 'Ali ibn Muhammad. *Al-Ahkam al-sultaniyya wa al-walayat al-'Arabiyya* (Cairo: Mustafa al-Babi al-Halabi, 1966).

Mubarak, 'Ali Basha. *Khitat al-jadida*. 20 volumes in 4 (Cairo, Buqlaq: al-Matba'a al-Kubra al-Amiriyya, 1888).

Muhammad, Suad Mahir, *Masajid Misr wa awliya'uha al-salihun* (Cairo: al-Majlis al-A'la lil-Shu'un al-Islamiyya, 1971).

Muhammad, Suad Mahir. *Mukhallafat al-Rasul fi al-masjid al-Husayn* (Cairo: Dar al-Nashr, 1989).

Murtada, Ibn al-'Afif, *L'Égypte de Murtadi fils du Gaphiphe*. Translated by Gaston Wiet (Frankfurt: Intstitute for the History of Arabic-Islamic Science at the Johann Wolfgang Goethe University, 2008).

Al-Nabulusi, 'Abd al-Ghani. *Hadra al-unsiyya fi al-rihla al-Qudsiyya* (Beirut: Al-Masadir, 1990).

Al-Nabulusi, 'Abd al-Ghani. *Al-Haqiqa wa al-majaz fi al-rihla ila bilad al-Sham wa Misr wa al-Hijaz* (Cairo: al-Hay'a al-Misriyya al-'Amma li-l-Kitab, 1986).

Al-Nahrawani, 'Ali Muhammad. *Kitab al-i'lam bi-a'lam bayt Allah al-haram* (Mecca: al-Maktaba al-Tijariyya, 1996).

Poole, Sophia Lane. *The Englishwoman in Egypt: Letters from Cairo* (Philadelphia: G.B. Zieber & Co., 1845).

Qadi 'Iyad, *Muhammad Messenger of Allah*. Translated by Aysha Bewley (Inverness: Madinah Press, 1991).

Al-Qalqashandi, Shihab al-Din. *Subh al-a'sha*. 14 vols. (Cairo: Dar al-Kutub al-Misriyya, 1922).

Al-Qifti, 'Ali ibn Yusuf. *Ta'rikh al-hukama* (Leipzig: Dieterichsche Verlagsbuchhandlung, 1908).

Qushayri, Abu al-Qasim. *Al-Qushayri's Epistle on Sufism: al-Risala al-qushayriyya fi 'ilm al-tasawwuf*. Translated by Alexander Knysh (Reading: Garnet, 2007).

Rif'at, Ibrahim. *Mir'at al-Haramayn*. 2 vols. (Cairo: Dar al-Kutub al-Misriyya, 1925).

Al-Sabi, Hilal. *The Rules and Regulations of the 'Abbasid Court*. Translated by Elie Salem (Beirut: American University of Beirut, 1977).

Sabri Pasha, Eyüp. *Mawsu'a Mir'at al-Haramayn al-Sharifayn wa Jazirat al-'Arab*. 2 vols. (Cairo: Dar al-Afaq al-'Arabiyya, 2004).

Sabri Pasha, Eyüp. *Mir'at al-Haramayn*. 5 vols. (Istanbul: Matbaa-i Bahriye, 1883).

Sadiq Basha, Muhammad. *Rihla mish'al al-mahmal* (Beirut: Dar al-'Arabiyya li'l-Mawsu'at, 2014).

Al-Sakhawi, Muhammad. *Al-Daw' al-lami'fi a'yan al-qarn al-tasi'*. 10 vols. (Beirut: Dar al-Jil, n.d.)

Al-Sakhawi, Muhammad. *Al-Tibr al-masbuk fi dhayl al-muluk*. 4 vols. (Cairo: Dar al-Kutub wa'l-Watha'iq al-Qawmiyya, 2002–2007).

Al-Samhudi, 'Ali ibn 'Abdallah. *Khulasat al-wafa bi-akhbar dar al-Mustafa* (Medina: al-Maktaba al-'Ilmiyya, 1972).

Al-Samhudi, 'Ali ibn 'Abdallah. *Wafa al-wafa bi akhbar dar al-Mustafa*. 5 vols. (London: al-Furqan, 2001).

Al-Sha'rani, 'Abd al-Wahhab. *Lata'if al-minan wa al-akhlaq fi wujub al-tahadduth bi-ni'mat Allah 'ala al-itlaq: al-ma'ruf bi al-Minan al-kubra* (Cairo: 'Alam al-Fikr, 1976).

Al-Sha'rani, 'Abd al-Wahhab. *al-Tabaqat al-kubra* (Beirut: Dar al-Jil, 1988).

Al-Subki, Taqi al-Din. *Shifa al-saqam fi ziyarat khair al-anam* (Haydarabad: Da'irat al-Ma'arif al-'Uthmaniyya, 1988).

Al-Suyuti, Jalal al-Din. *Husn al-muhadara fi akhbar Misr wa al-Qahira*. 2 vols. (Beirut: Dar al-Kutub al-'Ilmiyya, 1997).

Al-Suyuti, Jalal al-Din. "The Treatise on the Egyptian Pyramids *(Tuhfat al-kiram fi khabar al-ahram).*" trans. Leon Nemoy, *Isis* 30 (1939): 17–37.

Al-Tabari, Abu Ghafar Muhammad. *The History of al-Tabari.* 40 vols., various translators (New York: State University of New York, 1989–2007).

Al-Tha'labi, Abu Ishaq. *'Ara'is al-majalis fi Qisas al-Anbiya or "Lives of the Prophets."* Translated by William Brinner (Leiden: Brill, 2002).

Al-Tirmidhi, Muhammad ibn 'Isa. *Al-Shama'il al-Muhammadiyya.* 2 vols. (Beirut: Dar al-Hadith, 1988).

Ulaymi, 'Abd al-Rahman. *Uns al-Jalil bi-Ta'rikh al-Quds wa al-Khalil* (n.d., n.p.)

Wafa', 'Ali. *Wasaya Sayyidi 'Ali Wafa'* Paris: Bibliothèque Nationale, ms no. 1359.

Wafa', Muhammad. *Sha'a'ir al- 'irfan fi alwah al-kitman* (Beirut: Dar al-Kutub al-'Ilmiyya, 2006).

Al-Yunini, Qutb al-Din. *Dhayl Mir'at al-Zaman.* 4 vols. (Haydarabad: Matba'at Majlis Da'irat al-'Uthmaniyya, 1954–61).

Al-Yunini, Qutb al-Din. *Early Mamluk Syrian Historiography: Al-Yunini's Dhayl Mir'at al-zaman.* 2 vols. Translated and edited by Li Guo (Leiden: Brill: 1998).

INDEX

Abbasid dynasty
  flags and banners during, 107
  kiswa during, 38–39
  parades and processions during, 104–105
  Prophet's tomb during, dressing of, 56
'Abd, al-Majid (sultan), 35
'Abd, al-Malik (caliph), 37, 151, 162
'Abd, al-Sabur, 80–81
'Abd al-Aziz, (sultan), 35
'Abd al-Hamid, (sultan), 35
'Abduh, Muhammad, 76
Al-'Abidin, Zayd ibn Zayn, 159, 160
Al-'Abidin, Zayn, 151, 159
Abu al-Fadl (Wafa' shaykh), 126
Abu Hurayra, 67
Abu Sa'id (sultan), 210
Adorno, Theodor, 9–10
aesthetic objects, beholders of, 12
aesthetics. *See also* Kant, Immanuel
  Adorno on, 13–14
    of objects, 13
  Buck-Morss on, 14
  Eagleton on, 14
Ahmadiyya, 92, 97, 105, 115, 117
alms. *See* payment of yearly alms
animated relics, 122, 144–146
  as Sahkra Stone, 145
annihilation of self, as concept, 221
Al-Ansari, Abu Zakariyya, 95
Arabia, Wahhabism in, rise of, 56
artifacts, cultural. *See* devotional objects
artworks, autonomy of, 14
Asad, Talal, 4–5, 8
Ashraf, Amir al-Malik, 131, 132, 163, 165
Ashrafiyya, madrasa, 131, 163, 164
Asqalon sanctuary, 156–158
athar. See relics
Ayyubid dynasty, 158
Al-Azraqi, 24–25
Al-Baghdadi, 'Abd al-Latif, 186–187, 231

banners. *See* flags and banners
baraka (currency of blessings), 52
  contact relics and, 129
  stage relics and, 146

Bakris, 82, 97, 169
Barquq, Nasir al-Din Faraj ibn, 39, 93, 167
Barquq, al-Zahir, 39, 92–94, 99, 167
Barsbay (sultan), 33, 128, 196
Al-Batanuni, 59
Baumgarten, A. G., 10
Baybars, 33, 67, 105, 108, 190
Baybars al-Jashnakir, 197
beauty, 6–14
  Adorno on, 9–10
  aesthetics
    for Kant, 11–13
    recovery of senses and, 10–11
    scientific method and, 10
  aisthesis and, 10–11
    aesthetics, 10–13
    etymological history, 10
  Buck-Morss on, 8, 11, 13
  "The End of Art" idea, 8
  Kant on, 9–10
    on aesthetics, 11–13
  representation mechanisms, 7–8
  signification mechanisms, 6–7
    deflection in, 8–9
    in language and culture theory, 7
    meaning and, 6–7
    structuralism and, 7
Bell, Catherine, 148
Belon, Pierre, 34
Benjamin, Walter, 104, 176
Bennett, Jane, 205
betyls, 204–205
Bierman, Irene, 87
Al-Bistami, Sidi Abu Zayd, 72–73
Black Stone, of Ka'ba, 55–56
  defacement of, 173–174, 172–173
  Hajj and, 25
  re-signification of, 84
bodily senses, 11
Buck-Morss, Susan, 8, 11, 13
  on aesthetics, 14
Burhamiyya, 97, 105, 115, 117
Burton, Isabel, 44, 68, 144
Al-Busiri, 127
Butler, Judith, 102